KU-298-860

TEACHING GEOGRAPHY CREATIVELY

Edited by
Stephen Scoffham

Routledge
Taylor & Francis Group

LONDON AND NEW YORK

First published 2013
by Routledge
2 Park Square, Milton Park, Abingdon, Oxon OX14 4RN

Simultaneously published in the USA and Canada
by Routledge
711 Third Avenue, New York, NY 10017

Routledge is an imprint of the Taylor & Francis Group, an informa business

British Library Cataloguing in Publication Data
A catalogue record for this book is available from the British Library

Library of Congress Cataloging in Publication Data
Teaching geography creatively / edited by Stephen Scoffham.
p. cm.
Includes index.
Geography–Study and teaching (Primary) I. Scoffham, Stephen.
G73.T4216 2013
372.89'1–dc23
2012027245

ISBN: 978-0-415-50818-6 (hbk)
ISBN: 978-0-415-50819-3 (pbk)
ISBN: 978-0-203-12577-9 (ebk)

Typeset in Times New Roman
by FiSH Books Ltd, Enfield

MIX
Paper from
responsible sources
FSC® C004839
www.fsc.org

Printed and bound in Great Britain by
TJ International Ltd, Padstow, Cornwall

TEACHING GEOGRAPHY CREATIVELY

Incl

ractical ideas
also make its
en's lives and

Jniversity, UK

Tea   aphy education   bringing the
teac   aphy, human
geo   es and active
learı

                                            ontemporary,
cutt   al topics and
con: culum areas.
Key

                                            n-solving;

ok stories.

With a   s knowledge,
unders   eyond simply
offering   it respects the
integrity   n of education
which ha   d teachers alike,
encourag   asm and helping
to equip c   .

Dr Stephen Scoffham is Principal Lecturer in Primary Geography Education at Canterbury Christ Church University, UK, with a special interest in sustainability education, inter-cultural understanding and creative learning.

THE LEARNING TO TEACH IN THE PRIMARY SCHOOL SERIES

Series Editor: Teresa Cremin, The Open University, UK

Teaching is an art form. It demands not only knowledge and understanding of the core areas of learning, but also the ability to teach these creatively and foster learner creativity in the process. The *Learning to Teach in the Primary School* series draws upon recent research that indicates the rich potential of creative teaching and learning, and explores what it means to teach creatively in the primary phase. It also responds to the evolving nature of subject teaching in a wider, more imaginatively framed, twenty-first-century primary curriculum.

Designed to complement the textbook *Learning to Teach in the Primary School* (Arthur and Cremin), the well-informed, lively texts offer support for student and practising teachers who want to develop more creative approaches to teaching and learning. The books highlight the importance of the teacher's own creative engagement and share a wealth of innovative ideas to enrich pedagogy and practice.

Titles in the series:

Teaching English Creatively
Teresa Cremin

Teaching Science Creatively
Dan Davies

Teaching Mathematics Creatively
Trisha Pound and Linda Lee

Teaching Geography Creatively
Edited by Stephen Scoffham

Teaching History Creatively
Edited by Hilary Cooper

Teaching Music Creatively
Pam Burnard and Regina Murphy

CONTENTS

CONTENTS ▨ ▨ ▨ ▪

SERIES EDITOR'S FOREWORD

Teresa Cremin

Over the last two decades, teachers in England, working in a culture of accountability and target setting, have experienced a high level of specification both of curriculum content and pedagogy. Positioned as recipients of the prescribed agenda, it could be argued that practitioners have had their hands tied, their voices quietened and their professional autonomy constrained. Research reveals that during this time some professionals have short-changed their understanding of pedagogy and practice (English *et al*. 2002; Burns and Myhill 2004) in order to deliver the required curriculum. The relentless quest for higher standards and 'coverage' may well have obscured the personal and affective dimensions of teaching and learning, fostering a mindset characterised more by compliance and conformity than curiosity and creativity.

However, alongside the standards agenda, creativity and creative policies and practices also became prominent and a focus on creative teaching and learning developed. Heralded by the publication *All Our Futures: Creativity, Culture and Education* (NACCCE 1999), this shift was exemplified in the Creative Partnerships initiative, in the Qualifications and Curriculum Authority's creativity framework (QCA 2005) and in a plethora of reports (e.g. Ofsted 2003; DfES 2003; CAPEUK 2006; Roberts 2006). It was also evident in the development of the Curriculum for Excellence in Scotland. The definition of creativity frequently employed was creativity is 'imaginative activity fashioned so as to produce outcomes that are both original and of value' (NACCCE 1999: 30). Many schools sought to develop more innovative curricula, and many teachers found renewed energy through teaching creatively and teaching for creativity.

Yet tensions persist, not only because the dual policies of performativity and creativity appear contradictory, but also because the new National Curriculum draft programmes of study in England at least afford a high degree of specificity and profile the knowledge needed to be taught and tested. We need to be concerned if teachers are positioned more as technically competent curriculum deliverers, rather than artistically engaged, research-informed curriculum developers. I believe, alongside Eisner (2003) and others, that teaching is an art form and that teachers benefit from viewing themselves as versatile artists in the classroom, drawing on their personal passions and creativity as they research and develop practice. As Joubert observes:

> Creative teaching is an art. One cannot teach teachers didactically how to be creative; there is no fail safe recipe or routines. Some strategies may help to promote creative thinking, but teachers need to develop a full repertoire of skills which they can adapt to different situations.
>
> (Joubert 2001: 21)

However, creative teaching is only part of the picture, since teaching for creativity also needs to be acknowledged and their mutual dependency recognised. The former focuses more on teachers using imaginative approaches in the classroom in order to make learning more interesting and effective, the latter, more on the development of children's creativity (NACCCE 1999). Both rely upon an understanding of the notion of creativity and demand that professionals confront the myths and mantras which surround the word. These include the commonly held misconceptions that creativity is connected only to participation in the arts and that it is confined to particular individuals, a competence of a few specially gifted children.

Nonetheless, creativity is an elusive concept; it has been multiply defined by educationalists, psychologists and neurologists, as well as by policy makers in different countries and cultural contexts. Debates resound about its individual and/or collaborative nature, the degree to which it is generic or domain specific, and the difference between the 'Big C' creativity of genius and the 'little c' creativity of the everyday. Notwithstanding these issues, most scholars in the field perceive it involves the capacity to generate, reason and critically evaluate novel ideas and/or imaginary scenarios. As such, I perceive it encompasses thinking through and solving problems, making connections, inventing and reinventing and flexing one's imaginative muscles in all aspects of learning and life.

In the primary classroom, creative teaching and learning have been associated with innovation, originality, ownership and control (Jeffrey and Woods 2009) and creative teachers have been seen, in their planning and teaching and in the ethos which they create, to afford high value to curiosity and risk taking, to ownership, autonomy and making connections (Cremin 2009; Cremin *et al.* 2009). Such teachers, it has been posited, often work in partnership with others: with children, other teachers and experts from beyond the school gates (Cochrane and Cockett 2007). Additionally, in research exploring possibility thinking, which it is argued is at the heart of creativity in education (Craft 2000), an intriguing interplay between teachers and children has been observed; both are involved in possibility thinking their ways forwards and in immersing themselves in playful contexts, posing questions, being imaginative, showing self-determination, taking risks and innovating (Craft *et al.* 2012; Burnard *et al.* 2006; Cremin *et al.* 2006). A new pedagogy of possibility beckons.

This series *Learning to Teach in the Primary School*, which accompanies and complements the edited textbook *Learning to Teach in the Primary School* (Arthur and Cremin 2010), seeks to support teachers in developing as creative practitioners, assisting them in exploring the synergies and potential of teaching creatively and teaching for creativity. The series does not merely offer practical strategies for use in the classroom, though these abound, but more importantly seeks to widen teachers' and student teachers' knowledge and understanding of the principles underpinning a creative approach to teaching. Principles based on research. It seeks to mediate the wealth of research evidence and make accessible and engaging the diverse theoretical perspectives and scholarly arguments available, demonstrating their practical relevance and value to the profession. Those who aspire to develop further as creative and curious educators will, I trust, find much of value to support their own professional learning journeys and enrich their pedagogy and practice and children's creative learning right across the curriculum.

ABOUT THE SERIES EDITOR

Teresa Cremin (Grainger) is a Professor of Education (Literacy) at the Open University and a past President of UKRA (2001–2) and UKLA (2007–9). She is currently co-convenor of the BERA Creativity SIG and a trustee of Booktrust, The Poetry Archive and UKLA. She is also a Fellow of the English Association and an Academician of the Academy of Social Sciences. Her work involves research, publication and consultancy in literacy and creativity. Her current projects seek to explore children's make believe play in the context of storytelling and storyacting, their everyday lives and literacy practices, and the nature of literary discussions in extracurricular reading groups. Additionally, Teresa is interested in teachers' identities as readers and writers and the characteristics and associated pedagogy that fosters possibility thinking within creative learning in the primary years. Teresa has published widely, writing and co-editing a variety of books including: *Writing Voices: Creating Communities of Writers* (Routldge, 2012) *Teaching English Creatively* (Routledge 2009); *Learning to Teach in the Primary School* (Routledge 2010); *Jumpstart Drama* (David Fulton 2009); *Documenting Creative Learning 5-11* (Trentham 2007), *Creativity and Writing: Developing Voice and Verve* (Routledge 2005); *Teaching English in Higher Education* (NATE and UKLA 2007); *Creative Activities for Character, Setting and Plot, 5–7, 7–9, 9–11* (Scholastic 2004); and *Language and Literacy: A Routledge Reader* (Routledge 2001).

REFERENCES

Arthur, J. and Cremin, T. (eds) (2010) *Learning to Teach in the Primary School*, 2nd edn, London: Routledge.

Burnard, P., Craft, A. and Cremin, T. (2006) 'Possibility thinking', *International Journal of Early Years Education*, 14(3): 243–62.

Burns, C. and Myhill, D. (2004) 'Interactive or inactive? A consideration of the nature of interaction in whole class teaching', *Cambridge Journal of Education*, 34: 35–49.

Cape UK (2006) *Building Creative Futures: The Story of Creative Action Research Awards, 2004–2005*. London: Arts Council.

Cohrane, P. and Cockett, M. (2007) *Building a Creative School: A Dynamic Approach to School Development*. London: Trentham.

Craft, A. McConnon, L. and Mathews, A. (2012). 'Creativity and child-initiated play'. *Thinking Skills and Creativity*, 7(1): 48-61.

Craft, A. (2000) *Creativity Across the Primary Curriculum*. London: Routledge.

Cremin, T. (2009) 'Creative teaching and creative teachers', in A. Wilson (ed.) *Creativity in Primary Education*. Exeter: Learning Matters, pp. 36–46.

Cremin, T., Burnard, P. and Craft, A. (2006) 'Pedagogy and possibility thinking in the early years', *International Journal of Thinking Skills and Creativity*, 1(2): 108–19.

Cremin, T., Barnes, J. and Scoffham, S. (2009) *Creative Teaching for Tomorrow: Fostering a Creative State of Mind*. Deal: Future Creative.

Department for Education and Skills (DfES) (2003) *Excellence and Enjoyment: A Strategy for Primary Schools*. Nottingham: DfES.

Eisner, E. (2003) 'Artistry in education', *Scandinavian Journal of Educational Research*, 47(3): 373–84.

English, E., Hargreaves, L. and Hislam, J. (2002) 'Pedagogical dilemmas in the National Literacy Strategy: primary teachers' perceptions, reflections and classroom behaviour', *Cambridge Journal of Education*, 32(1): 9–26.

Jeffrey, B. and Woods, P. (2009) *Creative Learning in the Primary School*. London: Routledge.

Joubert, M. M. (2001) 'The art of creative teaching: NACCCE and beyond', in A. Craft, B. Jeffrey and M. Liebling (eds) *Creativity in Education*. London: Continuum.

National Advisory Committee on Creative and Cultural Education (NACCCE) (1999) *All Our Futures: Creativity, Culture and Education*. London: Department for Education and Employment.

Ofsted (2003) *Expecting the Unexpected: Developing Creativity in Primary and Secondary Schools*, HMI 1612. E-publication available at http://www.ofsted.gov.uk (accessed 9 November 2007).

Qualifications and Curriculum Authority (QCA) (2005) *Creativity: Find It, Promote It! – Promoting Pupils' Creative Thinking and Behaviour Across The Curriculum at Key Stages 1, 2 and 3 – Practical Materials For Schools*. London: QCA.

Roberts, P. (2006) *Nurturing Creativity in Young People. A Report to Government to Inform Future Policy*. London: DCMS.

ACKNOWLEDGEMENTS

This book has been a joy to work on. The affirmative nature of the subject and the unstinting engagement of all those involved in producing it have urged me on over many months. Teresa Cremin made the initial contact and had the vision to see how we could build on our joint research into learning and creativity. Helen Pritt (commissioning editor) responded to the proposal with enthusiasm from the very beginning. Meanwhile, Rhiannon Findlay has handled endless editorial queries tirelessly and with great good nature. The result is in front of you.

The idea for an edited (rather than a single-authored) book emerged at the research conference on primary geography held at Charney Manor in Oxfordshire in February 2011. It was the overwhelmingly positive response from friends and colleagues who were present at the time that convinced me to take on the task of editing the scripts. Some members of the writing team are experienced and well-established authors; others are writing a book chapter for the first time. All have contributed wonderfully imaginative ideas, responded positively to my suggestions and proved immensely quick to answer emails. Thank you for being such a pleasant, generous and agreeable author team. I truly believe this book is imbued with the spirit of the Charney Manor conferences, which have meant so much to all of us who have attended them over the years.

Stephen Scoffham
Faculty of Education
Canterbury Christ Church University
July 2012

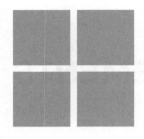

CONTRIBUTORS

Anthony Barlow is Senior Lecturer in Primary Geography Education at the University of Roehampton. He is Vice-Chair of the Early Years and Primary phase committee of the Geographical Association (GA). He is a regular presenter at the GA annual conference and has been involved with geography projects with the BBC, NESTA and Channel 4.

Jonathan Barnes is Senior Lecturer in Education at Canterbury Christ Church University. He writes regularly for the journal *Improving Schools* and lectures widely on his research into the relationships between the curriculum, the arts and well-being. He is the author of *Creative Teaching for Tomorrow* and *Cross Curricular Learning 3-14*.

Simon Catling was Professor of Primary Education in the School of Education, Oxford Brookes University, until his retirement in 2012. A past president of the Geographical Association, he is author of *Mapstart* and co-author of *Teaching Primary Geography*.

Anne M. Dolan is a lecturer at Mary Immaculate College, Limerick. Her research interests include primary geography, adult education, experiential learning and creative approaches to education. She is currently exploring the potential of picture storybooks as a creative approach for teaching development and intercultural education in primary classrooms.

Arthur Kelly is Geography Curriculum Leader at Liverpool Hope University. He is a member of the editorial board of the journal *Primary Geography* and is a moderator for the Primary Geography Quality Mark, a national scheme benchmarking geographical teaching and learning.

Margaret Mackintosh was Senior Lecturer in Primary Geography Education at Plymouth University. She is a member of the Geographical Association's Early Years and Primary phase committee and serves on the editorial board of *Primary Geography*.

Paula Owens leads primary education for the Geographical Association (GA) where she has responsibility for curriculum development and the Primary Geography Quality Mark. She is co-editor of the GA's award-winning Geography Plus series and a member of the Editorial Geography Primary Collective, responsible for editing the flagship journal *Primary Geography*.

Stephen Pickering is Senior Lecturer in Primary Education at the University of Worcester. He was the Education for Sustainable Development Officer for Worcestershire County Council. He is also a consultant for the Geographical Association (GA) and sits on the GA's *Primary Geography* editorial board.

Stephen Scoffham is Principal Lecturer in the Faculty of Education, Canterbury Christ Church University. He is also Honorary Publications Officer for the Geographical Association (GA) and an elected member of the GA governing council.

Julia Tanner works as an education consultant. She is a member of the Geographical Association's Early Years and Primary phase committee, and a trustee of the World Studies Trust.

Peter Vujaković is Professor of Geography at Canterbury Christ Church University. He has written widely on cartography and information graphics and has recently run a national workshop on primary school atlases as co-convenor of the British Cartographic Society's Map Design Special Interest Group.

Niki Whitburn is a visiting tutor at Bishop Grosseteste University College, Lincoln. She also works with the Earth Science Teachers' Association (ESTA), is a former chair of their council and an active member of their primary team.

Sharon Witt is Senior Lecturer in Education at the University of Winchester. Her research has explored children's personal geographies through scrapbooking, sense-of-place maps and den-building. She is a member of the Early Years and Primary phase committee of the Geographical Association.

Jane Whittle works at the International School of Bologna, Italy. Her research involves exploring the creative potential of internationalism in schools. She is a member of the Geographical Association's Primary School phase committee and the co-author of *Teaching Geography through Story*.

Terry Whyte is Senior Lecturer in the Faculty of Education, Canterbury Christ Church University. He has written in books, journals and electronic publications about his research and his approach to education in which learning, creativity and fun are intrinsically linked.

CHAPTER 1

GEOGRAPHY AND CREATIVITY: MAKING CONNECTIONS

Stephen Scoffham

This chapter explores what we mean by creativity. It begins by considering some of the different definitions and features of creative thought and how these might relate to classroom practice. It is suggested that creative learning experiences have the potential to enrich the curriculum and enhance personal well-being, but need to be placed in a values context. The rich possibilities that are offered by geography are outlined. The chapter concludes by focusing on how everyday artefacts can act as entry points to illustrate different aspects of geography, raise questions and suggest imaginative teaching ideas.

INTRODUCTION

Creativity is an elusive concept. It is treasured by many educationalists as one of the key elements of effective teaching, yet remains ill-defined and poorly understood. Historically, creativity was associated with the act of creation, which was seen as a divine gift. The notion that the world was created by God is a central tenet in many religious texts. We learn from the Bible, for example, how, in the beginning, God created the heavens and Earth, progressively adding light, water, sky and living things. Certainly, there are good reasons why people in the past might have wanted to invoke superhuman powers to explain the magic and beauty of life in all its diversity. How else could these wonders have come about? Interestingly, the association between creation and creativity is embedded in our language. Both terms are derived from the same Latin verb 'creare', which means to produce or to make. It is no coincidence that the word 'creature' also shares the same linguistic root. Small wonder then that we sometimes feel uncomfortable when we are invited to be creative. The student who, when asked to note her responses to a heritage site, roundly declared 'I don't do creativity!' was reflecting this unease. Her fear was that she would be unable to come up with something that required exceptional talents or gifts.

In modern times the meaning of creativity has shifted considerably. Whilst the idea that creativity implies a special gift still informs popular usage, it has also taken on a more prosaic dimension. Solving the problems that make up our everyday lives has come to be seen as a creative activity. As we think of solutions, come up with alternatives and imagine what might happen in the future, we are drawing on our creative powers. In education, especially, creativity has come to be associated with thinking and learning. Scoffham and

Barnes (2007), for example, argue that creativity is a 'fundamental aspect of human thought' (p. 13). This means that, rather than being restricted to the expressive arts, creativity has relevance for all curriculum areas.

The overlap between creativity and thought places it at the centre of the educational agenda. Moreover, there is an increasing realisation that creativity is not fixed. Some years ago, a key UK government report, *All Our Futures* (NACCCE 1999), made the point that 'all people are capable of creative achievement in some area of activity' (p. 28). It now seems that we can develop our creative capacities whatever area we are involved in. Drawing on research, Lucas and Claxton (2011) argue that our mental attitude and temperament are not set in stone but are capable of change. Not only do they offer compelling evidence to support this claim, but they also outline practical strategies for effecting change. This is encouraging news because teachers are in a prime position to construct situations in which creativity is likely to flourish.

DEFINITIONS OF CREATIVITY

There are many definitions of creativity. In educational circles the definition that was put forward by the National Advisory Committee on Creative and Cultural Education (NACCCE) in 1999 has gained considerable currency and has informed subsequent government thinking. The committee argued that creativity always involves the four following characteristics:

(a) thinking and behaving imaginatively;
(b) purposeful activity directed towards an objective;
(c) processes that generate something which is original;
(d) outcomes that are of value in relation to the objective.

This led the NACCCE to define creativity as 'imaginative activity fashioned so as to produce outcomes that are both original and of value' (p. 30).

The NACCCE definition places considerable stress on products and outcomes and underplays the role of experimentation and flexibility. Craft (2000) takes a different angle and draws attention to what she calls 'possibility thinking'. This involves both solving problems and raising questions. She also reminds us that creativity is not a single process but involves multiple dimensions that include looking into ourselves as well as outwards towards our surroundings. De Bono (2010), who has become associated with the notion of lateral thinking, takes a different approach when he highlights the importance of making connections and seeking alternatives. He stresses how creativity involves going beyond the obvious to generate novel solutions. One of de Bono's particular interests is to develop strategies that allow people to pool their thoughts. His 'thinking hats' is a neat device for avoiding the limiting effect of binary approaches. Another enduring insight comes from Koestler (1964), who emphasises the link between creativity, surprise and humour. The way that two ideas, often from different subjects or discipline areas, can come together to generate a creative spark underpins his notion of bi-sociation (Figure 1.1).

There is increasing recognition that creativity needs to be viewed in a cultural context. Western interpretations tend to emphasise the role of the individual and are orientated towards products and innovation. Eastern perspectives are more likely to focus on team and group endeavour. They may also emphasise personal fulfilment, the expression of inner truths and a sense of oneness with the world. Hinduism, for example, interprets

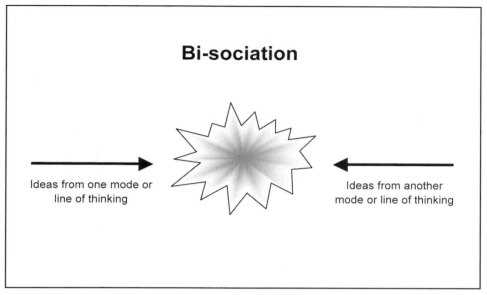

■ **Figure 1.1** When ideas from two different modes or lines of thinking interact it generates humour, surprise and creative sparks
Source: After Koestler 1964

creativity in spiritual or religious terms and sees time and history as cyclical. In education, where many teachers will be working with pupils from multicultural backgrounds, the dangers of adopting a one-size-fits-all approach to creativity will be immediately apparent.

To conclude, it is perhaps best to think of creativity as having a number of different dimensions ranging from the cognitive to the social and emotional. Choosing to focus on one aspect of creativity may lead us to neglect the others. However, it is generally accepted across cultures that creativity is a positive concept. There is also significant agreement that creativity is strongly associated with play, imagination and the emotions, and that it leads to new ways of seeing and thinking. These ideas are explored further in the following section.

Play

Young children are well known for their curiosity and their desire for play. They have a seemingly insatiable interest in the world around them and are constantly asking questions that adults find alternatively charming and annoying. Their questions appear charming because they often suggest unusual or unexpected connections. They are annoying partly because children ask them so persistently and partly because we often don't know the answers ourselves; or if we do, we find it hard to express them in terms children can understand.

One of the great qualities of play is that it is experimental, flexible and entertaining. Katz (2004) declares that play is about making and remaking the world. Young children are particularly good at this. Schools and teachers are sometimes accused of undermining children's natural capacity for inventiveness, but this is perhaps unfair. As children become older they come to recognise how ideas can fit together in useful patterns and networks. In other words, experience teaches them how best to approach different situations, and their capacity for unusual or divergent thought is reduced in consequence.

Generating ideas

Creativity is also strongly associated with generating new ideas. Some people, such as famous musicians, artists, scientists and mathematicians, have been so successful at devising new ideas that they have changed the way we see the world. This is sometimes termed 'big C' creativity, and it is, by definition, a comparatively rare phenomenon. By contrast, the kind of creativity we are likely to engage in on an everyday basis is known as 'small C' creativity. Both 'big C' and 'small C' creativity are about being original, even if the scale and impact are vastly different. It is also important to note that coming up with new ideas can be a highly stimulating and rewarding process. In his review of the primary school curriculum, Alexander (2010) reports that children 'valued those subjects that sparked their curiosity and encouraged them to explore' (p. 213). We are all attracted by novelty, and the complaint that something is boring usually arises because it is repetitive and lacks challenge. Developing new ways of thinking is stimulating even if it may also be unsettling.

Imagination

Using imagination is another aspect of creativity. This can take make different forms. It may involve asking unusual questions, envisaging alternatives or re-examining something that is taken for granted and seeing it in a different light. Coming up with new ideas can be fun, but unless these ideas are applied in some way they remain in the world of fantasy. The problem is that it is not always clear at the time whether a new idea is useful or not. Thus divergent thinking can oscillate between appearing highly creative on the one hand and whacky and weird on the other. Perhaps this is why genius and madness are often associated in the popular imagination. There are times when the boundary between the two is surprisingly thin.

Emotions

Creativity is not purely intellectual activity. Harnessing our emotional energies is an essential part of creativity and it involves accessing layers of thought that lie beneath the surface of everyday cognition. Drawing on evidence from neuroscience, Imordino Yang and Damasio (2007) argue that while creativity may be informed by high reason, it is fundamentally based on a platform of emotional thought in both social and non-social contexts. They go on to argue that motivation – the dynamo that drives our learning – derives from emotional rather than cognitive neural networks. Craft (2000) makes a similar point when she declares that the sources of creativity are not always conscious or rational. She reminds us that 'the intuitive, spiritual and emotional also feed creativity' and that these are themselves 'fed by the bedrock of impulse' (p. 31).

Intuition

There is a sense in which creativity involves a particular type of thought. It involves making links and connections, allowing ideas to emerge and being open to suggestion. Lucas and Claxton (2011) draw on a metaphor used by neuroscientists to suggest that we can view mental processes as a landscape that can be made either steeper or flatter according to our state of mind. Definite modes of thinking correspond to a steep, mountainous landscape while more playful and dreamy modes relate to a gentler, flatter terrain. There are times when we need focused thinking that channels our thinking down deep valleys, but the flatter terrain is better at handling ambiguities. As Lucas and Claxton explain, 'because the land is flat, neural patterns are much more able to bleed into one another, so you can find connections which are less stereotyped or conventional' (p. 75). It is also important to be able to switch between different modes so as to get the benefit of both. People who are less creative tend to be stuck in one mode. Being flexible and receptive to new ideas is part of a creative mindset.

CREATIVITY IN PRACTICE

So what does creativity look like in a classroom context? One distinction that has proved useful is the difference between (a) teaching creatively and (b) teaching for creativity.

Teaching creatively focuses attention on the teacher; it involves teachers drawing on their own skills and abilities to make learning more stimulating. Self-image is important here. Research shows that when teachers regard themselves as creative it can enhance their practice (Cremin *et al.* 2009). Confidence is important too. Working alongside other colleagues or with non-teacher practitioners such as artists, musicians, engineers and town planners is often an affirmative experience that can release latent talents. Your own enthusiasm, curiosity and desire to learn are liable to be much more important than being theatrical or showy.

Teaching for creativity, by contrast, directs attention to the learner and the quality of their experience. A focus on creativity is likely to involve giving pupils greater control over their learning. It may also favour collaborative and co-operative approaches in which children spark ideas off each other. Providing different entry points, encouraging pupils to ask questions and getting them to make connections are key strategies. Research suggests that a combination of teaching methods is likely to be more effective than any single approach. In their study of creative teachers, Cremin *et al.* (2009) found that over 30 techniques and activities were used in just a few lessons (Figure 1.2).

Teaching creatively is not an easy option. It requires good subject knowledge so that teachers are able to answer questions imaginatively, have the confidence to engage with unfamiliar material and identify new learning opportunities as and when they occur. It also requires careful lesson planning so that pupils are exposed to an appropriate stimulus and provided with a supportive environment in which they can develop their ideas. There will be times when individual study is appropriate but opportunities for group and team work also need to be exploited. Collaboration helps to trigger new ideas and sharing findings can prompt further thoughts. As Perkins (2010) points out, learning from 'the team' is often more effective than learning 'solo'.

It is also important to recognise that there are different stages in creative thought. An initial period of drafting and incubation is followed by a period of development and testing that leads eventually to some form of iteration. The timescale is very variable.

Child-initiated activity	Explanation	Library research
Discovery	Problem-solving	Personal computer
Reverse/open questioning	Investigations	Fieldwork
Music	Conversation	Breaks for 'brain gym'
Practical activities	Time for reflection	Photographs
Construction	Shared/individual writing	Videos
Demonstration	Stories	Map work
Electronic games	Poems	Competitions
Worksheets	Role play	Presentations
Edible and visual aids	Drama	Tests
Classroom displays	Dance	Class league tables
Interactive whiteboards	Crosswords	Merit marks

■ **Figure 1.2** Creative teachers use a range of techniques and activities to engage children
Source: After Cremin *et al.* 2009

Tentative ideas and suggestions can be extremely fragile and appear silly or inappropriate until they are refined. The final resolution will be much more robust. The NACCCE observe, 'At the right time and in the right way, rigorous critical appraisal is essential. At the wrong point, criticism and the cold hand of realism can kill an emerging idea' (p. 34). Judging the moment is one of the arts of teaching.

Creative teaching presents teachers with other challenges. When pupils engage in deep learning it leads them to reappraise their basic concepts. This can result in a period of uncertainty and confusion. Festinger (1957) uses the term 'cognitive dissonance' to describe. the disturbance that occurs when our assumptions and expectations are challenged in some way. Pupils need a supportive environment that encourages them to speculate and experiment. This in turn will serve to build their self-confidence and mental resilience. As one teacher remarked, 'It's all about taking chances...letting them take risks with their own learning' (Cremin *et al.* 2009: 25). In the way that they relate to pupils and structure learning, teachers can generate the social and educational environment that will provide the necessary nurture and support.

CREATIVITY MATTERS

Over the last decade central government has given increasing support for creative teaching. The Roberts report (2006) summarises some of the key arguments. It points out that the creative industries account for around 8 per cent of the UK economy and are important drivers of economic growth. But the report also stresses the moral case for giving children creative experiences. These help pupils to develop their sense of personal identity and can prepare them for twenty-first-century society. There is a further point that relates to the inclusion and diversity agendas. A focus on creativity has the potential to re-engage young people who are at risk of opting out of learning altogether (DfES 2006).

Technology is another powerful force that is serving to move creativity to the forefront of the educational agenda. Within a generation, electronic communications have come to dominate modern life. We are linked to people in different parts of the world through texts, emails, information searches, e-commerce, gaming and social-networking sites. We can develop ideas in conjunction with people we have never met and we can occupy multiple spaces and realities. Craft (2011) argues that the digital revolution is empowering children by extending their opportunities and developing their talents. It invites activity, participation, engagement and interpretation – all key elements of creativity. It also promotes possibility thinking by allowing us to hold ideas alongside each other, bring different pieces of information together and make leaps and connections between ideas. Technology is thus pushing the boundaries of both how we learn and how we understand the world. Digital environments favour parallel rather linear processing, emphasise graphics over text and invite collaboration rather than isolation. A major challenge for schools and educators is to decide how best to respond to these opportunities. The digital revolution is leading to patterns of thinking and ways of behaving that are difficult to control and hard to assess.

Creativity matters to us all. One leading psychologist makes the bold claim that creativity is a 'central source of meaning in our lives' (Csikszentmihalyi 1997: 2). It is through human ingenuity, he argues, that we have developed language, science, technology and all those other achievements that distinguish us from the rest of the animal kingdom. Furthermore, when we are engaged in creative activity we feel more fully alive than at other times in our lives. Csikszentmihalyi has coined the term 'flow' to characterise those moments when we are so deeply involved in something that nothing else seems to matter. On these occasions our self-awareness is diminished, time seems altered and action and awareness are merged. At the same time our motivation is so intense that we stop worrying about failure and we pursue what we are doing not because of any benefits it might bring but for its own sake. Csikszentmihalyi suggests that flow activities are most likely to occur when there is a reasonable balance between the skills we have at our disposal and the challenges that confront us. If there is too much challenge we are likely to give up. If there is too little, we tend to become bored (Figure 1.3). There are important implications for education. One of them is that creative activity is not a substitute for developing skills and knowledge. Quite the contrary: it thrives on them. Another is that creative activity is intricately linked with learning.

The link between creativity and well-being is one that merits further attention. It is tantalising to think that if we engage pupils in creative activities on a daily basis it could maximise their longer-term sense of fulfilment and satisfaction. This in turn has the potential to trigger an upward spiral of growth and personal development. At a time when there are considerable concerns about the quality and experience of childhood (Layard and Dunn 2009), a focus on creativity could offer a valuable way of enhancing well-being.

It is, however, important to sound a note of caution. Creativity on its own is not necessarily a force for good. Flow experiences can be derived from both worthwhile and distasteful experiences. Education and learning can be channelled towards indoctrination as well as enlightenment. Barnes *et al.* (2008) offer this advice:

> Before embarking upon any creative journey in schools we need first to discuss, agree and document what we believe is good and right and true and beautiful. This is not as difficult as it sounds in a school setting, but ensuring that creativity is used for the good of all is a major challenge for the future of our world.

(p. 133)

Creativity, then, is a capacity or capability we can harness in different ways. It is what distinguishes us from machines and has given rise to some of our finest achievements. We need to ensure that it is applied constructively and placed within a moral framework. As

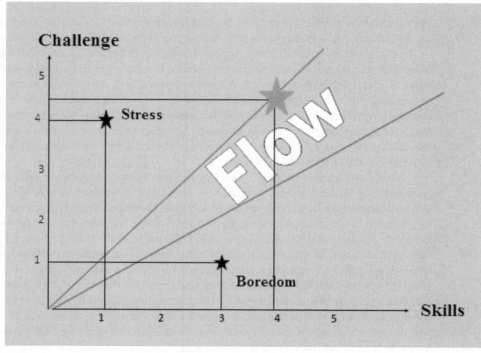

we enter the first decades of the twenty-first century, many people would argue that thinking creatively about sustainability and the environment should be particularly high on our list of priorities.

CREATIVITY AND GEOGRAPHY

So how can creativity and geography best be brought together? Once we acknowledge that in curriculum terms creativity isn't restricted to the performing arts, the opportunities immediately open out. To begin with, geography has a unique role as a synthesis subject. Historically, it has two major branches – physical and human. Physical geography studies the natural world and leans towards the sciences. Human geography studies how people live their lives and leans towards the humanities. The fusion of these two perspectives – how people affect the environment and how the environment affects people – stands at the heart of the subject. This means that there is an in-built creative tension. The different perspectives feed off each other.

At the same time, geography is about the contemporary world; what it is like today and how it might change in the future. Devising narratives to explain current events is a fundamentally creative endeavour. It includes drawing on different sources of information, offering alternative explanations, speculating about trends and acknowledging diversity and different cultural viewpoints. Digital technologies have a key role in helping geographers analyse and present data they collect. Modern geographers don't aspire to offer a single, immutable truth; instead they seek to provide a range of interpretations and perspectives that are systematic and rigorous, and which have validity within their own terms.

On a more practical level, geography is celebrated for its use of visual and graphical techniques such as charts and diagrams. Maps are its particular hallmark. Yet even the most accurate of these has a significant subjective element. For example, when making a map, the cartographer has to decide what to include, what to leave out and how best to portray information about places using signs and symbols. This means that as well as being an analytical tool, maps can be seen as an art form in their own right. A comparison between the different official map surveys of western European countries makes this point extremely clearly.

If the content of geography offers rich creative possibilities, the way that it is delivered and promoted in school can be equally fruitful. There are many different situations and environments that will provide pupils with creative learning opportunities. The skilful teacher will take pupils on a journey that involves not only finding out about the world around them in imaginative ways, but also learning about themselves as they probe deep into emotional and existential domains. Geography is as much about asking questions as discovering answers. It involves learning *from* the world as well as learning *about* it.

The connection between geography and creativity is affirmed by many leading specialists. For example, in a speech launching a new geography initiative, the broadcaster and presenter Michael Palin reflected on what geography meant for him. Geography, he declared, is 'a fusion of the power of the imagination and the hard truths of science'. It is about 'sunsets and eclipses, mountains, dreamlines, dancing dervishes, painted churches'. What could be more important, Palin asks, than exploring 'the living, breathing essence of the world we live in' and learning more about the past, present and future (2008: 5)? Using imagination and science to find out deeper truths about the planet is a highly creative endeavour. It certainly requires us to use our capacities to the full as we use different modes of thinking to make innovative links and connections.

TEACHING GEOGRAPHY CREATIVELY

Geography is an extensive area of study with many different branches. Creative learning experiences such as those suggested in this book have the potential to engage children and to lay the foundations for a deep and lasting interest in the subject. One way of structuring the curriculum is to think in terms of key ideas such as place, space, communication and the environment. This approach has the advantage of focusing on concepts that are central to geography. It also makes it possible to explore links and connections between different content areas.

Skills are important in geography. Learning to read and make maps helps pupils to think spatially. Fieldwork gives children opportunities to learn at first hand about their surroundings. ICT can help pupils record, analyse and process information. Encouraging children to ask questions and conduct their own enquiries and investigations also has a part to play. Through this work, pupils will learn about the world at a range of scales from the local to the global. As they develop their knowledge and extend their skills they will gain a deeper understanding of the processes that underpin both physical events and human activity.

There are many different ways to start creative geography teaching. The objects described in Figures 1.4 and 1.5 have been selected because they each relate to a different

Artefacts that tell the story of the world

1   A bottle of water   *Concepts: Water and the environment*

We depend on water in lots of different ways. We drink, cook and wash in it. Water irrigates crops, helps to run factories and provides the power to make electricity. Although seas and oceans cover nearly three quarters of the Earth's surface, fresh water represents less than 3 per cent of the total. Most fresh water lies deep underground or is frozen in the polar ice caps. Nevertheless, there is enough to meet our needs. The problem is that supplies are unevenly distributed and drought and erratic weather conditions are affecting people in many parts of the world. Obtaining supplies of clean drinking water is essential for health. Bottled water is one guarantee of quality. The label will also indicate the source, opening up a discussion about the water cycle, rivers and weather patterns.

2   A fossil   *Concepts: Rocks and mountains*

Fossils have been a key source of evidence for piecing together the story of life on Earth. They also show that the rocks that are now at the top of high mountain ranges were once under the sea. Children love collecting rocks and fossils and they make an excellent addition to any geography display. Ammonites, belemnites and other small sea creatures from the Jurassic period are quite common in many parts of the country. Fossilised dinosaur bones feature in museum collections and new finds are reported in the media from time to time as they are discovered. Extend the collection to include minerals and brightly coloured stones. You may not be able to identify them all but a simple collector's guide will certainly help.

3   A pair of woollen gloves   *Concepts: Weather and seasons*

The weather in the UK is notoriously variable. The interaction between warm air from the equator and cold air from the poles means that there are continual changes. Children are particularly responsive to the weather and enjoy learning more about it. There are plenty of opportunities for practical work. Recording the weather on a day-to-day basis links strongly with science while seasonal changes are revealed in longer-term patterns. A pair of gloves represents the winter just as a sun hat or sunglasses can symbolise the summer. Finding out what causes the seasons and how the seasons affect plants and creatures takes the work to greater depths.

4   A map of the London Underground   *Concepts: Maps, routes and journeys*

Geographers are particularly interested in where places and are and how they relate to each other. Maps are a powerful way of representing such spatial information. There are many types of map ranging from the personal maps we carry in our heads to the formal maps found in atlases and gazetteers. The London Underground map has become a classic because it is brilliantly effective at showing the sequence of stations and links between lines. If children are exposed to different types of map, it gives them models they can copy and adapt. There are a surprising number of occasions when you need to find out where places are. Finding out the answer and speculating over routes and connections can be a highly creative process.

5 A cuddly toy

Concepts: Habitats and biodiversity

Children have a deep-seated empathy for the natural environment and tend to be fascinated by living creatures. Finding out about animal habitats is one way of exploiting their interest. Celebrating the variety and wonders of the animal kingdom is also an excellent starting point for wider investigations. Four thousand million years of Earth history have given rise to great diversity. Sadly, many creatures are under threat, particularly due to human pressure and climate change. The cuddly toys that many children have treasured since they were toddlers symbolise not only their interest in animals but also issues to do with biodiversity. There are plenty of links to geography. Bears, for example, are found around the world – koalas in Australia, brown bears in the Rockies, polar bears in the Arctic. Identifying these places and finding out about their climate is an integral part of any study.

6 An energy-efficient light bulb

Concepts: Energy and global warming

One of the great challenges at the present time is to find ways of reducing carbon emissions. Scientists warn that without radical measures we face the prospect of damaging global warming and climate change. The humble energy-efficient light bulb could be part of the solution. These bulbs use a fraction of the power of incandescent bulbs, last much longer and give out roughly equivalent amounts of light. Other measures to save energy at home, school and work could make a really significant difference to our carbon emissions and be part of a battery of strategies to combat climate change. However, time is not on our side as levels of atmospheric carbon dioxide need to be drastically reduced to have any meaningful impact.

7 A banana

Concepts: Food, trade and global inequalities

Much of the food that we eat comes from other countries. We import grain from the USA and Canada and fresh fruit and vegetables from the Mediterranean. Some other products such as tea, coffee and pineapples come from the Tropics. Bananas make a particularly interesting case study. Supplies are shipped to the UK from the Caribbean, central Africa and parts of southern Asia and distributed to shops and supermarkets from warehouses. Some bananas are grown under fair trade agreements that ensure that producers receive a reasonable payment for their work. Others are sold on the open market where prices fluctuate. Finding out about the terms of trade raises questions about global inequalities. It also reminds us how we are linked to other people around the world through the food chain and how we depend on them for our survival.

8 A mobile phone

Concepts: Communication and the future

Mobile phones have not only become cheaper and more versatile in recent years, they have also become more powerful. As well as sending messages, mobiles are important for navigation and a significant number of internet searches are to do with location. The traffic is not all one-way. Any mobile that contains a battery is tracked by satellite, effectively monitoring the whereabouts of the vast majority of people in economically developed countries. Thus the children in your class are not only going to benefit from the information about the world that is now, literally, at their finger-tips, they are also going to have to come to terms with the privacy implications and learn how to cope with information overload. As a communication tool the mobile phone has eliminated distance and opened up enormous possibilities for intercultural dialogue. In this sense it is profoundly interesting to geographers.

■ **Figure 1.4** Many everyday artefacts relate to wider geographical concepts

Learning about geography from everyday objects

■ **Figure 1.5** Fridge magnets provide children with information about the world

aspect of geography and suggest a range of different questions and enquiries. They are also likely to be familiar to children and link directly to their everyday lives. Why not set up a geography display table of your own? This might perhaps take a theme or concept. Alternatively, it could focus on your local area, region or country or perhaps looking back to the past or forward to the future.

CONCLUSION

Teachers who specialise in primary geography often do not think of themselves as being particularly creative. This is partly because creativity is still widely associated with the expressive arts and partly because it is easy to overlook the creativity that is latent in many teaching situations. It is time for this to change. By devising a challenging but supportive teaching environment, teachers can help pupils to develop their creative potential and to actually become more creative in their thinking. Not only does this have the potential to yield rich educational benefits, it is also more fun and engaging for the pupils involved.

Recognising that geography, along with other subjects, is a highly creative endeavour is essentially liberating and will enrich your teaching. As we proceed through the twenty-first century towards a future that is increasingly punctuated by uncertainty, there are good reasons why we need to help pupils to develop flexible and responsive modes of thinking. Our ability to use information, rather than information itself, will be of crucial importance in solving problems and devising imaginative solutions to them. Digital technology has an important part to play in helping us to develop creative responses.

Creativity is one of the attributes that human beings possess in abundance. Thinking back to the start of this chapter, there can be no question that 'we don't do creativity'. The link between creativity and learning is so close that the two cannot be meaningfully separated. Creativity is central to geography just as it is to every other subject in the curriculum. Furthermore, harnessing our creative abilities is a highly fulfilling process. There is nothing conceited in recognising creativity in your teaching. Nor does it have to be daunting. As the following chapters indicate, there are lots of different ways of going about it.

REFERENCES

Alexander, R. (2010) *Children, their World, their Education*. London: Routledge.

Barnes, J., Hope, G. and Scoffham, S. (2008) 'A conversation about creative teaching and learning', in Craft, A., Cremin, T. and Burnard, P. (eds) *Creative Learning 3–11 and How We Document It*. Stoke-on-Trent: Trentham.

Craft, A. (2000) *Creativity Across the Primary Curriculum*. London: Routledge-Falmer.

Craft, A. (2011) *Creativity and Education Futures: Learning in a Digital Age*. Stoke-on-Trent: Trentham.

Cremin, T., Barnes, J. and Scoffham, S. (2009) *Creative Teaching for Tomorrow*. Deal: Future Creative.

Csikzenmihahalyi, M. (1997) *Creativity: Flow and the Psychology of Discovery and Invention*. London: HarperPerennial.

DfES (2006) *Government Response to Paul Roberts' Report on Nurturing Creativity in Young People*. London: DCMS.

De Bono, E. (2010) *Six Thinking Hats*. London: Penguin.

Festinger, L. (1957) *A Theory of Cognitive Dissonance*. London: Stanford UP.

Immordino Yang, M. H. and Damasio, A. (2007) 'We feel, therefore we learn: the relevance of affective and social neuroscience to education'. *Mind, Brain and Education*, 1(1): 3–10.

Katz, C. (2004) *Growing Up Global*. Minneapolis, MN: University of Minnesota.

Koestler, A. (1964) *The Act of Creation*. London: Hutchinson.

Layard, R and Dunn, J. (2009) *A Good Childhood*. London: Penguin.

Lucas, B. and Claxton, G. (2011) *New Kinds of Smart*. Maidenhead: Open University.

NACCCE (National Advisory Committee for Creative and Cultural Education) (1999) *All Our Futures: Creativity, Culture and Education*. London: DfEE.

Palin, M. (2008) 'Geography action plan at Speaker's House'. *Mapping News*, 33: 4–5.

Perkins, D. (2010) *Making Learning Whole*. San Francisco, CA: Jossey-Bass.

Roberts, P. (2006) *Nurturing Creativity in Young People: A Report to Government to Inform Policy*. London: DfES.

Scoffham, S. and Barnes, J. (2007) Written evidence to House of Commons Education and Skills Committee, in *Creative Partnerships and the Curriculum*. London: Stationery Office.

CHAPTER 2

FUN AND GAMES IN GEOGRAPHY

Terry Whyte

Activities and games are an excellent way of tapping into children's sense of fun and linking together both everyday and academic geography. They can be presented as warm-up exercises, provide the main focus for lessons linked to specific learning objectives or as a series of entry points either within or outside the framework of a normal lesson. This chapter focuses on the advantages of using games and play within geography teaching and the importance of developing starter activities and entry points for lessons.

INTRODUCTION

Children coming into the classroom on any day of the week will have been directly or indirectly affected by the geography around them. They will have experienced the start of a new day, eaten breakfast sourced from various local and global locations, made decisions about routes and journeys, interacted with issues such as road safety, communicated with others with similar or different cultures and identities, encountered a variety of landscapes and experienced the physical manifestations of the weather. Whether or not they identify it, geography is all around them.

Geography is often defined as the interaction between people and places. It follows that children (and adults) are geographers in an everyday sense of the word. These familiar experiences allow children to build up a useful knowledge base about their surroundings from which greater understandings can be developed. Such everyday geography can be seen as routine and taken very much for granted (Moran 2008) but it also can be 'novel, fascinating, wondrous and important' (Catling and Willy 2009: 9). Very often, children have a natural interest and curiosity for their world around them. Harnessing their enthusiasm can be a powerful and creative way to teach geography.

Using children's experiences and knowledge in isolation will not necessarily allow them to gain the skills required to understand geography as a discipline nor the ability to apply their understanding in practice. Catling and Martin (2011) argue that what is required is an equality between academic and everyday knowledge. Government requirements provide scope for this to happen. The Early Years Foundation Stage includes elements of geography in many of the learning goals (especially Knowledge and Understanding of the World) and supports the integration of subjects. The curriculum for

Key Stages 1 and 2 is underpinned by the notion that geography is about generating and asking questions as well as developing knowledge and inspiring children to think about their own place in the world. If we view creativity as dynamic and generative, and also perhaps intuitive, then being involved in games and fun activities has the potential to support imaginative teaching and learning.

WHY ENJOYMENT MATTERS

Children seem to have a natural sense of fun, often relate comfortably to their environment and enjoy games and play. Read and MacFarlane (2000) identify three dimensions of fun: expectation, engagement and endurability:

(a) *Expectation.* When they encounter a new activity, children have expectations of the degree of fun it will give them. These expectations can affect their level of engagement from the outset, and they often judge what happens against their expectations.

(b) *Engagement.* Engagement denotes the children's actual involvement where smiles, laughter and co-operation are evident (or not, as the case may be).

(c) *Endurability.* Endurability relates to children's memory of what they did and the enjoyment it brought them, which might hopefully be repeated. Ask children (or adults) to think about activities that they enjoy; their responses are likely to include the elements outlined above. Simply using humour as part of your everyday teaching is a good way to start.

Fun can be achieved through play. We all play, but children seem to be particularly good at it. What is play? Perhaps it can be seen as those activities that absorb children and in which they participate with enthusiasm. Csikszentmihalyi (1981) alludes to the freedom one can experience when playing when he describes it as a 'subset of life and arrangement in which one can practice behavior without dreading its consequences' (p. 14). Brown (2009) highlights the importance of the emotional side of play when he links it to stress reduction. Play is international. All children in all cultures engage in activities that could be construed as play and they all use pretence as a way of interacting with their world (Hyder 2005).

There are close links between play and creativity. Blatner and Blatner (1988) see play as being fundamental to fostering creativity. Through play, pupils and their teachers engage in a co-creative process that involves spontaneous originality, emotional reactions and the production of a range of outcomes. Russ (2004) talks about how play can promote divergent thinking while Wood (2007) argues that play and creativity, while not synonymous, share important characteristics.

The link between play and learning has fascinated psychologists. Piaget regarded play as a pleasurable process that allowed children to practise what had previously been learnt but which did not necessarily result in new learning. Vygotsky argued that it actually facilitates cognitive development. Dobson (2004) believes that play is important to a child's development and learning, encompassing creative, emotional and social aspects.

Work and play are not opposites but can be combined. Brown (2009) cites evidence from neuroscience that play stimulates nerve growth in the circuits of the brain where decisions are made and in the frontal cortex, which is linked to cognition. Koops and Taggart (2010), however, question the wisdom of using play to meet educational targets.

They worry that 'elements of play could be lost when it is a requirement or even hijacked for specific purposes' (p. 58). This could be said to be a situation that confronts the teacher in the classroom. There are goals to be met, learning outcomes to be achieved and 'work' to be done. It is important not to let these demands obscure deeper aspects of learning and to remember that children of all ages need to engage in play. It is just that with older children we tend to view play as childish and secondary to work, despite the benefits it brings.

If play is seen to be important in a child's development, how can we use this in teaching geography? One way to do this is through games and puzzles. Csikszentmihalyi (1997) argues that when children (and adults) are involved in a game and other purposeful activities they sometimes become so engrossed in it that they lose all sense of time. He uses the term 'flow' to describe this state of total engagement and goes on to argue that flow is strongly associated with creativity. It also provides optimal learning conditions and promotes our sense of confidence and well-being.

The use of games in geography has been seen as beneficial by Tidmarsh (2009) as they allow children to learn through co-operative experience rather than instruction and can allow them to have fun. Tidmarsh categorises four types of games that could be used in the geography context:

1 simulations ranging from sophisticated multimedia programs to modelling in class which replicate reality and real-life situations;
2 role play in which children take on the mantle of another person in a real-life context;
3 educational games that have a set of rules and are often linked to a particular area of knowledge and often involve either competition and co-operation;
4 simulation games that combine features of the other categories, incorporating rules as well as defined roles.

Being aware of different types of games is useful when it comes to planning a scheme of work. Games also have potential to assess children's progress and achievement. For example, having studied rivers, you might ask children to develop a 'consequences'-type game based around physical processes and the things people do. Younger children could construct a role play in which they pretend to be animals living along a riverbank. Both activities would reveal their level of understanding.

STARTER ACTIVITIES

The way a lesson begins will often affect the way children respond throughout the rest of the topic. Good starter activities can be the hook that pulls in the attention of children. When mixed with an element of fun, play and healthy competition, they can be strongly motivating. Gilbert (2002) cites research that shows that mental limbering-up makes for more effective learning. Starter activities can therefore be seen as exercising 'brain muscles' in the same way as an athlete limbers up for a race.

Gardner's (1991) idea of entry points is a useful reminder that children think and learn in different ways to adults and that there are different ways to engage them. Starter activities can include child-initiated activity, problem-solving, role play, questioning and discovery. Linking creativity with fun allows for a wealth of different activities that provide a stimulating way into the main body of a lesson. For example, try placing a dirty walking-boot on your desk without making any reference to it through the day. This will invite questioning, discussion, imagination, hypothesising, collaboration, frustration and fun. There is no real way of knowing how the children will react. The creative teacher will relish the different directions the children take and the interactions that follow before revealing that the boot is the clue to the work they are about to do on mountains.

Research suggests that a sense of fun, personal curiosity and desire to learn are important aspects of creative teaching (Cremin *et al.* 2009). It is also important to establish a classroom environment that is safe, open and emotionally supportive so that children feel free to indulge their natural curiosity. In this environment children will be prepared for the unexpected. A word puzzle on the board, picture clues on a slide show or a mini-test on previous knowledge can encourage the whole class to pool their thoughts and knowledge. The challenge for the teacher is to devise new activities and keep one step ahead of the game. The following sections outline some of the possibilities.

WORD GAMES

Word games work with a range of ages of children and help to build on and consolidate geographical vocabulary, thus assisting with general literacy skills. An added bonus is the fact that they are relatively easy to set up, many are downloadable from websites and, after a little practice, can be child-generated, which adds to motivation.

Jokes

Geographical jokes are a simple way to engage children and change their frame of mind (Figure 2.1).

Knock knock jokes	Jokes
Knock knock. Who's there? Alaska. Alaska who? Alaska later when I see her.	What is the fastest country in the world? Russia. What do Penguins wear on their heads? Ice caps.
Knock knock. Who's there? Francis. Francis who? France is a country in Europe.	What did the sea say to the shore? Nothing, it just waved.

■ **Figure 2.1** Geographical jokes are one example of word games

Word association

Word-association games or word chains can get children thinking about geographical vocabulary. Using the topic of weather as a stimulus, try taking the children on a journey across the world to places with different weather conditions. Each child has to think of a word that links with one previously used, such as: hot–desert–sahara–Africa–tropical–

rain–Amazon–humid–monsoon–India–flooding–wet. This activity can develop in many different ways, allowing a range of geographical features to be explored and perhaps explained along the way, and can be challenging. All children should be encouraged to participate, either in small groups or as a class. Another option, still using the idea of connections or chains, is to ask children to think of the next word that begins with the last letter of the previous one, e.g. street–traffic–cars–shop–parking–garage. You might show younger children linking pictures as clues with the words on an interactive whiteboard.

Anagrams

Mixing up the letters of a geographical term to make a puzzle allows children to investigate phonics and spelling skills as well as the vocabulary itself. Use this as an early morning starter before during or after teaching a specific topic. Children can make up their own anagrams to test their peers, e.g. tenrinnvoem, telicma, hewtera. A simple printed paragraph for early morning reading could also include a number of words jumbled up for children to solve. An alternative is to challenge the children to see how many words they can make using the letters of a long word or term such as preciptation or volcanic eruption. They get special praise for finding further geographical words.

Hidden countries

Look at this sentence: 'Using a webcam, Erica can adapt nice landscape pictures.' Now ask the children which three countries are buried in the letters. The answer is: 'America', 'Canada' and 'Iceland'. Once they have got the idea, children should be able to make up puzzles of their own.

Odd one out

Provide a set of words on any geographical topic and see if the children can guess the odd one out, e.g. London, Paris, Northampton, Berlin, Washington. The simple answer is Northampton because it is not a capital, but children might have other ideas. For example, all the cities are in Europe apart from Washington, Paris has the shortest name, Berlin is the only city containing the letter b. An alternative would be to use groups of photographs. If you put the photographs on a PowerPoint loop, the speed of the loop will be another challenge (Figure 2.2).

Definitions

Identify a range of geographical terms together with their definitions. You might take a theme such as coastal or river features and turn to a glossary for help. Write each term and each definition on a separate piece of paper, put them in a bag and mix them up. The children now have to match the word with the definition. These could then be fixed to a display board with drawing pins or Blu-tack. They could also be used as a bingo or snap game. An alternative is simply to put the terms in the bag. One child then takes a word, keeping it carefully concealed, and the others have to guess what it is with yes/no questions as in 20 questions.

Odd one out

			Answer
Sydney	Manchester	Norwich	Sydney (other two are in the UK)
River	Reservoir	Sea	Reservoir (other two are natural)
Hawaii	Canada	Alaska	Canada (other two are States of USA)
			Pyramids (other two in the UK) **Or** (other two older)
			Middle Symbol (windmill) (other two are places of worship)

■ **Figure 2.2** An example of an odd-one-out quiz

Call my bluff

Call my bluff is where children are given a new or strange geographical term and have to decide which is the correct definition out of three possibles. For example, is 'erosion' (a) listening carefully to the wind (b) the wearing away of rock and soil (c) a European money system? This game can be extended by getting children to make up the answers and having fun with terminology.

Vocabulary power

Select a range of vocabulary associated with the topic being studied and ensure that the children understand their meaning. Now challenge the children to use these words in everyday conversation as much as possible during the day, even if out of context with the subject matter. For example, how many weather words can be used? Depression, pressure, cloud, rain, precipitation, snow, heat, temperature . . . great fun!

Dingbats

A dingbat is a kind of picture puzzle. Each picture represents a word, phrase or name, and the picture can often be supplemented with a couple of letters to assist in the guessing. Dingbats are easy to construct with place names like Liver-pool, Black-burn, Corn-wall and Fin-land. They can also be useful for geographical terms associated with a topic such as waterfall, river, source, mouth and rainbow (Figure 2.3).

■ **Figure 2.3** Dingbats for Washing-ton and rain-bow

Alphabet

Get the children to make a list of words or names relating to a theme beginning with each letter of the alphabet, starting with A and finishing with Z. You might focus on countries, cities, rivers, the local area and so on. This activity can be turned into a game in which groups compete against each other, perhaps to find as many examples as possible for a certain letter. An extension would be to allow children to take photos around the school that fit into the A to Z format. Maybe pupils can create their own booklet. *ABC UK* (James Dunn 2008) provides an inspiring model that they could emulate. Alphabet games can also be played, like 'I spy'. This could be done in the classroom, outside in the schools grounds or beyond, and encourages observational and language skills. It is a simple yet effective way of getting children to focus and be a little cheeky with their clues! Like so many other games it allows assessment of knowledge and children's ability to think creatively.

Crosswords

Crosswords don't have to be as difficult as the one in *The Times*! Using simple clues and internet crossword creators (if required) makes using these word games accessible and fun for children. Crosswords also allow words to be seen in different contexts, mixed with others and in different orientations. Printed or displayed on a screen they make a good introduction to any geographical topic. Picture clues could also be used for differentiation. How about creating a giant wall-display crossword that develops over a week once the answers are discovered during lessons? A useful development is asking children to create their own crossword, which could be used to sum up their knowledge at the end of a topic. Crosswords often require a lot of thought to make them work. Providing a template and a list of suitable words is one way of supporting pupils who need help.

Word searches

Word searches seem to appeal to all ages of children as they hunt for hidden words or create puzzles for others. The obvious advantage of allowing children to create their word search is that they will know the answers (as long as the spellings are accurate). Their engagement comes in hiding the words amongst the letters. Again, this is a quick starter for an individual lesson or topic.

Acrostics

The acrostic format is a simple visual way to get children thinking around any geographical topic. If children illustrate their work it can make a very effective class display. One possible extension is to make pictures out of groups of words. For example, children might make a river shape out of a selection of words that describe river features (Figure 2.4).

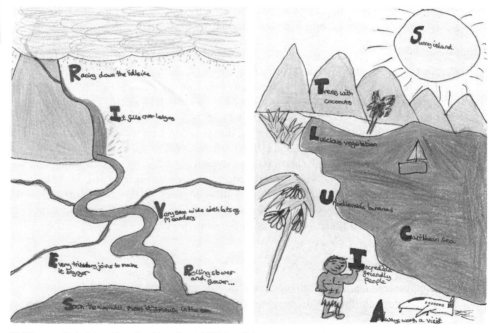

■ **Figure 2.4** Acrostics for 'river' and 'St Lucia'

STORIES AND POEMS

Children and adults like a good story and the anticipation that stories generate is a wonderful entry point for learning. Every story involves a place, either real or imagined, so the links to geography are immediately apparent. From the early years onwards, children listen to the tales about Red Riding Hood making her way through the forest to her grandmother's house, or how Jack climbed the beanstalk to enter the giant's house. They might find themselves going on a bear hunt in school, following the Gruffalo in the forest or joining the animals in *Handa's Surprise*. Older children might be engaged in Kensuke's kingdom, or travelling in the wonderworld of *The Lion, the Witch and the Wardrobe*. Once we realise the potential, we are able to use the stories that are read every day in every classroom to enhance geographical thinking.

Stories specific to locations can be linked to a piece of work or topic. With younger children, learning about the seaside can be enriched by picture-books such as *Sneakers the Seaside Cat* (Margaret Wise Brown), *Paddington: A Day at the Seaside* (Michael Bond) or *The Lighthouse Keeper* (Ronda and David Armitage). When studying a distant place, a well-chosen story can set the scene by describing the physical setting and the lives of the people who live there. Studying the environment can make much more sense if accompanied by a story.

Children can be very good at telling stories so the culmination of a unit of work might be in children creating their own. They could focus on everyday events such as a seaside holiday or family life in rural Kenya or take a theme such as waves fighting a battle against cliffs or the story of the gods of the storms. The imaginative possibilities are huge. How about street life around the school from a cat's point of view? There are obvious links between stories and role play/drama exercises, which might ultimately lead to a production, perhaps for a school assembly.

Using ICT to assist in visualising the story can also be motivating. Visualisers can magnify text and illustrations in a book, though there is often nothing better than firing up children's own visualisations through their thoughts and imagination. Photographs and video allow children to tell a story calling on their ICT skills. There is also the option of getting children to simply tell their story in the old-fashioned way.

Finally, it is worth remembering that you don't even need a book! Making up a story on the hoof requires confidence but it allows you to seize the moment and personalise experiences. Photographs and images can provide a degree of scaffolding and will support stories on subjects as varied as the story of a raindrop, city life in Mumbai, an island home, the pebble in the stream, the holiday journey or *Barnaby Bear at the Seaside*. As you gain experience your verbal artistry will develop. Why not encourage children to make up and tell their own stories in the same way?

Riddles

Riddles are statements that can have double meanings and are written to solve a puzzle. They allow children to investigate words and their meanings. Here are some examples:

I am tall and I often wear a snow cap. Who Am I? (mountain)
I am big and powerful and salty too. Who Am I? (ocean)
What has five eyes and is lying on the water? (the Mississippi River)
What stays in the corner, but travels around the world? (a stamp)
What happens to cows during an earthquake? (they give milkshakes!)
Where do cows go on holiday? (Moo York)

Limericks

Children take great delight in limericks. Limericks often include place names, which give them immediate geographical appeal. There is also good scope for making up your own to include local place names or to describe geographical processes (Figure 2.5).

There was an old man of Peru Who dreamt he was eating his shoe. He woke in the night With a terrible fright And found it was perfectly true.	There was a young lady from Niger Who smiled as she rode on a tiger. After the ride She was inside And the smile was on the face of the tiger.

■ **Figure 2.5** Examples of limericks that include place names

Haikus

Another poetic device is the haiku – a poetic form that originates from Japan. The simplest haikus have just three lines of five, seven and five syllables. They can focus on small details such as a pebble, leaf or speck of dust. The last line is sometimes a question or larger thought. Haikus provide a clear structure for children to follow and are a great way of getting children out of their classroom. Here are two examples that explore the environment:

Sand scatters the beach Waves crash on the sandy shore Blue water shimmers	Spring is in the air Flowers are blooming sky high Children are laughing

MUSIC

Music can conjure up a wide range of emotions and images. It can transport the child to a place associated with the sounds or take them on an imaginary journey. It can also widen their understanding of different cultures. Why not try to find a piece of music associated with your next geography topic? If the topic involves a distant locality, use music from that region to bring the place alive. For example, when studying an island home like the Isle of Coll in Scotland with young children, listening to fiddle and pipe music is an evocative way to introduce a cultural dimension. Similarly, the sound of steel drums will help to develop children's images of the Caribbean island of St Lucia. Another approach is to devise a quiz to see if pupils can recognise musical styles from around the world. You might also select songs and tunes that refer to geographical events. You will find that a surprisingly large number refer to the weather.

There is nothing quite like getting children to sing songs themselves. Singing local and global songs can bring in languages and different rhythms. There are a number of very good websites available to assist in finding the songs, so you don't have to be an expert. Why not create your own songs about the locality, perhaps after a field trail? Consider sound effects that might be appropriate. What sounds best represent your locality? What might it be like to be in the streets of New York or the wilds of Antarctica? What does the Amazon rainforest sound like? Consider using these sounds in a music/image presentation?

Let's take a break!

Remember to take a break in a lesson. This can have the effect of allowing you as the teacher to reflect on the feedback the children have given you and analyse the overall progress of the work. It will also give the children a physical and mental break and allows everyone to 'recharge their batteries'. Why not accompany the break with a blast of high-energy music that encourages everyone to move round, or calming music that serves to refresh? Ask children to get into a huddle to discuss their progress or talk to a partner about what they have learnt so far.

EXPLORING IMAGES

Every picture tells a story. Watching a video clip of polar bears in the Arctic or water toppling over the edge of the Angel Falls in Venezuela can evoke a powerful sense of awe and wonder. Images help to transport children imaginatively and to match their learning to the real world. This makes them a powerful teaching resource, particularly when learning about distant places in geography. However, as with reading, children need to be guided in the interpretation of what they see. Mackintosh (2010) reminds us that children tend to focus on details rather than whole scenes and that they do not always draw the conclusions you expect.

Photo packs and videos

Photo packs have traditionally been used in primary schools to examine a wide range of geography topics. Whilst they can undoubtedly help pupils learn about places, they quickly become dated. An alternative is to use images from the web or to create a locality pack based on your own experiences. (Children could create their own photo pack in the same way.)

Commercially produced educational videos are another way of bringing places alive, but be prepared to use the pause button rather than just viewing. The same also applies to websites. There is a lot of visual information available; the key is deciding how to use it creatively.

Single pictures

Using the single picture for any topic is a good way of encouraging children to ask questions. Get them to focus on the foreground and background, speculate about the motives of the photographer and consider what lies outside the frame. Try placing a silhouette of the child or group of children in the picture. What is it like being there? What can they see and how do they feel? Use cut-out speech bubbles to decide what conversations the people in the picture might be having. Another way to use a single picture is to imagine what the landscape might look like in the future. Using tracing paper can help children devise how a landscape may change?

Finally, you might want to use aerial photographs and images from Google Earth show different angles on places either familiar or unfamiliar. A simple game is to list all the places children can recognise and name on an image of the local area.

Photograph game

Use a photograph of somewhere famous to play a 'Where is this place?' game. Project an image onto the interactive whiteboard that only shows a small part of the picture. Get the children to guess the location. Gradually reveal other areas, getting the children to guess at each point until they get the right answer. Appropriate world landmarks include the Eiffel Tower, Houses of Parliament, Sydney Harbour Bridge and so forth. Again, children can make their own (Figure 2.6).

■ **Figure 2.6** Reveal picture of the leaning tower of Pisa

FUN WITH MAPS

Maps are an integral part of geography, and children tend to enjoy using and making them. Beginning a topic with maps can help them to locate and visualise their subsequent learning. This can apply to a local or distant place study as well as work on geographical features and processes. Children benefit from seeing many forms of map, so try to present them with examples that go well beyond the conventional Ordnance Survey and atlas formats.

Globes

Simply getting children to handle a large, plastic, inflatable globe engenders fun and encourages them to find out more about the world. You can focus their attention by asking questions. For example, can they find a country in Africa beginning with the letter Z, locate a small European country, identify the seas and oceans surrounding India or name a mountain range in each continent? Once engaged, children will soon want to devise questions of their own. As an extension you might decide to make a papier-mâché globe using a balloon as the base. Children can paint their globes to show land and sea and add small drawings of fish, boats and other items.

Atlases

Children's atlas skills can be enhanced using quiz cards. The questions can focus on a location, place or country and can be differentiated according to the age and ability of your pupils. At their simplest, the questions might just involve a page number or refer to an entry in the index. It is quite easy also to link questions to create a journey around the world using the atlas. Why not go on a journey around the world using Google Earth? Pretend with younger children to be seated on a plane and fly to places they name. Children can be the pilot and navigator and take everyone to Disneyland, Australia, the South Pole and then back home again to land in the street next to the school.

Flags

Flags are colourful emblems that serve to symbolise and identify different countries. Get the children to look at different designs, comparing their similarities and differences. Try playing a 'guess the flag' game as a quick-fire end-of-day activity (or at any time), using cards or the interactive whiteboard. Flags can also be used as an introduction to learning about the different countries that are competing in a sporting event or linked together in groups as in the Commonwealth or European Union. Use atlases to help children find out more.

Puzzle pieces

Cut up a photocopied map from an atlas, geographical textbook or suitable website. The children then have to reassemble it. This activity is particularly effective at consolidating their understanding of countries and can be adapted for a range of abilities.

Ordnance Survey maps

There are lots of different ways of introducing children to Ordnance Survey maps. One approach is to ask them to do a name search of the local area. (The popular 1:50,000 or 1:25,000 scale maps work well.) How many places can they find that include geographical words such as water, street, hill, ford or sand? Rather than scanning the whole map you might get pupils to focus on a block of a dozen or so grid squares. This initial focusing exercise will almost inevitably raise questions about symbols and other map conventions, paving the way for future work.

Map symbols

You can develop children's understanding of map symbols by playing matching games. To do this you will need a set of around 30 cards in which each symbol appears twice. You can make the cards yourself, download them from the internet (use the Ordnance Survey website) or get children to make their own. Remember, there is no reason why children have to follow the conventional symbols. Devising their own will involve them creatively and is likely to lead to lots of discussion.

Maps from memory

Getting the children to draw a map from memory is good for recognition and memory skills. Give them a distinctive map to look at for a specified period of time, say one minute, then ask them to draw what they have seen. You can differentiate this activity by using simpler or more complex maps and varying the time exposure.

Back-to-back mapping

In order to do back-to-back mapping you need to sit the children in pairs facing away from each other. One child describes a route taken, perhaps on the way to school, or in the locality or school grounds. The other tries to draw a map of the route (using a clipboard). The roles can then be reversed.

Maps of imaginary places

Do you remember creating your own treasure island map when you were young? Perhaps you made it look old by burning the edges and staining with tea or coffee. Why not make a large Treasure Island map covered with clues, riddles, instructions and pictures for a wall display? The links with literacy and stories are obvious and you need to be flexible enough in your planning to allow children to follow their own enthusiasms.

Monster map

Create a monster three-dimensional map of the locality in the school hall or playground using lots of cardboard boxes. There will be plenty of discussion as to where local roads end and begin. Add models of local landmarks using more boxes, then fix photographs of local scenes at appropriate places. A smaller, more permanent version of the map could be made with modelling clay or plasticine, then painted, decorated and celebrated. Remember to take photographs as memories and to inspire classes in the future.

Map corner

Have a map corner where children can find their own maps and set up map displays. They might select something from a newspaper or magazine or want to show where they have been for the weekend or on holiday. Remember to give children time to discuss their contributions. A map box may also be a good idea for children to look through in any spare moment.

OTHER SUGGESTIONS

Artefacts

Simply creating a stimulus display or table to begin a unit of work can get children motivated especially if they can get involved with the actual objects. Once the children have guessed the theme, get them to add their own artefacts. Very often what children bring in from home can alter what you have planned for future lessons, or perhaps it should do!

Quizzes

Children enjoy playing quizzes in whatever subject, so why not incorporate this into a geography topic, perhaps at the beginning as well as the end of a unit of work? Introduce an element of teamwork as well as a motive, perhaps a prize or a special concession. Try to organise questions to include all ability groups and emphasise participation rather than being correct all the time. Revising for a class quiz is more motivating than revising for a test. Try giving the quiz a theme, such as 'continents', or devise 'true or false' questions. Alternatively, you might focus on photographs or facts and figures.

Questions

Open and inviting questions are integral to eliciting wider thinking. Why not consider using a 'thunk'. A thunk, as Gilbert (2007) explains, is a 'beguiling, simple-looking question about everyday life that stops you in your tracks and helps you to start looking at the world in a new light' (p. 3). Examples of geographical thunks could be:

> What does the back of a rainbow look like?
> Can you step on water?
> Can you touch the wind?
> If I go somewhere by sat nav, who directed me there?
> Are you manmade or natural?
> If the water in a river changes all the time, what or where is the river?
> Is a wooden table still a tree?
> Can you always walk on the same beach?
> Can you weigh the sky? Would it be heavier on a cloudy day?

Board and card games

Children enjoy board games and many of these can have a geographical perspective. Monopoly is a particularly good example, but others like Mouse Trap, Cluedo, Romans, Labyrinth, Battleships and Snakes and Ladders involve maps, real places, imagined, journeys and spatial representation in some form or another. Why not apply the format of these commercially produced games to geographical settings? Can children think how to use Snakes and Ladders, for example, to illustrate processes of coastal erosion and deposition? Could Monopoly be used to envisage the locality in the future? Card games have similar potential. Popular games such as Snap and Top Trumps can be used for capital cities, countries, flags and landmarks. Making and using games in this way has considerable potential as formative or summative assessment at the end of a unit of work.

CONCLUSION

The ideas presented in this chapter could not possibly be comprehensive. They do however indicate some of the ways in which children can learn about geography in imaginative ways. More importantly, they suggest an ethos or a way of approaching learning which appeals to children and engages their enthusiasm. In an educational environment where learning is dominated by targets and assessment, it is all too easy to overlook how having fun can motivate children and improve their attainment. It can also serve to enhance their creativity and problem-solving skills. As Brown (2009) argues, creative activities can enrich pupils' learning.

You may not want to use these ideas exactly as they have been presented. They are intended to serve as frameworks and strategies that can be adapted to fit the needs of the individual class and children. They can also be child-led and child-initiated. Giving pupils greater responsibility for their learning and encouraging their intrinsic interest and motivation is an excellent way of bringing lessons to life.

Many primary school teachers are rather tentative and uncertain in their approach to geography teaching. Quizzes, games and imaginative starter activities are excellent ways to build up confidence, are easy to organise and can be extended or curtailed according to circumstances. An added advantage is that they appeal to different learning styles and ways of thinking. Stimulating children's curiosity and harnessing their enthusiasm makes it much easier to develop topics and themes in subsequent lessons. It is important not to be too serious. Having fun while pursuing educational objectives appeals to all those who are young at heart. That includes the teacher and learning assistants as well as the pupils themselves!

REFERENCES AND FURTHER READING

Blatner, A. and Blatner, A. (1988) *The Art of Play: An Adult's Guide to Reclaiming Imagination and Spontaneity.* New York: Human Sciences Press.

Brown, S. (2009) *Play: How it Shapes the Brain, Opens the Imagination and Invigorates the Soul.* New York: Penguin.

Catling, S. and Martin, F. (2011) 'Contesting powerful knowledge: the primary geography curriculum as an articulation between academic and children's (ethno-) geographies'. *Curriculum Journal*, 27(3): 317–35.

Catling, S. and Willy, T. (2009) *Teaching Primary Geography.* Exeter: Learning Matters.

Craft, A. (2001) 'Little 'c' creativity', in Craft, A., Jeffrey, B. and Liebling, M. (eds) *Creativity in Education.* London: Continuum, pp. 45–61.

Cremin, T., Barnes, J. and Scoffham, S. (2009) *Creative Teaching for Tomorrow.* Deal: Future Creative.

Csikszentmihalyi, M. (1981) 'Some paradoxes in the definition of play', in Cheska, A.T. (ed.) *Play as Context.* West Point, NY: Leisure Press, pp. 14–26.

Csikszentmihalyi, M. (1997) *Creativity: Flow and the Psychology of Discovery and Invention.* New York: HarperCollins.

Csikszentmihalyi, M. (2000) *Beyond Boredom and Anxiety: Experiencing Flow in Work and Play.* San Francisco, CA: Jossey-Bass.

Dobson, F. (2004) *Getting Serious about Play: A Review of Children's Play.* London: DCMS.

Dunn, J. (2008) *ABC UK.* London: Frances Lincoln.

Gardner, H. (1991) *Unschooled Mind: How Children Think and How Schools Should Teach.* New York: Basic Books.

Gilbert, I. (2002) *Essential Motivation in the Classroom.* London: Falmer.

Gilbert, I. (2007) *The Little Book of Thunks*. Carmarthen: Crown House.

Hyder, T. (2005) *War, Conflict and Play*. Maidenhead: Open University Press.

Koops, L. and Taggart, C. (2010) 'Learning through play: extending an early childhood music education approach to undergraduate and graduate music education', in *Journal of Music Teacher Education*, 20: 55–66.

Kratus, J. (1997) 'The roles of work and play in music education'. Paper presented at the Philosophy of Music Education. International Symposium III, Los Angeles.

Mackintosh, M. (2010) 'Using photographs, diagrams and sketches', in Scoffham, S. (ed.) *Primary Geography Handbook*. Sheffield: Geographical Association.

Martin, F. (2008a) 'Knowledge bases for effective teaching: beginning teachers development as teachers of primary geography'. *International Research in Geographical and Environmental Education*, 17(1): 13–39.

Martin, F. (2008b) 'Ethnogeography: towards a liberatory geography education'. *Children's Geographies*, 6(4): 437–50.

Moran, J. (2008) *Queuing for Beginners: The Story of Daily Life from Breakfast to Bedtime*. London: Profile.

Read, J.C. and MacFarlane, S.J. (2000) 'Endurability, engagement and expectations: measuring children's fun'. *Journal of Service Research*, 1(3): 196–214.

Russ, S. (2004) *Play in Child Development and Psychotherapy: Toward Empirically Supported Practice*. Manwah, NJ: Lawrence Erlbaum.

Scoffham, S. (2007) 'Geography and creativity: an overview', available at www.geography.org.uk (accessed 12 March 2012).

Tidmarsh, C. (2009) 'Using games in geography' (Think Piece), available at www.geography.org.uk (accessed 12 March 2012).

Vandenberg, B. (1986) 'Play theory', in Fein, G. and Rivkin, M. (eds) *The Young Child at Play*. Washington, DC: NAEYC.

Wood, E. (2007) 'Play and playfulness in the Early Years Foundation Stage', in Wilson, A. (ed.) *Creativity in Primary Education*. Exeter: Learning Matters.

Website

Ordnance Survey www.mapzone.ordnancesurvey.co.uk.

CHAPTER 3

EXPLORING GEOGRAPHY THROUGH STORIES

Anne M. Dolan

Picture storybooks have many unrecognised and underestimated qualities. Regularly used in literacy lessons, they also offer an opportunity to support creative geography teaching, since many feature a range of geographical ideas and locations. By connecting geographical ideas to children's personal experience, picture-books can accommodate different learning styles and help to promote creative and critical thinking. They also provide children with a range of windows through which they can view the world. Conversely, a range of different geographical perspectives can be filtered into the world of the child through the virtual lens of picture-books. The creative potential of geography teaching through picture-books is substantial. The degree to which this potential can be achieved lies in the skill and the perceptions of creativity held by the primary school teacher.

PICTURE-BOOKS IN THE CLASSROOM

Typically, a picture-book is 32 pages long with a balance between text and illustrations. In the better-quality picture-books the relationship between text and illustrations is tightly interconnected, complementary and seamless. This ensures that pupils 'read' both the words and the pictures. It is this relationship between pictures and words, this 'inter-animation', as Lewis (2001) calls it, that makes picture-books so special.

In high-quality picture-books, not only are the texts written in expressive, carefully crafted language, but also the illustrations are themselves accomplished works of visual and graphic art. According to Graham (2000) 'teachers and children can be caught up imaginatively through the creative talent of authors and illustrators' (p. 62). Picture-books thus demonstrate excellent examples of creativity by authors and illustrators, which can in turn inspire creativity among teachers and children. In Graham's terms, picture-books bring a second and third teacher into the classroom. Interestingly, it appears that many children's initial exposure to fine art is through picture-books. Evans (2009) describes picture-books as works of art in their own right, 'stimulating and demanding responses to their very existence in the form of their shape, form, feel, smell and overall presentation' (pp. 101–2).

The influence of the teacher is paramount in guiding how the child interacts with the picture-book. Arizpe and Styles (2003) underline the importance of teaching children to deconstruct pictures. Their research confirms that 'children can become more visually literate and operate at a much higher level if they are taught how to look' (p. 249). Hence, the challenge for the primary teacher is to interrogate images from picture storybooks in a manner that promotes enquiry-based learning and creative thinking, and develops skills of critical visual literacy (Figure 3.1).

■ **Figure 3.1** Through their drawings, children interpret and make sense of storybooks in different ways

Picture-books can bring the world into the classroom in a manner that makes sense to young children and enlarges children's ideas about places at a range of scales from the local to the distant. However, one of the greatest advantages of using picture-books in geography teaching is their potential to engage children imaginatively and creatively with abstract concepts such as movement, pattern and change. Responding to picture-books includes an analysis of illustrations and text, discussions about different places, and presentations based on 'What happens next?' This can prompt children to think about alternatives and relationships. Questions about how different characters might feel or respond can take their thinking further. There may also be opportunities to draw maps and plans to show the places that are mentioned in the story.

Picture-books feature in all preschool and early childhood classrooms. While often associated exclusively with younger children, some are appropriate for older children, adolescents and even adults. For example, although Anthony Browne's *Zoo* (2002) appeals to children at Key Stage 1, its anti-zoo message can more usefully be explored in depth across the curriculum at Key Stage 2. Indeed, it could be argued that because picture-books draw on previous experiences of people and places, they can be particularly effective in promoting creativity with older children. Nonetheless, they tend to be used less frequently at Key Stage 2 as other literary forms such as the novel take centre-stage. Furthermore, many early years and Key Stage 1 teachers see them as exclusively their jurisdiction.

Teachers need to ensure that they select high-quality picture-books for their teaching. Unfortunately, many primary teachers feel less than confident in their ability to select contemporary literature for children and tend to rely on the books they themselves enjoyed as children. In a survey of 1,200 teachers, the United Kingdom Literacy Association (UKLA) found that there was evidence that teachers relied on a narrow repertoire of children's authors and, in particular, had a very limited selection of poetry and picture fiction (Cremin *et al.* 2008). Hopefully, the ideas outlined in the following pages will provide some suggestions that will encourage the use of a larger repertoire.

EXPLORING EVERYDAY ENVIRONMENTS

It is the everyday themes of geography that are most successfully presented through a range of picture-books. Stories that focus on transport, communication, weather and the kinds of activities in which children are engaged on a regular basis, e.g. shopping, provide a mirror through which the children can reflect on what they already know.

The concept of posting a letter features in Janet and Allan Ahlberg's book *The Jolly Postman: Or Other People's Letters* (1999). The story follows a postman, known only as The Postman or The Jolly Postman as he delivers letters to various characters. All the recipients of the letters are characters drawn from popular fairytales or children's stories including *Goldilocks*, *The Gingerbread Man* and *Cinderella*. Throughout the story, after each page of narration, there is a page shaped like an envelope containing a letter that the postman has delivered. The letters that the postman delivers all have the same theme of either picking up where the fairytales ended, or creating an alternative perspective to an aspect of the original plot, e.g. Goldilocks writes a letter of apology to the three bears. The Ahlbergs have explained that the origins of the book lie in their own daughter's wanting to have letters of her own to open and read and the fantastic nature of this book lies in having such an activity embedded within the text. Cross-curricular opportunities for literacy and geographical learning emerge here through the creative presentation of the geographical concept of posting a letter.

A range of map skills can also be introduced to children creatively through picture-books. *Zoom* (1995) and *Re-Zoom* (1998) by Istvan Banyai are provocative wordless picture-books, with illustrations that slowly zoom out as though the viewer steps back from the previous pages. These are fantastic books for exploring perspective. Each frame yields to a progressively bigger view so that the net effect of moving through its expanding viewpoint is to loosen our imaginations about what we think is the ultimate environment. In another picture-book about maps, *How I Learned Geography* (Uri Shulevitz 2009), a boy and his family are living in poverty in Turkestan (modern-day Kazakhstan). Having fled from war in their troubled homeland, food is scarce, so when the boy's father brings home a map instead of bread for supper, the boy is at first furious. His mood changes, however, when the map is hung on the wall and it floods their cheerless room with colour. As the boy studies its every detail, he is transported to exotic places without ever leaving the room, and he eventually comes to realise that the map feeds him in a way that bread never could. This story, which is based on the author's memories of World War II, captures some of the key challenges in teaching geography. It stimulates the child's interest, takes the child on a journey and makes abstract concepts accessible.

Children have their own innate curiosity, inherent creativity and problem-solving skills. It is in the act of responding to the picture-book that the art of creativity and geographical enquiry lie. Responses can take many different forms: visual, aural, kinesthetic, gestural and spatial, as well as more traditional modes such as oral and written expression. There is a wide range of media that can be used by teachers and children to present children's responses e.g. role play, PowerPoint presentations, flash or multimedia presentations, blogs or websites, Claymation videos, soundscapes, films, plays, songs, poems, posters or advertisements. Some other strategies for promoting creative and critical engagement with picture-books include:

■ discussing personal reactions to books;
■ marking selections of text and illustrations with comments on post-it notes;
■ writing questions beside text or illustrations, e.g. a question for a character, a question for the author or a question for the illustrator;
■ using these questions to generate discussion;
■ discussing the use of illustrations;
■ trying to find alternative meanings for the illustrations;
■ thinking of an alternative title for the book;
■ writing the text and drawing an illustration for the next episode, i.e. What happens next?; and
■ finding difficult or interesting words.

FINDING OUT ABOUT DISTANT ENVIRONMENTS

Place has a very special resonance in picture-books in that stories need to be set in some kind of place, be it real or imaginary. The territory in which the story unfolds is more than just a decorative backdrop; it is, in many instances, the influencing frame of the story. The manner in which the place is depicted is governed by an array of artistic techniques employed by the illustrator. Therefore, place and setting in picture-books together provide fundamental aspects of the picture-book experience, hence underlying the immense geographical potential of using picture-books in the geography lesson. Picture-books bring a range of geographical locations into the classroom from Africa and Asia to America and the Antarctic. Armed with a globe and a map of the world, children can virtually travel around the world. Here are a few examples.

Starting in Europe, *Olivia Goes to Venice* (Ian Falconer 2010) introduces children to this remarkable Italian city. Olivia takes her discerning eye for architecture on a family vacation that involves dodging pigeons in the Piazza San Marco, gorging on gelato, and barely staying afloat in a gondola. Staying in Italy, *Pizza for the Queen* (Nancy Castaldo 2005) recreates the events of 11 June 1889 in Naples, Italy. Queen Margherita wants to taste what the people of Naples love to eat. So Raffaele Esposito, the owner of a tavern called Pizzeria di Pietro e Basta Cosi, sets out to get the finest ingredients, which culminates in the birth of a brand-new pizza, the pizza Margherita. To impress Queen Margherita, Raffaele topped the flat bread, so popular at the time, with ingredients in the colours of Italy: red tomato, white mozzarella and green basil. The book includes a recipe, and an author's note provides more information about pizza and this special pizzeria, which still exists today.

Further afield, readers can join Arusha, Mosi, Tumpe and their Maasai friends as they set out on a counting journey through the grasslands of Tanzania, *We all Went on Safari* (Laurie Krebs 2005). Along the way, the children encounter all sorts of animals including elephants, lions and monkeys, while counting from one to ten in both English and Swahili. The lively rhyming text is accompanied by an illustrated guide to counting in Swahili, a map, notes about each of the animals, and interesting facts about Tanzania and the Maasai people.

Many picture-books are based on journeys. The Dora the Explorer series (based on the Nickedeon TV programmes) is a good example. In every Dora book the Latina, bilingual cartoon character goes to a different location to solve a problem. 'Map' is a cartoon character who helps readers to follow directions. Through this series of books, young children are introduced to lakes and rivers, ponds and oceans, forests and swamps, hills and mountains as well as human features such as roads, bridges and playgrounds. Occasionally, we see Dora's house, school and her grandmother's house. In one book, *Dora the Explorer World Adventure* (2006), Dora needs to deliver friendship bracelets to boys and girls around the world. In this book Dora visits France, Tanzania, Russia and China.

CONSIDERING ENVIRONMENTAL ISSUES

Many picture storybooks deal with environmental issues sensitively, constructively and creatively. *The Curious Garden* (Peter Brown 2009), for example, is a magical story about a boy's dream and how the efforts of one small person can help change the world. Gradually the city is transformed as other citizens follow Liam's example and take up gardening. The illustrations present a veritable feast for the eyes, as the reader encounters the indomitable will of this little garden to go beyond the boundaries of the railway tracks and its bridge, to every little nook and corner of a dreary city, livening up its landscape, and spreading its curiosities and happiness to the local environment and the local community. This book focuses on the impact of people on the physical environment in a positive manner through gardening. This central message could be creatively reinforced by setting up a school garden.

This positive message of the power of citizens is reinforced by Jeannie Baker. In *Belonging* (2004), this Australian author/illustrator interrogates the theme of urban renewal through a series of scenes viewed through the same window over a period of several years. With the turning of every page, the years pass and gradual changes can be deduced. An alienating city street gradually becomes a place to call home. As little baby Tracy grows older, she begins to set about rescuing the street with the help of her neighbours. Together, children and adults plant grass, trees and bushes in the empty spaces. They paint murals over old graffiti. They stop the cars. Everything begins to blossom. *Belonging* explores the re-greening of the city: the role of community, the empowerment of people and the significance of children, family and neighbourhood in changing their urban environment. The streets gradually become places for safe children's play, community activity and environments for nature and wonder. This is a positive book about urban renewal that shows that each individual can make a difference. It demonstrates the complex concept of interdependence in a thought-provoking, challenging manner that children and teachers can use as a basis for further discussion and interrogation.

There is a range of excellent books that deal with the issue of recycling and positive actions to care for our environment. In *George Saves the World by Lunchtime* (Jo Readman 2006), the main character is determined to save the world by lunchtime but he's not quite sure how. Grandpa suggests they start by recycling his yoghurt container, putting his banana peel in the compost pile and hanging the washing to dry in the sun. On his bike, George discovers many more ways he can help save the world. A trip to the recycling bank, charity shop and local farmer's market shows how recycling and reusing materials can really help save the world. George even gets a favourite toy fixed!

Two books that deal with recycling on a micro-level, both by Alison Inches, are *The Adventures of An Aluminium Can* (2009) and *The Adventure of a Plastic Bottle* (2009). These stories are told from the point of view of the plastic bottle and the aluminium can whereby children can share their journeys through a diary. The plastic bottle goes on a journey from the refinery plant to the manufacturing line to the store shelf to a rubbish bin, and finally to a recycling plant where it emerges into its new life . . . as a fleece jacket.

Following the oil spill in the Gulf of Mexico in 2010, 11-year-old Olivia Bouler was inspired to take action. She wrote to a local bird conservation society and offered her own bird paintings to raise contributions. She embarked on a fundraising campaign and designed a picture-book called *Olivia's Birds* (Olivier Bouler 2011). Once again, this book clearly demonstrates that one person can make a real difference. Through her efforts, thousands of dollars were raised for the Gulf Oil Spill recovery initiative.

One of the reasons picture-books are so effective in exploring environmental issues is that they raise questions about the future. Dolan (2012) discusses the possibilities for using picture-books to promote future studies by considering what happens next? Allowing children to write the next chapter or the next instalment can facilitate a sense of agency and ownership over what lies ahead, even if only in the context of an illustrated storybook. Dolan takes Andres Melrose's book *Kyoto* (2010) as an example for promoting discussion about future scenarios.

Kyoto is a big story about a boy and a little story about global warming. The first scenes in the book feature the bear and the boy playing together until their iceberg breaks away and floats out to sea. They begin their long journey which takes them to another land. The illustrations and text show us a land that is dirty and strange, full of factory machines, coal lorries and dumping diggers. Once they locate a wooden palette they begin their journey home. The contrast between the illustrations of their homeland and new land are quite stark and the implicit message about climate change is communicated clearly. The name of the book, *Kyoto*, is also a clever play on the name of the Kyoto Protocol agreed at the United Nations Convention on Climate Change in 1997.

Picture-books can demonstrate creatively the beauty and uniqueness of our world. In Michael Foreman's *One World* (2004) the self-contained environment of the rockpool is used as a metaphor for the beauty and diversity of our oceans. Similarly, the text in Liz Garton Scanlon's *All the World* (2009) flows from one page to the next with a thoughtful tone that makes the reader pause to let the words sink in. The story follows the family's day beginning with a morning on the beach and their daily routine until the evening, which is spent with family and friends. The words are simple but convey the idea that each moment is special and should be relished. A further message is that we each have a place in this world and that we are all connected. Beautifully illustrated, the book is inclusive in that it shows pictures of the young, the elderly and people from different cultures. Many of the double-page illustrations capture entire landscapes, evoking the sounds of waves against a rocky shore, or a pond in a rainstorm at dusk. Picture-books can simultaneously demonstrate the beauty of our environment and our role in its conservation.

INTRODUCING A GLOBAL PERSPECTIVE

Picture-books include a variety of stories and illustrations from a range of different ethnic groups and cultures around the world. The beauty of the illustrations and the quality of the stories provide a strong visible statement that affirms the importance of valuing diversity. Increasingly, picture-books are also dealing with a range of complex geographical issues including interdependence, development, globalisation, justice and unequal distribution of resources in a manner that is accessible for young children.

The reasons why asylum-seekers seek refuge are often misunderstood. Many people do not realise how much suffering asylum-seekers, and especially children, have been through. Mary Hoffman's *The Colour of Home* (2002) tells, in simple language, the story of Hassan, a refugee from Somalia, who has witnessed things no child should ever see. When he arrives in England his life is so different that it is very difficult for him to respond to friendliness from his new classmates. His imaginative teacher invites him to paint a picture, and in this way Hassan is at last able to communicate the terrible things that happened to his family in Somalia when his home was burnt and his uncle was shot. Slowly, through the picture, his teacher and classmates begin to understand his story and why he must try to build a new life a long way from home. The clever use of colour – bright and happy for his home, red and black for anger and war, various tones of grey for his sadness and loss – explains Hassan's moods and feelings where words would fail. Towards the end of the story, colour and hope begins to return to Hassan's life. Another perspective on asylum-seekers is provided by Ben Morley. His book *The Silence Seeker* (2009) tells the story of two boys, Joe and the boy next door who is seeking asylum. When Joe hears his new friend is seeking asylum, he misunderstands the term and believes he wants 'silence' instead. The book tells of their quest for peaceful and quiet places in the midst of a noisy city.

There are a number of picture-books about the life of the 2004 Nobel Peace Prize winner Wangari Maathai. The first African woman to win the Nobel Peace Prize, Wangari's personal story from veterinary medicine to the foundation of the 'green belt movement', to halting deforestation in Kenya, is inspirational. *Mama Miti* (Donna Jo Napoli 2010) tells Wangari's story, aided by Kadir Nelson's stunning collage illustrations. Wangari grew up in the shadow of Mount Kenya listening to the stories about the people and land around her. As a young girl Mama Miti was taught by her tribal elders the significance of caring for the natural environment and, especially, trees. As trees were removed, the foundation of a community was also destroyed. Wangari carried this message into adulthood. Planting trees, one by one, she became involved in local community issues. When local women came to her for help with their families she told them to do the same. Soon the countryside was filled with trees. Kenya was strong once more. Wangari had changed her country 'tree by tree'. *Seeds of Change* (Jen Cullerton Johnson 2010), *Wangari's Trees of Peace* (Jeanette Winter 2008) and *Planting the Trees of Kenya* (Claire Nivola 2008) are other picture-books about her life. Background information (or teacher's notes) are included on the last two pages of each book. The books highlight the importance of trees in a global context. Their aesthetic value is presented through the beautiful illustrations and the delicate relationship between humans and nature is carefully considered. One note of warning is that the spelling in *Seeds of Change* and *Mama Miti* follows the American style, so observant children should be encouraged to spot these words. Children and teachers will be inspired to plant lots of trees following work based on these picture-books. These books demonstrate the potential of picture storybooks to introduce children to complex global geographical concepts in a way that makes sense to children.

WRITING A PICTURE-BOOK

Children who have had the opportunity to read and enjoy a variety of picture storybooks will have plenty of examples to work from when they come to write one of their own. This activity is one of the most creative activities in which a child can engage and can do much to enhance their knowledge and understanding of geography given an appropriate steer. Knowing about the codes and conventions used by authors and illustrators will assist teachers and children to create their own masterpieces. The first step is to show children a variety of different picture-books from different genres and styles.

Picture-books, in general, are extraordinarily diverse. Some picture-books have been created largely for humour while others present sensitive issues in a way that promotes empathy and understanding. Some books leave the reader reflecting about a particular perspective while others have no message at all. In some cases the pictures tell the story with a little assistance from the text and in other cases the text does most of the work with some help from the illustrations. Some picture-books include illustrations that are truly magnificent works of art in their own right, while other picture-books use photographs and digital media.

Many children's books tell their stories through double-page spreads, which may not obviously be organised on the left-to-right reading principle. Other codes and conventions are used to communicate the central message and to support the text and illustrations. These include the format of a book, i.e. whether the book is presented in portrait or landscape; the presence of a frame, i.e. a border around the illustration; whether pictures break through the frame or, in some case, the illustrations take up the whole page. Colour and tone or the level of brightness or darkness can be used effectively to support the central message. Viewpoint refers to the position from which the reader views the illustrations. The excitement and anticipation of picture-books are intensified through turning the page. The issue of page turning is crucial for the illustrator and author and turning the page requires the reader to pause and peruse the picture. Sometimes a sentence is continued over two pages, which urges the reader to turn the page to find out what happens next. The term 'peritext' refers to the physical features of a picture-book such as the front and back covers, dust jackets (if the book is a hardback), the endpapers and the title and dedication pages. Endpapers are the pages that are immediately inside the front and back covers. Knowing about these conventions will assist teachers and children to write and illustrate their own award-winning picture storybooks.

RESPONDING WITH PUPPETS (KEY STAGE 1)

An Irish development non-governmental organisation (Trócaire) and the Centre for Human Rights and Citizenship Education, Ireland (CHRCE) have devised a story sack called *Just Children* (Trócaire and CHRCE 2010). This is an excellent example of resources that can promote creative, enquiry-based responses to picture-book stories. The story sack contains a range of resources including 'Adiko the Puppet'. Aimed at preschool educators and Key Stage 1 teachers, the sack is built around the colourful children's story *Mama Panya's Pancakes*: *A Village Tale from Kenya* (Mary and Richard Chamberlin 2006). This story provides an opportunity to teach young children about Kenya. The story also enables teachers to bring a global dimension effortlessly into their teaching by highlighting concepts such as diversity and equality (Figure 3.2).

■ **Figure 3.2** A young girl talks to 'Adiko' the puppet
Photo: Anne M. Dolan

Mama Panya's Pancakes depicts a young Kenyan boy's experience of visiting the market with his mother. Along the way, Adika invites all their friends for pancakes, causing Mama to worry that she can't afford enough flour to feed the extra guests. However, everyone brings 'gifts' such as milk, butter and flour so that there is more than enough for everyone. The story highlights both the generosity and vulnerability of impoverished families, but the use of topics such as food and journeys allows children to identify similarities with their own lives.

The Kenyan landscape is presented in the book, as are sample Swahili words such as 'jambo' and 'harambee'. The book contains a map suitable for primary school children, which outlines some of the major geographical features located in Kenya, e.g. rivers, mountains and major cities. Additional information about village life in Kenya can also be found including animals, insects, reptiles, plants, instructions for pronouncing Swahili words and Mama Panya's pancake recipe.

The handbook and resources included in the sack build on this story. Developed in consultation with educators and early education experts, the handbook contains a programme of learning experiences designed to introduce children aged 3 to 7 to concepts such as fairness, interdependence, near and far, similarity and difference, and another perspective, in a global context. With a puppet, songs, a CD and photographs, the sack provides an example of how education for a just world can begin in preschool and Key Stage 1 educational settings.

The story sack is informed by research into young children's engagement with global justice issues (Ruane *et al.* 2010; Dillon *et al.* 2010). According to this research, young children already hold perceptions of the wider world and of Africa, and that before they start learning in school these perceptions are predominantly formed by media and fundraising campaigns. The research also indicated young children's ability to empathise, to articulate their own ideas in relation to justice issues and to recognise people's basic human needs.

The *Just Children* story sack provides resources for teachers to begin exploring with their children concepts, attitudes and perspectives related to global justice. The programme focuses on five dimensions identified as central to education for global justice:

■ an understanding of fairness;
■ the ability to empathise;
■ openness to and respect for diversity;
■ awareness of the connections between people around the world;
■ awareness of the wider world and of people living in developing countries.

The programme is divided into four modules:

Module 1 Near and Far	Module 2 Another Perspective	Module 3 Living with Poverty	Module 4 Exploring Fairness and Interdependence
1 Using a song to travel from Ireland to Kenya 2 Meeting the puppet Adika 3 Making baskets and puppets inspired from the story	4 Creating a life-size Adika and mapping his journey to the market 5 Creating and playing in a make-believe play area depicting the Kenyan market scene 6 Meeting Cecelia and exploring her photography	7 Investigating how food is produced 8 Exploring the tasks Adika has to do 9 Making and comparing Adika's and Cecelia's homes	10 Discussing fairness and helping Adika the puppet understand fairness 11 Looking at fairness in the Kenyan market scene 12 Using a song to bring foods back from Kenya for a pancake party.

ENGAGING WITH ISSUES AND DILEMMAS (KEY STAGE 2)

Anthony Browne's book *Zoo* (2002) offers a very interesting twist on the traditional visit to the zoo story. Two brothers and their parents spend a day at the zoo looking at the animals in the cages. They visit the elephant, giraffes, tiger, rhino, penguins, polar bear, baboons and orangutan and, finally, the gorilla. As the family walk around the zoo looking at the animals, the reader has an opportunity to observe their personalities. During the visit, Dad is bad-tempered and the children are badly behaved, because they are bored. Only Mum seems to have any empathy with the fate of the animals. Winner of the Kate Greenaway Medal, this book is a fascinating examination of the relationship between humans and animals, and the role of zoos.

Anthony Browne shows us, through illustrations and the behaviours and reactions of the individual characters to the animals in the zoo, the intricate dynamics of a family. Each character has a different perspective on the day at the zoo. The loud father has an image that takes up much of the page; the quiet, long-suffering mother is always to the back or side. The images of the depressed captive animals promote ample opportunity for children to explore what it must be like to be in a confined area such as a cage within a zoo.

The reader has to examine the pictures to find out what is really happening. The animals seem disaffected to the point of unhappiness. On one page we see the family and on the facing page we see the animals they are looking at. In the last few illustrations the family becomes more like the ones being watched by the primates. The dream the narrator has at the end reflects this idea of enclosure. It is a thought-provoking and moving story.

Browne's effectively stark, magnificently realistic illustrations of the zoo animals offer a distinct contrast to his clever renditions of the supposedly human visitors to the zoo, many of whom bear an uncanny resemblance to the creatures in the cages. The beautiful illustrations depict the visitors to the zoo with animal-like qualities (i.e. tails, ears, webbed feet etc.), while the depictions of the animals in the zoo are hauntingly realistic. Browne's sophisticated style, with its references to surrealism and his use of gorillas as interchangeable with humans, have made him one of the most intensely analysed and highly praised contemporary illustrators.

In terms of promoting creative geographical responses, I have developed a five-point response or a five-finger strategy for teachers (Figure 3.3). My strategy can be adapted for all picture storybooks.

CONCLUSION

Picture storybooks help teachers and children to engage geographically and creatively with the world. Through this creative engagement children can learn to enlarge their perception, to see things from alternative points of view, to predict the future and to identify relationships in their immediate and global environments. With careful planning, primary geography teachers can use picture storybooks to promote a wide range of skills including creative thinking, information processing, reasoning, enquiry and evaluation. This chapter has outlined a range of strategies for using picture-books to help children learn about geography. As with any recipe, the proof of the pudding is in the eating. Hopefully, you will be inspired by the suggestions presented here to test out some of the ideas for yourself.

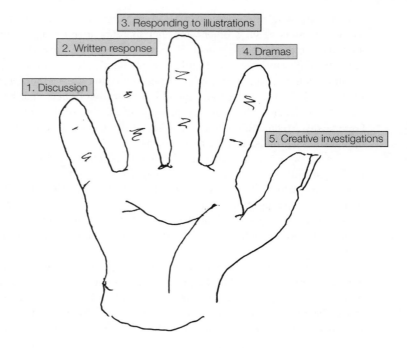

■ **Figure 3.3** Five-point response strategy (five-finger strategy)

1 Discussion: oral response
■ Initiate discussion about zoos. What do children think about a zoo? Have the children ever visited a zoo? Ask if any of the children have been to the zoo? Ask them to talk about their trip and what they enjoyed or what they disliked.
■ Read the story *Zoo* with the class and explore why Anthony Browne may have written it.
■ Focus on the behaviour of the people in the zoo and discuss whether they behave well or not. Ask children to justify their opinions by referring to the text.
■ Debate the topic: Zoos should be banned. Pair up students who then plan, present and contest points made by each other, drawing on and demonstrating their understanding and analysis of the issues developed through previous discussions.
■ After reading the book, make a list of arguments for and against zoos. This may be completed as concept or mind maps. Divide the class into two teams to debate the issues. For further ideas see Tony Buzan's (2003) work on mind maps.

2 Written response
■ Write a book review.
■ Write the story from the perspective of one character, e.g. mother, father, son, gorilla etc.
■ Write a thought bubble for each of the animals. Post-it notes in speech-bubble shapes can be used and stuck to the illustrations.

- Write character profiles for Mum and Dad.
- In *Zoo*, look at the pages where speech bubbles are used. Rewrite these as sentences using speech marks, then write them out again as reported speech. What effect does it have when you change the text in this way?
- Write a diary entry for one day in the life of a keeper at London Zoo. Imagine you were looking after the tiger cub that had to be fed every two hours!
- One of the animals has escaped from the zoo! Write a report for the local television news. This could be completed in groups and then videoed.
- Give children pictures of zoo animals and ask them to write a caption for each one. This could be to advertise the good features of the zoo, a fact about the animal or a commentary about what the animal is doing.

3   Responding to illustrations

- Examine the illustrations of the animals and the particular way that Anthony Browne has drawn them. How do the children feel about the animals? What do the illustrations convey about the animals?
- Should animals be kept in zoos? Ask children to design a poster which shows how they feel about the issue.
- Dreams: ask and talk about bad dreams the children have experienced. Draw and/or write about them.
- Create your own poster/image of a zoo using framing, colours and other devices to make the viewer think positively or negatively about zoos. Write about your poster/image.
- *Zoo* is a perfect book for examining inference in illustrations. How can we infer what the author thinks about zoos? What do the pictures tell us about Dad?
- Examine the double-page spreads. Why are the animal pictures (right-hand pages) full-size while the humans are in small blocks on the left-hand side? Compare the words with the pictures. Discussion: Who is trapped? Who are the animals? Does the author like people? Locate pictures of all the 'cages'; for example, Dad's jumper with 'bars'.

4   Drama: exploration of issues raised in the story

- This book raises issues about keeping animals in a zoo. By focusing on the text and illustrations children can discuss the feelings of characters. This can be expanded using hot-seating and still images. Pictures from the story could be used to investigate the thoughts of the animals and their feelings about being in captivity. In order to organise the debate, divide the class into two groups, one thinking about the positive reasons and the other thinking about the negative points for having zoos. The teacher can become a zoo inspector faced with the choice of leaving the zoo open or closing it down. The class forms a conscience alley to voice both sides of the argument, drawing on the discussion and written responses that have taken place earlier.

5   Creative investigation

- Make a survey in school of those people who are for and against keeping animals in zoos. Display this as a graph, complete with relevant comments – 'I don't like zoos because the animals look unhappy' or 'I think zoos do a really good job of helping to look after animals that might otherwise be dead.'
- Plan a trip to the zoo (this could be for real or hypothetical). The members of the class have to plan and organise the trip taking into consideration things like: health and safety, risk assessment, costs, supervision, transport, distance, food, itinerary, and expectations.

REFERENCES

Arizpe, E. and Styles, M. (2003) *Children Reading Pictures: Interpreting Visual Texts.* London: RoutledgeFalmer.

Buzan, T. (2003) *Mind Maps.* London: HarperCollins.

Cremin, T., Mottram, M., Bearne, E. and Goodwin, P. (2008) 'Exploring teachers' knowledge of children's literature'. *The Cambridge Journal of Education*, 38(4): 449–64.

Dillon, S., Ruane, B. and Kavanagh, A.M. (2010) 'Young children as global citizens'. *Policy & Practice: A Development Education Review*, 11, Autumn:. 84–91. Available at: http://www.developmenteducationreview.com/issue11-perspectives3

Dolan, A. (2012) 'Futures talk over story time'. *Primary Geography.* Sheffield: Geographical Association, 78: 26–7.

Evans, J. (2009) 'Reading the visual: creative and aesthetic responses to picture-books and fine art', in Evans (ed.) *Talking Beyond the Page: Reading and Responding to Picturebooks.* London and New York: Routledge/Taylor & Francis, pp. 99–117.

Goodwin, P. (2008) (ed.) *Understanding Children's Books: A Guide for Education Professionals.* Thousand Oaks, CA: Sage Publications.

Graham, J. (2000) 'Creativity and picturebooks'. *Reading,* 34(2): 61–7.

Graham, J. (2008) 'Picturebooks: looking closely', in P. Goodwin (ed.) *Understanding Children's Books: A Guide for Education Professionals.* Thousand Oaks, CA: Sage Publications, pp. 95–107.

Hicks, D. (2006) *Lessons for the Future: The Missing Dimension in Education.* Victoria, BC: Trafford Publishing.

Kiefer, B. (1993) 'Visual criticism and children's literature', in B. Hearne and R. Sutton (eds) *Evaluating Children's Books: A Critical Look.* Urbana-Champaign, IL: University of Illinois Graduate School of Library and Information Science.

Lewis, D. (2001) *Reading Contemporary Picturebooks Picturing Text.* London and New York: Routledge.

Mendoza, J. and Reese, D. (2001) 'Examining multicultural picture books for the early childhood classroom: possibilities and pitfalls'. *Journal of Early Childhood Research and Practice*, 3(2). Available at: http://ecrp.uiuc.edu/v3n2/mendoza.html

O'Neill, K. (2010) 'Once upon today: teaching for social justice with postmodern picture-books'. *Children's Literature in Education*, 41: 40–51.

Page, J.M. (2000) *Reframing the Early Childhood Curriculum: Educational Imperatives for the Future.* London: Routledge.

Ruane, B., Dillon, S. and Kavanagh, A.M. (2010) *Young Children's Engagement with Issues of Global Justice.* A report by the Centre for Human Rights and Citizenship Education, St. Patrick's College, Drumcondra and Trócaire. Available at: http://www.spd.dcu.ie/hosted/chrce/Uploads%20pdf%20doc%20ppt/Trocaire%20CHCRE%20report.pdf

Sipe, L. and McGuire, C. (2009) 'Picturebook endpapers: resources for literary and aesthetic appreciation', in Page, J.M. *Reframing the Early Childhood Curriculum: Educational Imperatives for the Future.* London: Routledge, pp. 62–80.

Trócaire and CHRCE (2010) *Just Children Story Sack.* Maynooth, Trócaire and Centre for Human Rights Citizenship Education, St. Patrick's College, Drumcondra. (Further information about the story sack is available on the Trócaire website: http://www.trocaire.org/resources/education-just-world)

Wolfenbarger, C.D. and Sipe, L. (2007) 'A Unique visual and literary art form: recent research on picturebooks'. *Language Arts*, 84: 273–80.

CHILDREN'S PICTURE-BOOKS

Alberg, J. and Alberg (1999) *The Jolly Postman or Other People's Letters.* Puffin.

Banyai, I. (1998) *Zoom.* Puffin.

Banyai, I. (1998) *Re-Zoom*. Puffin.
Nimm, S. (adapted) (2006) *Dora the Explorer: World Adventure*. Simon Spotlight/ Nickelodeon.

Books about the environment

Baker, J. (2004) *Belonging*. Walker Books.
Bethel, E. (2008) *Michael Recycle*. Meadowside Children's Books.
Brown, P. (2009) *The Curious Garden*. Little, Brown.
Browne, A. (2002) *Zoo*. Farrar, Straus and Giroux.
Bouler, O. (2011) *Olivia's Birds: Saving the Gulf*. Sterling.
Cullerton Johnson, J. (2010) *Seeds of Change*. Lee and Low Books.
Foreman, M. (2004) *Our World: The World in our Hands*. Andersen.
Garton Scanlon, L. (2009) *All the World*. Beach Lane Books.
Hoffman, M. (2002) *The Colour of Hope*. Frances Lincoln.
Inches, A. (2009) *The Adventures of an Aluminium Can: A Story about Recycling*. Little Green Books.
Inches, A. (2009) *The Adventures of a Plastic Bottle: A Story about Recycling*. Little Simon.
Melrose, A. (2010) *Kyoto: A Big Story of a Boy and a Little Bear, and a Little Story about Global Warming*. Polar Bear Press.
Morley, B. (2009) *The Silence Seeker*. Tamarind.
Napoli, D. (2010) *Mama Mia*. Simon and Schuster.
Nivola, C. (2008) *Planting the Trees of Kenya: The Story of Wangari Maathai*. Farrar, Straus Giroux.
Readman, J. (2006) *George Saves the World by Lunchtime*. Random House.
Lynn Cherry (2000) *The Great Kapok Tree: A Tale of the Amazon Rain Forest*. Voyager Books.
Winter, J. (2008) *Wangari's Trees of Peace: A True Story from Africa*. Harcourt Children's Books.

Books about places around the world

AFRICA

Alalou, A. (2008) *The Butter Man*. Charlesbridge.
Chamberlin, M. and Chamberlin, R. (2006) *Mama Panya's Pancakes*. Barefoot Books.
Cunnane, K. (2006) *For You Are a Kenyan Child*. Atheneum.
Diakite, P. (2006) *I Lost My Tooth in Africa*. Scholastic.
Krebs, L. (2003) *We All Went on Safari: A Counting Journey through Tanzani*. Barefoot Books.

ASIA

Ho, M. (2004) *Peek! A Thai Hide and Seek*. Walker Books.
My Cat Copies Me. Yoon-duck Kwon Kane/Miller Book Publishers.
Yangsook Choi (2010) *The Name Jar*. Knopf Books for Young Readers.
Recorvits, H. and Swiatkowska, G. (2000) *My Name is Yoon* by Farrar, Straus and Giroux.

AUSTRALIA

Bancroft, K. and B. (2000) *Big Rains Coming*. Clarion Books.
Bancroft, B. (2011) *Why I Love Australia*. Little Hare Books.
Lester, A. (2005) *Are We There Yet*? Kane/Miller.
Harvey, R. (2010) *To the Top End: Our Trip Across Australia*. Allen & Unwin.

EUROPE

Castaldo, N. (2005) *Pizza for the Queen*. Holiday House.
Banks, K. and Hallensleben, G. (2004) *The Cat who Walked across France*. Farrar, Straus and Giroux.
Falcone, I. (2010) *Olivia Goes To Venice*. Farrar, Straus and Giroux.
Castaldo, N. and Potter, M. (2005) *Pizza for the Queen*. Holiday House.
Fleming, C. and Potter, G. (2001) *Gabriella's Song*. Atheneum Books for Young Readers.
Sasek, M. (2004) *This is London*. Universe.

NORTH AMERICA AND THE ARCTIC

Bania, M.(2004) *Kumak's Fish: A Tale From the Far North*. Alaska Northwest Books.
Pitcher, C. and Morris, J. (2007) *The Snow Whale*. Frances Lincoln Children's Books.
Levison, N. and Hearn, D. (2002) *North Pole South Pole*. Holiday House.

SOUTH AMERICA

Krebs, L. and Fronty, A. (2011) *Up and Down the Andes*. Barefoot Books.
Morrison, P. and F. (2010) *For the Love of Soccer*. Hyperion Books.
Mitchell, S. and McLennan, C. (2007) *The Rainforest Grew All Around*. Sylvan Dell Publishing.
Rand, G. and Rand, E. (2005) *A Pen Pal for Max*. Henry Holt & Company.

Further resources

Shulevitz's, U. (2009) *How I Learned Geography*. Farrar, Straus and Giroux.
Ritchie, S. (2009) *Follow that Map: A first book of mapping skills*. Kids Can Press.
Leedy, L. (2003) *Mapping Penny's World*. Owlet Paperbacks.
Loewen, N. and Lyles, C. (2009) *Show Me a Story: Writing Your Own Picture Book*. Picture Window Books/Capstone Publishers.

PLAYFUL APPROACHES TO LEARNING OUT OF DOORS

Sharon Witt

Playful teaching and outdoor learning offer children and teachers opportunities to engage with the subject of geography in a creative manner. Playful learning is a powerful way to promote children's knowledge and understanding of their local landscapes and encourage them to make connections to people and places on a global scale, whilst promoting their well-being and happiness. This chapter provides examples to demonstrate that playful learning opportunities that immerse children in their surroundings can provide children with valuable geographical experiences throughout the primary years.

PLAYFUL LEARNING

Although in recent years play has become increasingly associated with the early years curriculum, the need for play does not disappear as children mature. The definition of play is much contested and it will depend on people's perspectives. Whilst play in its purest sense is associated with children being in complete control with the freedom to explore independently, it is questionable whether this is truly possible within a curriculum that is planned and delivered by the teacher and constrained by time, resources and health and safety requirements. Moyles (2010) suggests that within the classroom, playful learning can be defined as learning experiences that are child-led or adult-initiated or inspired when children engage in playful ways (p. 21).

Research findings

It is widely recognised that play and playfulness have a key role in learning. Moyles argues that it is through this process that children acquire knowledge and insights into themselves and their world. Furthermore, as the Geographical Association (GA) contends 'learning directly in the untidy real world outside the classroom' continues to be an essential component of a broad, rich geographical curriculum, which can motivate and engage children in their learning (2009: 23). Despite this, there is evidence that opportunities for geographical fieldwork are diminishing (Ofsted 2011: 6). At the same time, ongoing concerns regarding children's current and future relationships with the environment are well documented (Stewart 2008). Commentators note that children's play is increasingly moving indoors and onto electronic screens (Sobel 2002: xi). This may bring benefits, but it has also been argued that children who have less direct contact with nature are liable to suffer from 'nature deficit disorder' (Louv 2011: 3). Meanwhile, research by Play England found that 86 per cent of children preferred outdoor activities, including playing out with their friends and getting muddy, to playing computer games (Lester and Maudsley 2007). It would therefore seem appropriate to draw on children's natural desires to explore, play and transform outdoor places in order to develop opportunities within geography, which are built on their personal interests and experiences.

Geography and outdoor play

Playful outdoor learning is a valuable vehicle for teaching and learning geography as it provides the children with multisensory, first-hand practical experience of the real world; all features of good-quality geography provision. Play allows teachers to promote a sense of fun and enjoyment and, therefore, enables them to focus on children's well-being and feelings about places, as well as their knowledge and understanding of the world (Figure 4.1). I have decided to analyse approaches to outdoor play suitable for geographical learning using categories identified by Hughes (2002).

■ **Figure 4.1** Playful opportunities for place-making can promote 'happy geographers'
Photo: Sharon Witt

■ *Free exploration.* Free exploration is where children are encouraged to explore a place for themselves in order to discover, investigate, examine and ask questions. This utilises their innate curiosity. In one class the teacher urged her children to 'leave no stone unturned' as she gave them freedom to explore a local woodland. In the feedback session one child remarked: 'I liked going down here. There is a ditch and I think it was once where a river was and it was a really deep ditch . . . I like going down there because I like running from side to side.' As well as learning about landscape features this example also suggests that children enjoy the space and opportunities for movement in an unfamiliar outdoor space (Tovey 2007).

■ *Guided exploration.* Guided exploration occurs where children are guided by questions generated earlier, either by the class or by the teacher. Classic geographical enquiry questions include: What is this place like? How is this place connected to other places? How is this place changing? How does this place make you feel? What will this place be like in the future? Such questions encourage pupils to search for clues, collect data and draw conclusions. Contexts that are appropriate for guided exploration include: adventures, quests, journeys, voyages of discovery, treasure hunts, scavenger hunts and foraging for interesting/special objects.

One Reception class inspired by the Winnie the Pooh story (Milne 1995) went on their own 'expotition to discover the North Pole' in their school grounds. On this walk the children developed their powers of observation through sensory exploration, used geographical vocabulary and shared their personal stories of the experience. The session ended, much to the delight of the children, when they found a broomstick with the words 'the North Pole' written on it. This was an imaginative and memorable lesson that excited and engaged the children both playfully and creatively.

■ *Close encounter play.* Close encounter play is where children immerse themselves in the environment. This type of play encourages teachers to use a 'slow pedagogical . . . approach' enabling children 'to pause or dwell in spaces for more than a fleeting moment', promoting the development of place attachments through stillness, silence and reflection (Payne and Wattchow 2009: 16). Cloud watching, watching waves or admiring a beautiful view provide suitable contexts. Close encounter play may also involve active engagement with the outdoors, e.g. rolling down a hill, puddle jumping or natural sculptures in the outdoors (sandcastles, mazes and mud pies). Such activities encourage children to use their senses to engage with the natural world and communicate their responses to the landscape in different ways.

■ *Creative play.* Creative play is where children are encouraged to change their surroundings through adaption, construction and transformation. This offers opportunities for place-making such as making dens and building shelters, yurts and tree-houses. Transformation of an environment may be temporary or permanent, reversible or irreversible, and can encourage children to consider their impact on their surroundings. The possibilities for these transformations are only limited by the children's imaginations. Shirley (2007) neatly summarises the educational potential when he declares, 'We can . . . use the magic that is inherent in places' to foster genuine creativity within the geography curriculum (p. 10).

■ *Imaginative play.* Imaginative play happens when children engage in fantasy play to help develop their understanding of the real world. This type of play can be full of important geographical content that is rich in meaning for the children. It allows them, through storytelling and folklore, to develop a connection to what James (Jenkinson 2001: 67) describes as 'the authentic tidings of invisible things', i.e. the unseen forces of nature and the metaphysical world, which could be fairies, elves, giants, trolls and boggarts. McLerran (1991) details the true story of a group of children who constructed a magical imaginary town known as Roxaboxen in the desert around Yuma, Arizona. This fantastical world could be used as a stimulus for children to create their own special places. The classic story *Where the Wild Things Are* (Maurice Sendak) could also be used as a stimulus to inspire children to construct special places of their own.

■ *Simulations.* Simulations are where children use play to make sense of some real-life situations. For example, they might try to recreate the settlement of a rainforest community in order to develop an understanding of other people's lives and to consider problems that some indigenous communities are facing around the world. Playful learning can, therefore, provide children with the chance to 'put themselves in someone else's shoes and thus experience empathy with another point of view' (Walford 2007: 13). Creative teachers can also use playful learning to help children become involved in improving their local environment; it is therefore inclusive and participative. One teacher used the Planning for Real® approach where children use props to begin to make suggestions and plan improvements in their playground (Learning through Landscapes 2006). In this way, opportunities for play can encourage sites to become 'the canvas for the children's ideas' (ibid. 2006: 1). A plan for changing an outdoor space using flowerpots, carpet squares, cones and other materials can been seen in Figure 4.2.

In order for playful learning to thrive, the environment needs to provide opportunities for children to manipulate, construct, observe, listen and touch their world. Geographical play can therefore take place in the school grounds or during an educational visit in the locality, e.g. a visit to the park. The Geographical Association reminds us that 'Geography in schools . . . is concerned with perceptive and deep description of the real world (2009: 13). In addition to reading the landscape, we should be encouraging our children to be 'authors' who are writing the landscape, as it is through providing them with opportunities to create, imagine, reinvent and transform environments that children gain a deep sense of place (Tovey 2007: 55).

A playful approach to geography stands in contrast to traditional fieldwork, which can be a highly structured, adult-led activity and may involve worksheets to record observations and data collected. This is not to suggest that experiential, exploratory playful experiences are an alternative to fieldwork; they should be complementary. Placing the learner at the centre of the learning process utilises their personal geographies to enhance their knowledge and understanding of the world. Play enables children to develop their geographical thinking through participative enquiry, deep and purposeful observation and open-ended problem-solving. This provides children with the opportunity to shape their own environment by allowing them to express their ideas about the world in inventive and innovative ways.

A playful approach to learning within geography is underpinned by the theory of

■ **Figure 4.2** An example of using the Planning for Real® approach to create an outdoor performance area

Photo: Sharon Witt. Planning for Real® approach created by MA (Ed) students during a Learning through Landscapes course, University of Winchester

constructivism which highlights the way children learn actively through experiences. This helps them make sense of their world through existing and new ways of thinking (Roberts 2003). If we want our children to grow up caring about the environment and feeling empowered to change communities in the future, they need to have the opportunities that are afforded by playful activities in the outdoors. These activities allow them to experience and reflect upon the environment and enable them to develop an understanding of the dynamism and ever-changing world in which we live. As one 11-year-old stated: 'To respect nature – we learn it ourselves by being in such a nice place! By being in that place I want to look after it!'

PLACE-MAKING ACTIVITIES

Creative teachers recognise the potential that place-making activities can offer for children to achieve geographical outcomes through 'first-hand experience and practical work' (Richardson 2010: 303). Place is a key idea in geography, yet Ofsted found the development of knowledge and understanding about geographical concepts, including place, to be 'very limited' (2011: 9). The potential for children to create places has been demonstrated by Barlow *et al.* (2010) who acknowledge that practical place-making can enhance a child's understanding of scale and engage children in meaningful map-making activities. Playful place-making activities in the outdoors have the potential to actively engage children to think geographically. Below are some suggestions for a range of contexts that might be used:

■ *Creating a special place.* Children are free to explore the environment within given boundaries and utilise the natural resources in order to build a den.
■ *Creating a shelter to camp in overnight.* Children are asked to build a bivouac or hammock to sleep in overnight. Research suggests that these spaces 'are 'owned' by their creators, safe, organised, secret and unique' (Sobel 2002: 96). This was evident with one group of children who said their shelter 'just felt really homely and the people in my bivvy used it like a bathroom. We hung our towels over a branch and brushed our teeth and had fun.'
■ *A home for a bear.* This is an adaptation of the overnight camp idea where children are asked to construct a shelter for a teddy bear or a toy to spend a night outside. It requires the children to adapt their place-making skills to a smaller scale.
■ *Enquiry headquarters.* Children create a base camp for forays and expeditions into an area when pursuing an enquiry. The HQ can be a place for storing equipment needed for the enquiry, e.g. maps, books, magnifying glasses, compasses and notepads. It can also be a place where first-hand and sensory experiences can be recorded, field sketches and notes created and observations and findings analysed. It can be designed to keep the geographical investigators sheltered and their findings secure until their conclusions are ready to be shared with the group.
■ *Shelters from other cultures.* Children recreate shelters from other times and places such as a charcoal burner's hut from pre-twentieth-century England or an east-African boma.
■ *Homelessness.* Children are asked to build shelters and consider a real issue such as homelessness.

The opportunity for children to engage in place-making activities can be identified at the beginning of a unit work. At this point it can provide an initial stimulus to hook the children's interest and engage them in a motivating activity. Alternatively, place-making can be used at the end of a topic/unit of work in order to provide an opportunity to extend and deepen children's relationship with a place. Place-making also promotes strong links across the curriculum. Construction techniques relate to design and technology, work on materials and forces are part of the science curriculum and teamwork and co-operation are elements of PSHE.

DEN-BUILDING

Den-building is a universal experience of childhood, which, according to Sobel (2002), 'happens in both rural and urban settings around the globe' (p. 6). Primary school children have a genuine interest in constructing their own places outdoors and they are often rich and motivating contexts for playful learning. Noddings (2003) acknowledges the importance of enhancing 'the pleasure that pupils seem naturally to find in the places they love' (p. 122). When one child was asked whether he would like to make dens as part of his geography lessons he announced with enthusiasm, 'Wow that would be amazing! If there was a vote for that, I would vote!'

Place-making in the outdoors provides children with the opportunity to engage both physically and cognitively with a landscape. It also allows children to understand and explore place and environmental geographies through their own personal experiences and viewpoints. Creative teachers, Sobel (2002) argues, should acknowledge the unique place-making desires of middle childhood and shape the curriculum to provide appropriate environmental experiences in school. Catling and Pickering (2010) develop this argument by saying that teachers should provide opportunities for children to create places in order to develop their higher-order thinking skills and to ensure depth of learning.

Den-building activities help children to develop their sense of competence and personal order. This was evident with a group of pupils who were asked to construct a special place; they were keen to add cushions, windows and doorways once the frame of their den was built. The activity allowed them to experience a sense of home-making and to operate as shapers and makers in what Sobel (2010: 110) calls 'small worlds.' The detailed research of American youngsters conducted by Hart (1979) reveals that the physical object of the den has great meaning for children. This individual and shared den-making experience creates a sense of place (albeit on a small scale) as the den has a 'particular location, a physical structure and even meanings' (Cresswell 2008: 134). Sobel agrees that 'a sense of place is often born in children's special places (2002: 161).

Children's descriptions and feelings about the places they have constructed can be expressed in many different ways. Those that have particular relevance for geography include:

■ conversations with the teacher and between children sharing observations and experiences that develop geographical language;
■ creating and telling stories;
■ maps and plans;
■ scrapbooking responses to a place, which could include a colour palette, descriptive words, rubbings of textures, photographs or pictures;
■ field sketches;
■ postcards;
■ estate agent details or advertisement;
■ written descriptions of locations/settings;
■ self-assessment or evaluation of the quality of the construction;
■ photographs and videos;
■ drama/role play.

Creative teachers who provide opportunities for den-building within their geography provision can help children build a deeper knowledge and understanding of local places. Den-building also relates directly to the world of work. One group of children who completed place-making activities in their school grounds made constant reference to real life when constructing their dens. Some of the children took a futures-orientated approach and viewed the activity as preparation for adulthood. One child enthusiastically declared, 'I am going to be really good at this because when I am older I want to be an architect.' The places the children created reflected their current understanding and their geographical imaginations. This is evident in the following conversation when one of the children said, 'Ours is like a block of flats. Now let's make a wig-wam'.

It is important for teachers to remember that children see their environments differently to adults. Research suggests that many adults care about the aesthetic quality of an environment, which is in contrast to children who value a landscape for the activity that is possible within it (Lindholm 1995, in Kylin 2003). Children, especially those in urban areas, live and act in environments that have been planned and monitored by adults, yet they possess strong views about how they would like their places to be (O'Brien 2003 in Catling 2011). Den-building can lead children to consider the quality of their own locality. In turn, this may eventually prompt them to participate in the affairs of their local communities (McKendrick 2000 in Catling 2011). There are good reasons to conclude, along with Hart (1997), that active involvement in their local area can enhance children's self-esteem, help them adopt a more caring attitude to their school and neighbourhood and engender improved relationships.

IMAGINATION AND WELL-BEING

The provision of rich geographical outdoor play experiences can foster children's imagination. These experiences provide a strong vehicle for children to express how they feel about themselves and the world. Catling and Willy (2009) argue that children 'see places through two lenses': as real and imagined (p. 44). As they play, investigate and transform spaces, children construct narratives based on the possibilities and potential of the environment. One teacher asked her Year 3 pupils to create a favourite place; they could base their work on places they had read about in books or upon their geographical knowledge. The children built a variety of places, including a desert and a football stadium. Once constructed, the children had an opportunity to visit each other's places and time to play and explore. This activity allowed children to describe places and to identify similarities and differences. Constructing places on a large scale encouraged them to generate questions and to use geographical vocabulary as they played in their imaginary worlds.

Research suggests that primary-age children really enjoy using their imaginations and can benefit in terms of being more thoughtful, open and creative (Scarlett *et al.* 2005). The following excerpts are from conversations of six-, seven- and eight-year-olds, recorded during a den-building activity. They demonstrate that these primary-age children are using their experiences to make stories that bring together their inner and outer worlds in language and space (Sobel 2002).

> Child A: This is the time in the building process where we have the break!
> Child C: Shall we have a cup of tea and a jam tart?
> Child B: Egg sandwich anyone?
> Child B: I want some toast and electric power.
> Child A: Cor! Look at this! I'm a Viking, I am a Viking!

Creative geography teachers need to seek opportunities for children to use their imaginations through playful learning experiences. Inspired by Van Matre's 'earth education' approach in which children experience a series of immersion activities designed to develop their emotional attachment to a place, one school decided to answer the geographical question 'What is this place like?' by inviting classes of seven-, eight- and nine-year-old children to look for signs of elves on a woodland visit. Throughout the day, children were encouraged to explore the woods freely in order to develop a sense of place, to build houses to attract the elves to the wood and have moments to pause, be still and reflect. This imaginative work was built on woodland folklore and it was hoped that 'weaving a story, using clues and riddles, creating a special atmosphere, doing the unexpected' would 'enhance and intensify the magic of nature' (Van Matre 1990: 203).

The results were impressive. The teacher discovered that the children eagerly suspended their disbelief to engage with this fantastical experience. Recalling this event, one child said 'I remember thinking that I saw an elf... It had a bluebell hat on; it was a lady who had long hair on top and a green... grassy dress.' Another said, 'We knew we were like just pretending we were laughing about it. But it was like really fun! I learnt there are magical creatures. We got to use our imaginations – and when you don't use your imaginations you don't have much fun!' Imaginatively engaging in places can, as one child stated, 'enable you to see places in a different way'. It infuses children's experiences of place with wonder, beauty and enchantment and it truly involves teaching geography with a different view (Figure 4.3).

■ **Figure 4.3** Looking for signs of elves in Captain Phillimore's Woods, Hampshire. Captain Phillimore left the use of the woods to Swanmore CE (Aided) Primary School as a legacy in his will
Photo: Sharon Witt

Working in outdoor settings can also contribute to our sense of well-being. 'There is something about the intrinsic nature of places,' Ballas and Tranmer (2008) declare, 'which can influence happiness and well-being.' This becomes evident when teachers provide children with opportunities to engage playfully in the outdoors. These sensory, exploratory activities can promote insightful geographical experiences that contribute significantly to the children's developing knowledge of themselves and their world. This is beautifully summed up in the observations of an eleven-year-old girl:

> I think it is something to do with when you look at them you can sort of tell how bluebells are sort of in creation. You are seeing it actually happening – you see the place for real and it gives you a view that photos can't show because you are looking at it from every angle. You just notice things when you are doing an activity. Like when you are playing hide and seek you see how… plants grow to the light or there are lots of oddly shaped brambles growing, weaving through things.

As Tovey states, 'we must allow children the opportunity to develop an intimate relationship with nature to understand but more importantly to feel the interconnectedness of all living things and to see their own place in the world' (2007: 31). Furthermore, it is important to remember that teaching geography creatively is an emotional process that involves engaging the whole child. The senses, imagination and feelings are all involved.

THE ROLE OF THE TEACHER

The value of playful activity is sometimes underestimated, and its validity as a learning tool questioned. Not all teachers and schools will be comfortable with this experiential, explorative approach, particularly given the demands of an overcrowded, assessment-driven curriculum. The creative teacher who adopts playful pedagogies thus needs to be clear about the geographical learning that may result. Through modelling 'a spirit of playfulness', creative teachers can champion an open-ended, exploratory approach to primary geography. They can work alongside children to design, construct, produce and invent in order to promote new ideas and consider innovative ways of viewing the world. Yet the role of the creative teacher must be more than just a geographical playmate as they need to ensure, as Moyles (2010) points out, that 'tasks are planned and presented in an enjoyable and meaningful way and links are made to the required curriculum and assessment procedures' (p. 21). The challenge for teachers is to try to free up their planning to work with 'emergent purposes' rather than detailed learning outcomes. The ultimate prize must be to create 'spaces for growth' where learning from the children's exploration, ideas and interests can inform geographical curriculum-making (Clarke *et al.* 2006: 408).

Observing how children occupy spaces provides insights into what they consider important. However, this can be problematic as one of the reasons that children like to create places is so that they can escape the control of adults and feel free, uncontrolled and independent. There is an innate tension between children's natural desire to build a secret den away from adults, and health and safety concerns. When children at one school decided to seek a site for their den on the other side of the school field in the dwindling light of a winter afternoon, the teacher was quick to negotiate boundaries. This example demonstrates that playful geographical activities in the outdoors can only ever place the children in what Ba (in Catling 2011) describes as the role of 'supervised explorers'. They are monitored by teachers and other adults, rather than being the 'independent explorers' they naturally aspire to be. Does this limitation, then, change the real essence of playful learning – a freedom to explore? This needs to be carefully considered, but it is important to acknowledge that playful approaches, even when circumscribed, can place the individual child at the centre of high-quality, sensorial geographical experience, providing them with agency and ownership of their learning.

Working out of doors offers children the potential for powerful learning experiences. Within a broad and rich geography curriculum where play is valued, children have the opportunity to engage deeply with local places and consider geographical ideas of scale, interconnectedness and environmental change. Play is a strong vehicle for children's geographical learning as it 'empowers a child to be in tune with the whole self and the creative self' (Martin, in Moyles 2010: 109). Creative teachers recognise that children's emotional well-being can be enhanced through high-quality outdoor play. This motivates primary-age children to explore, manipulate, construct and respond to their surroundings, enabling them to build on and extend their personal geographies and celebrate the wonder of places whilst creating a lasting sense of stewardship for their world.

REFERENCES

Ballas, D. and Tranmer, M. (2008) *Happy Places or Happy People? A Multi-level Modelling Approach to the Analysis of Happiness and Well-being* (http://arxiv.org/ftp/arxiv/papers/0808/0808.1001.pdf).

Barlow, A., Whittle, J. and Potts, R. (2010) 'Messy maps and messy spaces'. *Primary Geography*, Autumn, pp. 14–15.

Catling, S. (2011) 'Children's geographies in the primary school', in G. Butt *Geography, Education and the Future*. London: Continuum.

Catling, S. and Pickering, S. (2010) 'Mess, mess, glorious mess'. *Primary Geographer*, Autumn, pp. 16–17.

Catling, S. and Willy, T. (2009) *Teaching Primary Geography*. Exeter: Learning Matters.

Clarke, H., Egan, B., Fletcher, L. and Ryan, C. (2006) 'Creating case studies of practice through appreciative inquiry'. *Educational Action Research*, 4(3): 407–22.

Cresswell, T. (2008) 'Place encountering geography as philosophy'. *Geography*, 93(3): 132–9.

Geographical Association (2009) *A Different View – A Manifesto for the Geographical Association*. Sheffield: Geographical Association.

Hart, R. (1979) *Children's Experience of Place*. New York: Irvington Publishers.

Hart, R. (1997) *Children's Participation: The Theory and Practice of Involving Young Citizens in Community Development and Environmental Care*. London: Earthscan.

Hughes, B. (2002) *A Playworker's Taxonomy of Play Types*, 2nd edn. London: PlayLink.

Kylin, M. (2003) 'Children's dens'. *Children, Youth and Environments*, 13(1).

Learning through Landscapes (2006) *Early Years Outdoors Planning for Real® for Real Groundnotes*. Winchester: Learning through Landscapes.

Lester, S. and Maudsley, M. (2007) *Play, Naturally: A Review of Children's Natural Play*. London: Play England/National Children's Bureau.

Louv, R. (2011) *The Nature Principle: Human Restoration and the End of Nature Deficit Disorder*. Chapel Hill, NC: Algonquin Books of Chapel Hill.

McLerran, A. (1991) *Roxaboxen*. New York: Harper Collins.

Milne, A.A. (1995) *Winnie the Pooh: The Complete Collection of Stories and Poems*. Godalming: The Book People.

Moyles, J. (2010) *Thinking about Play: Developing a Reflective Approach*. Maidenhead: Open University Press.

Noddings, N. (2003) *Happiness and Education*. Cambridge: Cambridge University Press.

Ofsted (2011) *Learning to Make a World of Difference*. London: Ofsted.

Osborne, M.D. and Brady, D.J. (2010) 'Constructing a space for developing a rich understanding of science through play'. *Journal of Curriculum Studies*, 33(5): 511–24.

Payne, P.G. and Wattchow, B. (2009) 'Phenomenological deconstruction, slow pedagogy, and the corporeal turn in wild environmental/outdoor education'. *Canadian Journal of Environmental Education*, 14: 15–32.

Rawding, C. (2007) *Reading Our Landscapes – Understanding Changing Geographies*. London: Chris Kington Publishing.

Richardson, P. (2010) 'Fieldwork and outdoor learning', in S. Scoffham, (ed.) *Primary Geography Handbook*. Sheffield: Geographical Association.

Roberts, M. (2003) *Learning through Enquiry*. Sheffield: Geographical Association.

Scarlett, W.G., Naudeau, S. Salonius-Pasternak, D. and Ponte, I. (2005) *Children's Play*. London: Sage.

Shirley, I. (2007) 'Exploring the great outdoors', in R. Austin, (ed.) *Letting the Outside In: Developing Teaching and Learning beyond the Early Years Classroom*. Stoke-on-Trent: Trentham.

Sobel, D. (2002) *Children's Special Places – Exploring the Role of Forts, Dens and Bush Houses in Middle Childhood*. Detroit, MI: Wayne State University Press.

Stewart, A. (2008) 'Whose place, whose history? Outdoor environmental education pedagogy as reading the landscape'. *Journal of Adventure Education and Outdoor Learning*, 8(2): 79–98.

Tovey, H. (2007) *Playing Outdoors: Spaces and Places Risk and Challenge*. Maidenhead: Open University Press.

Van Matre, S. (1990) *Earth Education: A New Beginning*. Greenville, WV: Institute for Earth Education.

Walford, R. (2007) *Using Games in School Geography*. London: Chris Kington Publishers.

CHAPTER 5

LEARNING ABOUT PLACES AROUND THE WORLD

Simon Catling

This chapter provides some creative approaches to developing locational knowledge at local and global scales. It outlines formal and informal approaches to learning locational knowledge using activities that can be adapted for the youngest and oldest primary children. Teaching and learning locational knowledge can and should be enjoyable, but we need to consider why this is important to us. It is not just about knowing the names of countries or capital cities.

INTRODUCTION

There used to be a car bumper sticker that proclaimed:

WITHOUT GEOGRAPHY YOU ARE NOWHERE!

The implicit message is that geography is about location. *Location* is about knowing *where* you are. People sometimes cite an old adage that claims that geography is 'about maps'! This infers that if you 'knew your geography' you knew where places are. Certainly geography is about using maps, but not maps simply for themselves. Maps help us in a number of ways. One is to locate where places are; another is to help us see and understand the nature and shape of places, whether the street map outline of our village, the landscape of a national park or the global pattern of urban settlements. Maps provide the basis for our knowledge and appreciation of what we call 'locational knowledge'. This is part of the core knowledge that is essential in helping us to make sense of the world.

Locational knowledge is vital for children in placing themselves and their geographical studies in local, national, international and global contexts. Studying any aspects of geography, whatever the scale, is missing something essential if you do not know where it is and how it relates to other places. Modern communications technologies recognise this. Our mobile phones are programmed to locate us and provide us with maps and other locational information. They use a global positioning system that can pinpoint our location and movement with remarkable accuracy. We cannot get away from location!

Locational knowledge about our home country and the continent we live in contribute to what might be called building a 'mental' or 'cognitive' map of the world

(Downs and Stea 1977; Gould and White 1986). It seems that children begin to construct their mental maps from an early age, though these are somewhat constrained by the places they have heard about and world maps that they have seen (Wiegand 2006). There is also evidence that schools need to do more to help children develop their sense of location. Ofsted (2011) reports that children study too few places around the world, that teachers often have weak locational knowledge, that maps and atlases are used infrequently and that the geography curricula and teaching are often unimaginative and uncreative.

WHERE IN THE WORLD?

Where do you live? Just write down your address, starting with your home on the first line and planet Earth on the last. This is a fun activity primary children have played for decades and it answers the question 'Where am I?' (see Figure 5.1). A key part of being who we are lies in knowing where we are. This involves more than saying 'I live in Newcastle' or 'Birmingham'. It enables us to affirm that we belong to a social group and say, 'I'm a Geordie' or 'I'm a Brummie'. Where we are from and where we live, locally and nationally, are important to us. Belonging is vital to our self-esteem and identity.

Places matter, and knowing where our place is matters. Saying 'I'm Welsh' helps to define us. Try not having a nationality! But if you don't know where Wales is or what it refers to, this statement does not amount to very much. We need to have a sense of what our 'place' is and how it relates to its surroundings. Being from Wales is not the same as being from England or Argentina or Vietnam. We position ourselves in relation to other people and other places. Our address represents this distinctiveness – it represents our *whereness* in the world. Even Barnaby Bear's address matters. He belongs to the Geographical Association! (Figure 5.1).

Barnaby Bear,
The Geographical Association,
160, Solly Street,
Sheffield,
South Yorkshire,
S1 4BF,
England,
The United Kingdom,
The European Union,
Europe,
Planet Earth.

▪ **Figure 5.1** Barnaby Bear's address tell us where to find him

We can write Barnaby Bear's address very succinctly, as 'Barnaby Bear, 160, S1 4BF, UK'. This is because we have developed coding systems to be able to define each global location with great precision. In the UK our postcode does this; in the USA it is the zipcode. To this code we simply add our nation's name. Global positioning systems (GPS) also locate us using satellite images and maps. When driving to unfamiliar destinations

we increasingly rely on GPS linked with a postcode to guide our route – though sometimes it does not always prove quite as helpful as we would like.

Addresses are invaluable. Almost all of us have or want one, however permanent,
transient or precarious they are. An address places us in the world. This is the heart of
knowing where we are. With young children we can write our addresses, not simply to
know where we live in case of an emergency but because it helps us think about the place
we live in. By sharing addresses and talking about each other's addresses, we can understand more about 'our place'. With older primary children we can investigate the nature
and uses of addresses and discuss their importance for everyone. Figure 5.2 illustrates this
through a sequence of activities.

Send a postcard map
Children can send a postcard map to a friend or to a link or partner school. Have them
include their own postal address so the recipient knows who sent it and can reply. You
could add a cross to show a little more precisely where you live.

The map locates you and your 'cross' says 'This is where I'm from'. It gives the
receiver a view – maps are very useful for this – of where 'your place' is. She or he can
then use it to look up where you live on a national map or a world map to see where you
are located. This is the nature of an address.

Make address maps
Create a series of maps of your address or of the place you sent your postcard to.
Include:

■ a local vicinity map to show the building and street;
■ a town or local area map to show the place lived at;
■ a national map to show where in the country;
■ a continental map to show where the country is;
■ a world map to show where the continent is.

These maps help to develop a sense of where we are in the world.

■ **Figure 5.2** Creative activities to explore the meaning of an address

Locational knowledge in the geography curriculum

National curriculum geography has always required children to develop a sense of where
they are in the world (DES 1991; DfEE/QCA 1999). This does not mean knowing where
everywhere is, but there is an expectation that children will be able to locate places, features
and environments on maps of different scales from the local to the global (Catling 2002). It
also involves building a vocabulary to describe different features and areas such as:

■ the continents and oceans;
■ major rivers, deserts, mountains and seas;
■ major countries and cities;

- places in the news;
- places children study in geography and other subjects;
- places, features and events that children might add themselves.

Similarly, core knowledge of the UK includes the chief cities and countries, some of the main rivers, islands and mountains and places featured in the news. To have a useful mental map of their local area we might want children to know the whereabouts of and relationship between the following:

- their own home and street;
- the road pattern in their area (pathways);
- the main intersections, or street corners (nodes);
- key landmarks such as churches, parks and hills;
- *personal landmarks* such as alleyways and play areas.

All these elements help children to locate themselves. As they build their experience and skills, they will then be able to apply this approach to how they understand other places that they visit (Kitchen and Blades 2002).

Research findings

Teaching locational knowledge builds on children's natural interest in knowing where places are. Children come to school with the capacity to locate themselves and navigate around their immediate environment. Their *mental maps* will include their home, local streets and other familiar nearby places (Matthews 1992). They will also have discrete mental maps of particular places elsewhere or abroad. They can draw these. As their experience increases during the primary years, their maps will become more accurate and detailed. Children learn about other places indirectly through the web, television programmes, computer games, books and stories. They develop a sense of the world map through exposure to world maps, such as in atlases (Figure 5.3). Their knowledge is augmented by informal interactions with family, friends, classmates and others (Reynolds 2004). Although their image of the world becomes more extensive, it is liable to be partial, and large areas will remain 'unknown' to them if they are left to their own devices (Wiegand 2006).

Research into the maps that young children draw from memory shows that their knowledge is built up of discrete 'chunks' or bits of information. Local maps often show specific features of interest to the child, perhaps with roads or pathways linking some elements, but are rarely accurate (Matthews 1992). When young children draw world maps they draw discrete and unconnected places to some extent at random on the page (Wiegand 2006). Knowing where places are involves understanding 'class inclusion' or 'nested hierarchy', where one place lies inside another and inside yet another, like the elements of an address or a set of Russian dolls (Harwood and McShane 1996). Young children quite reasonably have difficulty with the nested hierarchy relationship, so tend to see Sheffield, England and Europe as separate places. It takes time for them to understand their relationship.

Experience of their local area and of finding out about their own country and other parts of the world helps children to develop their understanding, as does regular exposure to national, continental and world maps (Kitchen and Blades 2002; Barrett *et al.* 2006).

■ **Figure 5.3** Africa and North and South America are key features in this map of the world, drawn by a seven year old from memory

For the youngest children, this must involve going out and about round school, visiting local places, playing with maps on playmats and soft toy globes, and nurturing their interest in maps by looking at atlases and exploring websites. For older primary children learning can focus on enquiries into the local area and other localities in national or global settings that develop their map skills. There is not an age when children can begin to learn locational knowledge; it is a matter of encouraging and refining the mapping and locational skills they need and bringing increased rigour to their growing understanding.

LEARNING ABOUT LOCATION

How can we help children to enhance their locational knowledge? It is evident that, left to chance, the development of local and global mental maps will be haphazard. While children undoubtedly construct their own 'personalised' mental maps, it is nevertheless vital that those maps have shared characteristics. After all, the key features of the Earth – such as the continents and oceans – are the basis for everyone's mental map of the world, just as the key patterns and features of a locality make up its shape and character.

Fieldwork

Fieldwork is the key to building young children's mental maps of their local area. Children bring some sense, even at entry to schooling, of places around the area, Fieldwork helps to extend this, fostering meaning as much as locational awareness. Figure 5.4 provides some pointers for this.

Local fieldwork

With Foundation Stage, Reception and Year 1 children, visits to selected places in and around the nursery or school help to focus their attention on what is there and what the place is like. Observing what is on the left, right, ahead, on the corner will develop their spatial vocabulary. You might walk round a route and ask the children to note the 'landmarks' they see, stop to work out where school is 'from here' and talk about which way they can go back. Similar activities that develop early notions of location and direction can be devised in the local park, play area or shops.

With children from Year 2 onwards, local studies should involve the use of maps. Children might draw their own maps or make large floor maps with models to show parts of their area. Using street maps while undertaking local investigations helps them identify their homes, key landmarks or favourite and less-liked places, It also develops their understanding of the connections between features and of the routes around the area. Devising a leaflet for new families to the area or a poster that shows where a new development is planned, as well as providing a creative challenge, will further clarify children's understanding of the layout of the area and its key features.

▪ **Figure 5.4** Local fieldwork helps to develop children's mental maps

Mental maps

It is useful to compare children's mental maps to see what they have in common and the ways in which they are unique. The purpose of 'My world, your world' (Figure 5.5) is to encourage children to think about familiar and unfamiliar places. It involves children in identifying places that have meaning or interests for them and it relates to developing their sense of identity and belonging. They also have to use maps and atlases to check their knowledge. The linked activity, 'My map, my gap', takes a different perspective and gets

My world, your world

This activity focuses on what 'I' know and what interests 'me', but also on what is common or shared. Each child either draws a local map, national map or a world map from memory or adds information to a blank outline. Below their map they then list places they cannot locate but want to add. They compare which places they have included, identifying those they have in common and those that are individual, explaining their choices. To conclude this activity they produce a list of local and global places they think it is useful for everyone to know.

My map, my gap

Across the age range, children list the places they know and find them on a local, UK or world map. They might create individual maps or use pins to show their knowledge on a poster display map or on cardboard cut-outs of the continents arranged as a world map. At intervals, look at the patterns of locations on the maps. Talk about why we know a lot about some places and nothing at all about others. Plan ways to investigate the 'gaps on the maps'. Periodically take digital photographs of the continents to show how information builds up. This might become a class project or can be a homework activity for older children.

▪ **Figure 5.5** Two ways to investigate my world knowledge

children to reflect on their current knowledge. Again, it can be personally focused or it can be a shared activity. Its purpose is to examine the extent of our locational awareness and identify the parts of the world that we are unaware of, which we might try to address.

Wider world

While children cannot readily explore the wider world, it can come to them. Globes and world wall maps are essential resources, as are atlases. From the earliest age children can search for continents, oceans and countries, or for cities, rivers, mountains, deserts and other landscape features. These searches can become more refined, focused and detailed with age but depend on the types of globes and atlases available in school. Google Earth, Google Maps and other internet sources offer alternative approaches. Figure 5.6 offers a number of games that can be used with children of all early years and primary ages.

Exploring the world

A large world map provides opportunities for children to undertake a variety of enjoyable and creative activities that will enhance their locational knowledge. Similar activities can be undertaken using large-size maps of the British Isles and the continents.

Using a large floor map such as MaxiMap
With groups, or a class, ask children to point to and sit or stand on named parts of the world. These might be continents or oceans, countries, mountains or deserts. Can they trace the line of a river or label a major city? Link this to using an atlas, and ask children about places they may not know or are uncertain of, so that they must use the atlas to find them and then locate them on the world map. Children can be asked to crawl, walk or fly from one location to another (see Figure 5.7).

Linking the globe and world map
Using large floor maps or poster (wall) maps with a globe, children can identify features and places on the globe and then point them out on the world map. For young children these might be the continents and oceans; for older children there should be more detail. An atlas should be available for reference.

Using a tabletop-size poster map
Children can use a set of place names, turned over one at a time, to label places on the map, using an atlas as necessary. They might use toy aeroplanes, ships, trains and vehicles to show journeys and routes across continents, oceans and seas. For all of these games you can ask the children to organise the activities – but they need to know where the places they include are! They must have prepared using maps and a globe.

Our connections
Using a poster or wall map, the children locate places they know, where relatives live, which they have visited, that are in the news, across a term or the year, where they would like to visit, or which they have come across for other reasons. Such locations can be marked by pins. They might be linked by a thread to a photograph, a postcard or some information around the map. Periodically discuss the pattern of locations and features marked. Where are most pins located, and where are the gaps? Can they think of reasons for this? Why do some places have no pins? Take photographs or mark a blank map with the named places and patterns.

■ **Figure 5.6** Games and activities to help children learn about the world

■ **Figure 5.7** Children using a Maximap¹ to explore the world map
Photo: Steph Pamplin

Using stories

Enhancing children's mental maps can also be fostered through stories. For young children, picture-books can offer a way to think about what places are like, what is there and how the different features and parts of an area relate to each other. Using the text and pictures enables children to begin to piece together the layout of an area, building a sense of what is where. Figure 5.8 notes some approaches. A selective list of stories is given at the end of this chapter.

Many storybooks have a global dimension. *Love Your Bear Pete!* involves children encountering different places; *The Great Round the World Balloon Race* links contrasting world environments; and *The World Came to My Place Today* illustrates global connections. These are enjoyable stories to read and show with children. This experience can be extended through spotting or finding out where the places mentioned in the stories might be. Children can also invent their own stories involving world journeys. They might tell these orally, using a globe, atlas or world map poster, or produce an illustrated book for younger children to follow.

Creating local maps from stories and experience

Using a picture-book such as *We're Going on a Bear Hunt*, *Roxaboxen* or *Guess Where I Live*, ask children to create a model, picture or map to show the location of the various features and places that are mentioned. Children can work in groups on a single story or work individually to devise their own images of the places and then compare them. What is it that has led them to create different mental maps of these imagined places? Can they agree what the 'true' map of the area might be?

These activities relate to making personal maps of familiar environments. Children often draw the route to school or the area around their school or home. When doing this, ask them to take their maps home with them to check their route or area and what they included. Usually they will improve them and redraw them. Make comparisons with Ordnance Survey or other local maps to see how their maps are similar or different. Why is this? Enhancing children's local mental maps involves them in imagining an overhead view. Sometimes stories such as *Small Bear Lost*, in which a character feels lost or cannot be found, help children to reflect on their own experience of places and extend their mental maps.

■ **Figure 5.8** Stories to introduce the *whereness* of places to children

The world map

Which way up in the Earth? Figure 5.10 shows two world maps. Map A is the one we are used to: north is at the top. Even when we look at a globe we tend to see it this way. In part this is because we use the axis of the Earth and its magnetic field as a point of reference, but this is also a Eurocentric perspective. When viewed from space, the Earth can, of course, be seen at any angle and there is no top or bottom. A different and fun way to challenge the perspective we assume is 'right' is to use the 'Australia-centred' world map illustrated in Map B. Figure 5.9 outlines an approach to using such a map to see where places are from a different perspective, where south provides the viewing base.

Which way is up? Does it matter?

Give the children two copies of the world map, one with 'north' marked at the top, and the other with 'south' at the top. Discuss which one the children feel more comfortable with and why? What is strange about the other one? Now ask them to name the continents and oceans on the south-orientated map. Conclude by talking about or investigating the following questions:

■　　Does it matter whether north or south is at the top?
■　　When and why did people start drawing world maps with north at the top?
■　　Why might people have wanted to put east at the top before magnetic compasses were invented?
■　　Enter 'world maps' into Google Images. How many different ways is the map of the world drawn? Which do you most like and which do you like least? Which fascinates you most? Explain why this is.

■ **Figure 5.9** Re-orientating the world map can be a highly creative process

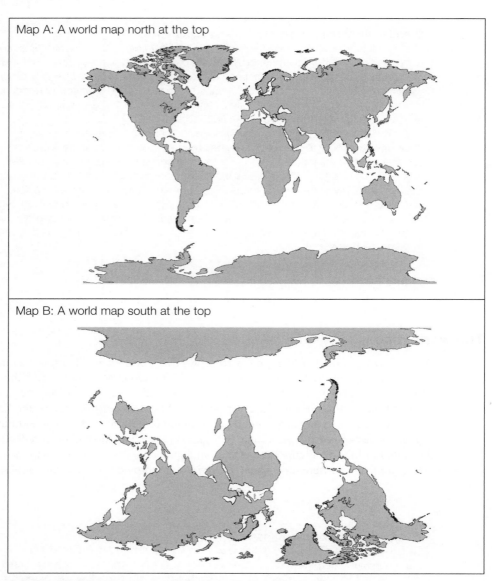

Map A: A world map north at the top

Map B: A world map south at the top

■ **Figure 5.10** Which of these world maps is the 'right way up'?

FURTHER ACTIVITIES

A variety of other approaches can be included within or alongside topics. They all use imaginative and creative responses. Problem-solving, investigation and enquiry are also highlighted. The activities outlined in Figure 5.11 might be the focus for a class activity, for a map club or as homework encouraging the children to find out about where places are and the value of locational knowledge. All 12 activities can be used to develop children's world locational knowledge.

Why should I know there?

This activity could focus on the local area or nationally, or be about world map knowledge. Encourage children to consider which features and places all children should know about, and which might be included individually to personalise maps. This can be an individual or group activity. They might focus on 'where should new people to our area know about?' or 'What are the places in the UK/world we should know about?' Have the children:

■ identify places they think everyone should know; debate and agree reasons to include them; create a map showing the places;

■ propose ways to learn where the places are on maps and how to show their learning;

■ develop criteria to choose places they want to add because they have a personal interest or meaning.

What's going on where – and why?

Use broadcasts, papers or websites to keep up to date with news reports from local to global. Mark the places that are mentioned on maps of the local area, British Isles, Europe and the world. Have different children write a brief summary, make a drawing or print off a captioned photograph about the event and link these to the locating map pin by string or cotton. Discuss why these places are in the news and why it helps to know where these events happen. Over a period of time, note which places are referred to more frequently. You might link this to the children's own maps of 'significant' places.

Atlas addicts

Encourage children to check the location of places they come across but do not know. They might use local street atlases, national road atlases and world atlases. (Refer to *The Times Atlas of the World* (Times Books) for places that are particularly obscure.) From time to time, ask the children about:

■ how many places they know the whereabouts of;

■ how they have discovered where these places are;

■ what sort of places they are;

■ the locations of the oddest, strangest or nicest places they have found;

■ what fascinates them about using atlases and finding out about places.

Atlas investigation

Use atlases to find out where places are and to develop children's map skills. For instance, they could:

■ use the contents and index pages to find particular maps and places;

■ learn to read alpha-numeric grids or longitude and latitude to locate places;

■ find out the longitude or latitude of key features such as the Equator, Tropics of Cancer and Capricorn and Greenwich meridian;

■ use the key to see how symbols show different types of features, including point features (like cities), line features (like rivers) or area features (like countries);

■ use the symbols to describe how the atlas map portrays an area;

■ use compass directions to say which direction places are from each other;

■ use scales to measure distances;

■ appreciate how atlas maps relate to the globe by comparing continent shapes.

■ **Figure 5.11** Twelve engaging ways to develop locational awareness

Atlas quiz

Children of all ages enjoy quizzes. Create quiz questions for groups to find out where places are and what they can say about these places. Once they have undertaken a few quizzes, children can set the questions themselves. A variation is to provide the children with atlas quiz questions for homework. In the quiz itself, in class, they cannot use an atlas but have to recall the answers. Children can work alone or in teams.

Country factfile

Make a factfile for different countries listing such things as the capital city, main physical features, population, language, neighbouring countries, main industries, farm products , habitats and environmental problems, Get the children to draw a map of the country together with its flag. Include its national flag, its population, what range of things its people do, where they live and how, its neighbour nations, what links it has with the UK, and what it is well-known for.

Country shapes

Provide cut-out shapes of a variety of countries on paper or card or give the children an activity sheet that contains the outline shapes/borders of a number of nations. Can the children identify them with the help of an atlas? You could restrict the activity to a single continent or to the regions within a country, e.g. UK counties or US states. Relate this to internet games such as those on the Ordnance Survey site www.mapzone.ordnancesurvey.co.uk/games.html.

United Nations

Find out how many countries are recognised by the United Nations. Find out about the UN as an organisation, its origins and role in the world today. How many countries are members and which nations want to join? A variation on this activity is to find out how the number of countries in the world has changed over time. Which are the newest countries in the world? Are there any others that are about to be created or want to be recognised?

World products

Where in the world are various products grown or made? Think about our daily foods, the toys and goods we buy, the television programmes we watch and so on. Highlight the places or countries involved on a map, perhaps as part of a cross-curricular or thematic topic

World environments

As a class exercise, ask the children to draw plants and creatures to add to a large world map. Show the children clips from wildlife films to extend their knowledge and fuel their enthusiasm. Find out some of the threats to different creatures or habitats. What are people doing to help preserve biodiversity?

Google Earth

Use the Google Earth website (earth.google.co.uk) to look at satellite views of the Earth and to zoom in to see where places are and what they look like from 'above' on the photographs. Use a map of the world to mark on the places you have looked at trying to include a variety of places. Now use Google Maps to look at maps of the same areas the satellite photos of which you have looked at.

■ **Figure 5.11** continued

Create your own globe

Children can create their own globes. They should blow up a (almost) circular balloon, cover it in papier-mâché and let it dry. Use a commercial globe to help draw on the 'globe' the continents and major islands of the Earth. Colour the land green and the sea blue, or create variations of colours to show major mountain areas, major deserts, major forests and so forth. Add the largest cities, lakes and some major rivers. Decide on what else to add to 'personalise' the globe.

■ **Figure 5.11** continued

CONCLUSION

This chapter has considered the rationale for teaching locational knowledge in geography, explored how to develop children's mental maps at local, national and global scales and outlined a number of stimulating and enjoyable activities. Not knowing where places are in the locality or around the world can be inhibiting, even embarrassing. Such learning does not happen unless children have the chance to explore places and use maps, globes and atlases from their earliest years. This requires careful planning. One of the pleasures for children in locating places lies in getting to know where they are. It requires increasingly effective map-reading skills and the building of ever more sophisticated mental maps. The objective should also be to ensure that children have fun with maps, that they value maps and atlases and that their world awareness is celebrated. Figure 5.12 outlines what is required to create such happy mappers.

Enjoying mapping and locating places comes about through children:

■ having local maps, road atlases, globes and atlases in class to pick up and explore, as well as to use in their investigations and projects;
■ learning the skills of map reading;
■ realising that maps and atlases matter for our daily lives;
■ being able to go and look up places when they hear about them to find out more, because there is map or an atlas to hand;
■ gaining pleasure from poring over a map just because it looks fascinating, there is much to see and it sparks their imagination;
■ realising it's fun to know stuff about the world.

For this to happen, ensure that:

■ there are atlases and maps of all sorts easily accessible in the classroom;
■ there is a globe (or two or three);
■ children know they can look at maps when they want to;
■ you include map skills and place learning in geography, other subjects and cross-curricular topics;
■ the children see you looking at maps and know you value them – and the world;
■ you celebrate your own and their knowledge of places locally and globally.

■ **Figure 5.12** Creating happy mappers

REFERENCES

Barrett, M., Lyons, E. and Bourchier-Sutton, A. (2006) 'Children's knowledge of countries', in Spencer, C. and Blades, M. (eds) *Children and their Environments*. Cambridge: Cambridge University Press.

Catling, S. (2002) *Placing Places*. Sheffield: Geographical Association.

DES (1991) *Geography in the National Curriculum (England)*. London: HMSO.

DfEE/QCA (1999) *The National Curriculum Handbook for Primary Teachers in England*. London: DfEE/QCA.

Downs, R. and Stea, D. (1977) *Maps in Minds*. New York: Harper & Row.

Gould, P. and White, R. (1986) *Mental Maps*. London: Routledge.

Harwood, D. and McShane, J. (1996) 'Young children's understanding of nested hierarchies on place relationship'. *International Research in Geographical and Environmental Education*, 5 (1), 3–29.

Kitchen, R. and Blades, M. (2002) *The Cognition of Geographic Space*. London: IB Tauris.

Matthews, H. (1992) *Making Sense of Place*. Hemel Hempstead: Harvester Wheatsheaf.

Ofsted (2011) *Geography: Learning to Make a World of Difference*. www.ofsted.gov.uk/resources/publications (accessed on 15 September 2011).

Reynolds, R. (2004) 'Where is that place? Primary children's attitudes to and knowledge of the world', Proceedings of the AARE Conference. http://ogma.newcastle.edu.au:8080/vital/access/manager/Repository/uon:3812/ATTACHMENT01 (accessed 26 September 2011).

Wiegand, P. (2006) *Learning and Teaching with Maps*. London: Routledge.

Atlases and globes

A range of atlases for all primary ages is available from the major school atlas publishers: Oxford University Press, Collins and Philips. Globes of many varieties can be obtained from the usual range of school suppliers. Look out for soft globes and inflatable globes that young children can hug, as well as for small and large globes on stands. Look also for globes that show the continents and oceans, unnamed, as well as those that show the Earth's physical features, countries and major cities.

Examples of locally based picture storybooks

Anni Axworth (2000) *Guess Where I Live*. Walker Books.

Anthony Browne (2004) *Into the Forest*. Walker Books.

Eric Carle (1996) *Rooster's Off to See the World*. Puffin Books.

Julia Donaldson and Axel Scheffler (2004) *The Gruffalo's Child*. Macmillan Publishers.

Julia Donaldson and Axel Schaffler (2009) *Stick Man*. Alison Green Books.

Emily Gravett (2006) *Meerkat Mail*. Macmillan Publishers.

Libby Hathorn and Gregory Rogers (1994) *Way Home*. Andersen Press.

Stephen King (2005) *Mutt Dog*. Scholastic Hippo.

Alice McLerran and Barbara Cooney (1991) *Roxaboxen*. HarperCollins

Inga Moore (2010) *Six Dinner Sid: A Highland Adventure*. Hodder Children's Books.

Michael Rosen and Helen Oxenbury (1993) *We're Going on a Bear Hunt*. Walker Books.

Examples of picture storybooks with a world focus

Paul Adshead and Toni Goffe (1996) *Around the World with Phineas Frog*. Child's Play International Ltd.

Hans de Beer (1994) *Little Polar Bear*. North-South Books.

Laurent de Brunhoff (2005) *Babar's World Tour*. Harry Abrams Publishers.
Sarah Fanelli (2006) *My Map Book*. Walker Books.
Brian Patten and Arthur Robbins (1993) *The Magic Bicycle*. Walker Books.
Jo Readman and Ley Honour Roberts (2002) *The World Came to My Place Today*. Eden Project Books.
Dyan Shedon and Tania Hurt-Newton (1994) *Love Your Bear Pete!* Walker Books.
Eve Sutton and Lynley Dodd (1973) *My Cat Likes to Hide in Boxes*. Puffin Books.
Jen Wainwright (2011) *Where's the Meercat?* Michael O'Mara Books.

NOTE

1   Maximap World and British Isles giant floor maps can be obtained from: sales@maximap.net.

CHAPTER 6

REPRESENTING PLACES IN MAPS AND ART

Margaret Mackintosh

This chapter aims to excite teachers and pupils with different and innovative pictorial ways of representing and communicating geographical spatial information, ideas and concepts. The way that we view the world from different perspectives creates strong links with both ICT and art. These links are explored here with particular reference to Aboriginal painting, Google Earth and the work of two artists, Friedereich Hundertwasser and David Hockney. The focus is on what some might call 'out-of-the-box' approaches, since more familiar ideas about using pictorial visual communication resources are published elsewhere, notably in the Geographical Association's *Primary Geography Handbook* (Scoffham 2010) and *Learning and Teaching with Maps* (Wiegand 2006). The aim is to give some practical, geography-led but interdisciplinary examples of how to be creative with spatial representation and communication. It is hoped that, as a result, children will develop enthusiasm for and enjoyment in looking at, reading and making different types and styles of spatial representation and a love of maps.

LANDSCAPE AND ART

'It was good fun, creative and geographical';
'I learnt to rely on other people, working in a team';
'I consider it both art and geography because I used both sorts of techniques';
'It was a good experience, fun, interesting and good inspiration – an art project with a geographical twist'.

What were these pupils talking about? What was the project? The pupils were commenting on a day's activity for a cluster of rural schools, 'Right or Left, Up or Down?', led by Kim Etchells, a practising artist and part-time tutor in north Devon. It was initially planned as an art project but the focus and potential was definitely geographical, so it is described here in some detail. In a fun, practical, creative and inspirational way it introduces, and provides opportunities to develop many concepts and techniques essential to representing geographical spatial information in maps, photographs and diagrams. The power of the geography in Etchells's approach was most evident when the work of the cluster of participating schools was brought together in an exhibition in Great Torrington, north Devon. Organising a similar event in your school would make a powerful impact, which, if accompanied by a display of all sorts of formal and informal maps, oblique and vertical aerial views, photographs and postcards, would highlight in a geographical context the importance of visual literacy, sometimes referred to as graphicacy (Mackintosh 2010).

There were three elements to the activity day: (i) landscape through maps, (ii) landscape through models, and (iii) journeys. In preparation, a map of the area centred on each school had been greatly enlarged, and the roads, settlements and field boundaries copied on to white paper. This was stuck on cardboard and cut into 15cm squares. A limited but appropriate colour palette was chosen involving greens, reds and browns.

Landscape through maps

The day started with a talk about land use, pattern and texture in the landscape. Pupils were already familiar with Google Earth, which they had used to explore features of the landscape in their local area and beyond. Now they looked at photographs of, for example, the pattern made by the bushes in a tea plantation, and other vertical and oblique aerial views. They were shown landscape paintings by artists such as Hockney and Hundertwasser. The children were encouraged to talk about their own area and the characteristics of their environment, and to collect descriptive words. They were asked to consider the meaning of the term 'rural'.

Each child was then given a 15cm square from the map of the area around their school and a palette of ready-mix colours. They each painted their square using the colours in a (fairly!) controlled system, leaving the roads white and giving the landscape colour and texture to indicate possible land-use. Further squares were painted as time allowed and the whole was assembled to recreate a map of each school's region (Figure 6.1).

In future geographical work children would be expected to look for pattern and texture in landscape on a range of photographs and maps. Using a restricted palette and indicative land-use textures on their own map helped them to understand the need for a key and symbols. Further discussion and practical work would lead to an eventual understanding of the significance of the stylised conventions used in OS maps.

■ **Figure 6.1** This close-up of some of the squares of the map created by pupils at Clinton C of E Primary School, Merton, Okehampton, Devon shows road and field patterns and uses texturing to indicate land use
Photo: Margaret Mackintosh

Landscape through models

The next part of the day consisted of a 'leap of freedom'. Using the same-size squares of card as for the earlier map exercise, the children were put together in teams to construct a model landscape (Figure 6.2). The possibility of including a river or lake – blue paint added to the palette – caused excitement and the children spontaneously wanted to relate one piece or square to another and to where they lived.

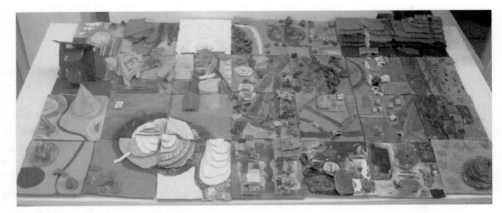

■ **Figure 6.2** Imagined landscapes by pupils from several participating schools in north Devon. Pupils created their model landscapes and appreciated the value of teamwork as they planned for adjacent squares to fit together
Photo: Margaret Mackintosh

In future geographical work, children would make drawings, diagrams and maps of the landscape in their models. Young pupils could also do this with model landscapes created in their sandtray and construct a model from a given landscape photograph. Older pupils could make models from maps and photographs and annotate photographs of their models to identify geographical features such as rivers, hills, routes and settlements. In doing this they would be exploring different ways of representing geographical information and beginning to appreciate the strengths and weaknesses of each. Children might also consider the need for a key, a scale and an indication of compass direction for the benefit of themselves and others, rather than because they had been told to include them by the teacher. In this way they will eventually begin to picture photographs and maps as three-dimensional 'models' by reconstructing or visualising the landscape represented. It is known that many children have difficulty interpreting the scale of geographical features they see in photographs (Lieben and Downs 1993). Creative teachers will provide fieldwork opportunities where children can see examples of streams, hills, cliffs and farms for themselves and bring photographs back to the classroom to relate to their models and maps.

Landscape through journeys

The afternoon activities focused on journeys. Pupils visualised a real or imagined journey of their own, which they depicted using collage and drawing techniques in a four-page concertina book. They thought about mode of transport, reason for the journey, the terrain, speed, destination, what they could see along the way, the season and the weather, and other geographical aspects. As the work was centred on collage, the children focused on how to use colour as a mosaic, rather than on drawing pictures of landmarks.

To generate ideas pupils looked at how different artists have depicted routes and journeys. Hockney's landscape paintings such as 'Winter Tunnel with Snow', 'Roads and Cornfields' and 'Road across the Wolds' (see Figure A in colour plate section and websites) provided a valuable stimulus. While some of Hockney's paintings depict hedge-lined tracks, others show a more elevated view over a road with the landscape and route disappearing into the distance. At times Hockney is more 'playful' with landscape, using photographs, as in his photo-collages and, more recently, an iPad. Following these inputs the children became more experimental, more open and playful themselves in their interpretation of their journey. Eavesdropping on conversation revealed the different scale of the journeys being portrayed, from transcontinental to a microscopic journey inside the human body.

The creative teacher might want to develop the visual communication of journeys in future geographical work. Children could look at some of the many ways of representing or communicating a journey pictorially. Young children could sequence photographs they had taken of landmarks seen on a class walk or journey. They could make a map of the journey, locate the landmarks on a large-scale map and look for them on Google Earth, using the satellite images and the facility Street View. Children might compile an album of photographs taken on a school residential visit and recreate the journey. They could look at journeys portrayed in art, in diagrams such as of the journey of a river or the London Underground, and in maps of many sorts, from pictorial oblique views to street maps and road and world atlases.

Map work is best not treated as an isolated and decontextualised exercise but related to real situations and needs. We use a dictionary or a calculator when we require them but seem much less ready to refer a map or diagram to support our work. The creative teacher will find many opportunities to use maps in connection with journeys. Whenever the class is going on a long or short journey, for whatever subject, an appropriate map should be consulted beforehand, to plan the 'best' route, taking distance, time, safety, mode of transport and cost into consideration. After the journey the route will be confirmed by again looking at the map. If the route is coloured on the map, pupils will be able to see the distance, direction and shape of the journey related to their school. This will help them to construct their spatial understanding of the school's surroundings.

Some weeks after the end of the project, pupils were asked for their reactions and responses. They replied:

'I learned about all different parts of the place where I live, but in a fun way'.
'I liked making my own map of somewhere – I enjoyed it'.
'I thought it was very interesting and fun – I most enjoyed creating my own little environment, a mountain'.
'I learned that there are so many different views in Devon'.
'You learn about the environment and can draw the/your surroundings – it was geography and art'.

The combination of geography and art provides the focus for later sections of this chapter. As well as being informative, maps can be beautiful works of art in their own right. Paintings and photographs can also communicate geographical information. Used creatively, separately or in combination, they can help to encourage a lifelong love of maps and geography.

STARTING WITH PAINTINGS

Many paintings have a spatial, almost map-like feel to them. This section suggests a range of paintings and artists that can be used as starting points for more geographical work on maps, diagrams and visual communication. Each painting could be used to encourage an interest in and enthusiasm for different ways of representing the three-dimensional world in two dimensions, ultimately to foster a love of maps.

Dreamings

Aboriginal 'dreamings' are timeless, spiritual and private creation stories, but some are now depicted in paintings. This map, diagram, plan or painting (does it matter what we call it?) relates to the Papunya community in Australia's Northern Territories desert and was produced around 1990. It tells a story using traditional symbols. The Aboriginal artist Nita Rubuntja has written the story on the back of her painting (Figure 6.3).

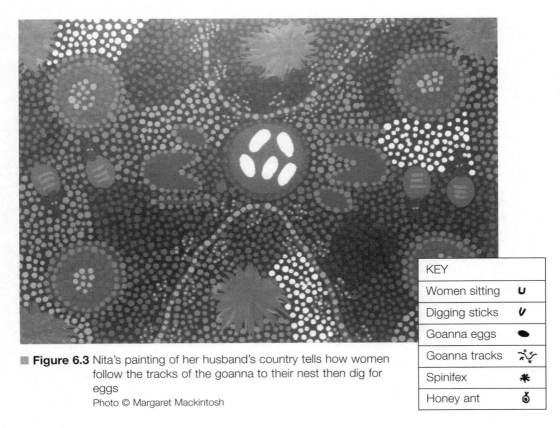

KEY	
Women sitting	U
Digging sticks	V
Goanna eggs	●
Goanna tracks	🐾
Spinifex	✳
Honey ant	☿

■ **Figure 6.3** Nita's painting of her husband's country tells how women follow the tracks of the goanna to their nest then dig for eggs
Photo © Margaret Mackintosh

Get the children to study the painting carefully but don't tell them the story yet. They could:

(i)   tell their own interpretation or story of the painting;
(ii) represent one of their own activities, journeys or personal stories in Aboriginal style for others to 'read';
(iii) create an alternative mapping of (i) or (ii) in their own personal, rather than Aboriginal, style.

Some children in Sheffield did this, making mappings of the Meadowhall Shopping Centre inspired by Aboriginal symbols, as part of work on Australia (Collis 2011).

Once they know Nita's story, encourage children to interpret the painting creatively in a western-style drawing or map. Needing to know the meaning of the Aboriginal symbols to read or tell the painting's story could create a memorable bridge or link with later work on keys and symbols. Letting the children into the secret of Nita's story vividly illustrates why we need a key to explain the symbols that we use. A key is a necessity if maps and diagrams are to communicate spatial information effectively and be fully understood.

Hundertwasser

Friedereich Hundterwasser was an architect, artist and environmentalist who used bright colours and organic forms to link humans and nature through his paintings, graphics and environmental posters. His works are a rich resource that cannot fail to interest and excite children and stimulate them to suggest their own interpretations. Some of the works are rural, others are urban, so will relate to schools in every setting. Some are from a street level (horizontal perspective), others are drawn from above (vertical perspective) and others are a combination of the two. Many of Hundertwasser's works make excellent starting points for exploring viewpoints. Here are a few you might like to try. Locate paintings 88, 125, 170, 241, 373, 433, 525 on the Hundertwasser website. Figures B and C in the colour plate section, show two Hundertwasser paintings: 175 An Almost Circle and 'City seen from beyond the Sun' (241).

Try to elicit the children's ideas about the paintings before giving them the title to encourage them to make their own interpretation. Once they know the title, 'City Seen from beyond the Sun' readily conjures up city streets circling a square city-centre piazza, park or even lake (it's painted blue), but children might have other ideas. 175 An Almost Circle looks very much like a map. It could be seen as an inner ring road or other major road with blocks of buildings, but are there faces, is there a central park or does it represent something entirely different to a child? A creative approach encourages a range of responses – there isn't one right answer. There are also plenty of opportunities to encourage children to create similar paintings of their own. Some pupils might want to overpaint a photocopy from a Google Earth image, photograph or map. Others may decide to follow their own creative ideas (Figure 6.4).

Further geographical work would include using different types of map, considering colour and texture and exploring the need for scales, compass directions and keys. Asking younger pupils to use a given palette to paint the roads, buildings, water, fields and woods in appropriate colours would check their understanding of a blank map. Studying Hundertwasser's works and their own artistic creations would encourage recognition and

■ **Figure 6.4** This ten-year-old's overpainting of an oblique aerial view of the Eden Project, Cornwall has some similarities to a Hundertwasser painting and emphasises the pattern of routeways in a map-like way
Artist: Alexander Mackintosh; photo © Margaret Mackintosh

understanding of pattern in both urban and rural environments. Depending on the stimulus used, children would be able to recognise the patterns made by motorways, streets, housing estates and more. Pupils could search for these in whatever maps, aerial photographs and satellite images they use in future geographical work. This would also serve to sensitise them to patterns, shapes and form and the way they are represented in more conventional maps.

Hockney

David Hockney's later work includes many magical paintings of landscapes and routes in the Yorkshire Wolds and other places (Figure A in colour plate section). Teachers can help children to identify the landscape features and land use, get them to 'walk into' the picture and imagine that they are travelling along the route. What would they hear, feel, see and smell around them? They could also create a map for someone else to use for the same journey. Elevated viewpoints increase the field of view and the complexity of the challenge.

Going further

The range of activities described will involve children looking at Aboriginal art, inspirational paintings, photographs, satellite images and maps in different and creative ways. The examples have focused on Hockney and Hundertwasser but there are many other artists who might also appeal to pupils and engage their imaginations. Developing pupils' interest in and enthusiasm for visual communication in many styles can establish the foundations for a lifelong love of maps, environments and geography. As one child with learning difficulties commented when doing this sort of work while he learned geography without realising it: 'I can DO pictures!'

STARTING WITH MAPS

Maps are informative and useful but they can also be wonderful works of art in their own right. Their essence and purpose is to represent a three-dimensional world in a two-dimensional format to communicate spatial information. Maps tell a story. Spatial thinkers are fascinated by this, but linear or sequential thinkers can find it challenging.

Maps, and also diagrams, tell a story that is represented, essentially, pictorially. Children need to be taught to read this pictorial story in much the same way as they are taught to read word stories. The term 'visual literacy' or, in a geographical sense, the word 'graphicacy' is often used to describe these skills. There are many different types, styles, perspectives and scales of maps, but in this section there is only room for a few cartographic styles, each fascinating in its own way, to be suggested as starting points. The message is to use as wide a range as you can.

It is easy to make people feel that maps are incomprehensible, and even to alienate them from maps for life. One explanation is that maps *per se*, and especially Ordnance Survey maps with their conventions, are sometimes taught to children too soon and in isolation rather than in a relevant context. Although some youngsters are able to complete the tasks associated with OS maps, their understanding is often limited. This negativity can be easily overcome by devising activities to foster and encourage children's innate love of, fascination for and curiosity about maps, especially if maps are used in association with other pictorial representations of places, spaces and environments.

Historical maps fascinate children both in content and style. The Hereford *Mappa Mundi* was drawn on vellum (calf skin) in about 1290AD and is one of the cathedral's treasures. Hereford appears in the map alongside the River Wye, its location marked by a drawing of the cathedral. As the cathedral website says, this circular map:

> reflects the thinking of the medieval church with Jerusalem at the centre of the world. Superimposed on to the continents are drawings of the history of humankind and the marvels of the natural world. These 500 or so drawings include around 420 cities and towns, 15 Biblical events, 33 plants, animals, birds and strange creatures, 32 images of the peoples of the world and 8 pictures from classical mythology.

Start by encouraging children to marvel at the intrinsic beauty of the map and at the way it records the known world of its time. Help them to recognise the continents, rivers, places and other geographical features along with the fantasy creatures. An exciting challenge would be for pupils to try to draw a map of their own known world in a similar style. Some children might try to draw a local map while others might work on a more global scale, perhaps related to their travel experiences. The *Mappa Mundi* is drawn with Asia at the top and Europe at the bottom. Surprisingly it is orientated towards the east – the direction of Jerusalem. This decision, which seems surprising nowadays, provides an opportunity to introduce children to the modern convention of putting north at the top.

Whatever locality is being studied, encourage children to look at as wide a range of maps as possible, helping them appreciate that there is not just one way to map a place. Compare the content of the maps. What do they all show? What does only one include? Maps show different features depending on the purposes, interests and choices made by the cartographer. This means that maps of the same place can look different even when they are drawn accurately. Using appropriate websites (see references) and other sources such as libraries, seek out maps from different dates. Children often find John Speed's seventeenth-century maps intriguing as they use pictorial oblique views. Such maps provide a natural opportunity to link history and geography. You might also encourage children to become time detectives by looking at, say, four maps of the same area at different dates in the past. Early maps of Hull, for example, only show buildings within the city wall. Subsequent maps show how the moat has been turned into docks and that the town is beginning to spread. When the railway arrives, the town grows still further, especially to the north and west.

Be on the lookout for maps in the street that convey information for visitors as well as local people. There are many information boards with pictorial maps at industrial and coastal tourist spots. A good example is in Leeds where the 'waterfront heritage' area has recently been improved. These maps are ideal for primary children because they are designed to be engaging and identify key landmarks. In recent years, pictorial maps have become increasingly available from bookshops, tourist centres and in tourist brochures. These employ a range of perspectives from horizontal to vertical and make valuable links between overhead views and OS maps, Aerial photographs are an additional resource accessible to the full primary age range, especially those by Arthus-Bertrand and Burleigh (2002), Experience suggests that children love looking at these – they should be in every school library, as should a full range of road and world atlases.

MISSING MAPS

Have you ever read a novel and thought to yourself 'this book needs a map'? A good example of a book that needs one is *Half of a Yellow Sun* (Adichie 2006), which is a story about eastern Nigeria before and after the Biafran war. There are some books that do benefit from maps, including the Beast Quest series, Arthur Ransome books, Winnie the Pooh stories and *Katie Morag in Struay* (Isle of Coll), although in some hardback library copies the dust jacket and date page are stuck down, obscuring the frontispiece map. The maps vary from rudimentary sketches to detailed pictorial representations but at least they communicate the spatial relationships of the places featured in the stories. Encourage children to visualise the setting and create maps to accompany stories they read. This requires them to think spatially and can help to indicate their understanding of place and story. The ability to visualise land- and town-scapes is an essential skill in reading and interpreting a conventional map.

CONCLUSION

Creative approaches will inspire other teachers and children to develop and foster a love of graphicacy in its widest manifestations and lead to imaginative work by teachers and children within and beyond geography. The suggestions presented in this chapter are deliberately divergent and possibly 'outside the box' to encourage imaginative and creative thinking and teaching. As a step towards developing the confidence to use visual communication more creatively, try using different graphicacy forms in combination to help children make the link between the horizontal, oblique and vertical viewpoints which are summarised in Figure 6.5).

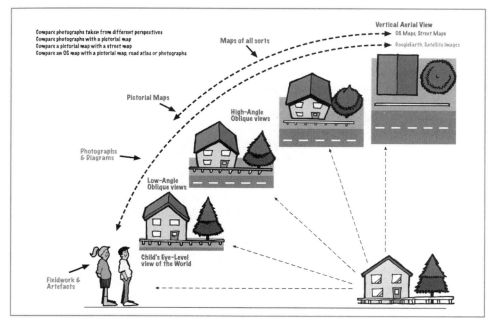

■ **Figure 6.5** It is important to encourage children to look at their surroundings from different perspectives

Source: *Primary Geography Handbook*, Geography Association: 122

There are several important points to keep in mind:

■ Use all sorts of maps and other geographical visual images as often as possible whenever the context is appropriate.

■ Help children to read and interpret a wide range of two-dimensional representations of three-dimensional spaces, places and environments.

■ Help children move from their everyday eye-level view of the world to the bird's-eye view of conventional maps by including images from the full range of horizontal to low- and high-angle oblique to vertical perspectives.

■ Use a wide range of styles and scales of image, including globes.

■ Include maps during fieldwork, and use photographs (from personal to satellite), drawings, diagrams, field sketches, paintings, maps of all sorts (pictorial, street, road atlas, OS, globes) in context to support and enhance geographical work.

■   aim to use different pictorial resources about a location in combination, rather than in a sequence. In combination, children can switch from one to another, can see the relationship between the photographic, satellite and pictorial, road and OS map representations and diagrams, so that clues from one representation can help understanding of another.

BUT, most of all, through creative teaching and creative activities that encourage creative responses, foster an enthusiasm for landscapes, a fascination for places, spaces and environments and a love of maps.

REFERENCES

Adichie (2006) *Half of a Yellow Sun*. New York: Alfred A. Knopf.

Arthus-Bertrand, Y. and Burleigh, R. (2002) *The Earth from the Air for Children*. London: Thames and Hudson.

Bridge, C. (2010) 'Mapwork skills', in Scoffham, S. (ed.) *Primary Geography Handbook*. Sheffield: Geographical Association.

Collis, S. (2011) 'Global mapping: looking at where I live with fresh eyes'. *Primary Geographer*, 75: 10–11.

Lieben, L. and Downs, R. (1993) 'Understanding person-space-map relations: cartographic and developmental perspectives'. *Developmental Psychology*, 29: 739–52.

Mackintosh, M. (2010), 'Using photographs, diagrams and sketches', in Scoffham, S. (ed.) *Primary Geography Handbook*. Sheffield: Geographical Association.

Mackintosh, M. (2011) 'Graphicacy for life'. *Primary Geographer*, 75: 6–8.

Rand, H. (2007) *Hundertwasser*. Cologne: Taschen.

Scoffham, S. (ed.) (2010) *Primary Geography Handbook*. Sheffield: Geography Association.

Stieff, B. (2008) *Hundertwasser for Kids*. London: Prestel.

Wiegand, P. (2006) *Learning and Teaching with Maps*. London: Routledge.

Websites

Aboriginal art
http://www.aboriginalarttreasures.com/symbols.php
http://www.thanguwa.com/symbols.htm
Mappa Mundi
http://www.herefordcathedral.org/visit-us/mappa-mundi-1
Maps and plans
http://www.google.com/earth/index.html
http://freepages.genealogy.rootsweb.ancestry.com/~genmaps/, http://www.cassinimaps.co.uk/shop/mapmaker2.asp
David Hockney paintings
Search for images of 'David Hockney landscape paintings', 'photocollages' and 'iPad art'
Friederich Hundertwasser's paintings
http://www.hundertwasser.com/

CHAPTER 7

LANDSCAPES AND SWEET GEOGRAPHY

Niki Whitburn

Rocks and soils are fundamental to life on Earth. They form the landscapes in which we live and provide nourishment for the plants on which we depend for food. Learning about rocks and soils can facilitate links between geography and other curriculum areas. An unusual way to introduce and develop this topic is to use food as an analogy. Children of all ages can relate to food, and using it in a creative way can enable them to build up their understanding of key geographical concepts. It was the Chinese philosopher Confucius who once said, 'I hear and I forget; I see and I remember; I do and I understand.' Bearing this in mind, the ideas presented here illustrate physical features and processes in a practical manner. They also provide a basis on which to develop and enhance the children's own creativity. Most can be delivered at various levels depending on the age and ability of your class.

LOOKING AT MINERALS (KEY STAGE 1)

Treasure chest

This is a sorting exercise, which can be turned into a game in which children create their own treasure chest of chosen 'jewels'.

AIM

To help children appreciate that there are different types of minerals.
To enable children to develop and discuss their likes and dislikes and relate these to sorting criteria.

WARNING

Take care when handling any minerals, rocks or soils. Ensure normal health and safety rules are applied and hands are washed afterwards

RESOURCES

Small boxes
Silver foil or coloured paper
Small mineral pieces of different colours and textures (obtainable from gift shops and educational suppliers)
Large tray and several smaller trays or boxes

Before the main activity the children could use the small boxes to make their own treasure chests and cover them with silver foil or decorated paper. Alternatively, they could be provided with pre-made ones.

THE CHALLENGE – THESE ARE MY TREASURES

Introduce the challenge to the children by showing them a large tray containing a large mixture of mineral pieces. Discuss how they look and feel and ask the children what they like and don't like about them. The mineral pieces can then be placed in 'mines' (small trays or boxes) at various places in the room. The children decide what criteria they will use to collect their treasure, e.g. a certain colour, clear ones, smooth ones, rough ones. The miners (children) then tour the country (classroom) to find the ones they have chosen, placing them in their treasure chests. Once all the children have collected their treasure, small groups can discuss what they have chosen and why, and describe the difference between the various minerals (Figure 7.1). The ensuing discussion can help to develop the children's knowledge and understanding of minerals and rocks and may provoke questions, which, in turn, will lead them to search for answers. (Alexander 2004, in Cremin 2009).

■ **Figure 7.1** The 'treasure chest' on the left has coloured minerals and the on the right sparkly minerals

EXTENSION

This activity can be progressive and lead into setting up a display table of unusual examples. Children will want to contribute their own specimens. Although you probably won't be able to identify these, the main teaching point is to draw attention to different minerals. Granite, for example, contains easily visible crystals of black mica and white/grey quartz. Shap granite also includes pink feldspar. This introduces the idea that rocks can be formed from several different minerals mixed together.

Rocks and minerals

We now come to the first analogy relating to food. Discuss with the children how biscuits can be very different depending on the ingredients. Get them to write down or produce a group list of as many different types of biscuit they can think of. Then discuss what the ingredients might be, e.g. chocolate chip biscuit has chocolate pieces added, fruit biscuit has sultanas, digestive has neither. Alternatively, with more able children, get them to write down their favourite biscuit and a list of what it is made of, then compare lists. All the above could be done using cakes rather than biscuits.

AIM

To learn that rocks are made of minerals (treasure).
To demonstrate that biscuits are different because they are made of different foods.
To link this analogy to the composition and appearance of rocks.

WARNING

With all food activities, check for nut and other allergies. Ensure normal health and safety rules are applied, e.g. hands are washed before and after and hair is tied back.

RESOURCES

Each child will need a biscuit or cake bar, a plate and lolly sticks or similar. The most suitable biscuits are those such as chocolate chip cookies, or fruit shortbreads. Alternatively, health-food bars work just as well. Small cake bars containing fruit or chocolate chips could also be used and may be easier for younger children to dissect. The activity works best if more than one type of biscuit or cake bar is used.

THE CHALLENGE – MINING FOR TREASURE

Ask the children what they can see in the biscuits/cakes – choc-chips, grains, fruit, sponge? The choc-chips or fruit represents the minerals that are valuable. Get them to break them up, or 'dissect' them, and sort them into the different components, so they end up with small piles of choc chip, grain, fruit, biscuit, sponge and so forth (Figure 7.2). Who has the most 'minerals' or which type of biscuit or cake bar has the most minerals? Ask the children questions to aid description and comparison such as:

Which component is the largest/smallest?
Do all the choc-chip ones have the same amounts of chocolate?

Do the fruit ones have more fruit than the chocolate in the choc-chip ones?
Do they think there is enough chocolate/fruit in the biscuits?
How would they alter them?

These questions could prompt children to design their own biscuits, which they might actually cook to see if they work. Remember that Robinson (2001) suggests that creativity involves both play and taking risks.

■ **Figure 7.2** Which biscuit is easier to break up?

EXTENSION

Explain that the choc-chips/fruit/grain is the mineral they want to find, the rest is the rock. Discussions could focus around the time it takes to 'mine' the mineral and the costs; how much money they could earn from the mineral; how much rock would have been wasted. Older or more able children could be given costs to enable them to calculate earnings.

Moving on

Work within Key Stage 1 forms an introduction to learning about the landscapes that are created by the rocks and soils around us. Within Key Stage 2, this can be developed further to enable the children to understand why the landscapes they see are like they are, and how they might have evolved. This can lead into questions relating to their surroundings and a deeper understanding of our physical world. Their imagination and creativity can be stimulated and they can be encouraged to develop their own expertise together with unusual ways to depict landscapes or demonstrate physical features and processes. As de Bono (1999) puts it, creativity goes beyond the obvious to generate novel solutions.

ROCKS AND THEIR PROPERTIES (KEY STAGE 2)

Erosion, transportation and deposition can all be linked to work on rivers and coastlines. Using the analogy of food can help pupils to relate rocks and their properties to their own experiences. Biscuits and cakes (as above) can be used to demonstrate how mixing different components together can result in a different end product with different properties. Fisher (1990) suggests a creative process that becomes a life skill – stimulus, exploration, planning, activity, review. Using unusual media can help develop these skills. Some basic information may help to underpin your understanding.

EROSION

Rocks are worn away or eroded over very long periods of time by the action of ice, water, wind, sun and chemical processes. Rocks break down differently depending on their strength, hardness and/or internal 'glue'.

TRANSPORTATION

Rocks that have been eroded are moved from one place to another by the wind, rivers, sea and other forces. Those that break down more easily are thus most likely to be transported.

DEPOSITION

Material that has been transported is deposited in layers to create sedimentary rock. The layers that are at the bottom will, unless disturbed, be older than the layers on the top.

The following activities explore these processes through practical work and discussion. The activities are all based on small group work, usually in competition with each other.

Sandstone crispie cakes

One type of rock that can help children understand more about rocks and erosion is sandstone. Making crispie cakes is a favourite classroom activity. However, very few teachers take the opportunity to use crispie cakes to help children understand more about the properties of rocks and why some erode more easily than others.

AIM

To demonstrate how sandstones are formed and particles bound together by a matrix (glue) using a food analogy.
To challenge the pupils to create their own edible 'rocks' with different properties.

INTRODUCTION

Discuss how sandstones and other rocks are composed of loosely bound grains, held together by a matrix or glue, and many are highly susceptible to erosion. If possible, demonstrate this by rubbing away the corner of a small piece of sandstone. Show how easily individual crispies can be knocked off a crispie cake by way of comparison.

RESOURCES

Plain cooking chocolate and crispies
A saucepan (to melt the chocolate)
A bowl (to mix the cakes in)
A spoon (to mix with) and two teaspoons
Paper plates and paper cases
Access to heat source (e.g. hot plate)

THE CHALLENGE – CREATING EROSION

Divide the pupils into groups. Their challenge is to make one crispie cake that is easy to erode but still holds together and one that is hard to erode but still has enough crispies to be called a crispie cake. Once they have made their cakes they present them to be tested. To ensure a reasonably fair test, each cake should be tested by the same adult. This adult might also decide which is the easiest and hardest to erode or the class could vote on it.

Each group reports back on how they decided what to do and what amount of each ingredient they used. Employ open-ended questions to aid this discussion and see that the children talk about what holds rocks like sandstone together and why some rocks erode more easily than others (Figure 7.3).

■ **Figure 7.3** The crispie cake on the left was easier to 'erode', it had less chocolate matrix to hold it together

FACILITATING THE ACTIVITY

Depending on their age and abilities the children may need adult support. You could suggest that they change the amount of chocolate or crispies that are included. Draw up a plan and think about how to test their results. Older pupils can work more independently on planning and testing with adult supervision rather than support. Suggest that within each group children might like to divide into two groups and focus on one type of cake each. Alternatively, the challenge could be divided over two sessions, one for each type of cake. Emphasise to the children that they don't need to use all the chocolate or crispies. You may decide to limit the number of paper cases as well as the amount of chocolate and crispies to create boundaries. You will naturally be limited by the resources you have in school and how easy it is to carry out this sort of activity.

As with others in this chapter, this activity includes, or has the potential to develop, cross-curricular links. These include:

■ Science – formation and properties of rocks and soils, and their subsequent uses; planning to solve challenges; changes of state;
■ Maths – weighing and measuring;
■ Design Technology – cooking, planning, experimenting;
■ Literacy – descriptive writing, vocabulary;
■ Art – recording by sketch and drawing;
■ IT – recording by photography.

What cross-curricular links can you make with the following activities?

Sedimentary layer biscuits

One idea that can be used to show how rocks can be eroded and deposited is to build a 'rockface' using various types of biscuit. A photograph of an actual layered eroding cliff would be a good starter. This can build into explanations relating to how the layers were deposited in different environments and are now being eroded differentially.

The activity can be facilitated as either a participatory demonstration or, preferably, a challenge, or challenge with adult support, depending on the age of the pupils, available assistance and resources. The rockface is constructed by using layers of different crushed biscuits mixed with melted fat (as in a cheesecake base). Suggested layers are: 1. choc-chip cookies; 2. digestives; 3. double choc-chip cookies; 4. fruit shortbreads (or similar).

AIM

To learn how different rocks can be deposited into and eroded from a rockface and have different strengths.
To challenge pupils to create and investigate their own 'food' rockface to demonstrate erosional properties.

RESOURCES (FOR ONE FOUR-TIER ROCKFACE)

One packet of each type of biscuit to be used
300g margarine
Saucepan; mixing bowl, spoon

Small, square or rectangular tin, minimum depth 12 cm, preferably with removable sides (this makes it easier to remove the cliff face) or a margarine tub or similar that can be peeled away once set.

METHOD

Each layer needs approximately 175g biscuit and 75g margarine. Melt the margarine and then mix with the crushed biscuits. Press the mixture into the tin. Repeat this with further layers using different biscuits. Chill or allow to set. Remove from the tin so that all sides can be used to test for erosion (this is best done with the back of a knife). Try to ensure the layers are a good thickness (minimum 2 cm) to aid investigation.

THE CHALLENGE – CREATING A CLIFF FACE

The level of this challenge will be different depending on the ages and abilities of the pupils. The older, more able children can be challenged with the whole of the activity, others may need to be introduced to it at different stages of its development. The challenge is to build a cliff that demonstrates how some layers erode more easily than others.

FACILITATING THE CHALLENGE AT DIFFERENT LEVELS

Pupils are told or shown how each layer is made and given the amounts to use plus necessary equipment. At whichever stage they are introduced to the challenge, they will need to predict which layer(s) will be easier to erode than others and decide how best they can demonstrate this, i.e. place one that is easier to erode between two that are harder to erode.

Level 1 (easiest) – As a class activity, pupils are given a fully built cliff of three or four layers such as choc-chip, digestive, double choc-chip, fruit shortbread. The pupils discuss which might be the easiest to erode and why. They then test them (see 'Method' above) and relate their findings back to the reasons they gave.

Level 2 (moderate) – In small groups or as a class activity, pupils are given a partially built cliff – two layers are ideal – and asked what type of layer to place on top and why. If the first layer is choc-chip, the second digestive, the best third layer is another choc-chip or similar as digestives are easier to erode. Using a fruit shortcake layer would place two that are easier to erode next to each other and possibly not demonstrate the erosional qualities so well.

Level 3 (hardest) – In small groups the pupils are given three (or four) different types of biscuits and asked to build a cliff that demonstrates different erosional layers. They will need to discuss how to make it a fair test, and in which order to build the layers. Once built, they will need to demonstrate the erosion and discuss why they built the layers as they did. Linking them to the original deposition environment. Hint: if more 'glue' is added to the mix in the form of chocolate, the layers stick together very well.

Conglomerate cakes

Pupils sometimes bring rocks into school to see if you know what they are. These often contain a mixture of materials including concrete that has been manufactured by people.

Rocks that are composed of pieces of other rocks are called conglomerates. These demonstrate how previously formed rocks can be broken down into fragments and then stuck back together in a new form. They are often found in riverbeds where components have been brought downstream, particularly in an estuary where there may be different river sources.

INTRODUCTION

This activity is for more able upper Key Stage 2 pupils, after studying rocks. Discuss how conglomerate rocks are formed, and allow the use of books and the internet to aid research if necessary. If possible, show them some examples of conglomerate rocks.

AIM

To demonstrate how many different types of rock can be deposited and re-formed within a matrix to create a new type of rock.
To investigate how easily conglomerates can be broken down further.
To show how cakes can be used to demonstrate erosion processes.

RESOURCES

Plain chocolate cake covering
Fruit and biscuit or fruit and nut or plain fruit chocolate bar
Margarine
Saucepan, heat source, large mixing bowl, large spoon and tinfoil

SUGGESTED INGREDIENTS FOR ROCKY LINKS

Digestive biscuits – sandstone
Glacé cherries – pink feldspar from granite
Raisins – dark mica from granite
Dates or sultanas – minerals
Mini pink and yellow marshmallows – softer more pliable rocks
Nuts – harder rocks; these could be included by using fruit and nut choc bar as part of a chocolate matrix

THE CHALLENGE – CREATING CONGLOMERATE

Divide the pupils into groups. Pupils are challenged to design and make their own conglomerate rock using different sorts of food to represent the different fragments of original rock. Provide a choice of chocolate or margarine – to use as a glue or 'matrix'.

Provide a choice of ingredients to represent the various rock components. Pupils then choose the appropriate components and the type of glue. This will involve them deciding what they want to create and what 'rocks' it should include: Once this is decided they need to work out amounts of 'matrix' in relation to 'rock fragments'.

Encourage the pupils to invent/create their own special conglomerate. They may also try to relate their cakes to some actual examples. The key idea is that they should argue about and discuss the properties of the 'rock' fragments that they select and why some might be smaller and smoother than others.When they slice their rock, what does it show? Are all parts of the 'rock' as easy to slice as others? Learning flourishes when children generate and seek to answer questions of this type. As Scoffham (2003) reminds us, 'creativity prospers when there is a flow of ideas between people who have different visions and expertise'.

For guidance, here is a basic recipe for the conglomerate cake:

- Melt 200/250g plain chocolate cake covering; 200g fruit and biscuit milk chocolate bar (or fruit and nut or plain fruit or similar) and 50g margarine.
- Break 200g biscuits into small pieces (not crumbs).
- Chop 50g dates (or sultanas) and 50g cherries into irregular sizes and add to biscuits with 50g raisins; add 50g small marshmallows, or any mix of these amounting to approximately 200g.
- Stir well, then add melted chocolate and mix well together until all ingredients are coated.
- Place on tin foil and mould into the desired shape using the foil to help keep the shape. The mixture could be shaped into one large roll (or rock) or smaller ones.
- Chill then slice.

SOILS (KEY STAGE 2)

The formation of soils is linked to the erosion of underlying rocks. Soils consist of five elements: weathered fragments of rock, humus (dead plant and animal remains), living organisms, water, and air. The mixture of these five elements and the resulting soil type tends to limit the plants that will grow and food that can be produced. Some plants thrive in well-drained sandy soils, others like the moist environments that are associated with clay soils.

Soils also vary in their chemical composition depending on whether they are acid or alkaline. This is expressed as a pH number which ranges from strongly acidic (1) to strongly alkaline (14), with neutral point of 7. Peaty or sandy soils tend to be acidic as do waterlogged ones, chalk soils are alkaline. Peas, beans and cabbage grow well in alkaline soil but are averse to acidic soil. Potatoes prefer acidic soil either sandy or peaty.

Will it grow?

Pupils can try growing different vegetables in different soils in order to see what happens. The food they produce could then be used in the school kitchen. Depending on resources and space, this is probably best done as a whole-class activity, with pupils looking after the plants in turn.

AIM

To investigate if a specific plant grows better in one type of soil.
To see if other plants also prefer that same soil.

RESOURCES

Different types of soil, e.g. one sandy acidic soil, one clay-ey waterlogged soil, one chalky alkaline soil and one loam soil

Some grow bags or large plant pots
Vegetable seeds (peas or beans) or cabbage seedlings. For a longer-term project try potatoes.

THE CHALLENGE – WHICH SOILS AND PLANTS DO WE WANT FOR OUR GARDEN?

The school is to develop a vegetable garden and wants to know which type of soil to use and which plants to grow. We have several types of soil samples and different vegetables. How can we find out what would be the best for us? Pupils should decide how to set up their experiment. The amount of support needed depends on their age and ability. Ideally, each type of soil should have samples of each type of seed/seedling; positioning and watering should be the same. Pupils could devise a rota to care for the plants and guidance or rules for doing so. Records should be kept of any differences, size and growth monitored, and a weekly update discussed in class. Digital cameras could be used to record changes. Once there are visible results they can decide why plants have developed as they have and produce a plan for their garden.

EXTENSION

Pupils could investigate the properties of the soils either beforehand or afterwards, looking at texture, colour, porosity and permeability. They should also establish their pH level using a simple testing kit. This may help them to decide why plants are growing well or not so well and what environment the plants prefer.

Artistic soils

Soils vary in colour and texture and some very interesting art work can be achieved by exploiting their properties. Soil colours differ from being almost black through dark brown, tan, red and gold to almost white in chalky areas. Textures can be from the very fine clay soils to coarser loams through to very coarse sandy soil. Pure sand can be used with glue to form a coarse texture. Soil can be mixed with very little water to make a thick painting material almost like a sludge in order to produce more solid shapes or with more water to make a colour wash that can be used in a background or any consistency between these two extremes, depending on what you want the pupils to achieve. You may decide to provide pupils with ready-made consistencies or allow them to make their own mixtures. Depending on age, ability and assistance available, it could be a good idea to let them practise a little first to explore the medium.

AIM

To understand that soils have many different colours and textures.
To learn to use these colours and textures to produce a natural painting.

RESOURCES

A selection of as many different coloured and textured soils as possible (ready-mixed, or not, depending on the situation)
Pots for mixing soil and water
A selection of different-sized paint brushes and sheets of paper (at least A4)

CHALLENGE – SOIL PAINTING

To produce a painting using only soils. You may wish to add further criteria such as making a link to a topic you are currently studying, or to restricting the focus to landscapes or plants or creatures.

EXTENSION

You could enhance the work by getting the children to include other natural objects such as leaves and bark in their paintings. Upper Key Stage 2 could investigate why the soils are the colours they are – a result of original compounds and specific mixtures. The links to history, cave paintings and Aboriginal art are particularly fruitful and an excellent way of extending the creative possibilities (Figure 7.4).

■ **Figure 7.4** Soil and sand seascape painting

MAPS

Creating maps – then eating them

Maps are creative documents. They are imaginative images, and rather than being the absolutes we might expect, they are actually, as Barnes (2003) argues, the products of creative minds. There are several foods that you can use to make maps with, either ready-made, such as different-coloured fondant icing or marzipan, or made in the classroom, such as biscuit dough. The food you use will depend on aims and availability plus the age and ability of the pupils.

Maps can be produced at different scales, such as your locality, the United Kingdom, a continent such as Europe or the whole world. They can be created to show a variety of features or information such as different areas, topography, products or population, again all depending on your topic and aims. Here are just a few basic ideas that could be developed and adapted to suit different challenges.

AIM

To learn about the shape of countries and how they fit together.
To learn about the features of different countries.

RESOURCES

Maps of the local area, UK or wider world
A variety of colours of fondant icing or marzipan
Large, flat baseboard for mounting
Rolling pin, greaseproof paper and a knife to cut shapes
Tracing paper and cocktail sticks (optional).

THE CHALLENGE – CREATE AN EDIBLE MAP

Challenge the pupils to produce a map of the local area, UK or other parts of the world using the icing or marzipan to create the base, to which they add details. Before beginning, the children will need to discuss how they are going to tackle the challenge. Consider the appropriate colour to use for each country, perhaps reflecting the national flag. Pupils might also add small flags on cocktail sticks to identify each of the countries on their map. You can differentiate or extend the work with younger or less able pupils, suggest they work to the same scale as the map provided; with older or more able children, suggest that no country should be the same colour as the ones it borders.

FURTHER MAP CHALLENGES

- Research products and use foods to depict them on the map, e.g. popcorn for corn, chocolate chips for coal.
- Research populations numbers and devise a way of demonstrating this with food. Jelly babies are useful here, possibly using one jelly baby per ten million of population, with an extra challenge to pupils to decide how to represent a population of say five million.
- Research topography and introduce this by adding layers, where the layers of food correspond to contour lines. This works well when an individual country is depicted, or for the United Kingdom.
- With a map of your own locality, pupils could depict routes to school using small sweets such as dolly mixtures.
- If using a biscuit dough, shapes could be cut relating to different countries of Europe then baked in order to be used as a jigsaw. Biscuit dough maybe more popular if the pupils are going to eat their maps, and fondant icing could be used here to add the topography.

CONCLUSION

Some ideas suggested here may seem rather unusual in relation to physical geography. However, if children are to be creative they need to be given the opportunity to extend their ideas in a variety of ways. By approaching the teaching of physical geography creatively, teachers can enhance children's ability to bring their own ideas to activities, which can aid understanding and promote further investigation and creativity. Children need to be given the chance to take risks and become confident in doing so.

This chapter has provided some ideas to help develop creativity using analogies that children can relate to within their everyday lives. They are aimed at providing a stimulating starting point for practical activities that can be used flexibly within any curriculum, providing children with the opportunities they need to become truly creative.

REFERENCES AND FURTHER READING

Alexander, R. (2004) 'Towards dialogic teaching', in Cremin, T. (ed.) (2009) *Teaching English Creatively*. London: Routledge.

Barnes, J. (2003) 'Creating the world in the mind'. *Primary Geographer*, 50: 17–18.

De Bono, E. (1999) 'Six thinking hats', in Scoffham, S. (2003) 'Thinking creatively'. *Primary Geographer*, 50: 4.

Fisher, R. (1990) 'Teaching children to think', in Bridge, C. (2003) 'Creating the space to think'. *Primary Geographer*, 50: 19.

Robinson, K. (2001) *Out of Our Minds: Learning to be Creative*. Chichester: Capstone.

Scoffham, S. (2003) 'Thinking creatively'. *Primary Geographer*, 50: 5.

Scoffham, S. and Vujaković, P. (2006) 'Edible maps'. *Primary Geographer*, 60: 23.

Websites

Australian ideas (http://www.slideshare.net/ansley22/australia-edible-maps-2010).
Earth Science Teachers' Association (ESTA) (www.esta-uk.net).
Marzipan Europe (http://bigthink.co./ideas/21275).
TTS (www.tts-group.co.uk).

Acknowlegements

These activities have been developed by the ESTA primary team for use in workshops for physical geography (estaprimary@hotmail.co.uk). Those relating to maps were developed from an idea by Scoffham and Vujaković (2006).

Resources

1   Small pieces of polished minerals can be obtained from gift shops, and could be mixed with other pieces of minerals found as chippings in order to obtain a mix of colours and types. Educational suppliers also have sets of minerals and gems, e.g. TTS (0800 318 686).

2   A variety of soils can be obtained from educational suppliers, garden centres or collected by pupils or staff from the local area or more distant places. You mix garden soil with sand, chalk or clay to create varieties of your own.

■ **Figure A** 'Winter Tunnel with Snow' (March 2006) is one of a number of Hockney paintings that suggest routes and journeys. Oil on canvas 36" x 48".

■ **Figure B** Hundertwasser's (1953) 175 An Almost Circle. Does this look like a map or aerial photograph of an urban area, or something very different?
© Hundertwasser Archive, Vienna

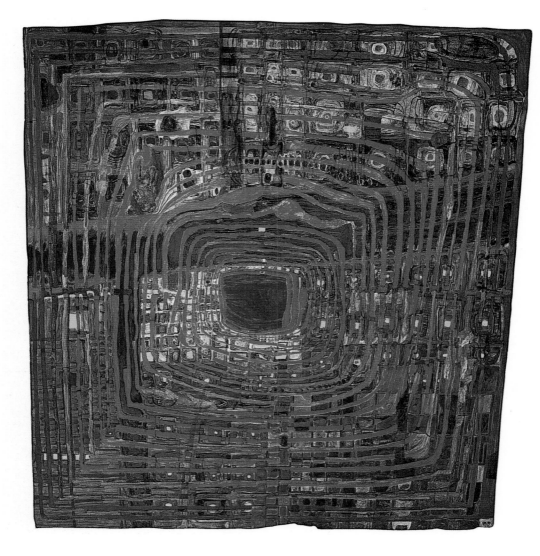

■ **Figure C** Hundertwasser's (1955) 'CITY SEEN FROM BEYOND THE SUN' (241). Is this the street pattern of a city with building between, or something very different?
© Hundertwasser Archive, Vienna

Time, Life and Landscape: Waiving to Mr Henshaw

Peter Vujaković

If there is one common theme that unites most young children, it is an abiding fascination with lost landscapes and animals of the past. Dinosaurs, trilobites, mammoths and saber-toothed cats populate their imaginations of 'deep time' and appear to have particular appeal in middle childhood. Understanding life and landscapes can be enhanced through this fascination, by encouraging children to see themselves as part of a grand narrative; as occupying a point in both space and time from which they have a grandstand view of environmental processes, and an understanding of the geology beneath their feet.

This theme offers wide scope for use of visual material; on video and in dioramas published in popular books on the subject. Fossils and models of extinct or speculative organisms can be deployed creatively in the class ('show and tell') or even outside. Pupils can be engaged by asking what it would have been like to live in these environments (consider climate, vegetation and habitats), and prompted to question the veracity of 'staged' constructions. Is nature always 'red in tooth and claw' as many images of 'deep time' suggest?

During key stage one, children are encouraged to investigate their local area. They can carry out geographical enquiries inside and outside the classroom by creatively thinking about past *and* future environments. The UK's rich and complex geological heritage presents teachers everywhere with a wonderful resource, literally beneath their feet. Draw a line in chalk 90 metres long across the playground to represent 4.5 billion years of the Earth's existence, and stand Mr Henshaw at the far end when the Earth began. At this scale each metre will represent 50 million years. Ask the children to place fossils, toy dinosaurs and other animals where they think they should exist in time. The first five metres should be fairly cluttered. The first ten will include all significant fossilised life. A murky bottle of water, representing early life, can be placed within twenty metres of Mr Henshaw. Everyone wave to Mr Henshaw, a very lonely mammal indeed!

At key stage two, water and its effects on landscapes, including the physical features of rivers and coasts and the processes of erosion and deposition, are a major geographical theme. Engagement with past landscapes provides a route to understanding the impact of slow but continual changes. Recent BBC programmes on dinosaurs (*Planet Dinosaur*) and very early life (Attenborough's *First Life*) indicate the continued public engagement with natural histories and 'deep time' tableaux, and provide a ready resource for discussion.

Another creative approach is for children to project their understanding of landscape and life into the future. What might new life forms look like? How are they adapted to the world around them? Children can be engaged creatively by constructing their own speculative organisms ('sporgs'), then placing them in real environments and habitats to create dioramas. Pupils can use a digital cameras and video to record these 'habitats' for display. This exercise encourages children to think deeply about the links between place and resources. The models can be collected into a 'cabinet of curiosities' as a permanent record of the learning process, pupil's creativity, and as a talking point.

References
David Attenborough, *First Life*. First broadcast by the BBC in 2010.
Nigel Paterson, *Planet Dinosaur*. First broadcast by the BBC in 2011.

CHAPTER 8

GEOGRAPHY AND HISTORY IN THE LOCAL AREA

Anthony Barlow

This chapter recounts my experiences of developing a cross-curricular study of a small village in northern England for children in Key Stage 2. The framework I outline could be applied to many other situations as it highlights the power of experiential learning, harnessing and developing the pupils' powers of observation and developing their thinking.

PRINCIPLES

> Younger children's daily lives are lived in their home localities...Neighbourhoods provide their home, schooling and community – key elements of their local attachment and identity. They are the sites of friendships and acquaintances, of early and later play and social activities...Neighbourhoods are places of smells and textures...
> (Catling 2010: 16)

Using what is familiar to children, such as their neighbourhood, should be a central feature of primary education. To give pupils some understanding of what they can see from their window, teachers need to have some sense of the geography and history of the area. They need to understand the continuum linking the past, present and future. Allowing pupils to gain a sense of place through the hands-on 'enquiry' process gives them opportunities to develop relevant knowledge, skills and understanding. Integrating geographical learning with other subjects provides a powerful nexus where pupils can develop a deeper understanding of what it means to live there and be 'rooted' in a place within the world. As a teacher it is important to enter into the process of curriculum-making yourself, especially when you first join a school. It is sometimes through such a process that your teaching gains relevance. There are also rewards in terms of fulfilment that can be found in few other classroom endeavours.

The desire to engage pupils in purposeful, real-world enquiry was central to my planning. There are various models to choose from. I opted for Margaret Roberts's version (2003) as it is both simple and adaptable. This outlines four stages to enquiry learning: (a) creating the need to know; (b) using data; (c) making sense; and (d) reflecting on learning (Figure 8.1).

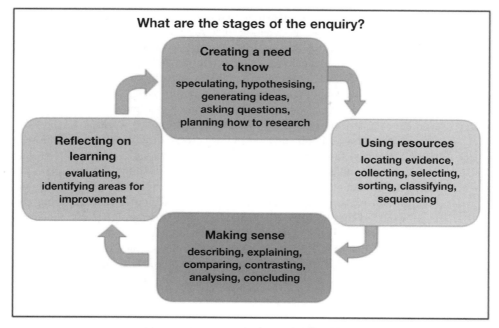

■ **Figure 8.1** Roberts proposes a concise framework for enquiry learning
Source: Adapted from Roberts 2003: 44

The enquiry process enshrines the idea that the teacher is not the sole repository of information. If it is to work effectively, pupils need to be supported to ask geographical questions that then help to develop their geographical thinking. It is through asking questions that the pupils develop a sense that there is so much to explore, find out and realise; and that as agents in the enquiry, they can comment on, assess, make new discoveries and even influence change. The initial lessons where we create a 'need to know' before embarking on fieldwork studies are thus very important in a scheme's success.

A key aim of my project was to help pupils understand that places are constructed, created, shaped and moulded by forces. I wanted my pupils, for example, to know factual knowledge (the names of streets named after notable historical figures), to understand about the landscape (how the valley was formed) and have the skills to be able to carry out fieldwork and speculate about why a place has changed. Our study involved various primary sources (e.g. visiting the local area, local speakers) and using secondary sources (studying photographs and maps). Our task was then to get the pupils to envisage alternative futures for the area.

PUPILS' GEOGRAPHICAL AND HISTORICAL WORLDS

the locality is more likely to be experienced from the car, necessarily in the company of adults, rather than alone or in the company of other children. The car then functions as a protective capsule from which the child observes the world but does not experience it directly through the experience of others.

(Sibley 1995: 136, cited in Bowles 2004)

Most pupils in my study lived within two miles of the school and local village. However, pupils' knowledge about the location, features and history of the village was often poor. Key features (such as the chimney of the bleach works) were visible from the playground and so were an excellent first stimulus. Also, as the area was a local beauty spot, some went on walks there. However, most children knew more about the local retail park than the immediate surroundings. Perhaps this is unsurprising, but it highlights the challenge of local area work. One way of engaging children is to put them in the role of detectives who have the task of uncovering the story of a 'forgotten world'.

With many schools now pursuing cross-curricular studies, following various models, the past few years have been a time of flux and uncertainty. For teachers fully confident in a subject area this might have been liberating, but how many teachers *are* fully confident in all the different subject areas? The relevance of my study, and the argument of adherents to a constructivist model of teaching, is that enquiring about pupils' experiences of the world is a key starting point of learning. Many pupils have limited experience of fieldwork. Ofsted (2011) reports that fieldwork happens more often in Reception classes and Key Stage 1 than at Key Stage 2 and that 'opportunities for fieldwork have decreased substantially in recent years' (p. 41). Maybe Key Stage 2 teachers have not appreciated how fieldwork can add to studies undertaken in the earlier years of schooling

PLANNING AND PREPARING FOR FIELDWORK

It is often claimed that geography is best learnt through the 'soles of your boots' (Steel 2010). Fieldwork is a fundamental part of geography and one of the most effective and inclusive ways to teach it. As Steel puts it, 'doing' helps pupils to understand. Since the National Curriculum was first devised, enquiry and the use of sources have featured in the programmes of study for both geography and history. Fieldwork is the most obvious example of a primary source as it allows pupils to connect with the natural and built environment round them.

Substantial evidence exists to indicate that fieldwork, properly conceived, adequately planned, well taught and effectively followed up, offers learners opportunities to develop their knowledge and skills in ways that add value to their everyday experiences in the classroom (Rickinson *et al.* 2004: 5). The challenge for me, as it is for any teacher, is how to develop an understanding of familiar landscape features with children. The 'wow' factor of the exotic – the mountain glacier or parched desert scene – is immediately obvious. However, it is much harder for us to tell the story of the familiar, everyday landscapes that have changed over long periods of time, or scrape away the layers of a derelict or wild place and tell of the forces that made them.

Learning about Barrow Bridge

My fieldwork case study was just a mile's walk from school, the small hamlet of Barrow Bridge. On the outskirts of Bolton, this northern England mill town was created from the early 1800s as a site-specific centre for early ventures in cotton spinning and weaving. As technology advanced and requirements changed, the mills did not adapt, and went into terminal decline. By 1910 the hamlet was largely abandoned and much of the evidence for the mills' existence was gone.

The study concerned what is visible of a much altered valley landscape: a diverted brook and storm drain, a few minor mill buildings and all the workers' houses. As is the case with places of this vintage, what rose and fell has risen once again as a desirable, gentrified residential setting. However, nestled as it is in the shadow of the West Pennine Moors, where William Blake's 'dark satanic mills' once stood, the valley is an increasingly wild and overgrown oasis.

I asked myself a range of questions at the start of the study to inform my planning (Figure 8.2). I decided to introduce the study by asking the children this question: Why did people move and settle in the valley? Figure 8.3 indicates the range of their responses.

These pupils' responses showed that they were thinking about what Barrow Bridge is like now – green and pastoral. I realised that they had not grasped the layers of history that have left their mark on this environment over time. They could not see the slowly evolving story of the place. To them the roads could be described as old or new, good or bad; but the concept that the roads had never been there and that someone decided to put them there for a purpose did not occur to them. Changing land use over time was a difficult concept. However, as soon as I introduced some postcards and linked them to dates and times, the concept of a very different place a hundred years ago started to form in their minds. So, simply starting with an open question (before we had looked at any resources) really gave me a baseline to understand pupils' preconceptions and misconceptions.

Smithills Dean Brook

Most local areas have a dominant or key feature such as a building, hill or stream. These allow us to work with pupils to start to construct a picture of *what*, *how* and *why* places are like they are. In Barrow Bridge, the brook provided the fast-flowing water for industry alongside the (more intangible) damp, valley climate this corner of the country provides, which favours cotton spinning.

A key question for the pupils is where the stream comes from. Answers ranged from 'the sky' to 'a big reservoir on the hill'. I needed my pupils to understand that the brook's source was in the hills above the school. It then flows through the town, joining numerous other rivers, and ends up as part of the River Mersey, finally flowing out into the Irish Sea. What a journey for a small brook near our school! The problem was that the children had mostly never even seen the hill in question and we certainly could not visit it. I therefore devised an activity to illustrate the journey that the water is taking.

The children were divided into groups, shown photos and given a section of the river system to draw (hill, upper valley, valley in the village, storm drain, drainage lake) and some characteristics to include. The results, when joined up, showed not just what they could see but where the brook had come from and where it went (Figure 8.4). Pupils used their own knowledge and creative licence to include extra details. As much of the brook was inaccessible for our fieldwork, this was, in fact, a fantasy map.

DEVELOPING CREATIVITY IN FIELDWORK

Fieldwork enquiries are hard! They can have varying degrees of success and are dependent on a range of factors such as the pupil grouping, the weather, planning and preparation, the quality of adult support and other unforeseen circumstances. Fieldwork is often used at the start of an enquiry but can also be appropriate at later stages. In teaching children about Barrow Bridge I used the fieldwork visit at the beginning of the unit to stimulate interest and at the end to consolidate learning.

What natural features are there?
The brook
What built features are there?
Houses, roads, street furniture.
Can we say how the area has been altered over time?
It has gone from being undeveloped to being heavily populated, then falling back into decline and now repopulated.

What photographic evidence can we find for the area?
Use local archives online to find period postcards when it was a beauty spot. Allow children to search too.
Can we collect new photos ourselves?
Compare and contrast. Ask parents and grandparents to send in photos.

What shape does the settlement have? Is there a reason for this?
It is built on the surrounding hills with the factory owners' large houses in prime spots at the head of the valley.

Is there a local expert (primary source) or resource we can draw upon to help us?
Use the local history society and the school governor who has lived here all his life.

How does it look on a map?
Very blue and green, overgrown.
What sort of map would be best?
Look for a range of maps both paper and online.
Can we compare it with an aerial photo?
Use Google Maps as well as photos taken for school project.

Has the area changed regularly, periodically or gradually over time?
Create a simplified timeline for the wall. Things did not happen evenly!

Are there documents (secondary sources) that describe the place?
Create a fictional diary of the place and use children's fiction based in workhouses.

Are there any creative surprises that we can use to engage pupils?
Show a video tour, dress up as a Victorian, open a long-lost letter, use a photo of a person, have an announcement from the head teacher, show an artefact, show previous students' work.

■ **Figure 8.2** Questions about Barrow Bridge that informed my lesson planning

They wanted somewhere new to live.	People liked the trees.	They went to church there.	They wanted fresh air.
People wanted to grow vegetables.	They liked the stream.	They liked the countryside.	The children wanted somewhere to play.

■ **Figure 8.3** Children's initial ideas about why people settled in Barrow Bridge

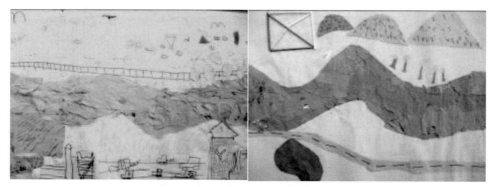

■ **Figure 8.4** Pupils made drawings of different sections of the river, which they joined together
Photo: Anthony Barlow

Successful fieldwork depends on good preparation. It is very easy to get involved with collecting information and ignore things that are not immediately apparent. As well as focusing on 'facts', such as date stones, symbols, signs and street furniture, we must get children to see deeper into the place. If they are adequately prepared beforehand they will see the significance in the patterns in a field or the course of a stream, which they might otherwise overlook. As shown above, I quickly realised that I needed to teach pupils some basic physical geography, such as why rivers create meanders, if they were to make the most of their visit.

Making the pupils 'active' agents in the enquiry

A common mistake, in my experience, is not making the pupils active enough in the enquiry. The first time I undertook the Barrow Bridge project, other than sketching, the children were expected to listen just like they might in the classroom. Worse, the pupils had to stand up for the whole trip! The result was that the learning was limited as the outcomes were predetermined and set by me. My solution was to be more flexible in my planning. As Roberts points out, teachers need to be aware of opportunities to enable students to participate in important decisions about enquiry work. She states:

> A constructivist view of learning recognises that students must be actively engaged in making sense of the world for themselves, they need to be able to connect new knowledge to what they already know and construct their own meanings.
>
> (Roberts, cited in Davidson 2006)

What can the pupils do in the 'field'?

In planning the fieldwork activities I needed to consider different stages in the pupils' knowledge about the place. Some things they could observe from stimuli, some from fieldwork, and some would only come after in the presentation phase. I was particularly keen to create opportunities for data collection and to show pupils that we can categorise what we see and draw conclusions. I also wanted all pupils to take part and be engaged (Figure 8.5).

Place knowledge	Place research	Post-visit thinking
Personal pupil knowledge	Look and listen	What might possible,
Family knowledge	Read and research	probable and preferable
Expert knowledge	Discuss	futures look like?
Oral history	Collect data (e.g. sketch,	What would happen if . . . ?
Also through:	count)	What might . . . say if . . . ?
Maps, plans	Hypothesise, fantasise,	Would you like to . . . ?
Photographs	synthesise	Can you place . . . in
Stories/imagined worlds	Understand	context?
	Surveying (e.g. using an	
	environmental index)	

Re-presenting the place creatively
Demonstrating knowledge and understanding through:
Writing stories and poems
Drawing maps and recording the journey
Using ICT to display, interpret and explain
Fieldwork as a spur for further research
Drama, dressing up and role play (e.g. having a 1900 day)
Examining found and collected artefacts
Making maps and models
Collecting opinions and questionnaires
Interpreting fieldwork data

■ **Figure 8.5** How pupil responses and creative engagement was part of the enquiry and fieldwork process

Place knowledge: developing vocabulary

Fieldwork generates discussion and allowing pupils access to difficult vocabulary is something geographers should not shy away from. In Literacy, pupils are introduced to terms such as alliteration. Developing a sense of a place is so much easier when children have the words they need to express themselves. Developing vocabulary was one of the aims of my field trip and it contributed significantly to the success of the work.

One way of supporting vocabulary development is to get pupils to contribute to a blog. Below are some examples of where (without notes or prompting) pupils showed what they had learned (Figure 8.6). I have highlighted the geographical vocabulary and other significant language used in these pieces. Of course, pupils will not all use language equally fluently.

Place research: encouraging engagement

Involving pupils in fieldwork increases their motivation. Assessing the environment at different points on their journey is the most obvious example of getting the pupils involved.

I decided to ask the pupils to focus on four discrete areas and asked them to record their responses using a writing frame. To extend this process and create numerical data,

11 June, 10:25 a.m.

Post 7 **Barrow Bridge** I learned about lots of different things with Clive, Mr Stockton and Mr Perris told us lots about **Barrow Bridge**. They told us about the **mills** and I found out that they were **six floors high.** I was amazed. I also found out where the **1st, 2nd, 3rd, 4th** and **5th** street are. My group with Mr Perris went up the 35 steps which led to the 1st, 2nd, 3rd, 4th and 5th street. But we did not go up the 63 steps because we did not have time. Finally there was the **river** the **river** was very important to the people in Barrow Bridge because it made all the **machinery working in the mills** and it is right under the **mission** which can also be called **the church**.

11 June, 10:31 a.m.

When we went to **Barrow Barrow Bridge** we learned lots about. The **post box** and that it was made in victorian time when the **mill** was built. It was on the **old shops wall**. we also went up some **steps to Bazley street** I counted **36** of them and turned it around it it made **63**. We looked up **Bazley street** and could just see the **garden center** and **tennis courts**.

Next we went to the 63 steps and after a breath taking climb we arrived at the top and we where told about the **pub** called the **kicking donkey** and that it was the only place that you could go and have a drink.

* * *

Lower achievers showed a poorer response, but still showed a sense of chronology on the journey and a sense of place names.

11 June, 10:30 a.m.

Post 11 **All about Barrow Brige!**

Next we saw lot's of nummber's around and on wall's just like nummber 1096. There was a **river** right at **Barrow Bridge Misson** on one side children where throwing leave's on one side of the river and going to the other side of the river to see the leave's coming under the river. We went up the 63 step's we saw a sine near the tree it said the best mum in the world. and we saw **two big water fall rither's.** Next we saw some dog's and a high **litter** on the floor. After That we saw some house's and athe **letter box** whitch is the **post office** letter box. By MS.

■ **Figure 8.6** Extracts from the blog about the Barrow Bridge fieldwork by Year 3 pupils, with key vocabulary highlighted

pupils can use a data-logging device (such as *Log-it Explorer*) that shows the light, heat and sound in a given area. Easy to use and read, the data that is recorded in this way can then be presented in bar charts and graphs. In some cases, collecting numerical data helped pupils change their minds about what they thought of an area. It also allowed them to start to address a teaching target: 'Use skills and sources of evidence to respond to a range of geographical questions'.

Throughout an enquiry it is important to keep linking back to the fieldwork experiences to refresh pupils' memories about what has been seen. Using a program such as 2Simple's 2DIY you can create a labelling exercise where pupils can add labels to a map (Figure 8.8).

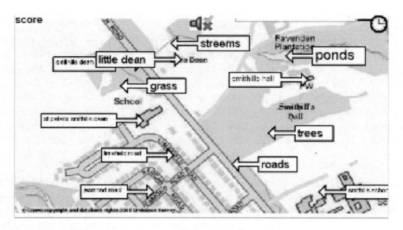

■ **Figure 8.7** Pupils created a map game using 2DIY software

RE-PRESENTING 'PLACE' CREATIVELY

The work that the children did as the result of the study visit was, for me, one of the most important parts of the project and demonstrated its impact as a learning experience. This work also provided evidence for summative assessment.

1 Drawing maps

In order to develop their map skills and abilities, children need to use and make maps in a variety of contexts. In my project, children drew labelled maps to show roads, buildings and items of street furniture. Some pupils could not recall the journey we had taken and said there were too many twists and turns, so we used photos in consecutive order instead. Pupils also made sketch maps to show the course of the stream. This extended their field-work observations and reinforced the notion that the water originates from a source.

It was important to give pupils a reason for creating a map. As part of the follow-up work to my project, I asked the children to devise a treasure map to illustrate an imaginary story about the long-demolished mills. This led the children to include the real places they had visited alongside imaginary characters they had created based on documentary photographs of millworkers.

2 Stories and imagined worlds

Using a mix of fieldwork, historical photos of real people and artefacts worked brilliantly to provide the children a real context and stimulus for writing. This is an extract from two Year 3 boys' playscript. The mill in the play is the demolished Barrow Bridge Mill; the tunnel really exists, as does the brook that flows through it. The map that the children refer to was their imaginary treasure map, which led to artefacts the (real) mill owner was hiding.

BARROW BRIDGE ADVENTURE PLAYSCRIPT BY TED AND SAM

Child 2: Let's go and look in Mr Bazley's office.
Child 1: OK, let's go then!
Child 2: It's still not there!
Child 1: I know.
Child 2: Let's look at this map.
Child 1: Where does it go?
Child 2: It looks like it goes to the cigarette tunnel.
Child 1: Let's go then!
Child 2: But how can we get out.
Child 1: We are going to have to sleep here until the morning for this place to be open again.

3 Junk models

We used aerial photographs and Ordnance Survey maps before, during and after the fieldwork visit. This allowed pupils to revisit their experiences, thus stimulating discussion and further thought. However, to really emphasise their journey and take them beyond the usual, I encouraged them to use junk modelling to create a 3D portrait of the area. The children responded to this exercise with great enthusiasm and the quality of their work was extremely high (Figure 8.8). Some pupils even decided to create a game based on their journey to Barrow Bridge. What impressed me was that this was based on the story that one boy had written the previous week and included the places we had visited.

The importance of thinking about the future of our place was key to the later stages of my enquiry. It tied in especially well with our work in history. Some of the old photographs that we studied showed bank holiday celebrations at Barrow Bridge when the village was packed with tourists. A few of these had even been turned into postcards. This prompted many questions about why people produce postcards. Where might the visitors have come from? One attraction would have been the large mills in their relatively incongruous surroundings. Another would have been the model village and stream. In further discussions we talked about which buildings we go to in our free time nowadays and what we do there.

4 Historical research

Barrow Bridge used to have a funfair and recreation area that was used by many people on public holidays. In a futures-based enquiry session I asked pupils to think about what local residents might think if these returned. This led to a very good discussion about the pros and cons of having an amusement fair. The reason the discussion was so animated was that the children were able to draw on their earlier creative responses. Their maps, drawings and models had engaged them in depth, as had their historical investigations. The discussions prolonged their memories of the field trip and engaged them both cognitively and emotionally. In these sessions, the fourth stage in the Roberts enquiry process, 'reflecting on learning' was really brought to life.

■ **Figure 8.8** Junk model of Barrow Bridge
Photo: Anthony Barlow

CONCLUSION

The old adage declares, 'There's no place like home'. Where is your home? It may not be where you are teaching, and that presents a challenge. Do you, then, feel part of the community? In many schools today, fostering a sense of community is crucial to pupil attainment and knowing each other is about knowing the place *as well as* its people. This is where cross-curricular studies that scratch beneath the surface and begin to peel back a place's shiny exterior are so vital for schools to engage in during pupils' formative years. Learning about communities and neighbourhoods is especially important when, as in many areas, a mobile and transitory population means that the story of a place is no longer passed on as a collective memory through the generations. Current debates about citizenship, multicultural Britain and identity reinforce the idea that schools have ignored parts of our 'island story'.

Through this chapter I have shown how using fieldwork and enquiry as a stimulus can lead to creative approaches encompassing literacy and drama, art and ICT. Such an approach starts to reveal the story behind a place. This is not easy, and you will need to do a lot of personal research. However, the rewards, as I hope this chapter shows, are immense.

BIBLIOGRAPHY AND FURTHER READING

Bowles, R. (2004) 'Children's understanding of locality', in Catling, S. and Martin, F. (eds) *Researching Primary Geography*. London: Register of Research in Primary Geography.

Catling, S. (2011) 'Children's Geographers in the Primary School', in Butt, G. (ed.) *Geography, Education and the Future*. London: Continuum.

Davidson, G. (2006) 'Geographical enquiry'. *Geographical Association*. http://www.geography.org.uk/gtip/thinkpieces/geographicalenquiry (accessed 21 July 2011).

Dillon, J., Morris, M., O'Donnell, L., Reid, A., Rickinson, M. and Scott, W. (2005) 'Engaging and learning with the outdoors – the final report of the outdoor classroom in a rural context action research project'. NFER. http://www.bath.ac.uk/cree/resources/OCR.pdf (accessed 9 August 2011).

Hopkins, D. (2008) *Teacher's Guide to Classroom Research*. Oxford: Oxford University Press.

House of Commons Education and Skills Committee (2005) *Education Outside the Classroom: Second Report of Session 2004–05 Report*. London: Stationery Office.

Kelly, A. (2009) 'GTIP think piece – every child matters, geography matters'. Geographical Association (http://www.geography.org.uk).

Mackintosh, M. (2005) 'Children's understanding of rivers'. *International Research in Geographical and Environmental Education*, 14(4): 313–22.

Malone, K. (2008) 'Every experience matters: an evidence-based research report on the role of learning outside the classroom for children's whole development from birth to eighteen years'. *Farming and Countryside Education*. http://www.face-online.org.uk/face-news/every-experience-matters (accessed 10 August 2011).

Ofsted (2011) 'Geography learning to make a world of difference'. http://www.ofsted.gov.uk/resources/geography-learning-make-world-of-difference (accessed 8 August 2011).

Rickinson, M., Dillon, J., Teamey, K., Morris, M., Young Choi, M. Sanders, S. and Benefield, P. (2004) 'A review of research on outdoor learning'. National Foundation for Educational Research and King's College London. http://www.field-studies-council.org/documents/ (accessed 15 August 2011).

Roberts, M. (2003) *Learning Through Enquiry*. Sheffield: Geographical Association.

Steel, B. (2010) 'Primary fieldwork'. *Geographical Association*. http://www.geography.org.uk/gtip/thinkpieces/ (accessed 17 July 2011).

Weeden, P. (1997) 'Learning through maps', in Tilbury, D. and Williams, M. (eds) *Teaching and Learning Geography*. London: Routledge.

Useful websites

Maps of different places in the UK (www.ordnancesurvey.org.uk/opendata).

Historic photographs of Barrow Bridge (http://www.boltonmuseums.org.uk/collections/local-history).

Educational software (to create maps) (http://www.2simple.com/2diy/).

GEOGRAPHY AND MATHEMATICS: A CREATIVE APPROACH

Jane Whittle

A creative approach to teaching encourages pupils to apply wonderings and skills in varied contexts. In this chapter I explore the potential for creative connections between geography and mathematics to motivate pupils to participate in active, lively and engaging lessons. I also consider the impact that this may have on the teacher with regards to their practice and planning. The main focus is on using maths trails to foster creativity. This serves as a practical example that could either be applied directly or to many other classroom situations.

A CASE FOR CROSS-CURRICULAR WORK

The skills and attitudes required to be successful mathematicians and geographers have some similarities. Both subjects encourage discussion, sorting and description of ideas – mathematics can be applied through geographical stimuli whilst mathematics can support the understanding of geographical principles or help to solve an enquiry question. As Barnes (2010) states: 'while creativity varies in degree and impact, it always involves making connections between two previously unconnected items or ideas' (p. 25). The importance of connections is also highlighted by Pound and Lee (2011) who explain how pupils need to use mathematics in 'meaningful, relevant and real contexts' (p. 86). As primary school teachers, we aim for children to acquire skills that they can apply creatively and in real-life and other contexts.

Geography encourages the study of local to global and is rooted in purposeful and realistic issues to provide the 'real contexts' that Pound and Lee argue are necessary for the effective learning of mathematics. There are powerful arguments to support the cross-curricular teaching of mathematics, which when integrated with geography provides opportunities for pupils to present their understanding in creative ways. Boaler (2009) highlights this explicitly when she argues that 'when we work as mathematicians in solitude, there is only one opportunity to understand the mathematics' (p. 44). However, when we combine the two subjects, exciting opportunities for creative links can be found, whilst maintaining the integrity of both subjects in their own right.

WHAT DO CREATIVE MATHEMATICS AND GEOGRAPHY LOOK LIKE?

Creative mathematics

Haylock and Thangata (2007) and Wyre and Dowson (2009) explain creativity as a new way of thinking, described by Askew (2003) as 'the process of mathematizing' (p. 85). Creative mathematics encourages pupils to make meaningful connections beyond the 'now complete page 50' approach to teaching mathematics. In our youngest pupils, Briggs (2009) suggests 'mathematical creativity occurs anywhere young children make connections between what they see and their emerging knowledge of mathematics' (p. 97). To summarise these findings, creative mathematics teachers give students time and space to make their own meanings in numerous and realistic contexts.

In planning for creative mathematics, Briggs (2009) builds on the ideas from Robinson and Koshy (2004) to suggest three elements that need to be considered. These are:

1 procedures – the area of mathematics involving facts, skills and concepts, for example, probability;
2 application – putting the skills into practice, extending students through higher-order thinking activities;
3 elegance – perhaps the more challenging element for non-maths specialists, mathematical elegance involves students making personal values and judgements of the procedures and application of mathematics. It encourages an appreciation for the creative nature of the subject. (pp. 70–1)

Thinking about mathematics in this way gives teachers scope to reflect on the potential for creativity in planning mathematical activities and helps to better understand the cross-curricular potential that mathematics has.

Creative geography

All the material in this book has been motivated by a concern for creative geography teaching. Catling (2009) neatly summarises the underlying argument when he states: 'Geography is an active subject, at the heart of which lies creativity' (p. 189). Creative geography involves viewing the world from different perspectives to develop broader and deeper understandings. It can be fostered, as Martin (2004) contends, 'through devising activities that are motivating, inspirational and in which children work collaboratively' (p. 129). Geography has great power to engage students in exploratory and evaluative talk. This allows teachers to observe students making connections and to document their developing understanding of their world.

Creativity

There are similarities between creative mathematics and geography. In order to foster creativity, both subjects require pupils to make connections. As well as being personal and global, these connections involve the materials presented and the strategies used to complete an activity. In a cross-curricular approach pupils also begin to see the connections between subjects, especially in seeing the world with 'maths eyes'. In order to do this, children need to have higher-order thinking modelled to them by the teacher and their peers. As Cremin (2009) writes: 'leaving space for pupils to think, connect and voice their thoughts is a crucial element of creative practice' (p. 48). This idea is echoed by Wyre and Dowson (2009) who believe the role of the teacher is to provide pupils with the ability to create.

WHAT ARE MATHS TRAILS AND WHY EXPERIMENT WITH THEM?

Maths trails in their simplest form are explorations in an area of the school locality, which focus on selected mathematical themes. They can be both indoor and outdoor. The concept of a 'trail' can take two forms:

(a) pupils can freely explore a place, such as the playground; or
(b) pupils can be given a map or objects to follow along a route specifically designed by the teacher.

Giving pupils the freedom to roam a place in search for mathematics gives them opportunities to make personal connections. They may be brave enough to venture to an area that once frightened them or see that the hopscotch game painted on the floor is in fact made of squares. In a more focused, teacher-designed trail, the teacher has the opportunity to make observations of children and their mathematical behaviours in a realistic geographical context. As Milner and Jewson (2010) write: 'trails can be an excellent way of structuring local area work and serve to focus attention on specific themes or issues' (p. 190). In terms of providing a cross-curricular approach, maths trails focus on discovering mathematics in a place. This requires pupils to form judgements and challenge their perceptions of a place. Maths trails support the following:

Procedures. Maths trails can involve practising the skill of one-to-one correspondence or looking for geometrical shapes in the corridor. It can involve recording the flow of vehicles or people past a point or hunting for number bonds attached to trees in the playground. Pound and Lee (2011) provide a neat summary: 'everyday mathematics,' they declare, is 'about allowing pupils to explore and make sense of the numbers, patterns, shapes and measures they see in the world around them. Mathematics is everywhere' (p. 56).

Application. By completing a trail, pupils gain a stronger sense of the environment around them, both physically and spatially. Pound and Lee (2011) argue this is important in making mathematics relevant to children and their world. A key part of applying maths is in the language pupils use to describe and explain. In undertaking a trail, the teacher has the opportunity to observe how children use and apply language in a real context.

Elegance Through maths trails, pupils have the opportunity to think positively about the elegance of mathematics. Geography aims to promote a sense of awe and wonder in children. Mathematics, too, can introduce an aesthetic and existential dimension by focusing on real and purposeful contexts. Boaler (2009) describes the contrast of 'fake' maths versus 'real' maths and argues that the latter must be brought into classrooms 'as a matter of urgency' (p. 13).

Enquiry into the locality. A fundamental feature of creative geography teaching is to provide pupils with experiences in their familiar environment – the locality of the school.

In using maths trails, pupils extend the scope of their enquiries into a related curriculum area, gaining timetable time in the process. A tally chart trail of transport along the high street may lead to a discussion of the number of cars on a road. Is this something that could be addressed further through enquiring into issues in the school locality, for example?

Sense of place. Writing in the *Primary Geography Handbook*, Paula Richardson (2010) declares: 'The buildings, streets and environment around your school are a valuable learning resource. Whatever their age, pupils can undertake a great variety of activities outside the classroom. This work stimulates their curiosity, promotes creative engagement and leads them to value their locality' (p. 135). Pupils need time to find the elegance in mathematics, they also need time to reflect on and build personal attachments to a place. This appreciation of place as explained by Buxton (2006) and Ashbridge (2006) is crucial to a child's development both geographically and psychologically.

Creativity. As the following sections explain, trails can be planned with creativity in mind, or alternatively, the creativity can arise from the pupils' explorations, discoveries and wonderings. In either event, maths trails provide opportunities for a new way of seeing, allowing pupils to take mathematics from the classroom and connect it to the natural and built environment. In being given time to create their own trails, pupils are encouraged to think and search for mathematics. Maths trails are flexible in their approach and thus are suitable for any age of the primary years. Haylock and Thangata (2007) recognise the importance of mathematical play in order to develop concepts in younger children, which can be addressed more formally in later years. Thus maths trails can form the foundations for a child's creative view of mathematics and local area study. It is sometimes tempting for Key Stage 2 teachers to assume play and local area study have been covered in the early years and that pupils should now be proceeding to more 'grown-up' work. However, maths trails always give pupils the possibility to learn or find something new, because their locality is never static and neither is a child's passion for enquiry.

USING A MATHS TRAIL WITH A YEAR 3 CLASS

Maths trails can be one-off events, stimuli for a maths week, or they can form a natural part of a teacher's repertoire of techniques for supporting pupils' mathematical understanding. The following case study shows how maths trails were introduced at the beginning of a school year to form the basis of local area enquiry and exploration of mathematics with my Year 3 class.

Being passionate about teaching mathematics creatively and making it accessible for my students aged 7–8, I began the year with a maths trail around the class and school corridors. In taking this approach, I wanted to introduce my class to the feeling of participating in a trail whilst gauging an understanding of their opinions and knowledge of mathematics.

1 Discussion

I began by asking the class, 'What is maths?', asking them to draw on prior experience of home and school mathematics. Figure 9.1 shows the responses that were recorded. Generally the pupils tended to focus on the procedures in mathematics and made only limited connections to the elegance of mathematics in context.

- All with numbers – you don't need anything else (Child A)
- Calculations, sums, minus, counting
- Adding and subtraction
- In maths, we can do things like sums and counting
- Times tables
- Symbols (+ x ÷ –)
- Maths means to learn
- It's an activity
- Numbers are in the date, the clock and the dice
- It's problems
- It's sorting
- It's putting numbers and things in their place
- Without numbers and years, we wouldn't be alive
- Years are made with days and days are numbers

■ **Figure 9.1** Pupil's responses to the question 'What is maths?'

2 Preparing the trail

I explained to the pupils that we were going to enquire and explore around school, looking for examples of mathematics. In order to keep the integrity of geography, I explained the concept of searching a place and finding new things. The children then made a simple 'Maths mask' to help with their searching. This mask needs to be no more than a paper plate with eye-holes that children fix to their face with string. My children decorated their masks to make them look 'mathematical', which allowed me to gauge their individual ideas and understanding of the subject.

3 The trail

The trail started in the classroom and moved into the corridors with pupils recording examples of mathematics in their own way. They were encouraged to look high and low, and even under furniture. In doing the trail, most children showed a more developed understanding of the breadth of mathematics, by including geometrical shapes. This allowed me to reinforce mathematical language and terms such as 'symmetry' and 'tessellation'. The trail took place in the first week of the school term and children were constantly commenting on changes to displays or the ways in which new teachers had changed the furniture around in the class. A curious teacher asked one boy 'What are you doing?' to which he replied, 'We are discovering the school'. This child had recognised the sense of awe and wonder in this activity.

4 Back in the classroom

With the maths mask off, we reflected on the trail in two ways. I began with the thinking routine, 'I used to think, but now I also think . . .', in order to help pupils make deeper connections and responses to the question 'What is maths?' The responses showed they were now more curious about everyday mathematics in the school locality (Figure 9.2). Following this discussion, I asked the children about the place we had explored and the things they had noticed. Their responses showed that whilst they were searching for mathematics they were also able to think and reflect on the locality of the school.

I used to think . . . , now I also think . . .
- It's about shapes – everything has a shape (Child A had now been convinced that there was more to maths than just numbers)
- Big and little
- It's about objects
- It's sizes and symbols
- It's about signs – they have a shape

- We can count a lot of things
- We use numbers and letters
- The world has lots of shapes – even the plants, planets, the sun and the galaxy
- It's not just about numbers, it's about shapes, numbers and patterns
- Why did somebody invent maths? Because they wanted to learn

■ **Figure 9.2** Pupil's reflection ideas following the trail

5 Going further

By introducing the children to trails, I set up an expectation that the maths they were going to do in the coming year was not going to be a 'sit-down' subject. Two terms later, the children are now familiar with many types of trail, and, following each one, always have something to add to our original discussion on what mathematics is and what was learnt about place.

MATHS TRAILS

The following section gives examples of maths trails that can be adapted to cater for the needs of different classes. Trails can be completed individually to allow for individual assessment by the child and teacher, or collaboratively. In collaborating and interacting, children construct meaning together and begin to recognise that creativity is not always an individual feat. The following trails aim to integrate creative mathematics and geography, and through this fusion, learning, motivation and a response to the environment can be fostered.

Counting trails

In the indoor and outdoor environment of a school, there is a wealth of counting opportunities. Materials, letters, door numbers, gateposts, trees – all give potential for counting. Counting trails can take the form of counting objects as a class or pupils could be asked to record how many of something they see. For example, children could have a map of the outdoor area, count how many minibeasts are found at each point marked on their map, and record their results using their own method. As Robinson and Koshy (2004) remind us, 'creative behaviour in mathematics may be seen when a child uses a new way of recording something' (p. 74). Skinner (2005) adds that recording numbers should be done in a practical situation. In formal recording, counting trails provide an opportunity to apply the skill of making tally charts.

Shape-hunting trails

Enquiry into shapes in the environment can lead to an interesting discussion about why some shapes are more common in the playground or in buildings. Pupils can look for shapes in the environment or, alternatively, the teacher can hide shapes for pupils to find. Directional vocabulary is an important part of both the geography and mathematics curriculum, and planning a shape hunt/trail allows for questions such as 'What shape was *behind* the bin?' Alternatively, pupils could hide the shapes and set clues for their friends with the focus being on both shape and the acquisition of directional vocabulary.

Peg trails

Peg trails are fun to organise and extremely effective in promoting learning. Prior to the lesson, the teacher needs to hang cards on trees, fences or benches in the area to be explored. Pupils then have to respond by pegging up a card of their own in the correct place. Peg trails for early years children could involve the numbers one to ten – each child has a number and they must peg their number to the matching hanging card. You could adapt the trail to focus on number bonds to ten, or to reinforce odd and even numbers; the scope is endless. Older children could be given the answer to a mathematical sum that they have to match to the correct calculation (Figure 9.3).

■ **Figure 9.3** A Year 2 student from International School of Bologna, racing to complete the peg trail in under two minutes
Photo: Jane Whittle

Once children are familiar with this sort of trail, it can easily form a weekly starter/plenary or formative assessment activity. Exploring and venturing into new areas is important in geography and using a peg trail can encourage children to go to places they do not normally visit. Peg trails allow for a competitive element in that the teacher can challenge their pupils – perhaps to finish a trail in less than three minutes. Peg trails also provide instant assessment of pupils' mathematical application of skills in that the teacher can view the pegs and the pupils' responses before taking them down to try the trail again.

Pattern trails

'Children are natural pattern spotters' (Swan 2003: 114) and their curiosity for finding patterns in the built and natural environment can form the basis of many maths trails. In the classroom, pupils can replicate the patterns they have found. Alternatively, pupils could photograph the patterns they find on the trail and insert their photographs into a Word document to make a digital map. Another option is to print the photographs, which can then be made into maps and combined to make a class 'atlas' of patterns.

Trails with maths maps

■ **Figure 9.4** An example of a maths map, completed by a Year 3 student

In this trail pupils investigate an area such as the playground, and, armed with a clip-board, make a map of the mathematics they find. In the example above (Figure 9.4) pupils had the option to create their own map or use a teacher-produced one. Pupils were also given a tape measure to aid their enquiries and encouraged to work collaboratively to measure more challenging objects (Figure 9.5). To develop their mapping skills, children could be asked to make a mathematics route map around part of the school. Teachers of Key Stage 2 pupils could also create maps and routes for pupils to follow and include co-ordinate questions as an extra challenge (Whittle 2010). Pupils have an innate curiosity for map-making and the freedom of these activities allows them to demonstrate their ability in both mathematical recording and mapwork.

■ **Figure 9.5** International School of Bologna Year 3 students measuring the height of a bush
Photo: Jane Whittle

Measuring trails

Measuring trails encourage creative ways of applying the skill of measuring whilst giving pupils an opportunity to recognise the elegance of using measuring equipment and different materials. Delaney (2010) states that children need opportunities to engage with a resource to allow them to make connections. When they measure different objects, pupils begin to do this through problem-solving. For instance, they need to choose the appropriate resource – a ruler, metre stick or tape measure if they are investigating distance. Pupils can also be encouraged to find examples of right-angles around the school and record their results. A more challenging exercise, which will probably involve a lot of discussion, is to measure the height of a tree (see websites). The teacher could design a trail of trees for pupils to measure to allow for discussion of height and to stimulate questions about trees in the locality.

Leaves and sticks trails

■ **Figure 9.6** International School of Bologna Year 1 students sorting leaves into different types
Photo: Jane Whittle

Autumn is the ideal time for collecting leaves and sorting them by colour, size or type (Figure 9.6). Pupils have the right to explore and understand the natural world around them and a creative teacher will find opportunity to do this through a combination of mathematics and geography. Alternatively, leaves and sticks could be measured. The problem-solving teacher could pose the question, 'How can we find the perimeter/calculate the area of this leaf?' Data collected could be presented in a bar graph and saved to compare to next year's leaf fall. Running around collecting leaves can motivate the disaffected learner and encourage timid children to use maths equipment in a non-threatening situation. Pupils can consider the Countryside Code and reflect on a responsible use of the natural environment during a trail. Respect for the environment is a crucial aspect of geography.

Trails starting from a story

For younger children especially, the world of fiction can be used as a gateway into the world of mathematics. In their role play or free play, pupils can create trails for characters in the stories they read or they can create mathematical worlds for them to roam in. For example, using a traditional counting book such as *Over in the Meadow: A Counting Rhyme* (Louise Voce 2011), pupils could create the meadow in the classroom and make the characters that they saw in the book. In this way pupils will apply counting skills as they make animals in the meadow. This sort of role play allows the teacher to question pupils about how many of something is in the meadow, taking the book as a stimulus. A further idea is for the teacher to hide characters or objects from a story around a place for pupils to hunt out, thus bringing the fictional world to life. Using books with a journey focus allows pupils to recreate this journey with a mathematical focus. An ideal text for this would be *A Friend Like You* (Julia Hubery 2010). Pupils can create the route Panda and Monkey took using toys or puppets to move the characters through the route. A maths trail could also be created by hiding many purple butterflies (like the ones in the story). The pupils use their toys of puppets to help find the butterflies, describing where they found them along the route. Using a story in this way encourages pupils to delve straight into the mathematical and geographical activity because they already have an understanding of the sense of place from reading the book so personal connections have been made, thus allowing for creativity in a natural sense.

Glow in the dark trails

Skinner (2005) explains how luminous paint could be used to mark out a trail for children to explore. Alternatively, the tables and chairs in the classroom could be rearranged into a maze with a map given to the children. Using torches, pupils could guide themselves around the maze and mark on the map things they find. In this way, the teacher could adapt the focus to finding shapes, solving calculations or finding symmetrical patterns. Incorporating map work encourages recording and allows pupils to feel like explorers (Figure 9.7).

A story with a related theme, which is suitable for younger children, is *Can't You Sleep Little Bear?* by Martin Waddell. The teacher could hide stars made of silver foil around the classroom. Using torches, pupils could take a teddy bear around the room pointing out the stars and explaining that bears don't need to be afraid of the dark. This trail obviously requires a teacher's discretion, in terms of age-appropriateness, concerning venturing into the dark.

■ **Figure 9.7** An International School of Bologna Year 3 student working on a glow in the dark trail
Photo: Jane Whittle

Land-use surveys from trails

As part of a child's geographical experience in the primary years, opportunities should be given for enquiry into land use in the locality. The trail will involve following a predetermined route and recording different land use using a key. The main land-use categories are housing (include gardens), shops/businesses, transport, park and farmland. When it comes to analysing the results, mathematics will come into play as pupils make graphs and interpret any numerical data they have collected. The teacher can draw out patterns and connections in an extended plenary. Displaying the work alongside photographs will demonstrate the impact of this combined mathematical and geographical learning journey.

Designing a trail

Pupils can be encouraged to design trails for their peers, younger pupils or even their parents, for a family maths day, for example. Milner and Jewson (2010) suggest that 'pupils learn best when activities revolve around their own interests and concerns' (p. 183). To ensure pupils understand the cross-curricular nature of the activity, in planning their trail they can complete a writing frame, which asks: 'What is the maths focus of the trail? What might you discover about the place? What geographical and mathematical skills will you need to complete your activity? How will you know if your trail was successful?

Assessment

As a teacher becomes more familiar with using trails they will find creative ways of assessing pupils. One option is to film a particular group of pupils during a trail to collect evidence of their performance. Alternatively, the pupils could watch the film as a means of self-assessment and reflect on the activity. Pupils and teachers could also take photographs while doing the trails for a maths trail scrapbook to share with other classes. This book could stay with the class as they move through the school and develop their maths trail expertise. The above examples are flexible in their design, and teacher and pupils' creativity can become the driving force for a synergy between mathematics and geography. In order to document creativity in pupils, the teacher needs to plan times to step back, observe and allow children time for originality. This notion is, of course, in contrast to that of the hourly numeracy lesson and will require teachers to be flexible in their approach. One way to set up this routine may be for the teacher to wear an item of clothing, which sends a message to the children and teacher that this is observation time.

OTHER APPROACHES

Geographical and mathematical stimuli can be used to engage the creative learner in more ways than can be described in this chapter; however, the following examples aim to give a sense of more creative partnerships between the two subjects.

Mental maths – compass points

The concept of the compass can be brought to life in creative ways using a selection of materials such as maps or perhaps hoops from the PE cupboard to represent places on a world map. In order for pupils to practise this skill, the teacher can ask pupils to point to a country on a map, which, for example, is south of England. This activity can also be taken outside making different-scaled maps with chalk or by using hoops in which pupils move around according to the compass-point direction instructed by the teacher.

Problem-solving

At the heart of creativity is the ability, curiosity and drive to pose questions and solve problems. Problem-solving is a key characteristic of the mathematics curriculum and it is common to find problems with a geographical context. There are plenty of opportunities for teachers to devise problems that are meaningful for children. For example, pupils could be asked to consider the following problem: 'How can we better fit everyone in the hall at lunch?' Another challenge would be to draw a plan to show how to accommodate three new pupils in your class. This would encourage pupils to reflect on the effectiveness of the classroom space, measure table and chair lengths and devise possible solutions to the problem.

Mathematics and weather

Weather is part of a child's everyday experience and can be used as a stimulus for collecting data and finding patterns, providing opportunities for cross-curricular discussions. Pupils can measure rainfall and record their data or observe patterns in cloud formations.

Pound and Lee (2011) remind us that imagination is 'a vital element of mathematical thinking' (p. 5), so rather than staying indoors, pupils should go outside when possible to engage with the elements. The creativity in these activities lies not in the richness of the stimulus but in the analysis of the data. In classrooms where year-long data is kept, pupils will begin to acquire a stronger sense of the geography of weather.

Education for sustainability

Sustainability is an important geographical concept and it involves mathematics both explicitly and implicitly. In discussing energy and water use in school, pupils are encouraged to become active members of their community and enquire into the use of lights or taps being left to run. This allows for real data to be collected and classified using mathematical strategies. In terms of encouraging sustainability, pupils could create a mathematical, sustainable garden, perhaps involving the planting of vegetables and measuring their growth, providing more scope for mathematics in the environment. Older pupils could measure the area of the garden and make plans or maps of how the area could be used effectively. Alternatively, pupils could be challenged to make recycled sculptures or use Unifix cubes to create homes for creatures living in the garden. This could be extended further by setting criteria for the area used for the homes.

World maths map

Children have an innate curiosity for patterns and places around the world and this allows the creative teacher to plan opportunities to enquire into global mathematics. Haylock and Thangata (2007) write about a teacher's responsibility to open up a 'world of delight and beauty to our pupils' (p. 5). Mathematics can be taught from a multicultural perspective, and thinking about the internationalism of the subject across different age phases of a school could lead to a whole-school world mathematics display. This could include:

■ examples of tessellation, polygons and non-polygons in flags;
■ how numbers are written in other languages (particularly those of non-English pupils in the school);
■ the world in numbers (number of countries, city populations, longest rivers, heights and distances, and so forth, displayed around a world map);
■ children's own holiday photos showing maths (their own maths trails);
■ maths textbooks and resources used around the world;
■ famous mathematicians across the globe;
■ patterns in materials and artwork, both modern and historical;
■ significant data about the globe.

In creating such a display, pupils will improve their locational knowledge whilst at the same time moving away from a very British-orientated approach to mathematics to a more geographically sensitive one.

THE ROLE OF THE TEACHER – WAYS OF SEEING

Creative links between geography and mathematics, and the promotion of creative explorations of the child, have been the focus of this chapter. However, in order for the ideas presented to be brought to life, teachers need to re-examine their current practice. In particular, practitioners need to reflect on their willingness to:

(a) 'trust in the children' (Pound and Lee 2011: 132); and
(b) consider the curiosity, awe and wonder they have for the world.

Loveless (2009) states that the challenge for schools in planning for creativity is 'to promote imaginative use of school environments as extensions to the physical space of classrooms'(p. 34). Skinner (2005) explains that teachers need the courage to learn alongside the child, whilst Robinson and Koshy (2004) explain that a 'creative outcome will only occur if the teacher fosters the innate creativity in the child' (p. 80).

Traditionally, mathematics has been seen as a 'right or wrong', passive subject, based on recall, but a shift towards a more creative approach is occurring. It is the role of the primary teacher or geography specialist in a school to ensure that geographical activities help pupils to experience and appreciate mathematics. Through using maths trails, exploring the natural environment and taking an international perspective, we, as primary practitioners, have the chance to support our pupils to become life-long creative enquirers into the mathematical world. Both subjects are driven by a desire to make sense of the world, and they have a surprising amount in common.

REFERENCES

Ashbridge, J. (2006) 'Is geography suitable for the foundation stage?', in Cooper, H. *et al.* (eds) *Geography 3–11*. London: David Fulton.

Askew, M. (2003) 'Word problems: Cinderellas or wicked witches?', in Thompson, I. (ed.) *Enhancing Primary Mathematics Teaching*. Maidenhead: Open University Press.

Barnes, J. (2010) 'Geography, creativity and place', in Scoffham, S. (ed.) *Primary Geography Handbook*. Sheffield: Geographical Association.

Boaler, J. (2009) *The Elephant in the Classroom*. London: Souvenir Press.

Briggs, M. (2009) 'Creative mathematics', in Wilson A. (ed.) *Creativity in Primary Education*. Exeter: Learning Matters.

Buxton, C. (2006) 'Sustainable education: What's that all about and what has geography fieldwork got to do with it?', in Cooper, H. *et al.* (eds) *Geography 3–11*. London: David Fulton.

Catling, S. (2009) 'Creativity in primary geography', in Wilson, A. (ed.) *Creativity in Primary Education*. Exeter: Learning Matters.

Cremin, T. (2009) *Teaching English Creatively*. London: Routledge.

Delaney, K. (2010) 'Making connections: teachers and children using resources effectively', in Thompson, I. (ed.) *Issues in Teaching Numeracy in Primary Schools*. Maidenhead: Open University Press.

Haylock, D. and Thangata, F. (2007) *Key Concepts in Teaching Primary Mathematics*. London: Sage.

Loveless, A. (2009) 'Thinking about creativity: developing ideas, making things happen', in Wilson, A. (ed.) *Creativity in Primary Education*. Exeter: Learning Matters.

Martin, F. (2004) 'Creativity through geography', in Fisher, R. and Williams, M. (eds) *Unlocking Creativity: Teaching across the Curriculum*. London: David Fulton.

Milner, A. and Jewson, T. (2010) 'Using the school locality', in Scoffham, S. (ed.) *Primary Geography Handbook*. Sheffield: Geographical Association.

Pound, L. and Lee, T. (2011) *Teaching Mathematics Creatively*. London: Routledge.

Richardson, P. (2010) 'Fieldwork and outdoor learning', in Scoffham, S. (ed.) *Primary Geography Handbook*. Sheffield: Geographical Association.

Robinson, D. and Koshy, V. (2004) 'Creative mathematics: allowing caged birds to fly', in Fisher, R. and Williams, M. (eds) *Unlocking Creativity. Teaching across the curriculum.* London: David Fulton.

Skinner, C. (2005) *Maths Outdoors*. London: BEAM.

Swan, M. (2003) 'Making sense of mathematics', in Thompson, I. (ed.) *Enhancing Primary Mathematics Teaching*. Maidenhead: Open University Press.

Waddell, M. (1988) *Can't You Sleep Little Bear?* London: Walker Books.

Whittle, J. (2010) 'Maths and geography – making connections'. *Primary Mathematics,* 14(2): 4–8.

Wyre, D. and Dowson, P. (2009) *The Really Useful Creativity Book.* London: Routledge.

Further reading

Alexander, R. (2008) *Towards Dialogic Teaching: Rethinking Classroom Talk.* Thirsk: Dialogos.

Barmby, P. *et al.* (2010) 'Teaching for understanding/understanding for teaching', in Thompson, I. (ed.) *Issues in Teaching Numeracy in Primary Schools.* Maidenhead: Open University Press.

Briggs, M. and Davis, S. (2008) *Mathematics in the Early Years and Primary Classroom.* London: Routledge.

Craft, A. (2009) 'Changes in the landscape for creativity in education', in Wilson, A. (ed.) *Creativity in Primary Education.* Exeter: Learning Matters.

Fisher, R. (2004) 'Creativity across the curriculum', in Fisher, R. and Williams, M. (eds) *Unlocking Creativity Teaching across the Curriculum.* London: David Fulton.

Higgins, S. (2003) 'Parlez-vous mathematics?', in Thompson, I. (ed.) *Enhancing Primary Mathematics Teaching*. Maidenhead: Open University Press.

McClure, L. (2007) *Primary Project Box: KS1. Units 1 and 2.* Sheffield: Curriculum Partnership/Geographical Association.

Useful websites

http://kidsactivities.suite101.com/article.cfm/measuring_big_trees
http://www.ianthompson.pi.dsl.pipex.com/index.htm
http://numeracy.cumbriagridforlearning.org.uk/

CHAPTER 10

GEOGRAPHY AND THE CREATIVE ARTS

Julia Tanner

This chapter focuses on the role of the creative arts in geographical education in the primary school. In the first section I explore creativity in geography and the role of the creative arts in education, including their contribution to children's well-being. This leads to a discussion about how the creative arts can motivate and engage children, thereby raising achievement. In the second section I consider the implications for classroom practice and suggest a variety of practical ideas for teachers who wish to develop imaginative cross-curricular approaches. These include creative practices drawn from movement and dance, drama and role play, and visual art. In the conclusion I focus on the exciting possibilities for using creative arts approaches to communicate the results of geographical enquiries in rich and meaningful ways.

CREATIVITY

There are many definitions of creativity, which variously emphasise that it can be seen as 'a property of people (who we are), a process (what we do), or products (what we make)' (Fisher 2004: 8). The cognitive aspect of creativity is important and was emphasised by the 2000 version of the National Curriculum, which included creativity within the thinking skills section, defining creative thinking skills as those that 'enable pupils to generate and extend ideas, to suggest hypotheses, to apply imagination, and to look for alternative outcomes'. The definition that I adopt here comes from the National Advisory Committee on Creative and Cultural Education (NACCCE) who defined it as 'imaginative activity fashioned so as to yield an outcome that is of value as well as original' (NACCCE 1999: 29).

Creativity and geography

Creativity, when it is broadly conceived, has natural synergies with geography. Geography is a subject that is driven by curiosity about the world as it is now and how it might become. Good geographical learning involves an enquiry process in which children (1) ask questions, (2) use a wide variety of sources to find the answers and (3) record and report their findings. Each of these stages offers possibilities for creative rather than routine approaches, such as asking quirky and unexpected questions, seeking unusual sources to provide answers and communicating findings through innovative media.

The best geographical enquiries are constructed as authentic learning activities – that is, learning activities that have real purposes, real audiences and real outcomes (Tanner 2012). Authentic learning activities provide meaningful and relevant contexts for the development of children's knowledge, understanding and skills. They are also motivating for children and teachers alike. A striking example concerns local road safety (Figure 10.1). An authentic enquiry such as this offers many opportunities for the application of creative thinking skills in the processes of planning the investigation, designing fieldwork and questionnaires, deciding how to analyse and present the data, imagining and evaluating possible solutions and devising the campaign. This final aspect, devising a real campaign, offers particularly rich prospects for fostering creativity as defined by NACCCE, and for applying the creative arts to communicate a powerful message to real audiences. It vividly illustrates Martin's argument that 'creativity in geography can be fostered through devising activities that are motivating and inspirational, and in which children work collaboratively (Martin 2004: 129).

Improving road safety

A Year 5 class was concerned about road safety issues following a road traffic accident near the school. They decided to investigate the nature and scope of the problem by conducting fieldwork and issuing questionnaires, identifying specific issues (lack of safe crossing points, speeding, the location of, and poor behaviour at, a bus stop), and analysis of the data collected. They then generated and evaluated possible solutions to the specific problems they identified.

The outcome was a multifaceted campaign aimed at those who had it within their power to improve the situation, e.g. parents who park inconsiderately, drivers who speed, high-school pupils, the bus company, and local councillors and planning officers. The campaign included a banner designed for the railings outside the school; an exhibition in the local library of posters about the dangers of speeding and inconsiderate parking; a DVD sent to local politicians, planning officers and the director of the bus company; and a performance at the local high school conveying the children's feelings about some secondary pupils' unruly behaviour at the bus stop.

■ **Figure 10.1** Authentic learning experiences can engage and motivate pupils

The creative arts

There is a rich literature attesting to the value of creative and expressive arts for well-being (Maslow 1971; Csikszentmihalyi 1992; Arts Council 2012). There is also a long tradition of using art, drama, music, dance and movement in therapeutic contexts to address psychological illness and distress (Levine and Levine 1999; Jones 2005). Recently, with the rise of the positive psychology movement, more attention has been paid to the role of creative arts in promoting the active well-being of individuals and communities. The Arts Council contends that the value of the arts is threefold:

1   to enhance people's capacity for life by helping them to understand, interpret and adapt to the world around them;

2   to enrich people's experience, bringing colour, beauty, passion and intensity to lives; and

3   to provide a safe context for the development of skills confidence and self-esteem.

Human societies have always used the arts. They can capture the beauty of nature, places or noble ideas; reflect on and question cultural values; unite people in public and private celebrations; express and interpret anguish; and bring profound pleasure and joy.

The value of the arts is manifold. While I was writing this chapter I went to an exhibition of David Hockney's innovative and magnificent new paintings. Many of them, such as 'Winter Tunnel in Snow' (see Figure A in colour plate section) portray ordinary country scenes. Like other people in the gallery that afternoon, my partner and I discussed the pictures at length, noticing different elements, studying the details and viewing them from various perspectives. Later I found myself noticing the beauty of the ordinary winter trees in the ordinary suburban roads in a new, more appreciative way. Hockney's pictures had made me see things differently and also tempted me to pick up some oil pastels to try some sketching.

The arts have the capacity to enrich and enhance our lives. They can focus our attention, provoke us to see things differently, allow for alternative interpretations, elicit unexpected responses, expose new insights, pose new questions and inspire creative thought and activity. There is a dynamic reciprocal relationship between the practical process of making art (the generative aspect of creativity) and experiencing art created by others (the evaluative aspect of creativity). In this way, existing works of art or performances can be revelatory and act as a powerful inspiration for the children's own creative work. One excellent example of this is the National Gallery's project 'Take One Picture' (see page 138). It is also possible for teachers and schools to create vivid and memorable learning experiences that provoke imaginative and creative responses (Figures 10.2 and 10.3).

Young children are innately creative, with a natural tendency to fantasise, to explore their physical and social environment and to experiment with things, processes and ideas. They express these creative impulses through their desire to play, move, draw and paint, their urge to make and do and their propensity for speculating and asking questions. In the creative arts curriculum we build upon these innate tendencies by introducing children to major cultural traditions. In promoting the role of the creative arts in education, Deirdre Russell-Brown argues that:

> Children need to experience and understand the complexity and beauty of the world of music, drama, dance and the visual arts for themselves. Being involved in the arts gives children the tools for lifelong learning within the arts so that they have the opportunity for pleasure and for self-development, creativity, self-expression, opening up a range of new experiences and opportunities they may never have known existed.
>
> (Russell-Brown 2009: 299)

The value of creative activities for young children's development has long been championed by early childhood and progressive educators, such as Frobel, Dewey and Vygotsky. More recently, significant international reports have investigated the role of the arts. For example, UNESCO (2006) identified how good-quality arts education is a key component of both formal and informal holistic education. Additionally, a report from the USA,

Kinaesthetic Adventure Learning Park

Lower Fields Primary School in Bradford is a school that takes kinaesthetic leaning seriously. In September 2010 it opened its Kinaesthetic Adventure Learning Park. This is described by the school as an 'outdoor arena which can become an environment from any time or place in the universe'. It comprises a large open space enclosed by walls. At one end is an enclosed area that can be turned into different imaginary places, such as a tomb, a cottage, a coalmine or a cave. The purpose of the Learning Park is to provide direct, first-hand experiences to ensure learning is memorable, meaningful and fun. The area is used by every year group in school for one week each term.

The creative approach to learning adopted by the school is illustrated by the events that led up to the formal opening event. During the construction of the Learning Park, the contractors apparently unearthed a strange map (see Figure 10.3). This event was witnessed by a Year 4 class who, needless to say, were eager to study the map and discover its secrets. As it was a map unlike any other, this proved an exciting challenge. Later, all classes in the school speculated on the meaning of the map and on other mysterious objects – including an old manuscript recounting a fantastic legend – which have subsequently been found. At the opening event, a time traveller unexpectedly burst into the event, and children and visitors had the opportunity to discuss the map and manuscript with him. At the time of writing, 18 months later, the meaning of the map remains unknown. It is on display in the school reception area, together with some examples of children's responses to it.

As a confirmed cartophile, I can confirm that I have never seen a map like it. The more I studied it, the more details I saw, and the more mysterious it seemed. It provokes the fundamental questions we often forget to ask about maps: Where does it show? Who made it? Was it commissioned by somebody? For what purpose? Who or what was the intended audience? What is its significance? What is its value?

The location in which the map was found provokes further questions. How did it end up in a school field in Bradford? Did it somehow get lost, or thrown away, like many archaeological artefacts? Was it hidden there deliberately, and if so, why? Did whoever hid it expect to retrieve it themselves, or was someone else intended to find it, and when? Is it significant that it was discovered in 2010? Is someone seeking it? If so, why? Are their motives good or bad?

I have little doubt that this map, and the manner of its finding, will continue to excite children's interest and stimulate their critical and imaginative thinking for many years to come.

■ **Figure 10.2** A Kinaesthetic Adventure Learning Park can create engrossing and memorable learning experiences

Reinvesting in Arts Education (President's Committee on the Arts and Humanities 2011) presented strong research evidence that arts teaching increases academic achievement and that integrating the arts into other subjects can dramatically improve results, particularly for 'disengaged' learners. In Britain, too, a government review (Henley 2012) affirms that cultural education including the creative arts is a 'strong influence on wider academic attainment in schools and helps to grow a child's interest in the process of learning' (p. 17). Significantly, the Cambridge Review of Primary Education (Alexander 2010) also highlighted the crucial role of arts in the primary years, arguing strongly that primary children are entitled to a genuinely broad and balanced curriculum.

■ **Figure 10.3** The mystery map that the contractors claimed to unearth when they built the park
Source: © John Edwards

Geography and the creative arts

Geography is concerned with the study of places and environments and the interaction between people and places. The relationship between geography and the creative arts is strong and enduring. Many public sculptures are created for specific sites, often reflecting their unique qualities or what is valued in the place. Throughout history, many artists, musicians, dramatists, choreographers, novelists and poets have been inspired by places, or moved to represent them in their work. The works of art they have produced are testimony to the power of places to excite emotions and provoke responses. Furthermore, many artists and writers have imagined and fashioned powerfully evocative fictitious places with their images and words. While some of these, such as Dickens's London, are based on recognisable places, others are conceived as fantastical worlds, such as C.S. Lewis's Narnia or Escher's drawings of impossible landscapes and buildings.

I have explored the ways in which geographical teaching and learning can contribute to children's well-being by providing opportunities for children to explore, acknowledge and express their feelings about places and geographical issues in my previous work (Tanner 2010). In particular, I have drawn attention to the significance of children's attachment to places that have personal significance for them, and how this can be nurtured and fostered through meaningful first-hand learning experiences and expressed through creative activities (Tanner 2009). The wider application of the creative arts to primary geography is a fertile interface, which suggests ways to enrich, enliven and enhance geographical learning and teaching. The value of such approaches is that they:

■ build on children's natural desire to move, do and make;
■ engage and motivate children;
■ provide for holistic learning, which engages the head, heart and hand;
■ nurture personal, social and emotional development;
■ stimulate creative thinking, experimentation and critical evaluation; and
■ offer thrilling possibilities for innovative cross-curricular projects.

USING THE ARTS TO ENHANCE LEARNING IN GEOGRAPHY

Most primary teachers appreciate the value of the creative arts in motivating and engaging children; in deepening and enriching their learning; in enabling them to express their feelings; in fostering their personal, social, emotional, cognitive and physical development; and in providing non-written modes of communication. In this section, I explore some of the approaches teachers can use to exploit creatively the potential of movement and dance, drama and role play, and all forms of art in primary geography.

Movement and dance

It is said that human communication is more about body language than the words we use. The way we move, the postures we adopt and our gestures and facial expressions convey much about our feelings and thoughts. Very young children can communicate their desires and emotions effectively through non-verbal sounds and their bodies, and as they grow, they delight in their ability to move in new ways, such as running, jumping and skipping.

In primary education, we build upon children's innate desire to move and experiment with their bodies through movement, mime and dance. These provide opportunities for children to explore the potential of their bodies for expressing feelings and communicating with others. They can experiment with using movement to express emotions, capture a mood, represent an idea or tell a story.

There is much potential for using movement, mime and dance to deepen and enhance children's understanding of physical geography. The processes that shape the land often work over very long time-frames (such as river valley formation), which cannot be directly observed (for example, the build-up of pressure before a volcanic eruption). Children can use dance/movement to explore, represent and communicate physical geography processes such as:

■ the journey of a pebble from a stream spring along a river course (via waterfalls, rapids, meanders and lakes in times of low and high flow) to the estuary;
■ the movement of the waves on a beach, in calm and stormy weather;
■ the violence of volcanic eruptions and earthquakes;
■ a hurricane or tsunami crossing the ocean and hitting land.

In human geography, movement or dance can be used to explore the idea that our environment may affect how we feel, to try to imagine ourselves in other places or in 'other people's shoes'. Some ideas include:

Devising place 'freeze-frames'. Invite the children to imagine a familiar place, such as the playground, in different sorts of weather (e.g. a hot sunny day, a very blustery day, a snowy day) and to experiment with moving as appropriate. Use 'freeze-frame' to capture the stance, and ask children to say how they feel in this pose. Discuss the impact of the different types of weather on how they move and feel.

Imagining unfamiliar places. A similar approach can be used to help children imagine themselves in an unfamiliar place, provided you have an evocative stimulus (e.g. a picture-book, a painting of a landscape, a piece of music) with a strong sense of place as a starting point. Ask the children to imagine themselves transported to that place. What can they see, hear, smell? Invite them to start moving, exploring the place. How do they feel, finding themselves in this place?

Making dances from paintings. The previous activity could be developed into a more collective piece, focusing on the social interaction between people in the place. Artworks that depict highly peopled landscapes, such as Breugel's winter landscapes or Lowry's industrial townscapes, can be an excellent stimulus for this. Careful study of the picture will reveal people engaged in all sorts of activities, and the children can experiment with holding their stances and then creating a movement or dance piece that conveys the mood of the picture, or develops a story that takes place there.

Miming journeys from picture-books. Many story- and picture-books for young children involve journeys, which can be mimed to imagine the experience of moving in or travelling through different sorts of environments. Good examples include *We're Going on a Bear Hunt* (Michael Rosen and Helen Oxenbury 1993), *Rosie's Walk* (Pat Hutchins 2009) and many traditional stories.

Traditional dances from overseas. It may be possible for children to work with a creative practitioner to learn and recreate the traditional dances or music of places they are studying as overseas localities. Such activities are excellent motivators and can lead to valuable new learning as long as stereotypes and post-colonial images are avoided.

Drama and role play

Drama presents extensive possibilities for exploring the nature of places and people's responses to them, including the conflicts and tensions associated with environmental challenges. Some of the best dramas involve discovering the unknown rather than acting out what has already been decided. Cremin (2009) argues that drama gives children the opportunity to engage with fictional situations and investigate the issues within them before returning to the real world with more understanding and insight (p. 26). In delineating what she calls the 'primary drama continuum', Cremin points out that drama encompasses a very wide range of activities from the informal (e.g. playground games, small-world play and puppetry) to more formal events (e.g. school performances and theatre outings). As she points out, most of these activities trigger children's imaginative involvement, offering rich opportunities to explore different possibilities and perspectives.

Many common drama activities identified on the primary drama continuum could be harnessed to enhance and extend geographical learning.

SMALL-WORLD MODELS

Younger children may enjoy creating their own version of real places such as towns, parks, farms or zoos, or fantasy worlds with small-world equipment, and playing out different scenarios with people and animal figures.

ROLE PLAY

Role-play areas can be created to represent significant aspects of common geographical topics, such as an estate agent's office (houses and homes), a local TV studio (change in the local area), a school/home/shop (overseas locality) or an environmental campaign office (rainforests).

ANIMAL PUPPETS

Animal puppets or masks can be used to support exploration of issues of animal habitats, perhaps based on a storybook (e.g. *We All Went on a Safari*, Laurie Crebs 2003), or *Backyard Bear* (Anne Rockwell 2006). Puppets and masks can serve as helpful 'props', enabling children to embody alternative personas and explore scenarios from different perspectives.

IMPROVISED OR 'PROCESS' DRAMAS

Improvised classroom drama, individually, in groups, or with the whole class and teacher in role, provides many opportunities for children to use their imaginations, consider situations, exchange ideas, try alternative perspectives and envision and rehearse possibilities. Improvised drama is commonly used in conjunction with fiction, which, typically, contains many moments of tension (e.g. conflict, misunderstandings and dilemmas), which can be explored through common drama conventions such as tableaux, thought-tracking, hot-seating, freeze-frame or improvised flashback/flash-forward. These techniques can be deployed to help children explore how they think and feel about the issue when they are in character, and the consequences of their thoughts and feelings.

DEBATES OR SIMULATIONS

With careful use of resources and detailed preparation to build belief in the scenario, role play or simulation can be used to debate a controversial issue. Examples include plans to redevelop derelict sites, building a supermarket on open land or creating a new wildlife area. You could collect information giving different perspectives from newspaper cuttings, campaign group leaflets or your local government planning department. Pupils could then adopt different roles, design campaign materials and prepare for a simulated TV studio discussion with the teacher in role as the presenter of the programme, inviting contributions from interested parties and the audience.

FIELD VISITS

Field visits to locations with a strong sense of place can offer powerful stimuli for drama activities. Many National Trust and English Heritage properties have education programmes that include place-specific role-play activities, but your local open spaces or woodland or derelict sites could also prove fruitful locations for exploring geographical issues through drama.

The visual arts

The visual arts offer numerous opportunities for exciting geographical and cross-curricular work. Visual materials such as photographs, diagrams, pictures, charts and maps are key geographical resources, used both to find and present geographical information. In this section I explore possible approaches to working with two- and three-dimensional art, textile art, photography and environmental art in primary geography (see also Chapter 6: 'Representing places in maps and art').

We live in an environment saturated with visual images, and as Sara Lipati points out, children possess very high levels of unconscious and often unacknowledged visual literacy (Lipati 2004: 133). Visual literacy is the ability to interpret, negotiate and make meaning from information presented in the form of an image. The concept is based on the idea that images can be 'read' and that meaning can be communicated through visual media. The practical implication of this is that children are highly skilled in decoding visual clues, and, as Lipati illustrates, well able to discuss the meaning of images they encounter.

The emphasis on images in geography offers rich opportunities for children to develop skills in critical visual literacy. These include adopting a critical approach in interpreting, negotiating and making meaning from images, and understanding that all images are created/constructed and selected, often with a particular purpose and/or audience in mind (Tanner 2012). Questions about the creation of an image include: Who created this image? What was their purpose in creating it? What audience did they have in mind? Were they trying to provoke a particular response, such as awe and wonder, sympathy, or anger? Questions about the interpretation of an image include issues of response and meaning: What do I see when I look at this image? What do others see? How do I feel when I look at this image? How do others feel? What does it mean?

Artists working in all media have been inspired by the world around them to try to represent particular places, or to capture their sense of place. They have produced drawings, paintings, prints, photographs, collages, embroideries, banners, ceramics, models, sculptures and, more recently, digital images. Primary school children can experiment with all these materials and processes in exploring the relationship between landscape and people, and its representation.

SPECIAL PLACES

Ask the children to think about a place that is special to them, and to create a sketch or painting of the place. Invite individuals to talk about their place, saying why it is special. Discuss the sorts of things that make places special, and explore the range of emotions that special places can invoke.

CAPTURING A SENSE OF PLACE

Visit somewhere with a strong or dramatic sense of place (for example, an old or religious building, clifftops, a local forest, a wild space, a historic townscape) and focus on experiencing it with all the senses, and on talking about how the children feel in this place. Discuss the emotions they experience. Use this as a stimulus for individual or collective art work that captures the spirit of the place, such as a mural, wall hanging or clay frieze (Figure 10.4).

■ **Figure 10.4** Making a model of Tower Bridge
Photo: Paul Owens

PHOTOMONTAGE

Ask children to take surprising/unexpected/quirky photographs of places around the school and grounds, or the local area, and create a photomontage.

LOCAL ARTISTS

Use the internet or local contacts to identify artists or photographers who create images of the local area, and invite the children to consider their work. Discuss why they may have chosen the particular sites to illustrate or represent. If possible, invite the artists into school to discuss their work. If you have the opportunity to work with a creative artist in school, consider the possibility of working with a place/geographical theme, perhaps celebrating the unique features of the local area.

ENVIRONMENTAL ART

Look at images of environmental art (e.g. Andy Goldsworthy) and use found materials such as stones, sticks, leaves or litter to create environmental art in the school grounds or a local open space. Invite the children to consider how it feels to create art that is temporary, and may be altered by the weather or the actions of others.

MODELLING

Older primary children may appreciate the opportunity to the use small-world equipment usually found in Foundation Stage or Key Stage 1 classrooms to create a model of a proposed development, or to envision how the world might be if, for example, their community committed itself to halving its carbon footprint.

IMPROVEMENT PROJECTS

Plan and undertake an environmental improvement project that involves the creative arts, such as creating an embroidered wall-hanging for the school hall, a mural for the playground, a storytelling chair or an open-air theatre in the school grounds, or get involved in local community arts environmental projects.

RESPONDING TO PAINTINGS

Study a picture depicting a landscape. Ask the children how they feel when they look at the picture. Can they guess how the artist felt about the place? Do they know any places that make them feel like this? Create pictures in the style of the artist/ picture.

COMPARING LANDSCAPES

Compare landscape pictures of the same sort of environment (rural, urban, coastal) by different artists and notice the geographical features they show. Discuss the differing ways the artists represent the similar features, e.g. cliffs, stormy seas, clouds, trees and buildings. Which do the children find most appealing, most accurate or most effective at conveying what it might be like to be there? Provide opportunities for the children to experiment with creating their own pictures incorporating landscape features.

TAKE ONE PICTURE

This National Gallery project offers many stimulating ideas for using individual pictures, including several landscapes, as the stimulus for cross-curricular work. Figure 10.5 lists some artists whose work has a strong sense of place, which could be used to explore a variety of different aesthetic and geographical issues.

Visual artists who convey a strong sense of place

Pieter Breugel the Elder – highly peopled sixteenth-century Flemish rural scenes
John Constable – early nineteenth-century East Anglian rural landscapes
Canaletto – highly detailed architectural paintings of eighteenth-century Venice and London
MC Escher – fantastical geometrically 'impossible' buildings
David Hockney – bold and colourful contemporary images of California and east Yorkshire
Edward Hopper – early/mid-twentieth-century (mostly urban) USA townscapes
Thomas Gainsborough – eighteenth-century English rural landscapes
LS Lowry – early twentieth-century northern English cityscapes
Claude Monet – nineteenth-/twentieth-century French impressionist paintings of outdoor scenes
Marianne North – nineteenth-century rural botanical landscapes of the Americas and Far East
Henri Rousseau – French post-Impressionist, exotic jungle scenes
William Turner – early nineteenth-century impressionistic British landscapes
Vincent van Gogh – Post-Impressionist, later nineteenth-century Dutch and French landscapes

■ **Figure 10.5** Artists whose paintings have influenced our perceptions of places

CONCLUSION

In this chapter, I have explored the contribution of the creative arts in primary geography, suggesting that they can be used:

■ to enhance children's learning about places, physical and human geography and environmental issues by providing approaches that deepen understanding;
■ to enrich and enliven geographical topics by extending their scope through creative cross-curricular approaches; and
■ to convey the outcomes of geographical learning in novel and engaging ways.

I conclude by focusing on exploring the communicative power of the creative arts. In developing my thinking on this topic I have drawn on the long tradition in arts practice of working across different art forms, and the concept of 'remodelling' developed by the Exeter Extending Literacy Project (EXIT). Amongst many stimulating ideas for supporting children in reading and writing non-fiction, Wray and Lewis (1997) suggest a wide range of activities to promote interactive reading, which, in a geographical context, can be applied to the full range of resources commonly used, such as books, maps, diagrams, websites, photographs and artefacts. Remodelling activities require children to restructure information from one format or genre to another, such as using prose text in an information book to produce a grid, diagram or board game. The extensive text-restructuring list of possible formats offered by Wray and Lewis involves mostly verbal and/or graphic forms, but I believe there is enormous potential in working with the freer, more creative approaches that the arts offer.

In a seminal work on the nature of creativity, Koestler (1964) argued that originality, discovery or creativity occurs through the dynamic interaction of discrete frames of reference. In Figure 10.6, I have experimented with this idea in the application of the creative arts to authentic geographical enquiries. I have listed possible learning activities drawn from creative arts practice, and some ways in which these can be presented and used to communicate with real audiences.

Remodelling offers many possibilities. Could children transform the information in standard geographical resources such as maps, photographs, information books, websites, field data, and photographs, into a puppet show, a mime or an art exhibition? Could their response to new experiences on a residential field trip be expressed in a handmade memory book, an installation in a corner of the school hall or a rap performance? Could the outcome of a study of some threatened local woodland be an environmental art trail, a piece of street theatre, a textile collage, an art exhibition or a multimedia presentation? I believe that the creative arts have much to offer primary geography and hope that the ideas in this chapter will inspire you to adopt creative approaches in devising exciting and meaningful learning experiences for the children you teach.

Possible approaches	Possible outcomes	Possible audiences
Movement	Dance performances	Peers in the class
Mime	Drama performances	Peers in the year group
Dance	Poetry performances	Older children
Sculpts	Simulated events	Younger children
Role play	Puppet shows	School Council
Improvisation	Playmats	Class teacher
Puppetry	Art exhibitions	Other teachers
Masks	Handmade picture-books	Head teacher
Drama performance	Photography exhibitions	Pupils in other local
Mark-making	Sculpture exhibitions	schools
Paper craft/bookmaking	Exhibition of models	Pupils in twinned school
Drawing	Installations	Parents and carers
Painting	Sculpture trails	Governors
Printing	Poetry trails	Members of local
Photographs	Environmental	community
Collage	improvements	Local community groups
Textile art/embroidery	Environmental art trails	Local councillors
Sculpture	Published storybooks	Local planning officers
Modelling	Published poetry books	National politicians
Clay work	Campaigns	
Installations	Websites	
Environmental art	Multimedia presentations	
Poetry and raps		
Stories		
Posters and leaflets		
Maps and diagrams		
Animation		
Video		

■ **Figure 10.6** Some opportunities for applying creative arts approaches in authentic geographical learning experiences

REFERENCES AND FURTHER READING

Alexander, R. (2009) 'What is primary education for?' *Times Education Supplement*, 20 February.

Alexander, R. (ed.) (2010) *Children, their World, their Education*. London: Routledge.

Arts Council (2005) *Children, Young People and the Arts*. London: Arts Council.

Arts Council (2012) *Be Creative, Be Well*. London: Arts Council.

Boniwell, I.. (2008) *Positive Psychology in a Nutshell*. London: Personal Well-being Centre.

Carr, A. (2005) *Positive Psychology*. London: Brunner-Routledge.

Catling, S. (2009) 'Creativity in primary geography', in Wilson, A. (2009) *Creativity in Primary Education*. Exeter: Learning Matters.

Craft, A., Jeffrey, B. and Leibling, M. (eds) (2001) *Creativity in Education*. London: Continuum.

Cremin, T. (2009) *Teaching English Creatively*. London: Routledge.

Csikszentmihalyi, M. (1992) *Flow: The Psychology of Happiness*. London: Rider.

Fisher, R. (2004) 'What is creativity?', in Fisher, R. and Williams, M. (eds) *Unlocking Creativity: Teaching Across the Curriculum*. London: David Fulton.

Henley, D. (2012) *Cultural Education in England*. London: DCMS.

Jones, P. (2005) *The Arts Therapies: A revolution in Health Care*. London: Brunner-Routledge.

Koestler, A. (1964) *The Act of Creation*. London: Hutchinson.

Levine, S.K. and Levine, E.G. (eds) (1999) *Foundations of Expressive Arts Therapy: Theoretical and Clinical Perspectives*. London: Jessica Kingsley.

Lipati, S. (2004) 'Creativity in music and art', in Fisher, R. and Williams, M. (eds) *Unlocking Creativity: Teaching Across the Curriculum*. London: David Fulton.

Martin, F. (2004) 'Creativity through geography', in Fisher, R. and Williams, M. (eds) *Unlocking Creativity: Teaching Across the Curriculum*. London: David Fulton.

Mackintosh, M. (2003) 'The art of geography'. *Primary Geographer*, 49: 36–37.

Maslow, A.H. (1971) *The Farther Reaches of Human Nature*. Harmondsworth: Penguin.

NACCCE (National Advisory Committee on Creative and Cultural Education) (1999) *All Our Futures: Creativity, Culture and Education*. London: DfEE.

Ofsted (2010) *Creative Approaches that Raise Standards*. London: Ofsted.

President's Committee on the Arts and Humanities (2011) *Reinvesting in Arts Education: Winning America's Future through Creative Schools*. Washington, DC: May, available at: www.pcah.gov (accessed 30 March 2012).

QCA (2005) *Creativity: Find It! Promote It! Promoting Pupils' Creative Thinking and Behaviour Across the Curriculum at Key Stages 1, 2, and 3*. London: QCA.

Robinson, K. (2011) *Out of Our Minds: Learning to Be Creative*. Chichester: Capstone.

Russell-Brown, D. (2009) 'Learning to teach the creative arts in primary schools through community engagement'. *International Journal of Teaching and Learning in Higher Education*, 20(2): 298–306.

Tanner, J. (2009) 'Special places: place attachment and children's happiness'. *Primary Geographer*, 68: 5–9.

Tanner, J. (2010) 'Geography and emotional intelligence', in Scoffham, S. (ed.) *Primary Geography Handbook*. Sheffield: Geographical Association.

Tanner, J. (2012) 'How do you see it? Using geographical images to promote meaningful talk'. *Primary Geography*, XX. Sheffield: Geographical Association.

Snyder, C.R. and Lopez, S.J. (2002) *Handbook of Positive Psychology*. New York: Oxford University Press.

UNESCO (2006) *World Conference on Arts Education* (available at: portal.unesco.org/culture/.../BOOKLET_world%2Bconference.doc).

Wilson, A. (ed.) (2005) *Creativity in Primary Education*. Exeter: Learning Matters.

Wray, D. and Lewis, M. (1997) *Extending Literacy: Children Reading and Writing Non-fiction*. London: Routledge.

Acknowledgement

Many thanks go to John Edwards, Head Teacher of Lower Fields Primary School, who had the vision and drive to create the Kinaesthetic Adventure Learning Park.

GEOGRAPHY AND MUSIC: A CREATIVE HARMONY

Arthur Kelly

This chapter starts by discussing the relationship between music and geography. It draws, in particular, on a literature base relating to cultural geography, which, over the past few decades, has shifted attention towards social interactions. It moves on to discuss the relationship between music, memory and geographical learning, focusing on the role of the affective domain, imagination and emotion. An ethnographic approach (Martin 2008), where music is employed to engage with pupils' geographical imaginations (Massey 2005) through dialogic teaching (Alexander 2008), is advocated. It is argued that such a strategy could empower teachers to become architects of a more relevant and creative curriculum. The chapter concludes by outlining a range of practical ideas that teachers can use with their pupils to develop geographical knowledge, understanding and skills. There are also suggestions for further activities, such as creating music in response to place.

OVERTURE

> Music is by nature geographical.
>
> (Connell and Gibson 2003: 280)

The word 'music' derives from the ancient Greek *mousike*, art of the muse, the muses being the goddesses who inspired creative practices. This chapter outlines the creative synergy between geography and music. This synergy has the potential to create high-quality, meaningful, enjoyable and memorable learning experiences across the primary age phase at the same time as providing teachers with insights into contemporary geographical understandings. It is argued that the use of music as a cultural artefact can be a springboard for two different aspects of creativity: (a) teaching creatively; and (b) teaching for creativity.

GEOGRAPHY AND MUSIC

> One might wonder what geography can say about music and vice versa.
>
> (Crang 1998: 89)

There is a developed academic interest in how music is geographical. Studies include the way music is linked to space and place, how music has geographical roots and the routes music takes around the world. This section aims to provide a brief overview of some relevant literature. This body of work is situated within the field of cultural geography, which was revitalised in the late twentieth century and continues to thrive. These trends are in line with the wider expansion of cultural studies. While definitions of culture are diverse and complex, the importance of place and identity, the relationships between the local and the global and the links between culture and economy have all been explored from a geographical standpoint (Mitchell 2000).

Music is an aspect of culture that has been studied by geographers. A range of themes has been explored including:

■ the relationship between music, identity and nationhood (Stokes 1994);
■ music practices as a challenge to spatial hegemony (Anderson *et al.* 2005);
■ music and the production of space and place (Connell and Gibson 2003);
■ the role of music in the structuring of community and identity (Whitely *et al.* 2005); and
■ the links between music and geographies of emotion (Wood and Smith 2004).

Much of this work is concerned within an exploration of 'popular' music as a cultural artefact, but, as will be seen below, this does not preclude the use of other musical genres in teaching and learning geography. Three interrelated areas are of particular relevance to the primary context and are explored in more detail: (a) music and place; (b) music and identity; and (c) music, emotion and the geographical imagination.

Music and place

Place is a fundamental geographical concept and has been described by Matthews and Herbert (2004) as a 'unifying bond' that links disparate studies, particularly in human geography. Understanding the relationship between place and music can deepen our understanding of the concept. As Matthews and Herbert explain:

> The unique quality of place is that it goes beyond the objective and has affective meanings...Place catches the very basis of the geography around which we build out lives.
>
> (Matthews and Herbert 2004: 165)

Identity and belonging are central to our concept of place, as are meaning and experience. Furthermore, Connell and Gibson (2003) suggest that auditory media, such as music, are involved in the generation and articulation of narratives about place. They contend that many everyday understandings about place are mediated through popular music. This argument builds on the work of Cohen (1995), who suggests that music plays a role in socially producing place in a number of ways. For example, a concert venue such as the O2, the Liverpool Echo or the Manchester MEN arena has a physical, economic and social impact.

In recent decades many English cities have sought to develop music as a cultural commodity and as a driver for economic development and regeneration. Cohen (2007) uses Liverpool as a case study to highlight the relationship between musical, social and economic change within the city, going on to make comparisons with other cities in the UK and north America. In Liverpool there is an economic and social impact beyond the 'Beatles legacy', and Cohen (2007) contends that there is a reciprocal relationship between music and the city:

> The city is not simply a place where music happens, or a container or inert setting for music activity. Instead music can be conceived of as contributing to the making or 'social production' of the city.
>
> (Cohen 2007: 35)

The economic and social impact of musical consumption on places within and beyond cities can be considerable, particularly with the recent growth in 'stadium venues' as loci of consumption. At the same time, music festivals have become increasingly popular, as indicated by the Glastonbury Festival in Somerset and the V Festival, which is held in August at venues in Essex and Staffordshire.

Music is rooted in culture, which is traditionally linked to place. This relationship is often expressed through musical styles and genres that include Mersey beat, Jamaican reggae, Irish music, New Orleans jazz, Chicago blues, and so forth. The symbolic representation of place is also evident in western classical traditions; for example, Rodrigo's *Concierto de Aranjuez* is a musical articulation of the town and landscape of Aranjuez in Spain. Additonally, the relationship between music and place may be apparent in the lyrics. At a simplistic level, this takes the form of 'name-checking' particular locations, as in songs such as 'New York, New York', 'The Leaving of Liverpool' and 'Carrickfergus'. The use of place names in song may also contribute to the construction of images of the place. Frank Sinatra created his idea of New York from a fusion of words and music. Paul Simon has given us the image of the Mississippi delta 'shining like a national guitar'. Meanwhile, Bruce Springsteen has constructed a particular notion of blue-collar America (Figure 11.1).

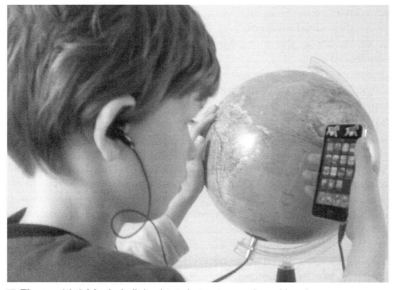

■ **Figure 11.1** Music is linked to place at a profound level

Geographers have long recognised that the nature of place is both multifaceted and contested. Some of these complexities can be highlighted by examining the relationship between music and geography. Cohen (1995) reminds us that the production of place through music has always been a political and contested process and that music is implicated in the struggle for identity and belonging. Music may also link us to past places as well as where we are now in an almost Flaubertian manner. As he puts it, 'many people maintain a link with their past through attachment to specific places and music is often used to remember such places' (Cohen 1995: 437). Many of us share the experience of hearing particular pieces of music or songs and being transported to particular places (and people) in our past. In addition, music may also transport us to places we have never been to or places in our geographical imaginings.

Music and identity

There is no doubt that music – in both its production and consumption – can be an important influence in shaping the typically hybrid identities of people and places, of engendering a sense of place and deep attachment to place.

(Hudson 2006: 633)

There have been a number of studies that explore the relationship between music and identity. This relationship operates on a range of scales – individual, community, regional and national. Taking a biographical approach, Cohen (1995) provides a case study of the relationship between music, place and identity, which illustrates its multifaceted nature. Stokes (1994) suggests that identity can be influenced through listening to, performing, dancing to and even thinking about music. Music, he suggests, can be the prison bars or the key to freedom. Many teenagers have gained freedom from their parents' world through discovering 'their' music, which then plays a part in establishing their identity.

Music plays a role in production of distinct cultural identities within which individual identities may be framed. Leonard (2005) examines how music and dance are used to construct an Irish 'cultural identity' by second- and third-generation Irish immigrants living in Coventry and Liverpool. Her research suggests that the role of music as a connective tissue among diaspora populations is important in establishing a collective identity and shared sense of community. Other displaced groups such as Jamaicans and Africans use music in similar ways to maintain their links with their country of origin. It is also recognised that the cultural heritage of the homeland can become fossilised as it travels through time and space, thus losing its dynamism and fluidity and that these constructions of community and the past form a series of overlapping and competing narratives (Bennett 2005).

There are many examples of the role music plays in confirming ethnicity and regional and national identities. Baily (1994) provides a historical overview of how music was used in a series of attempts to construct Afghan national identity while Mach (1994) explores how national anthems are one of three emblems that represent the interplay of nation and state symbolically. Bennett (2005) also points out that music can be particularly important in times of war and national crisis: Vera Lynn's 'White Cliffs of Dover' and Elvis Costello's 'Shipbuilding' provide different temporal and political examples. Interestingly, the hymn *Nkosi Sikelel'i Afrika* changed from being an act of political defiance against apartheid to being part of the South African national anthem. The way it mixes languages and forms is designed to attempt to reflect the plurality of the 'rainbow nation'.

Music, emotion and the geographical imagination

> It is probably now well accepted, though it is still important to argue, that a lot of our geography is in the mind.
>
> (Massey 2005: 48)

Emotion and imagination are recognised as having a role in geography. There is a grow-ing appreciation that our emotions influence how we engage with the world, and that emotional ways of knowing enable us to form unique personal geographies. This interest in emotional geographies is relevant across a range of themes and scales, from the emotional aspects of social life in the city to the role of emotion in building our sense of identity and nationalism. Wood and Smith (2004) explore the relationship between music and geographies of emotion, making interesting links between music, emotion, well-being and quality of life that echo the links between creativity and well-being. They point out that part of the power of music is that it expresses a range of emotions that we cannot rationalise. In this way it 'communicates something which tells us who people are, what has happened to them, where they are going, why and how' (Wood and Smith 2004: 544).

The complexity of how and why music evokes emotion has been the subject of extensive research by music scientists. While there seems to be a broad consensus that most people are moved by music, we need to be careful of attributing a simple cause-and-effect relationship. Ball (2010) reminds us that rather than being passive recipients of music, we construct our own interpretations. It has the ability to evoke memories that may be either personal or communal, and that lie outside the music itself.

THE POWER OF MUSIC

> Understanding why we like music and what draws us to it is a window on the essence of human nature.
>
> (Levitin 2008: 7)

Music is a powerful form of communication, which is universal across human cultures and seems to be related to basic human needs and expression. It can provide a deep response at an individual level but also acts as a glue that binds us together. Levitin describes it as 'the most beautiful human obsession' (2008: 11).

There is a significant body of research rooted in neuropsychology and music cogni-tion, which explores the relationship between music and the human brain. Levitin (2008) points out that listening to music involves the oldest and newest parts of the brain as well as prediction and emotional reward systems. There is a logical structure to music but the affective element is also important and the links to memory are clear. As Levitin puts it, 'when we love a piece of music, it reminds us of other music we have heard, and it acti-vates memory traces of emotional times in our lives' (2008: 192).

Ball (2010) provides an overview of how our minds respond to and come to under-stand music, and provides evidence to support the claim that music is 'part of what we are and how we perceive the world' (p. 31). MRI scans suggest that listening to music is an integrative activity that links left and right brain areas, utilises cognitive and emotional systems, and engages both the heart and the mind. This may be contrasted with the brain areas to do with language, which seem to be more strongly lateralised. Ball contends that, as a stimulus, music is like a 'gymnasium of the mind' and plays a key role in develop-ment, cognition, education and socialisation.

Film directors and advertising executives utilise the power of music to influence our emotional responses and buying preferences. Both are aware of the power music has to influence us, from the creation of catchy jingles to the use of a wide range of music to create mood. Educators, too, should be taking the power of music more seriously and using it to promote interest and engagement. Studies suggest that in listening to music the brain is far from passive. It is involved in seeking patterns, looking for clues, unpacking sensory data, accessing old stories and constructing new ones. Even if the music appears to be 'aural wallpaper', brain activity is still stimulated.

DIALOGIC ETHNOGRAPHY

> Dialogue is the antithesis of a state theory of learning, and its antidote.
>
> (Alexander 2010: 307)

What model of learning would enable teachers to construct a curriculum that recognises the importance of music in geography and its relevance in children's lives? The past 25 years has taught us that curriculum is mutable, but it is argued here that a curriculum built upon the enquiry process and embracing what is termed 'dialogic ethnography' would be exciting, stimulating and relevant. It is further suggested that such an approach could impact favourably on the decline in standards of teaching and learning in primary geography, which seems to be linked in part to teachers' weak subject knowledge (Ofsted 2011).

Martin (2008) argues that teachers often fail to realise that geography is part of everyday life. Furthermore, they tend to have a limited and outdated view of the subject, which they pass on to their pupils. One of the results is that they are reluctant to engage in creative practices. However, contemporary constructions of both music and geography emphasise the relevance of real-world experience. Also, as previously discussed, music is a cultural form, which interests, stimulates and engages most people. This fits in with the new paradigm that Martin (2008) proposes for primary geography. She calls this 'ethno-geography', or geographies of people and their cultures. As Martin argued in an earlier piece:

> There is . . . a real need to re-connect people with the subject in ways that recognise what their starting points might be . . . Everyday geography means . . . connecting the knowledge that teachers and pupils bring with them from their daily experiences to the knowledge and ways of understanding that geographers have developed over the years.
>
> (Martin 2006: 5)

This argument places an emphasis on children's everyday worlds and experiences. However, as Catling (2005) points out, the curriculum distances pupils from their interests and opts instead for comfortable topics based around safe questions and safe answers. This dislocation could be ameliorated by creative approaches, such as the integration of music and geography, which are child-centred and involve an appreciation and celebration of personal geographies (Kelly 2009).

School geography makes extensive use of enquiries and investigations. The basis of the enquiry process is that pupils should be supported in asking geographical questions, which thus develop geographical knowledge, understanding and skills. The nature of these questions may vary from the generic to the specific. The power of a questioning approach is that it recognises that geographical knowledge is dynamic rather than static. Putting it another way, Roberts (2003) reminds us, 'all geographical knowledge has been generated by someone, who at some time . . . has been puzzled and has wanted to know and understand more' (p. 39).

Within the ethnographic model, the relationship between teacher and learner is characterised by dialogue and co-construction rather than monologue and delivery. Alexander (2008) has championed dialogic teaching. He declares, 'dialogic teaching harnesses the power of talk to engage children, stimulate and extend their thinking, and advance their learning and understanding' (p. 37). Martin (2008) takes the notion of dialogue to a higher level by suggesting that the curriculum should be designed to harness the dialectical relationship between children's everyday geographies and the academic discipline. It is suggested here that the use of music as a stimulus for dialogic enquiries into children's lived geographies is an exemplification of this process.

Dialogic ethnography is not without its criticisms. It is argued that the focus on the everyday may be limiting in scope and may fail to provide opportunities to teach a full range of geographical skills and concepts. There are also fears that this approach may shift attention away from knowledge and the epistemological base of geography. However, such arguments emphasise transmission models of learning and assume that children's everyday knowledge is mundane. Ultimately, it is for teachers to decide on the relative merits of different pedagogies and the approaches they want to adopt.

CLASSROOM APPLICATIONS

The following teaching and learning ideas are not presented in any particular order. They are designed to make learning enjoyable and memorable while promoting empathy and understanding. They can be adapted to suit different abilities according to the professional judgement of the teacher. All are intended to harness the energy generated by the emotional link with the music to stimulate geographical enquiry.

Favourite music

If we are to pursue an ethnographic approach, we need to start with the pupils themselves. Ask the children to discuss the music they like listening to. Encourage them to consider what appeals to them about particular songs or compositions. Are they influenced by their family, friends or faith community (i.e. their cultural background)? This can lead to an exploration of the places where they listen to music and links to particular people and memories. Pupils could bring examples of music to share with the class. Similarly, they could survey their parents' or family's preferences. The key point here is to celebrate the diversity of preferences and the shared enjoyment of music. Children's use of technology could also be explored. How do they listen to music? Do they have personal stereos/MP3 players? Are there issues in listening to music in public places (noise pollution) or the outdoors (safety)?

Describing music

Music can also be used to develop pupils' 'emotional palette'. Some pupils may have difficulty expressing emotional responses beyond 'happy' or 'sad'; many others will find themselves at a loss for suitable words. One way to address this problem is to provide a vocabulary bank to describe the emotions, feelings and moods evoked by music. This can be developed by playing pieces from around the world and getting pupils to choose words that describe how they feel about them. The life, vibrancy and emotional palette of music from different parts of Africa can provide a stark counterpoint to the negative media images of that continent. Exploring different musical traditions can help to convey how diverse Africa is. This strategy can help develop emotional literacy at the same time as exposing pupils to diverse cultures. You could also use 'classical' music to introduce children to other cultural traditions and to develop their historical perspective.

Music and place

The strong link between music and place is relatively easy to explore as there are many examples. Most countries and regions have their traditional folk music and many have particular types of music or instruments associated with them. For example, the tango is rooted in Argentina, flamenco in Spain and samba in Brazil. The harp is seen as a symbol of Welsh culture just as the bodrhan represents Ireland. Let children listen and respond to music from different places, then use this to develop their knowledge of places around the world. A display could be made locating the musical styles or instruments on a world map. Once pupils have addressed the fundamental enquiry question 'Where is this place?', they could use secondary sources (e.g. maps, photographs) to explore further geographical questions. In addition to recognising different types of music from around the world, pupils could also explore the breadth of music from within individual countries.

Musical stereotypes

An issue that may arise is that children will develop musical stereotypes if they listen to just one type of music from a particular place, e.g. accordian music from France or digeridoo music from Australia. Initially, these simple images can be useful reference points and raise their awareness of other people and cultures. However, to avoid stereotyping, children need to hear a range of music from a particular country. This will help them to appreciate that there is diversity within other places, just as there is in their own. As well as listening to different styles and tempi, you could explore the emotions that music conveys – joy, sadness, loss and hope – and the way that this is part of our common humanity. I have used this strategy successfully in teaching about diversity within particular African countries. Music from different cultures can also be played ambiently in lessons or assemblies, perhaps linking to an overseas locality. This can be useful in encouraging pupils to accept and respect cultural differences – the 'other' becomes part of their world. Always ensure that children are given an opportunity to discuss how the music makes them feel and ensure that they know where it comes from, using maps and globes to help.

Musical journeys

Some pieces of music depict journeys through sound; 'Route 66' (Chuck Berry) is an obvious example from popular music. The 'Little Train of the Caipara' from *Bachianas Brasileiras No. 2* (Villa-Lobos) is another. This describes a journey through rural Brazil. Given pictures of the landscape, pupils could imagine themselves on the journey and create a map showing what they might see. You could extend this idea to musical representations of landscape and weather. *Fingal's Cave* (Mendelssohn) was inspired by the basalt columns in the uninhabited island of Staffa in western Scotland, Beethoven's Pastoral Symphony depicts a passing storm, Vivaldi's *Four Seasons* chronicles changes over a 12-month cycle. There are many other examples.

National anthems

National anthems are often not the most inspiring or emotionally stirring pieces of music (to the outsiders at least). However, listening to national anthems and their lyrics can be linked to work on overseas localities and introduces aspects of culture. For example, if the class is studying Mexico, then this is a natural opportunity to listen to the Mexican national anthem. The key point is to try to understand the music and its significance for the people who live in or originate from the country concerned.

Places in songs

A fun way of developing map and atlas skills is through a focus on lyrics in songs. Places are often mentioned in song lyrics but tend to go unnoticed. You could play the children extracts from selected songs and challenge them to find the places on a map. Examples include 'London Town', 'We're Going to Jamaica' and 'Barcelona'. When the children have found all the places mentioned, they could plot them on a world map and plan a journey linking them together. How would they travel? What would they see? Vocabulary relating to compass points, distances and obstacles such as mountains and deserts can also be developed through this exercise. Extend the work with home learning by asking pupils to find as many songs as they can that mention places. Can they find a way of going around the world in 80 songs? As always with these ideas, get children to discuss how the music makes them feel.

Creating music

The preceding ideas have involved pupils in listening to and responding to recorded music. In other words, they have been consumers. However, there is also huge potential for pupils to create their own music in response to place and to make up their own songs. An obvious stimulus for composition would be the school itself. One way to do this would be to compose different pieces based on places within the school. For example, how would pupils evoke the character of the dining-hall at lunchtime or the classroom during lesson time through music? Maybe they could devise a *Playtime Concerto*, which could either tell the story of the playground activities or capture the mood of relaxation and leisure. Children could also compose musical responses to other places using photographs as a stimulus. The contrast between a bustling urban scene, a stormy seashore or a sunny day in the country can be expressed in many different ways and make a really creative contribution to work in related geography topics.

CODA

This chapter has explored the relationship between music and geography and suggested that music is a fundamental human disposition with deep emotional resonance, which has the potential to create meaningful, enjoyable and memorable geographical learning experiences. Music, with its dynamism, hybridity and multiplicity, could almost be a metaphor for more nuanced understandings of place and geography. The academic case is grounded in a pedagogy that embraces dialogic teaching, and an ethnographic approach that supports teachers in both teaching creatively and harnessing children's creativity. The chapter has also exemplified some teaching strategies, all of which have been applied in the classroom. The harmonies and resonances between music and geography have the potential to bring excitement and relevance to teaching and learning. These harmonies operate at a number of different levels ranging from individual emotional impact to intercultural understanding. Ultimately, music is part of what it means to be human, just as the desire to explore, know and understand is, too. I would argue this is what geography is all about.

REFERENCES

Alexander, R. (2008) *Towards Dialogic Teaching: Rethinking Classroom Talk*. York: Dialogos.
Alexander, R. (ed.) (2010) *Children, their World and their Education*. Oxford: Routledge.
Anderson, B., Morton, F. and Revill, G. (2005) 'Practices of music and sound'. *Social and Cultural Geography*, 6(5): 640–3.
Baily, J. (1994) 'The role of music in the Creation of an Afghan national identity, 1923–1972', in Stokes, M. (ed.) *Ethnicity, Identity and Music*. Oxford: Berg.
Ball, P. (2010) *The Music Instinct*. London: The Bodley Head.
Bennett, A. (2000) *Popular Music and Youth Culture: Music Identity and Place*. London: Macmillan.
Bennett, A. (2005) 'Music, space and place', in Whiteley, S. *et al.* (eds) *Music, Space and Place: Popular Music and Cultural Identity*. Farnham: Ashgate.
Bonnett, A. (2003) 'Geography as the world discipline: connecting popular and academic geographical imaginations'. *Area*, 35(1): 55–63.
Catling, S. (2005) 'Children's personal geographies and the English primary school curriculum'. *Children's Geographies*, 3(3): 325–44.
Cohen, S. (1995) 'Sounding out the city: Music and the sensuous production of place'. *Transactions of the Institute of British Geographers*, 20: 434–46.
Cohen, S. (2007) *Decline, Renewal and the City in Popular Musical Culture*. Farnham: Ashgate.
Connell, J. and Gibson, C. (2003) *Sound Tracks: Popular Music, Identity and Place*. London: Routledge.
Crang, M. (1998) *Cultural Geography*. London: Routledge.
Davidson, J. and Milligan, C. (2004) 'Embodying emotion sensing space: introducing emotional geographies'. *Social and Cultural Geography*, 5(4): 523–32.
Duncan, J. and Ley, D. (1993) *Place/Culture/Representation*. London: Routledge.
Hudson, R. (2006) 'Regions and place: music identity and place'. *Human Geography*, 30(5): 626–34.
Kelly, A. (2009) 'Sounds geographical'. *Primary Geographer*, 68: 34–6.
Leonard, M. (2005) 'Performing identities: music and dance in the Irish communities of Coventry and Liverpool'. *Social and Cultural Geography*, 6(4).
Levitin, D. (2008) *This is Your Brain on Music*. London: Atlantic Books.
Mach, Z. (1994) 'National anthems: the case of Chopin as a national composer', in Stokes, M. (ed.) *Ethnicity, Identity and Music*. Oxford: Berg.
Martin, F. (2006) 'Everyday geography'. *Primary Geographer*, 61: 4–7.
Martin, F. (2008) 'Ethnogeography: towards liberatory geography education'. *Children's Geographies*, 6(4): 437–50.

Massey, D. (2005) *For Space*. London: Sage.

Matthews, J. and Herbert, D. (2004) *Unifying Geography: Common Heritage, Shared Future*. London: Routledge.

Mitchell, D. (2000) *Cultural Geography: A Critical Introduction*. Oxford: Blackwell.

Ofsted (2011) *Learning to Make a World of Difference*. London: Ofsted.

Roberts, M. (2003) *Learning through Enquiry: Making Sense of Geography in the Key Stage 3 Classroom*. Sheffield: Geographical Association.

Stokes, M. (ed.) (1994) *Ethnicity, Identity and Music*. Oxford: Berg.

Whiteley, S., Bennett, A. and Hawkins, S. (eds) (2005) *Music, Space and Place: Popular Music and Cultural Identity*. Farnham: Ashgate.

Wood, N. and Smith, S. (2004) 'Instrumental routes to emotional geographies'. *Social and Cultural Geography*, 5(4): 533–47.

Websites

http://www.singup.org/   Sing Up is an organisation that provides tools, songs and music linked to geography (and other curriculum areas).

www.songlines.co.uk   Songlines is a journal that focuses on the genre of world music, and the sampler CDs can provide a way in to this area.

http://www.putumayo.com/en/putumayo_kids.php   Putumayo is a source of a range of resources relating to music and multicultural understanding.

http://www.oxfam.org.uk/education/resources/   Oxfam Education provides ideas for using music as a stimulus to develop global citizenship.

www.youtube.co./xl   YouTube is a source of a wide range of music but there are issues about use in the classroom. YouTube XL is a safer source.

http://audacity.sourceforge.net/   Audacity is an excellent piece of freeware that allows you to edit and shape sounds for the classroom.

http://www.globaldimension.org.uk/news/item/?n=15046   A useful site providing more general advice on using sound more generally to explore the world near and far.

http://www.woodlandtrust.org.uk/en/campaigning/woodwatch/woodwatchers/Pages/Musicins piredbywoodsandtrees.aspx   The Woodland Trust website includes examples of music and songs inspired by trees and woodland.

CHAPTER 12

GEOGRAPHY AND SUSTAINABILITY

Paula Owens

This chapter discusses how creative geography teaching can help children understand and engage with sustainability issues and be genuinely involved in designing outcomes with future well-being in mind. Young children have a good deal of curiosity about the world that they live in but they also worry about the future of the planet. When they are given opportunities to participate in relevant creative and critical problem-solving enquiries, their learning can become powerful. Such teaching helps children to be better informed and thus more able to tackle issues such as climate change, unequal development and loss of biodiversity, which may otherwise seem daunting. It also provides an agenda of hope.

GEOGRAPHY AND ESD

'Education for sustainability' (ESD) is a term used to describe an approach to education that considers how we might better look after the planet we have inherited for the benefit of future generations. It has a wide remit and takes into account ideas such as equity and stewardship. Although there are many definitions of ESD, they all involve thinking about the future and how we might change it through our actions to offer a preferable quality of life for everyone. Thinking about how we might be best equipped to make decisions that will impact on our own and others' everyday lives, and the environments that sustain us, are powerful and relevant ideas for education, requiring both creative and critical thought. Owens (2011: 8) raises the following questions:

- What is education for if it is not to empower us with the knowledge, skills and values to live well on this Earth and with each other?
- What good is education if it does not build the capacity to question and change lifestyles and habits that threaten the one planet that sustains us?
- How effective is education if it does not carry a message of hope – that we can make a difference?

Sustainable development is commonly thought of as having three mutually supporting economic, social and environmental aspects. These work together and link to the idea of quality of life for all, recognising that we live in an interconnected world. They also relate to some of the 'big' questions that geography seeks to answer, namely:

- Where is this place? What is it like and why?
- Why and how is it changing? What will it be like in the future? What kinds of futures do we want?
- What do people do here? How are their actions influenced by, and how do they impact on, environments at different scales?
- How is this place connected to other places? How am I connected to other people and places?
- Who gets what, where, when and how? Who decides?
- What's it got to do with me? Why should I care?

Sustainability is relevant across the entire curriculum and is best approached through holistic teaching and learning. It has a particular association with geography and requires careful underpinning with geographical thinking and knowledge. Issues concerning sustainability and the environment have a values-led and emotive base, often articulated as a need to 'care for the world', which can sometimes eclipse other necessary components of knowledge and critical thinking. While values and emotions are intrinsic and inescapable facets of sustainability, being properly equipped to respond to these issues also demands some degree of understanding about how and why human, biological and physical worlds interact with and affect each other. This is part of the remit of geography education. Melding these ingredients together successfully to produce new ways of thinking about the world and some of the daunting issues we face requires creativity of approach, thought and deed.

TEACHERS' KNOWLEDGE OF ESD

Research by Symonds (2008) found that the majority of teachers had limited knowledge of ESD and that it was often piecemeal and impacted only on small groups of pupils. However, surveys of school practice in ESD by Ofsted between 2003 and 2009 found that there was some improvement in the teaching of sustainability and that this was more noticeable in primary than in secondary schools (Ofsted 2003, 2008, 2009). This finding was tempered by the observation that 'while a small number of schools were doing this well, many schools were only doing this as a peripheral activity and not through the mainstream curriculum' (Ofsted 2008: 5).

In addition, Ofsted (2011) remarked that too many schools were not doing geography to a high-enough standard and that in some schools geography was even disappearing from the curriculum. Unfortunately, a climate of poor geography teaching does not bode well for successful work on sustainability. As Martin and Owens (2010) note, '. . . if you are doing ESD then you're probably doing geography!' (p. 9). Imagine, for example, trying to teach about sustainability without understanding how local and global events are connected or how human, physical and environmental processes interact. If we need to improve ESD, we also need to improve the teaching and learning of geography.

Some of the barriers to successful engagement with ESD have been identified as: a lack of understanding of what this concept means; too little time or encouragement for teachers to think 'outside the box', and a lack of opportunity to make connections with relevant initiatives (UNESCO 2005). More recently, a survey by WWF (2010) into pedagogical approaches to sustainability found that success was dependent on teachers' subject knowledge; the support structures in schools; and teachers' capacity to root learning within the knowledge and skills of the curriculum. The WWF report recommended that both initial training and ongoing CPD should develop teachers' ability to engage with successful pedagogical approaches and build the subject knowledge necessary to support pupil enquiry, independent thinking and debate.

Many of the teaching and learning strategies that underpin quality geography are consistent with those that encourage effective ESD. These include (a) developing autonomy and critical thinking; (b) developing skills of enquiry, creativity and imagination; and (c) collective decision-making and using a range of media and text resources (Smith 2012). The 2011 subject report from Ofsted specifically mentions sustainability as a component in several examples of good practice observed. This adds weight to the argument that sustainability is an indicator of high-quality geography. Sustainability offers a real context for learning and enables pupils to make links between their own and others' lives in meaningful ways.

Many schools are enthusiastic about the idea of a 'creative curriculum' although Ofsted (2010) warns that successful creative curriculum practice is dependent on teachers' subject knowledge. When teachers are confident in their understanding of geography as a subject they are better equipped to make and apply relevant and powerful links to other curricular areas. Successful geography teaching requires that pupils know some 'core knowledge' about the world, but it also draws on other kinds of knowledge, such as that provided by personal and everyday geographies, which help to develop deeper *understanding* about the complex nature of the world we live in. Core knowledge on its own is useful, yet it can be static if not viewed in contexts of diversity, conflicting opinions and change. Personal and everyday geographies recognise the interpretations and experiences gathered through our everyday transactions. These latter kinds of knowing are, by definition, varied and subjective, yet they are hugely pertinent to the way that learners perceive, interpret and imagine the world around them.

In addition, it is important to note that the 'creative' aspects of exploration and imagination need to be complemented by critical thinking to avoid learning becoming 'woolly'. When creativity and critical thinking work together they generate purposeful learning that can be applied to real-world contexts. This can be thought of, diagrammatically, as a diamond-shaped process in which divergent and creative ideas are honed and focused towards a purposeful outcome (see Figure 12.1).

TEACHING GEOGRAPHY AND ESD CREATIVELY

Geography enables creative enquiry opportunities when taught well because it offers investigations into real places, situations, and issues and invites active agency, giving children a real voice (Catling 2009). It has also been suggested that geography is particularly well suited to promoting creative thought because it synthesises material and ideas from different subject areas (Scoffham 2003), thus helping pupils to 'think outside the box' when, for example, imagining how issues are connected and how problems might be tackled. Making connections, envisaging futures, problem-solving and collaboration in purposeful contexts are all indicators of creative activity (Hicks 2012). Indeed, where schools have developed their approaches towards sustainability, an increasing emphasis on creative thinking has been seen as a result (Ofsted 2009). The following headings indicate some of the key areas through which creativity can be developed.

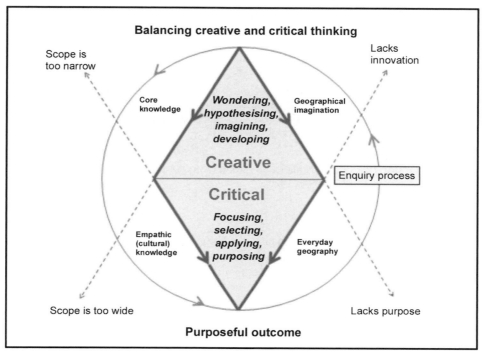

■ **Figure 12.1** Creativity and criticality are complementary but different aspects of purposeful learning

Making geography enjoyable and relevant

The Geographical Association manifesto (*A Different View*) puts forward ideas about the nature and relevance of modern geography as a 'living' subject (Figure 12.2). Geography uses an enquiry approach to support and encourage curiosity about the wider world and aims to develop pupils' ability to give creative and critical responses to everyday issues. Starting from what pupils know, and want to know, provides intrinsic motivation. It makes learning enjoyable as pupils can investigate aspects of life that are relevant to them. You might start by asking pupils to tell stories about who they are and where they come from. Sharing stories about who we are can build social bonds in the classroom and contribute to ESD: it helps us to understand more about the characteristics of places from our own and others' perspectives; deepens feelings of value, and strengthens notions of national identity. Mapping and explaining where we live, play and shop is also an important part of geography, developing our geographical imagination, or ways in which we view the world.

Fieldwork

Children today have less first-hand contact with outdoor environments than previous generations. This can be partly explained by the pull of indoor virtual lifestyles, reduced access to outdoor play spaces and increased parental concerns about safety (Pretty *et al.* 2009). Yet children enjoy being out-of-doors where there is often far more scope for

Living geography:

■ is directly relevant to people's lives and the world of work;

■ is about change – recognises that the past helps explain the present, but is current and futures-orientated;

■ has a scale 'zoom lens', so that the local is always set in a global context;

■ is 'deeply observant' – it looks beneath the surface to identify the mechanisms that change environments and societies; and

■ encourages a critical understanding of big ideas like 'sustainable development', interdependence' and 'globalisation'.

■ **Figure 12.2** Some principles of 'Living geography'
Source: GA 2010: 13

exploration and discovery than in the home or classroom. Fieldwork immerses pupils in experiences that allow them to engage with their local environment and better imagine distant ones. We also learn more about our environment when we experience it at first hand and have the opportunity to use all our senses. The process of immersing ourselves in such experiences helps to develop positive values and feelings towards the world around us and provides us with incentives for stewardship. Fieldwork, Lambert and Owens (2013) argue, is an essential aspect of engaging with sustainability and promoting creativity.

Being outside can open up new experiences: sights, smells, touch, sounds and feelings that stimulate the imagination and heighten awareness (Figure 12.3). Research has shown that fieldwork promotes vocabulary acquisition so necessary for engaging with environmental dialogues (Ward 1998). It can also provide an affective component, through positive emotional experiences that promote the development of deep and lasting memories. Such memories can positively influence adult values and attitudes (Catling *et al.* 2010). These days, teachers are more wary of taking children beyond the school gates even just to walk around the local area because of safety concerns, yet even this is an opportunity for creative teaching and learning. You might, for example, involve pupils in their own risk assessments before venturing outside, using digital images and maps to allow pupils to identify possible hazards and think about how they will keep themselves safe. This allows pupils to be creative in their solutions to everyday hazards in ways that they may not have thought of before. It also develops relevant geography as pupils recognise and discuss specific environmental features using maps and diagrams, and relevant ESD as pupils learn to take responsibility for their actions.

Investigating the locality through first-hand exploration is one of the best ways of developing knowledge about local issues. You might have already identified an issue that requires focused enquiry, such as the closure of a local shop or a proposal to build new houses or roads; or you might discover an issue whilst exploring the local area: for example, a walk around the school to record good and negative aspects of the local environment will produce many ideas about how the area might be improved. You could also undertake simple explorations of the school grounds in which pupils are free to collect and record sights, sounds and other phenomena that interest them (Figure 12.3). This is a simple awareness technique that develops pupils' capacity to see their surroundings in new ways and to begin to think critically about the quality of an environment. Such explorations encourage children to make careful and deep observations, raise questions and make connections of which they were not previously aware. One of the other benefits is the sense of awe and wonder that can be found from being outside, which might stem from noticing everyday natural phenomena such as the patterns of clouds, spiders' webs or the colour of autumn leaves. Or it might be discovered in the complexity and beauty found in some parts of the built environment. Awe and wonder are, in themselves, powerful motivators for imaginative thought and response. They remind us that the world is an amazing place.

■ **Figure 12.3** Year 3 student, International School of Bologna, collecting information about the school grounds
Photo: Jane Whittle

Investigating current issues

Flexibility is a key feature of effective planning for creativity as everyday events and issues can crop up that trigger sparks of curiosity and motivation in children, offering fruitful and creative sources of enquiry. Flexibility is especially relevant for geography as it deals with the 'here and now', and so is particularly susceptible to the need to be 'current'. Very often, unplanned learning opportunities emerge from news stories, often, sadly, because of a disaster such as a volcanic eruption or a tsunami, where lives have been lost and livelihoods threatened. Even very young children can be aware of these events, which they can find worrying as they fear for their own safety. Using such stories to start a geographical enquiry can help children make sense of them and feel less threatened. It also helps to empower them as they become actively engaged in tackling a problem perceived as a threat.

In one Year 2 class, children discussed the effects of a volcanic eruption and, particularly, how it had disrupted air travel. One of the consequences was that tourists had become stranded, including some teachers following a holiday period. In addition, some fruit and vegetables started to run low in supermarkets. This led pupils to develop all kinds of interesting ideas about how the stranded teachers might be able to get home and led them to think about why we rely on certain fresh foods to be transported by aeroplane. The new thinking by pupils enabled them to appreciate the importance of interdependence and how we are globally connected to each other.

Many classes use the 'What's in the news?' approach in geography, but few develop this further to actively investigate a particular news topic. Using sources of information such as newspapers and television media can provide a starting point for pupils to voice their concerns and pose their own questions. Sometimes a simple image can be used to ask pupils, 'What's going on here?' and 'How do you feel about . . . ?', which is enough of a hook for pupils to begin to imagine and respond to what might be happening. Using a mix of knowledge and emotional response in connection with issues-based thinking is also a very powerful way to create new understanding.

Sometimes children can be fired up by exposure to a particular issue. For example, when a Year 4 class learnt, through a speaker from the Hawk and Owl Trust, how barn owls were losing their natural habit and were in decline, they wanted to know more. Such was their enthusiasm that planning was adapted to make the most of their curiosity and drive. This example is typical of how geography can provide a real focus point for cross-curricular work. Instead of designing money boxes, children designed owl boxes, and the study of habitats in science was given a new slant through a real-life problem. The geography involved active fieldwork to investigate the kinds of habitats favoured by owls, and to decide where to site the owl boxes, whilst it was also necessary to find out about the human and physical pressures that had led to this environmental problem (Figure 12.4).

Some issues are current but also long-term, which gives ample scope for planning, although they can be daunting to tackle. Perhaps the most contentious is global warming. There is still some debate over the extent to which global warming can be attributed to human activity but the consensus of scientific opinion is that a casual link exists. Understanding the language of this debate requires sound underpinning with subject knowledge and facts before the more value-laden aspects of how we might respond are explored.

'Climate change' refers to the fluctuation of climate conditions on Earth over varying periods, and we know that this has always happened. 'Rapid climate change'

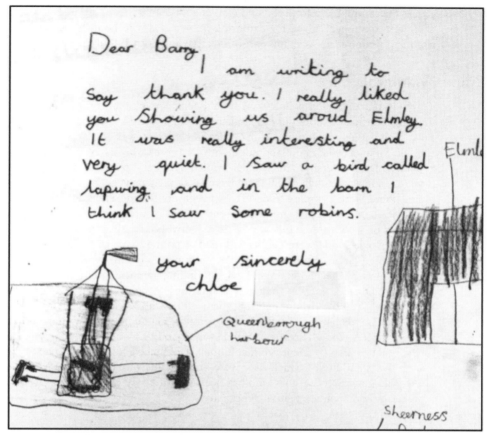

■ **Figure 12.4** Finding out about birds at a local nature reserve. A letter from a Year 3 pupil, Eastchurch School, Isle of Sheppey, Kent, following a visit

differentiates the unexpectedly fast pace of change, which is leading to environmental conditions to which humans and other living creatures may find it hard to adapt. 'Global warming' is a natural phenomenon thanks to the presence of carbon dioxide, which means that our planet has just the right conditions for life to flourish, whereas 'enhanced global warming' refers to the human-induced build-up of carbon dioxide, methane and other gases in the Earth's atmosphere that is causing global temperature rise. Understanding the terminology of complex processes such as this can seem anything but creative, yet creativity flourishes where there is secure subject knowledge, so helping pupils to differentiate between, and use, appropriate vocabulary is vital.

Drama can be a useful method for exploring some of these processes. Pupils could act out, through dance, for example, how carbon dioxide in the Earth's atmosphere captures some of the sun's energy reflected back from the Earth. This would allow pupils to see in a concrete way how much more energy can be captured if the amount of (e.g. number of dancers) carbon dioxide increases. Encourage pupils to think of good questions to ask that allow them to probe and challenge assumptions about issues such as climate change: a dialogical space for exploring known or given boundaries between accepted truth and fiction is an essential part of creative and critical thinking.

Empathy and role play

Trying to imagine other people's views and perspectives can be difficult, especially when there are conflicts of opinion. Empathising through role play can be one way in which this kind of imaginative thinking can be developed, and was the approach used by class teacher, Sarah Lewis, in collaboration with Dr Emma Mawdsley, a lecturer in geography at Cambridge University. This teacher wanted her Year 4 pupils to develop more complex thinking, and accept that, often, there were no simple answers to environmental problems; rather, there were complex trade-offs between conflicting areas of need. To this end, a group of characters representing different aspects of life on the island of St Lucia were portrayed on a website. Pupils were able to learn about their life, ask Dr Emma questions about their needs and were challenged to take on the 'Role of the Mantle' by becoming experts about environmental policy. The culmination of this work was a presentation to visiting 'ministers' where the pupils would outline identified policies.

Through this activity, innovative solutions to conflicts on St Lucia, such as the tensions between the fishing industry, the health of the reef and tourist yachts, were identified. The pupils used a variety of maps, graphs, 3D models and written and oral reports to present their work. They demonstrated their ability by not only achieving complexity of thought but also by identifying solutions such as beach zoning, which are actually in use on the island but of which they were hitherto unaware (Lewis and Mawdsley 2007). 'Empathic geography' of this kind has been identified by Lambert and Owens (2013) as a powerful approach to creative geography.

Using storybooks

Stories about place can be powerful and stimulating influences on the geographical imagination (Rawling 2011) and invite personal responses. They take us out of our place in the world and help us to imagine other situations, landscapes, cultures and contexts. In this way they can help to scaffold enquiry, interpretation and learning. Cremin (2009) notes how the choice of text is important for enabling creative engagement and how picture-books can be especially powerful in facilitating a range of responses and meaning-making. Picture-based and other relevant storybooks can provide examples of features and environmental vocabulary that can set children off on an enquiry bolstered by relevant knowledge and their own questions.

Books by authors such as Jeanne Baker are particularly evocative through their use of illustrations, which invite children to enter into a futures-orientated world. For example, *Where the Forest Meets the Sea* (1987) and *Window* (2002), are both enduring and relevant tales of our time in which the story is set in the context of an encroaching built environment.

Some books have the power to enchant and inspire us to think about the diversity and beauty of the wider world, for example *Ben's Magic Telescope* (2003) by Brian Patten. Others help us learn where everyday resources come from such as in *The World Came to My Place Today* by Jo Readman (2004). More recent books that have captured concerns about global issues such as climate change include *Who Will Save Us?* by

Rebecca Morch (2007) and *The Trouble with Dragons* by Debi Gliori (2009), while *Dolphin Boy* by Michael Morpurgo (2004) invites us to discuss the impacts of change at a local scale. Books that deal with changing environments and other issues offer a safe space for children to explore and respond to scenarios that they might hitherto have been unable to imagine. They can also allow children to apply some of these ideas to help them better imagine other scenarios.

Even traditional tales can be used in creative hands as a starting point for sustainability enquiries. Jonathon Kersey subverted the story of Little Red Riding Hood to develop an idea with his Year 2 pupils in which the big bad wolf became the good wolf who helped Little Red Riding Hood to successfully recognise and negotiate dangers in the neighbourhood (Figure 12.5). This was developed through active fieldwork and made into a film through a cross-curricular project with a geography focus. The creativity of this project was inherent in how pupils had collaborated to create new meanings from their locality through a mix of fieldwork and film, while the sustainability dimension arose from pupils' new perspectives and identified actions with regard to the quality of their environment (Lambert and Owens 2013).

Geographical skills and fieldwork
- Identify locations within Southborough that present dangers or difficulties for pedestrians.
- Use maps and plans to mark a route to visit these locations and use them as film locations to retell a narrative story.
- Visit locations and record film footage.
- Record environmental hazards and dangers with photography and sketches.
- Identify the causes of some of the environmental hazards in Southborough.
- Recognise how aspects of the environment can be sustained, developed and improved.

■ **Figure 12.5** Extract from initial planning sheet, Southborough Primary School: the true story of Little Red Riding Hood

Pupil participation

Genuine participation is an essential part of both the process and outcome in sustainable learning and typifies high-quality geography. It is really important that pupils feel that they have a genuine voice, share responsibility and have the freedom to suggest outcomes that are taken seriously. Building this aspect into teaching and learning can seem risky initially, but jointly constructed curricula can help to develop children's sense of autonomy and improve motivation.

Children need to feel that they can make a difference and they need to value the learning. This means it is important to use pupils' starting questions to frame enquiries. Equally, you need to listen to their suggestions as to how data might be collected and presented and who might be interested in the outcomes. Finally, you need to decide if there are realistic actions that might be taken. For example, some Year 4 pupils gathered data about litter in the environment and provision was made for them to work with the local council in deciding where new bins ought to be sited. If you were doing this kind of activity in the school grounds you might want to collect pupils' ideas as to what might actually be done to combat this, and decide as a class which were the most achievable, then follow these ideas up. Alternatively they could make a presentation to school governors. Enquiries set in purposeful contexts tell pupils that their work and opinions matter and are a powerful driver for creative work.

Collaborative learning

Working together is a vital part of sustainable thinking and learning, and of creativity too. Collaboration happens easily in classroom situations, less often through links with the local community, and is even rarer with distant communities. Yet, in our globalised world, where our actions impact on local and global environments, learning from people who live in other parts of the world is valuable as it helps us to imagine a wider range of acceptable responses to local problems.

Many schools now have links with schools overseas or, at the very least, study contrasting localities overseas, and this provides a huge potential to promote learning from and about other cultures. While we cannot actually go to overseas localities and experience them at first hand, we can employ empathic geographies to help us learn about them. We can also employ creative techniques such as 'hot-seating' and 'putting ourselves in the picture' to imagine what life is like there, having securely underpinned imaginative thought with background information from as many sources as possible, e.g. sights, sounds, tastes, artefacts and stories.

It is essential to challenge stereotypical thinking about others' lifestyles, especially when there is a stark contrast in material wealth (Scoffham 2013). Try to focus on questions such as 'What can we learn from this community?' rather than the shallow and often inaccurate stance, 'How can we help this community?' The best school partnerships are equal in terms of learning and giving and provide enormous motivation for pupils to respond to and learn from other cultures. True, collaborative geographies can help to mutually develop and enhance geographical imagination and widen perspectives.

Campus, community and curriculum

Learning about ESD does not only happen in the classroom and designated curriculum activities; it also emerges in hidden agendas, such as the way the buildings and grounds are managed and the quality of the links with the community, both local and distant. Many schools have found that they can clarify what they do using the following three headings: care: caring for oneself, caring for others, and caring for environments. This approach can be neatly combined with the idea of working across the campus, community and curriculum. Ideally, sustainability needs to be embedded within the curriculum; apparent across the school campus in both deed and ethos, and achieved through collaboration with local communities.

One area that rightly warrants a lot of attention is our use of resources especially that of energy. Our energy use has many geographical implications, such as, for example: How do we source our energy? How does energy use impact on local and global environments (e.g. global warming)? Why do some people in other parts of the world not have ready access to electricity? How do other people and communities solve their energy problems? How do we travel to school? Several schools now have 'energy monitors' who help ensure that their class takes every precaution against wasting energy. It is important that laudable initiatives of this kind are built into the curriculum. Ofsted (2009) has highlighted how, in some examples of best practice, schools are influencing the local community to act more sustainably. How can this be achieved? And how can we get pupils to think creatively around the idea of energy use? Making it real and current through geography helps pupils to identify with the issues.

Some Key Stage 2 pupils were investigating wind energy as their school was going to have a wind turbine installed. They were asked to consider the pros and cons of this type of energy use from different perspectives. In particular, they were asked to think about their own opinions, those of neighbours and how some of the wildlife in the school grounds might be affected. These pupils were engaging with sustainability through creative and critical thinking rather than being 'greenwashed' into merely making positive comments about a technology that the school had chosen to adopt (see Figure 12.6).

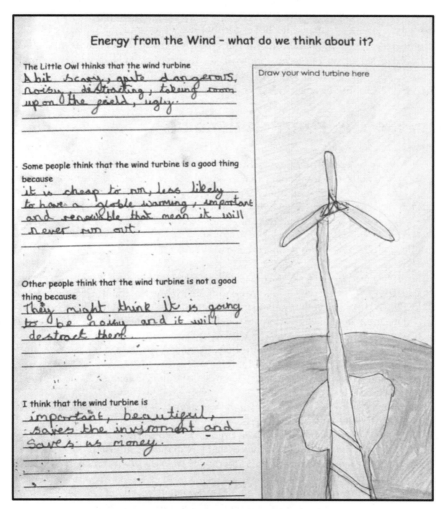

Figure 12.6 Thinking about wind turbines from different viewpoints – from a Year 4 pupil from Eastchurch School, Isle of Sheppey, Kent

CONCLUSION

Sustainability and the environment are key ideas for geography and require a creative approach in which children are enabled to:

▪ envisage previously unimagined places and futures;
▪ empathise and understand other viewpoints and perspectives;
▪ think about possible solutions that might help solve local and global issues; and
▪ imagine themselves as capable agents of change.

It also requires a critical approach to received wisdom and an ethos in which children feel free to question and enquire about alternative explanations and actions. It is a most important and relevant aspect of our children's education.

Sustainability is about considering a range of opinions and recognising that sometimes we do not have all the answers or that our knowledge may be uncertain. It is also about recognising that people have conflicting views and that these may be value-led: solutions to conflicting opinions may involve trade-offs and compromise and it is often difficult to select an outcome that will suit everyone. This is why sustainability is so complex, yet it is all the more important to provide children with the necessary skills and knowledge to think about it creatively.

REFERENCES AND FURTHER READING

Catling, S. (2008) *Young Geographers: A Living Geography Project for Primary Schools, 2008 – An Evaluation Report*. Sheffield: Geographical Association.

Catling, S. (2009) 'Creativity in primary geography', in Wilson, A. (ed.) *Creativity in Primary Education*. Exeter: Learning Matters, pp.189–98.

Catling, S., Greenwood, R., Martin, F. and Owens, P. (2010) 'Formative experiences of primary geography educators'. *International Research in Geographical and Environmental Education*, 19(4): 341–50.

Cremin, T. (2009) *Teaching English Creatively*. Learning to Teach in the Primary School Series. London: Routledge.

DfEE (1999) *Geography: The National Curriculum for England*. London: QCA.

GA (2010) *A Different View: A Manifesto for Geography*. Sheffield: Geographical Association.

Hicks, D. (2012) 'The future only arrives when things look dangerous: reflections on futures education in the UK'. *Futures*, 44(1): 4–13. http://teaching4abetterworld.co.uk/docs/download17.pdf (accessed 15 February 2012).

Lambert, D. and Owens, P. (2013), in Jones, R. and Wyse, D. (eds) *Creativity in the Primary Curriculum*. Abingdon: David Fulton.

Lewis, S. and Mawdsley, E. (2007) 'Geojoes St Lucia Challenge'. *Primary Geography*, 64: 19–21.

Martin, F. and Owens, P. (2010) *Caring for Our World: A Practical Guide to ESD for 4–7 Year Olds*. Sheffield: Geographical Association.

Ofsted (2003) *Taking the First Step Forward – Towards an Education for Sustainable Development* (HMI 1658) (www.ofsted.gov.uk/publications/1658).

Ofsted (2008) *Schools and Sustainability: A Climate for Change* (www.ofsted.gov.uk/publications/070173).

Ofsted (2009) *Education for Sustainable Development Improving Schools – Improving Lives*.

Ofsted (2010) *Learning: Creative Approaches that Raise Standards*.

Ofsted (2011) *Geography Learning to Make a World of Difference*.

Owens, P. (2011) 'Why sustainability has a future'. *Primary Geography*, Spring: 7–9.

Pretty, J., Angus, C., Bain, M., Barton, J., Gladwell, V., Hine, R., Pilgrim, S., Sandercock, S. and Sellens, M. (2009) 'Nature, childhood, health and life pathways'. Interdisciplinary Centre for Environment and Society Occasional Paper 2009–02. University of Essex.

Rawling, E. (2011) 'Reading and writing place', in Butt, G. (ed.) *Geography Education and the Future*. London: Continuum, pp. 65–83.

Scoffham, S. (2003) 'Thinking creatively'. *Primary Geography*, 50: 4–6.

Scoffham, S. (2012) 'Why stereotypes are so pernicious', in Sangster, M. (ed.) *Developing Teacher Expertise*. London: Continuum.

Smith, M. (2012) *GTIP Think Piece – Education for Sustainable Development* http://www.geography.org.uk/gtip/thinkpieces/esd/#4 (accessed 15 February 2012).

Symonds, G. (2008) *Barriers and Enablers in ESD and EE: A Review of the Research A Report for Sustainability and Environmental Education*. SEEd Practice.

Tilbury, D. (2011) *Education for Sustainable Development: An Expert Review of Processes and Learning*. Paris: UNESCO.

UNESCO (2005) 'Guidelines and recommendations for reorienting teacher education to address sustainability'. *Education for Sustainable Development in Action*. Technical Paper No 2. UNESCO Education Sector.

Ward, H. (1998) 'Geographical vocabulary', in Scoffham, S. (ed.) *Primary Sources: Research Findings in Primary Geography*. Sheffield: Geographical Association, pp. 20–1.

WWF (2010) *Learning for Sustainability in Schools: Effective Pedagogies*. Godalming: WWF.

Storybooks

Baker, J. (1987) *Where the Forest Meets the Sea*. London: Walker Books.

Baker, J. (2002) *Window*. London: Walker Books.

Gliori, D. (2009) *The Trouble with Dragons*. London: Bloomsbury.

Morch, R. (2007) *Who Will Save Us?* Rebecca Morch Publishing.

Morpugo, M. and Foreman, M. (2004) *Dolphin Boy*. London: Andersen Press.

Patten, B. (2003) *Ben's Magic Telescope*. London: Penguin.

Readman, J. (2004) *The World Came to My Place Today*. Eden Project Books.

Acknowledgements

Thanks to:

■ The Geographical Association and their Quality Mark Schools.

■ St Joseph's Catholic Primary School, Surrey, Dr Emma Mawdsley and teacher Sarah Lewis.

■ Teacher Jonathan Kersey and pupils at Southborough Primary School, Kent.

■ Jan Austin and pupils at Eastchurch Primary School, Isle of Sheppey, Kent.

CHAPTER 13

KEEPING GEOGRAPHY MESSY

Stephen Pickering

One of the main ideas in this chapter is that geographical themes and issues involve complex problems that rarely have precise or clear-cut answers. This chapter also highlights how learning is itself an untidy process that does not fall into the neat and orderly sequences that many would have us believe. Finding out about the real world is, inevitably, a much messier process than studying sanitised textbook examples. If the curriculum is to be meaningful it involves, as Catling and Pickering (2010) argue, investigating real issues rather than separating children from them. Getting your hands dirty is part of the process of engaging with this fascinating subject.

CREATIVITY: A MESSY BUSINESS

When Phineas Gage set out to work on the railway early one morning in 1848 he had no idea that he was about to lead the way in brain research. His job was to clear rocks so that the railway tracks could be laid, but on 13 September (an unlucky day for Phineas) a spark from the rock set off the gunpowder too early and the metal bar he used for tamping down the explosives was blown straight through his head and out of the top of the skull with such force that it landed 30 metres away. Undeterred, he hitched a ride into the nearest town where a doctor tried his best to cover the hole. Amazingly, Phineas lived for a further 12 years with a hole in his head. But his personality changed from a happy, generous soul to one who was quick to anger and who lacked all inhibitions. Constant swearing was the least worrying of his new personality traits. But this messy accident also heralded the realisation that different areas of the brain are responsible for different emotions and learning, and the start of modern neuroscience.

The findings emerging from modern research confirm that the brain, as well as being little understood, is indeed a messy organ. There are multiple links and connections; neural pathways vary from one individual to another and brain areas that appear to have one function are sometimes recruited for other purposes. The evolutionary processes that have resulted in overlaps and multiplicity help to give the brain its resilience. In this chapter we investigate how the messiness of geography and the messiness of learning can combine in creative approaches to teaching. Children think in a variety of ways: intuitively, cognitively and emotionally. One of the advantages of creative approaches to teaching is that they draw on a range of different capacities and challenge children to marshall their thoughts in new configurations. If children are made aware of the way in which they learn and which type of thinking they have been engaged in, then they will be better placed to apply these thinking skills to new situations.

TEACHING MAP SKILLS CREATIVELY

Messy maps

Villages, towns and cities often develop haphazardly over long historical periods. Indeed, pupils may discover that their own school is a bit of a mess, consisting of higgledy-piggledy buildings that have been put up for different purposes at different times in the past. You might begin by asking the children to define what they understand by the term 'mess'. They will probably start with untidiness and images of their bedroom and move (perhaps with a bit of teacher input!) towards a more general idea that things that are messy lack a sense of order. Now look at local maps and plans, perhaps focusing on the school and its surroundings, a local attraction like a theme park or the area in which children live. This is a great way for children to discover the apparent chaos in the roads, highways and infrastructure that actually give order to their lives. Can they identify any loose or abandoned spaces? Why do they think these areas have become neglected and how might they be used in the future?

Physical maps, particularly when you consider landscape and relief, or even a meandering river, provide further examples of 'messy geography'. Try zooming in and out of an area using Google Earth to view images at a range of scales and perspectives. Make comparisons with traditional maps and discuss the things that seem odd. Can the children explain how the odd and illogical things might have come about? Can they see any order within the apparent mess?

It is important for children to understand that places are complex, particularly as they develop haphazardly over time. You can help them to move beyond simple 'yes/no' answers to more nuanced and evaluative modes of thinking. Embracing complexity and accepting that there are not necessarily clear-cut or definitive solutions to problems is part of creative thinking. Additionally, learning is almost always enhanced if pupils can understand *why* they are learning. Pupils need to see the relevance of the subject. Indeed, neurologist Howard Gardner (1999) asserts that, as an organism, the brain learns best when it is exploring situations and asking questions to which it actively craves the answers. The following exercises show how mapwork can be both relevant, providing a local focus, and challenging – the challenge of creative interpretations.

MAP DETECTIVES

This is a super activity that helps children to make links between maps and the places they portray. It can be easily adapted to suit a range of ages. Arm each small group of children with a digital camera and ask them to take six photographs of small, interesting details around the school grounds (examples might include a special bench, places where the playground markings have been rubbed off or the area under a bench). Older children can mark where they have taken their photos on an outline map of the school. Put each photograph onto a PowerPoint slide and print off as a slideshow (six slides to a page). The children swap sheets, are given an outline map of the school and set out to discover where the photos were taken and mark them on the map. You could ask pupils to take photographs that illustrate a theme such as sustainable practice, messy places or favourite places. The aim is to connect real places to maps. Children might work with maps of different scales, e.g. classroom or school grounds, depending on which is most appropriate.

MAKING MESSY MAPS

Pupils love to do things differently. Challenge them to create a messy or unusual map of their local area (Figures 13.1a and 13.1b). They could use chalk and the playground, or arrange tables and chairs – anything they can utilise – to create a map of the local area in their classroom or hall. To do this they will need to collaborate, discuss features, describe the local area to each other, use artistic licence and consider what makes their local area distinctive. They can follow this up by taking groups on a guided tour of the area, highlighting distinctive features, or even create a documentary film.

■ **Figure 13.1a** Year 3 and 4 children recreated their home town with everything they could lay their hands on

■ **Figure 13.1b** The children raided the PE store to create their maps

LIVING MAPS

One way to help children become familiar with Ordnance Survey maps if they personalise them. Use the set of cards shown in Figure 13.2 with pupils at Key Stage 2. Children will need to read and interpret the map in order to choose appropriate places to apply the statements. You can challenge the children further by getting them to write their own statements to test each other. These questions might be structured around skills. For example, pupils could write two cards that focus on each of the following: scale, signs, symbols and map-reading.

The cards in Figure 13.2 encourage children to evaluate the places shown on the map. (The train station is 3.5 km SW as the crow flies.) They imagine what they are like (this is my favourite spot because...). This calls for both cognitive and emotional responses and draws on different neural networks. The exercise works best if you use a map local to your school and create your own appropriate 'living map' cards. You can develop this further by using maps of different scales and compare how the statements vary. The exercise can also be linked with Modern Languages, using, for example, a French map and creating simple French phrases.

What a great place for a picnic!	The church is only 2 km away, but it is much further if you travel by road.	I can't see the town because of the hills.	The slope is really steep here: great for sledging in winter.
This is the centre of the wood.	If you travel due east for 5 km you will reach the centre of town.	Isn't this spot beautiful?	This is probably the busiest road.
I wouldn't like to stay here in the middle of the night!	The train station is 3.5 km south-west as the crow flies.	I think the views from here are best.	If you want a good job you should come to this place.
I wouldn't be able to see this on a larger-scale map.	The bypass is best placed here.	If we are to develop this area, we need a shopping centre here.	This is my favourite spot because...

■ **Figure 13.2** Statements that might be used in a set of 'living map' cards

Messy scale

Scale can be quite a difficult concept for children, particularly those who may not have travelled far in their young lives or who fall asleep as soon as they set off on a long car journey! It is rare for children to engage with maps when travelling in order to gain a sense of distance or scale, yet these fundamental skills are necessary for both understanding maps and developing knowledge of places. They also feature as part of a balanced geography curriculum. Traditionally, scale is often taught as a classroom activity that dovetails mathematics and mapwork. However, children's understanding of scale can be greatly enhanced by fieldwork in the local area. This can, quite literally, be a messy business in which pupils get stuck into their surroundings. However, practical activities help them gain a sense of place and space, which they can then apply when the look at maps when they return the classroom.

GOOGLE EARTH

Google Earth is a fantastic tool to develop the notion of scale in a local, national or global context. Images from Google Earth can be easily transferred onto an interactive white-board using the camera tool and then annotated by the children. Pupils might add a set of research questions or add speech bubbles and thoughts to the map. Using the Street View tool, the children can act as if they are taxi drivers taking the class on a guided tour of virtually any major road network in the world. All it takes is that creative spark from the children, but it develops deep (and quick) thinking as children base their commentaries on previous knowledge, connect learning from different subjects and start thinking about places in a more holistic sense. The idea outlined in 'map detectives' (see p. 169) can also be explored on computer by cropping, cutting and pasting parts of Google Maps at different scales for children to identify. Additionally, you might use a free download called Scribble Maps, where you can draw over Google Maps, highlight various areas and complete a wide range of map exercises.

MAPPING OUR WORLD

There are some excellent games for the interactive whiteboard that explore scale at a continental and global context. The Oxfam website has activities appropriate for children in Year 1 to Year 6. In a section called 'Mapping Our World', children can flatten out a globe, view the world as an alien might see it at a range of scales and challenge each other to dig through the centre of the Earth and guess where they will emerge! This award-winning site encourages children to engage with and learn about the world in a thoroughly creative and imaginative manner.

TRAVEL AGENT

Put children into groups of five. Each group needs to have two travel agents and three customers. See that the travel agents are armed with an atlas (or Google Earth), a ruler, a calculator (unless you want to encourage mental maths skills) and perhaps some old travel brochures. Each customer takes one of the traveller cards (Figure 13.3) and becomes that person when they enter the travel agents.

The travel agent has to find the best place for each customer to take a holiday and also answer all the questions they may have. As an additional challenge, pupils could be encouraged to make up some cards of their own. This will help them to appreciate that different people have different requirements and also to view alternative perspectives. The children will quickly learn to pore over the atlas, refer to climate graphs and find out interesting facts and statistics. They will learn to how to conduct research and present their data clearly and effectively.

TEACHING CREATIVELY ABOUT THE EARTH AND ENVIRONMENT

The messy Earth

It can sometimes be helpful to use objects as metaphors to illustrate complex or abstract ideas. You can use an apple, for example, as a way of getting children to think about the Earth. An open-ended question such as 'How is the Earth like an apple?' will get them

Explorer	Family	Student	Vulcanologist
Personality: Adventurous	*Personality*: Varied (mum, dad + 4 children)	*Personality*: Intelligent	*Personality*: Fiery
Special requirements: Somewhere exciting with extreme climate	*Special requirements*: Fun for all, not too far to travel, something for everyone	*Special requirements*: Wants to travel across at least two climatic regions, meet interesting people and visit places of culture	*Special requirements*: Likes barbeques and chilli
Type of holiday: Wild	*Type of holiday*: Something different	*Type of holiday*: Touring	*Type of holiday*: Wants to explore an active volcano
Needs to know: Climate, distance, equipment needed to survive	*Needs to know*: Where, distance to travel, what they can do for fun (for the whole family)	*Needs to know*: Cheap way to travel and live, places to visit, people to see, climate and environment	*Needs to know*: What to wear, climate, typical food of chosen region
Old person	**Alien**	**Chef**	**Head teacher**
Personality: Inquisitive	*Personality*: Different	*Personality*: Happy and fun	*Personality*: Grumpy
Special requirements: Frightened of flying	*Special requirements*: Brings own human disguise	*Special requirements*: Exotic food	*Special requirements*: Away from children and families
Type of holiday: Cultural, city and rural Not too hot Likes views	*Type of holiday*: Wants to find out about the human race	*Type of holiday*: Touring	*Type of holiday*: Open to suggestions
Needs to know: Total itinerary and distance to travel Weather and the best time to travel.	*Needs to know*: At present, the alien knows nothing – looks to you to plan the perfect holiday to investigate human beings	*Needs to know*: The typical food of the chosen area and the best things to eat Distance to travel and weather	*Needs to know*: Everything (the head teacher is likely to ask lots of questions)

■ **Figure 13.3** Person specifications for the travel agent simulation speculating. At first, children generally give straightforward answers based on the core and the skin, and these can be used to develop their knowledge. But when given encouragement, children's ideas will extend far beyond the obvious. The apple is a living thing. Is the Earth? This leads into an interesting discussion on what it means to be alive and whether the Gaia hypothesis rings true or not (Figure 13.4). There are many other instances where open-ended questions and prompts can help stimulate creative responses. You can find out more about strategies and techniques from the Philosophy for Children website.

■ **Figure 13.4** How is the Earth like an apple?
Source: adapted from Deborah Haines

HOW IS THE EARTH LIKE AN APPLE?

Draw the outline of the continents on an apple (boardmarker pens work well) or get the children to draw outlines on apples of their own. Now ask them to consider how the apple resembles the Earth. In my experience, if you ask the question with the correct emphasis, the class is usually divided over the answer. This means you can then challenge the children to suggest similarities and enhance their geographical knowledge as they investigate further. Here are some interesting facts that may surprise children:

1   The peel of an apple is, proportionately, the same thickness as the Earth's crust.
2   Both the apple and the Earth contain water. Apples are about 75 per cent water: the oceans cover about 71 per cent of the Earth's surface.
3   They both contain life. All sorts of creatures live and breathe on and within the Earth and, of course, on and in apples!

4   Both are alive in some sense. The Gaia hypothesis by James Lovelock and Lyn Margulis describes the Earth as a living system, just like an apple (Lovelock 1979).

5   They are both spheres. Additionally, neither is a perfect shape. The Earth is an oblate sphere, being very slightly flattened at the poles by millions of years of spinning and bulging at the equator. Apples, of course, are distorted by all sorts of events over their growing life. It is even possible to grow a cubed apple!

Climate change

■ **Figure 13.5** Climate change could have disastrous implications for wildlife
Source: adapted from Deborah Haines

No one knows for sure what the future may bring and this uncertainty can be quite hard for children, particularly when they hear stories of doom and gloom through the media. Climate change is a particular area of concern where children often view adults as spoiling the world they are due to inherit. The threat of flooding, drought and other catastrophes can be really frightening and the media seems to delight in bleak and emotive imagery (Figure 13.5). Such media coverage can be disempowering for children and their worries tend to be exacerbated by their lack of knowledge. Research shows that prolonged or inappropriate stress can have significant negative physiological and cognitive effects (Goswami 2004). Furthermore, it has been established that when schools place too much emphasis on troubling problems, young people tend to become increasingly worried and disinterested (Scott 2010). An alternative is to engage children creatively and to empower them with knowledge. When children can see through the mess of a 'problem' and are given the chance to develop possible solutions, they become troubleshooters rather than victims. The following activities provide examples of a constructive and positive introduction to developing a creative response to environmental issues and sustainability issues.

MESSING WITH CLIMATE CHANGE

Start with a selection of photographs that all relate to climate change. It helps if these are not immediately clearly linked. For example, you could choose from images of a coal-fired power station, a dried-up reservoir, a flooded town, a traffic jam, a city at night, alive with lights, or a solar-powered cooker. Cut each of the chosen images into a jigsaw of four or five pieces, one for each child in the class. The first task is for the children to complete the jigsaw and form a group with those who have other parts of the same picture. This is a great way to split children up and get them talking. Now give each group a large sheet of paper and coloured pens and ask the pupils to answer the following questions using their photograph:

■ Describe the photograph. What can you see? What questions would you like to ask about it?
■ Can you identify any issues – good or bad – connected to this photograph?
■ What has this issue got to do with our lives?
■ What can I do to make things better?

Give the children a few minutes to think about each question before you go on to the next. You can choose whether to have a class feedback session after each question or save this till all the questions have been tackled. The last question is vital. It provides the link between the children's own lives and abstract concepts. Climate change, for example, isn't only something that happens to other people thousands of miles away; it affects us too.

The final challenge is to ask pupils to design a creative solution to climate change. It could be anything at all, inspired by the photographs or not. It may be helpful to describe some of the creative solutions already in place around the world like children's roundabouts in playgrounds in arid areas of South Africa, which pump water up into a tank as the children play, or lamp-posts in England that have a solar panel on top and a wind turbine in the crook so that they become net contributors to the electricity grid.

Sustainability

Sustainability starts at home. It is also a messy and complex issue, often simplified in schools to turning off lights and not wasting paper. But it is far more than the way in which we create and manage mess. We produce vast amounts of rubbish and waste that we subsequently have to manage. Each item, however, has a long tale behind it that relates to sustainable production, distribution and discard. The issue of using local food over international supplies to reduce food miles becomes more complex if local production involves a greater carbon footprint, with heating costs and large-scale greenhousing, than importing produce from southern Europe. It is important for children to learn to ask questions and challenge ideas, both to enable them to become more effective learners, but also to gain a broader and deeper understanding of complex processes. Sustainability can be portrayed in a very simple way for the children, which, curiously, opens the door to deeper thinking. The diagram below (Figure 13.6) defines sustainability in terms of care (DfES 2006).

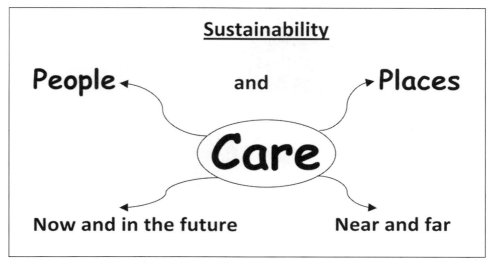

'Care' is a term of which all children are fully aware. Indeed it is used in many contexts throughout early life and this makes it a far more comfortable and easily understood word than 'sustainability'. It is still very important for children to learn and use the term 'sustainable', but the word 'care' can be used to remove some of the myth and confusion. Care also refers to people as much as places and, hopefully, children will be better-placed to move beyond the ideas around recycling and saving energy to working to providing a better life for people around us. The notion of care can be an excellent vehicle for pupils to investigate sustainability with their own sustainable audit following an enquiry cycle designed to allow children to develop creative solutions (Figure 13.7).

DOES OUR SCHOOL CARE?

Challenge the children to present their head teacher with a plan to make their school more sustainable under the mission title 'Does our school care for people and places, near and far, now and in the future?' Children should investigate as much as they can about how the school cares for people and places by asking questions, researching, observing and analysing. It helps if they structure their investigation under the following headings: People, Places, Near, Far, Now, Future. Once they have discovered all they need to know, pupils should work together to *dream up* ways to improve things. This is where the children should be allowed to let their creativity run wild; let them think of the most amazing ways to improve their school. The third stage is the testing one. This is when they have to rein in their creativity alongside actualities. Deep thinking is called for when children

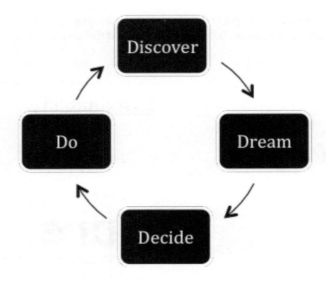

■ **Figure 13.7** The four Ds of the enquiry cycle
Source: Adapted from Cooperrider and Whitney 1999

have to decide which of their ideas are truly viable and how they could adapt their dreams to make them a reality. The final stage is the 'do'. In this example, the *do* is to present their action plan to the head teacher to make the school more sustainable, thereby helping it truly care for people and places, near and far, now and in the future.

OUR MESSY WORLD

Every day we learn through the media about geographical events that are unfolding around the world. Children naturally want to find out why volcanoes erupt (earth movements), why some places are very wet (climate patterns), why some people dress so strangely (global cultures) and why tigers are becoming extinct (habitat loss). You can build on their enthusiasm by setting up a 'News from around the World' noticeboard in your classroom. Encourage children to bring newspaper cuttings about geographical events and processes from the local to the global. Everything from sporting occasions like the Olympic Games to floods in Asia can generate great interest in the world and its people. This ongoing activity provides rich opportunities for children to ask the questions that lurk at the back of the mind. It also helps to open their eyes to the wonderful world we inhabit for inspection and debate.

CONCLUSION

Children love mess, be it a messy bedroom, a messy river to scramble around or a muddy field, and this notion of mess really should be embraced within learning too. If children are given the opportunities to accept that there are some patterns and processes, issues and concerns around the world that are 'messy' and for which there is not necessarily a single solution, then they will also find it easier to understand this messy world of ours. But there is a fundamental learning element to this idea of mess as well: mess encourages investigation. It encourages critical thinking and, crucially, it encourages learners to start to think for themselves, to sort in their minds which elements of the mess could be important information and how the mess might mean different things to different people. In other words, accepting that the world is a messy place and getting involved and trying to find creative solutions, or at least reason within the mess, helps children to develop as critical thinkers and effective learners.

REFERENCES AND FURTHER READING

Catling, S. and Pickering, S. (2010) 'Mess, mess, glorious mess'. *Primary Geographer*, 73: 16–17.

Cooperrider, D. and Whitney, D. (1999) *Collaborating for Change: Appreciative Inquiry*. San Francisco, CA: Berrett-Koehler.

DfES (2006) *National Framework for Sustainable Schools*. London: DfES. Archive address: https://www.education.gov.uk/publications/standard/_arc_SOP/Page20/DFES-04231-2006 (accessed 4th May 2012).

Gardner, H. (1999) *The Disciplined Mind*. New Jersey: Prentice-Hall.

Goswami, U. (2004) 'Neuroscience and education'. *British Journal of Educational Psychology*, 74(9): 9–46.

Goswami, U. (2008) 'Principles of learning, implications for teaching: a cognitive neuroscience perspective'. *Journal of Philosophy of Education*, 42(3–4): 381–99.

Lovelock, J. (1979) *Gaia: A New Look at Life on Earth*. Oxford: Oxford University Press.

Pickering, S. (2008) 'Pupils advise on sustainability'. *Primary Subjects* 2, DfCSF/CfSA. Northwold: Buxton Press.

Scott, W. (2010) *Sustainable Schools: Seven Propositions around Young People's Motivations, Interests and Knowledge*. London: SEED.

Websites

Google Earth
Oxfam (www.oxfam.org.uk)
Philosophy for Children (www.philosophy4children.co.uk)
Scribble maps (www.scribblemaps.com/)
World Wide Fund for Nature (www.wwf.org.uk)

Acknowledgement

The idea for 'Messing with climate change' is adapted from the World Wide Fund for Nature (WWF) Reaching Out programme with thanks to R. Brakspear and the Worcestershire County Council sustainability team. I am grateful to Anthony Barlow, Jane Whittle and Ruth Potts for their ideas on messy maps, which appear in *Primary Geographer*, 73, Autumn 2010. Finally, I would like to thank children and staff at Upton Primary School, Upton-upon-Severn, Worcestershire and the Wyche C of E Primary School, Malvern, Worcestershire.

CHAPTER 14

GEOGRAPHY, CREATIVITY AND THE FUTURE

Jonathan Barnes and Stephen Scoffham

This chapter explores how geography and creativity can be combined to build a preferred and hopeful future. It focuses especially on the way that places and environments can be a catalyst for creative thinking. A series of simple but powerful fieldwork exercises are included to illustrate the possibilities. These 'focus exercises' involve collecting sensory and emotionally significant data from the environment, which can then be used to develop geographical understanding. We argue that such activities stimulate imaginative thinking and can help children develop their sense of identity and responsibility. It is precisely these qualities that children will need to draw on as adults as they negotiate the challenges of an uncertain world.

GEOGRAPHY AND PLACE

Geography is a constantly evolving discipline. The earliest geographies date back to classical times and were largely descriptions of different, and often unknown, parts of the world. In the sixteenth century, geographical knowledge played a crucial part in the voyages of exploration as it did in subsequent colonial adventures. Today, geographers continue to investigate and interpret the world around us, though the tools and methods that they use have changed beyond all recognition. What unifies these endeavours is an enduring interest in place – what places are like, where they are found and how they inter-relate.

Place is a complex notion, which can be interpreted in different ways. Place can be a physical entity like a town. It can be as small as a street corner or as large as a continent or ocean. Some argue that place is best understood as the intersection and meetings of people. For example, Massey (1999) points out that a village is a node for a network of connections reaching out thousands of miles, brought together at a specific moment in time. With digital technology allowing us to occupy multiple spaces, the notion of place is becoming ever more diffuse. Certainly, we need to recognise that different groups and individuals will be set within the community in contrasting ways and have different understandings of it. Such cultural and social definitions highlight aspects of human geography and draw in some of the complexities of the modern world. However, from a teaching point of view, it may be best to start with physical definitions of places as these have the advantage of being visible, before proceeding to more sophisticated conceptions. In either event, place studies offer rich opportunities for creative teaching and learning.

As well as being rooted in space, places are located in time. There will be observable clues that link them to different periods of the past, whether this is measured in terms of hours and days or the great expanses of geological history. Places also anticipate the future in the potential they have for change and development. At the same time, places exist at different scales, from the microscopic to the global. The processes of weathering and erosion, for example, can affect a school wall, a rock face or a mountain range. An awareness of these different dimensions significantly deepens our understanding of place. A mature understanding challenges our imagination to envisage possibilities and alternatives (Figure 14.1).

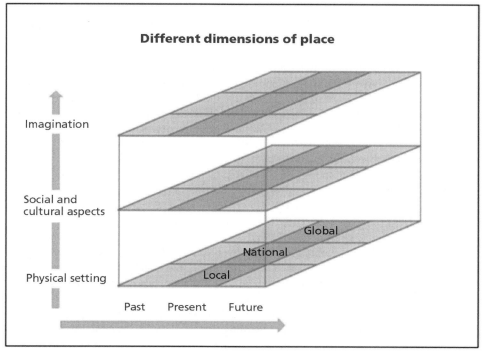

Figure 14.1 The various dimensions of place can be viewed through different scales and time-frames

© Stephen Scoffham

CREATIVE GEOGRAPHY AND THE FUTURE

Everything we do happens in the context of places. As adults we remember places that were special to us in childhood and we can often map significant childhood locations with surprising accuracy. Tanner (2009) reports that when teachers and other education professionals are asked to nominate a special place, they usually choose locations that:

(a)   are associated with positive childhood memories;
(b)   are linked to people they love; or
(c)   have intrinsic landscape qualities.

The enduring resonance of these memories suggests that the foundations of place attachment are often laid in childhood. Tanner goes on to argue that teaching that starts from children's own geographies has an important role in enhancing their personal well-being. The implication for schools, she declares, is that 'we should seek to ensure children have plenty of opportunities for authentic first-hand learning outside the classroom' (p. 7).

Play is one of the ways in which we explore our relationship with place. It is also the medium through which we envisage future possibilities and is closely associated with creativity. Play is disinterested and rarely purposeful – in school playgrounds we see it as a fully engaging present-tense experience. Teachers often remark on how immersed children seem to be in games they play outside the classroom. Think how much more potential could be released if schools could harness the level of motivation evident in the playground. Geography is in a good position to generate such motivation through fieldwork and study visits.

When they are working out of doors, it is important that pupils have a reasonable scope to explore the things that interest them. Intrinsic motivation is much more likely to lead to lasting learning than externally imposed targets. This suggests that teachers need to build a degree of flexibility into their planning. To put it another way, outdoor work can provide pupils with powerful and immediate feedback. We need to allow them to benefit from this, rather than discounting it.

Fieldwork may sound daunting, conjuring up images of residential trips to isolated moors and mountain ranges. However, fieldwork can take place in any location, however near and small. When children gather first-hand data from any real place, they engage in fieldwork. The classroom, corridor, playground and school grounds are the most immediate, safe and accessible fieldwork settings. Other convenient locations include local streets, shops, churches, parks and development sites (Milner and Jewson 2010). As well as discovering information about the present, fieldwork can draw us into speculating about the future. Questions to do with change, the quality of the environment and sustainability are particularly likely to lead to a futures perspective (Figure 14.2).

Geography for a better future suggests that schools need to do more fieldwork. Moving outside the classroom takes children and teachers to a neutral and inclusive space in which informal and formal learning may be brought together. Activity and conversation in the 'real world' can also promote purposeful discussion, creative thinking and genuine engagement. Research has indicted that some of the best work in geography occurs when children investigate actual and proposed changes in their community such as the closure of a post office or the construction a high-speed rail line (Ofsted 2008; Ofsted 2011). Envisaging different possibilities and playfully considering options stimulates deep thinking. A developed geographical imagination offers solutions, establishes relationships and powers positive change in places that are perceived as relevant to both learners and teachers. However, if the decisions we make are to positively affect the well-being of the planet, they need to be made within an agreed moral framework. Geography teachers therefore have to be clear about the values that drive the curriculum.

Schools have a key role in helping pupils lead more fulfilling lives. In a world characterised by environmental and ecological stress, engaging with our surroundings matters. Bonnet (2004) reminds us that our relationship with our environment is an important

■ **Figure 14.2** Children at Woolmore Primary School, Tower Hamlets, listen to sounds and assess the quality of the environment while on a trail
Photo: Jonathan Barnes

aspect of our aspect of our identity. This means that it also sets 'the contours for what can count as human flourishing' (p. 130). Law (2010) takes this argument a stage further when he argues, from a theological stance, that education is about 'coming to understand one's existence within a total ecology'. The idea that geography is a journey of self-discovery is acknowledged in academic and professional circles. As we construct the narratives that make sense of our lives, our interactions with place are one of the strands that are of special significance. These interactions are also a powerful catalyst for creative thinking, not just about the external world but also for making sense of who we are.

RESEARCH FINDINGS

Place-based experience can engage children in a way that is significantly different to classroom studies. The multifaceted nature of the immediate environment is a rich stimulus that has the potential to raise problems and provoke creative thinking. In the following section we examine a range of research studies that support the argument for fieldwork and a future-oriented geography.

1 Knowledge is based in activity

Research into the operating systems of the brain is now beginning to yield empirical evidence that has significance for education. It seems that when we engage in activity, it literally shapes our brains – sculpting neurons, synapses and brain activity. By contrast, when we are simply exposed to events and information in a passive manner our brains and bodies are not much affected (Fischer 2009). Neuroscience is thus confirming what cognitive science has demonstrated for over a century. Learning and teaching require the active construction of knowledge. Fieldwork is part of this process – simply memorising facts is not enough.

2 We are naturally curious about our surroundings

Jaak Pankseep (2004) is one of a number of researchers who has focused on the role of the emotions. Pankseep describes four primal circuits – fear, seeking, rage, and panic – which appear to have a particularly powerful influence on our behaviour. Out of these four, it is the 'seeking' system that is of particular interest to educationalists. This is the system that drives animals to explore their world and sustains curiosity and learning in humans. The seeking system also helps us to prioritise events by automatically evaluating their importance. It appears that humans, like other creatures, have a deep-seated urge to investigate their surroundings – fieldwork exploits this fundamental biological drive.

3 Deep learning involves using all our senses

The Cambridge Primary Review (Alexander 2010) draws on neuroscience research. One of the findings it highlights concerns the value of using all our senses in learning. As the report puts it, 'learning is strengthened not only in relation to how many neurons fire in a neural network, but also by how they are distributed across different domains, such as the motor and sensory cortices . . . In other words, multi-sensory approaches are to be encouraged' (pp. 96–7). Again, environmental work scores highly here. One of the arguments that has been consistently advanced in its favour over the past few decades is that fieldwork provides children with rich sensory stimuli and immediate feedback. Another line of thinking stresses the importance of vivid and memorable experiences.

4 The environment provides a neutral 'third space' for learning

There is a rich literature on children's relationship with the environment that has been explored by Cobb (1977), Chawla (1992) and others. More recently, Catling (2003) has documented the role of play experience in young children's environmental learning. A further dimension is provided by Wason-Ellam (2010), who combines her classroom experience with a literary perspective. She recalls how the children in one elementary school found a big boulder by the river where they could go to be quiet when they were distressed. She reflects, 'I wanted children to have a "third space", an in-between dialogic space, somewhere between formal schooling and home that negotiates broader crosscultural and creative interactions and allows low stakes exploration of emerging ideas' (pp. 284–5). The idea that children need a neutral space in which they can process their ideas supports a broader vision of fieldwork and environmental investigation. The argument that she presents adds extra strength to the case for outdoor experience. It is a vision that we need to hold onto particularly vigorously in the current climate of accountability and measurable objectives, and increasing pressure on curriculum time.

5 Places can provoke creativity

There are suggestions that the environment plays a part in stimulating creativity. In his study of exceptionally talented individuals, Csikzentmihalyi (1997) concluded that there are some places that are important because they act as hot spots where information and ideas grow quickly. Furthermore, Scoffham and Barnes (2011) argue that when fieldwork is set within a secure social environment it is more likely to promote creativity, positive dispositions and lasting learning experiences. The larger point is that places help to provoke imaginative and unusual responses and act as a catalyst that stimulates thinking (Figure 14.3).

■ **Figure 14.3** Pupils at Woolmore Primary School, Tower Hamlets, exploring textures and surfaces
Photo: Jonathan Barnes

6 Our relationship with places links closely with our sense of identity

There is growing debate surrounding issues of identity and our relationship with places. Greenfield (2003), for example, argues that sustained exposure to cyber worlds could have lasting (and possibly damaging) impact on children's thinking. The Children's Society is concerned about the changing nature of childhood (Layard and Dunn 2009). Other studies focus on the restrictions placed on children nowadays and argue that young-sters need greater freedom to explore their surroundings (Malone 2007). The general conclusion is that the amount of time spent out of doors, especially in natural surroundings, affects children's brain function and contributes to their healthy emotional, social and cognitive growth. Fieldwork has a part to play in addressing the current imbalance.

7 Our relationship with the environment is linked to our sense of well-being

Some readers will be familiar with the notion of 'nature deficit syndrome' proposed by Louv (2008). Louv argues that 'a growing body of research links our mental, physical and spiritual health directly to our association with nature' (p. 3). If we become alienated from nature, then we pay the price. The costs include 'diminished use of the senses, attention difficulties and higher rates of physical and emotional illnesses' (p. 36). The National Trust has drawn on Louv's ideas to make a more general case for the benefits of childhood interactions with the natural world (Moss 2012). Here again is powerful argument for engaging children with their surroundings through fieldwork. It is an argument that resonates strongly with the sustainability and ESD (Education for Sustainable Development) agenda.

8 We are more interested in our environment when we are in positive states

Children often report that they enjoy fieldwork. Fredrickson (2004) and other positive psychologists have recently made an important contribution to our thinking in this area. Fredrickson has established that when we are in a positive frame of mind we are more outgoing, exploratory and interested in our surroundings. Two mutually reinforcing processes are involved. As we *broaden* our experience and thought-action repertoires, we also *build* enduring resources for the future. This in turn helps us to flourish both physically and emotionally and initiates an upward spiral of well-being. While there are ideas here that apply to learning in general, Fredrickson specifically mentions how positive emotions prompt individuals to engage with their environment (2004: 1368) and how broadening includes social and environmental knowledge, e.g. knowledge of places (2005: 679). Interestingly, Alexander (2010), who comes from an entirely different starting point, draws a similar conclusion in the Cambridge Primary Review when he concludes that 'a sense of agency is vital for both learning and well-being' (p. 489). It is also worth noting Nundy's (1999) research, which suggests that residential fieldwork is capable of generating positive cognitive and affective learning.

FOCUS EXERCISES

If geography teachers are to encourage thinking in, about and through places, then they will need a range of strategies to support children's learning. Our own experience and research indicates that there are advantages in starting with activities that involve physical, sensory and emotional engagement with place. Before or after using these focus exercises, the teacher should plan appropriate geographical follow-up work. It is important to identify the new knowledge that children will require in order to build effectively on their practical experiences. We offer case studies to illustrate how some classes have addressed issues in the follow-up session to raise questions about the future.

The activities described below are designed to help pupils make full use of their sensory and social faculties in constructive interaction with their immediate environment. Although the activities are tightly framed, the geographical follow-up is left to teacher, child or group. Essentially, these focus exercises are data-collection exercises. Using touch, smell, sight, hearing, social and emotional entry points, they encourage the child to experience the detail of different places at an age-appropriate level. They can be applied in any environment, inside or out, in familiar or unfamiliar places. They are also open-ended and can be followed up in a wide variety of ways.

Experience over ten years of using these focus exercises has shown that they frequently generate conditions of 'flow'. Flow is the term coined by psychologist Csikszentmihalyi (1997) to describe the sense of timeless involvement we sometimes feel when we are deeply engaged in an activity. Psychologists argue that these occasions are optimum times for deep learning, connection-making and creative thought (Fredrickson 2009). Participation in the exercises also provides opportunities to draw on what is known as 'distributed intelligence' (Lucas and Claxton 2011). This is the type of thinking that arises when we use tools and devices invented by others to augment our ideas. In other words, it occurs when we are sharing and communicating thoughts rather than working in isolation.

Health and safety

Children's physical and emotional safety needs to be every teacher's primary concern. Fieldwork will not constitute any extra risks to the child if the following simple checks are carried out:

1   Know and follow the health and safety policies of the school/local authority.
2   Always make a preliminary visit to the site to be visited with another person to assess any potential hazards.
3   Note the potential hazards and enter them on the school health and safety documentation.
4   Communicate potential hazards to all adults supervising and all children participating.
5   Speak to children about their responsibility to keep themselves safe and be aware of dangers for others.

Preparing to teach and learn from the focus exercises

The exercises in the table below are set alongside geographical follow-up ideas and suggestions of the skills and knowledge the teacher should acquire before the session. The exercises are divided into those that describe places and those that respond to places.

Describing places

Focus exercise (Creative stimulus)	Follow up (Geographical focus)	Skills (Teacher and pupils)
Emotional map Ask pupils to record their feelings about their school or local area with words or colours on an outline map (sad, happy, lonely, frightened, excited and so on).	Get pupils to report back on their findings and present information in posters.	Understanding plan views
Sound map Make a map using symbols or words to record the dominant sound in each area.	Make large composite maps to the show the character of the area you have surveyed.	Locating places on a map
Smell map Get pupils to mark the location of the smells.that they identify in each place. Show the boundaries between them.	Discuss any changes that could be made to the area to address any negative features, e.g. unpleasant sounds and smells.	Adding labels to a map
Touch map Make a map to show different textures and surfaces along a journey.	Create a local map for someone in a wheelchair or with a visual impediment.	Using map symbols
Panorama Select a place where you can see in different compass directions.	Assemble and present a collection of different 360-degree drawings of the area.	Using a magnetic compass
Ask pupils to draw an outline of what they can see on the skyline to the north, east, south and west. Use thick marker pens and large sheets of kitchen paper.	Add a large movable arrow to show wind direction. Paint a continuous skyline to create a freeze to decorate the school.	Identifying compass directions Using geographical language, e.g. direction, boundary, view, skyline

Focus exercise (Creative stimulus)	Follow up (Geographical focus)	Skills (Teacher and pupils)
Sound diagram Ask pupils to draw a small circle to represent a plan view of their head, adding ears at the side and a nose at the front. New get them to listen carefully to the sounds around them. They should now mark the location of each sound on their diagram, using arrows to show moving sounds such as cars and aeroplanes.	Devise a walk across the school site to make a sound transect or cross-section of quiet and noisy places. Compare how the sound environment of the school changes during the day. Discuss noise pollution or the contribution sounds make to the character of the environment. Make a musical map of the area to reflect local sounds and noises.	Using a diagram to record information about the environment Making comparisons over time Devising a transect Comparing the quality and character of environments
Colour match Ask children to use paint swatches (available in different colours from DIY shops) to find matching examples in natural and built environments. They should attach around half a dozen examples to a length of double-sided tape attached to a cardboard strip (no living animals please!).	Discuss the colours that were easiest and hardest to find. Consider how colour contributes to the quality of the environment. Devise a short trail focusing on a specific colour such as red or yellow.	Exploring the environment Devising the route for a trail Using descriptive vocabulary

Case study 1: Describing an urban area
Three-hundred-and-twenty children walked excitedly and carefully along Robin Hood Lane to visit Canary Wharf in the London Docklands less than 500 metres from the school gates. Nursery children were paired with Year 6 pupils, Reception with Year 5 and the Year 1s held hands with Year 4s. The children worked in mixed-age groups of six with the support and care of teachers, teaching assistants and adult helpers. The aim of the visit was to collect as much information as possible about the area. Children conducted traffic surveys, made rubbings, noted the routes taken by people, hunted for geometric shapes, took photographs and absorbed sights and smells. None of this information could have been gathered from a website or written sources. For some pupils it was the first time they had really looked at the shiny glass-and-steel office blocks or seen the River Thames. Back at school their work blossomed as they recalled and recounted their experiences in the following days.

Responding to places

Focus exercise (Creative stimulus)	Follow up (Geographical focus)	Skills (Teacher and pupils)
Journey sticks Individual children use a strip of card with double-sided tape on the front to collect five small items from a short walk. Get them to theme their collection (e.g. life, decay, same colour etc.) or simply collect items at random. Discuss the choices and compare results. Do not collect any living creature.	Using the journey sticks as a prompt, pupils describe and/or map the route they followed. Make up a story that links the different items collected in an imaginative way. Talk about the landmarks that help us find our way between places, e.g. journey from home to school.	Describing a route or journey Recognising and sequencing landmarks Drawing a map
Haiku Write your own haiku (a three-line classical Japanese poem that uses only 17 syllables; five in line one, seven in line two and five in line three). Start by choosing a tiny detail of the environment. Describe it in the first two lines and then lift it to a higher philosophical plain by asking a deep question arising from it. Traditionally, Japanese haikus make some mention of the seasons too.	Working in groups, ask the children to share their haikus with each other and the rest of the class. Take photographs or make drawings to illustrate or complement the haikus. Make a display of haikus that give poetic impressions of the local area.	Describing and responding to places Using geographical vocabulary Identifying seasonal characteristics
Fridge-magnet poems Fold an A4 sheet into 16 rectangles, then unfold it to reveal the spaces. Ask pupils to explore their surroundings and write down 16 random words that relate to their chosen spot and environment.	Get the children to arrange their words into a meaningful poem or sentence. They could add extra words and they don't have to use all the words they have collected. Repeat the exercise, restricting children to geographical words and ideas.	Knowledge of the features of the local area Understanding that places change over time

Case study 2: Using a local street
In one school, a Year 4 teacher developed a project to enhance her students' connection with their community. The children began by discussing their ideas of community before considering the question 'How is our street a community and how can I impact upon it?' They then divided into small groups and ventured into the street in small groups (each supervised by an adult) to collect data from different angles and perspectives. One group focused on the changing sounds, a second group noted traffic hazards and talked about how to solve them, while a third group used small items of litter to deduce something about the life of the street. Others photographed houses of different ages. One pupil commented, 'I really enjoyed today because it got me looking at the street in ways I don't normally'. Back at school, each group used a planning sheet to develop a project they felt would create a positive change in their local community. They were supported by a town planner, an architect, a geography lecturer and a scientist (gathered from the teacher's friends and school governors) to develop their project.

ETHICAL ATTITUDES FOR THE FUTURE

The case studies and exercises outlined above all focus firmly on place. They are also about developing particular attitudes and values. The growth in human numbers over the past few centuries is putting planetary systems under increasing strain. Accelerating climate change, rapid economic growth, the unsustainable exploitation of natural resources and the dramatic decline of wildlife and biodiversity all require the next generation to be confident, values-literate citizens. Craft (2011) points out that these challenges, which are both local and global, will require us to draw on our creative potential perhaps more urgently than at any other time in our history. Building a better future also leads us into an ethical domain in which we are obliged to clarify our values. Geography, with its focus on place and the future is centrally placed to explore these issues and is particularly well positioned to provide a suitable context for critical debate.

Learning about sustainability and environment also raises questions about inclusion. Booth and Ainscow (2011) make a powerful point when they argue that a commitment to inclusive values implies a commitment to the well-being of future generations. This is a commitment that cannot be postponed. Earth's resources are already very unequally shared and the damage caused by human activity is undermining the lives of millions of poor people around the world on a daily basis. Schools cannot avoid taking a moral stance.

There are those who would rather avoid teaching children about controversial issues and argue that they are too complex for them to understand; but this is not the case. Without an early exposure to their surroundings and a grounding in aspects of biodiversity and human stewardship, children are less likely to appreciate their environment and engage with it as they grow older. However, rather than teaching about catastrophe, it is important to teach in a spirit of hope. This is why creativity is so important: it engages us with learning and empowers us to envisage alternatives and to propose imaginative solutions.

A positive future requires people with a high degree of respect for each other and their environment. To be respectful, students need to learn self-confidence as well as sensitivity to others. They need to take an interest in both local and global issues. Self-confidence and sensitivity to the lives of others may both be supported by the increased sense of belonging to a locality and by appreciating the unique patterns and relationships evident in every place. The details of a locality can only be fully appreciated by understanding how it links with the global.

Geography asks and answers questions about place. To participate in a relevant and responsible geography curriculum, learners must ask similar questions as those at the frontiers of the subject. Even Earth's wildest places are affected by human influences and this impact needs mediation in order to be positive and sustainable. The built environment is full of examples of creative endeavour. The questions that stimulate creative thinking about places are simple and fundamental: 'Where exactly is this place? What characterises it? What are its links to other places? How is it changing? How can we protect it or change it for the better? How can I contribute? These and other similar questions have occupied geographers for centuries and are best addressed by creative, collaborative thought and action. The future of every place on this planet is therefore the central concern of geography education. It is our hope that creative geography teaching will foster creativity and knowledge in pupils and, in turn, play a part in building a world where fairness, sensitivity and kindness to each other and the environments that sustain us become our guiding values.

REFERENCES

Alexander, R. (2010) *Children, their World, their Education*. Report of the Cambridge Primary Review. London: Routledge.

Booth, T. and Ainscow, M. (2011) *Index for Inclusion: Developing Learning and Participation in Schools*, 2nd edn. Bristol: Centre for Studies on Inclusive Education.

Bonnet, M. (2004) *Retrieving Nature: Education for a Post-humanist Age*. Oxford: Blackwell.

Catling, S. (2003) 'Curriculum contested: primary geography and social justice'. *Geography*, 88(3): 164–210.

Chawla, L. (1992) 'Childhood place attachments', in Altman, I. and Low, S. (eds) *Place Attachment*. New York: Plenum.

Cobb, E. (1977) *The Ecology of Imagination in Childhood*. Dallas, TX: Spring.

Craft, A. (2011) *Creativity and Education Futures*. Stoke-on-Trent: Trentham.

Csikszentmihalyi, M. (1997) *Creativity: Flow and the Psychology of Discovery and Invention*. London: HarperPerennial.

Fischer, K. (2007) 'Building a scientific groundwork for teaching and learning'. *Mind, Brain and Education*, 3(1): 3–14.

Fischer, K. (2009) 'Mind, brain and education: building a scientific groundwork for learning and teaching'. *Mind, Brain and Education*, 1(1): 3–16.

Fredrickson, B. (2004) 'The broaden and build theory of positive emotions'. *Philosophical Transactions of the Royal Society*, 359(1449): 1367–77.

Fredrickson, B. (2009) *Positivity*. New York: Crown.

Fredrickson, B. and Losada, M. (2005) 'Positive affect and the complex dynamics of human flourishing'. *American Psychologist*, 60(7): 678–86.

Gardner, H. (2005) *Five Minds for the Future*. Cambridge, MA: Harvard Business School.

Greenfield, S. (2003) *Tomorrow's People*. London: Penguin.

Law, J. (2010) 'A Distinctive vocation: serving the economy of life', in Wright, M. and Arthur, J. (eds) *Leadership in Christian Higher Education*. Exeter: Imprint Academic.

Layard, R. and Dunn, J. (2009) *A Good Childhood*. London: Penguin.

Louv, R. (2008) *Last Child in the Woods*. Chapel Hill, NC: Algonquin Books.

Lucas, B. and Claxton, G. (2011) *New Kinds of Smart*. Maidenhead: Open University Press.

Malone, K. (2007) 'The Bubble-wrap generation: children growing up in walled gardens'. *Environmental Education Research*, 13(4): 513–27.

Massey, D. (1999) 'The social place'. *Primary Geographer*, 37: 4–6.

Moss, S. (2012) *Natural Childhood*. Swindon: National Trust.

Milner, A. and Jewson, T. (2010) 'Using the school locality', in Scoffham, S. (ed.) *Primary Geography Handbook*. Sheffield: Geographical Association.

Nundy, S. (1999) 'The fieldwork effect: the role and impact of fieldwork in the upper primary school'. *International Research in Geographical and Environmental Education*, 8: 190–8.

Ofsted (2008) *Geography in Schools: Changing Practice*. London: Ofsted.

Ofsted (2011) *Geography: Learning to Make a World of Difference*. London: Ofsted.

Pankseep, J. (2004) *Affective Neuroscience: The Foundations of Human and Animal Emotions*. Oxford: Oxford University Press.

Scoffham, S. and Barnes, J. (2011) 'Happiness matters: towards a pedagogy of happiness and well-being'. *The Curriculum Journal*, 22(4): 535–48.

Tanner, J (2009) 'Special places: place attachment and children's happiness'. *Primary Geographer*, 68: 5–8.

Wason-Ellam, L. (2010) 'Children's literature as a springboard to place-based learning'. *Environmental Education Research*, 16(3–4): 279–94.

INDEX

Escape
from Shangri-La

EGMONT

Escape
from Shangri-La
MICHAEL MORPURGO

EGMONT

For Conrad and Anne

EGMONT
We bring stories to life

The extract (p76) of 'Little Gidding' from *Four Quartets*,
Collected Poems 1909-1962 by T.S. Eliot is reproduced by permission
of Faber and Faber Limited.

First published in Great Britain in 1998 by Heinemann Young Books
This edition published 2018 by Egmont UK Limited
The Yellow Building, 1 Nicholas Road, London, WII 4AN
Text copyright © 1998 Michael Morpurgo
Cover illustration copyright © 2006 Lee Gibbons

ISBN 978 0 6035 6834 3

A CIP catalogue record for this title is available from the British Library

Printed and bound in Great Britain by the CPI Group

55241/007

Stay safe online. Any website addresses listed in this book are correct at the time
of going to print. However, Egmont is not responsible for content hosted by third
parties. Please be aware that online content can be subject to change and websites
can contain content that is unsuitable for children. We advise that all children
are supervised when using the internet.

Egmont takes its responsibility to the planet and its inhabitants very seriously.
All the papers we use are from well-managed forests run by responsible suppliers.

CONTENTS

1 A BIT OF AN OLD GOAT

I WAS KNEELING UP AGAINST THE BACK OF THE sofa looking out of the window. Summer holidays and raining, raining streams. 'He's been there all day,' I said.

'Who has?' My mother was still doing the ironing. 'I don't know why,' she went on, 'but I love ironing. Therapeutic, restorative, satisfying. Not like teaching at all. Teaching's definitely not therapeutic.' She talked a lot about teaching, even in the holidays.

'That man. He just stands there. He just stands there staring at us.'

'It's a free world, isn't it?'

The old man was standing on the opposite side of the road outside Mrs Martin's house underneath the lamppost. Sometimes he'd be leaning up against it, and sometimes he'd be just standing there, shoulders hunched, his hands deep in his pockets. But always he'd be looking, looking right at me. He was wearing a blue donkey jacket – or perhaps it was a sailor's jacket, I couldn't tell – the collar turned up against the rain. His hair was long, long and white, and it seemed to be tied up in a ponytail behind him. He looked like some ancient Viking warlord.

'Come and see,' I said. 'He's strange, really strange.' But she never even looked up. How anyone could be so obsessively absorbed in ironing was beyond me. She was patting the shirt she'd finished, sadly, her head on one side, just as if she was saying goodbye to an old dog. I turned to the window again.

'What's he up to? He must be soaked. Mum!' At last she came over. She was kneeling beside me on the sofa now and smelling all freshly ironed herself. 'All day, he's been there all day, ever since breakfast. Honest.'

'All that hair,' she tutted. 'He looks a bit of a tramp if you ask me, a bit of an old goat.' And she wrinkled up her nose in disapproval, as if she could smell him, even from this far away.

'And what's wrong with tramps, then?' I said. 'I thought you said it was a free world.'

'Free-ish, Cessie dear, only free-ish.' And she leant across me and closed the curtains. 'There, now he can look at the back of our William Morris lily pattern to his heart's content, and we don't have to look at him any more, do we?' She smiled her ever so knowing smile at me. 'Do you think I was born yesterday, Cessie Stevens? Do you think I don't know what this is all about? It's the "p" word, isn't it? Pro . . . cras . . . tin . . . ation.' She was right of course. She enunciated it excruciatingly slowly, deliberately teasing the word out for greatest effect. She was expert at it. My mother wasn't a teacher for nothing. 'Violin practice, Cessie. First you said you'd do it this morning, then you were going to do it this afternoon. And now it's already this evening and you still haven't done it, have you?'

She was off the sofa now and crouching down in front of me, looking into my face, her hands on mine. 'Come on. Before your dad gets home. You know how it upsets him when you don't practise. Be an angel.'

'I am not an angel,' I said firmly. 'And I don't want to be an angel either.' I was out of the room and up the stairs before she could say another word.

I was ambivalent about my mother. I was closer to her than anyone else in this world. She had always been my only confidant, my most trusted friend. Whatever I did, she would always defend me to the hilt. I'd overhear her talking about me. 'She's just going through that awkward prickly stage,' she'd explain. 'Half girl, half woman. Not the one thing, nor the other. She'll come out of it.' But sometimes she just couldn't stop playing teacher. Worst of all, she would use my father as a weapon against me. In fact, my father was never really upset when I didn't practise my violin, but I knew that he would be disappointed. And I hated to disappoint him – she knew that too.

Whenever he could, whenever he was home, my father would come up to my room to hear me play. He'd sit back in my chair, put his hands behind his head and close his eyes. When I played well – and I usually did when he was there – he would give me a huge bear hug afterwards, and say something like, 'Eat your heart out, Yehudi.' But just recently, ever since we moved house, my father hadn't been able to hear me that much. His new job at the radio station kept him busier than ever – he had two shows a day and some at weekends too. I'd listen in from time to time just to hear his voice, but it was never the same. He was never my father on the radio.

I was ambivalent about my violin too. The truth was that I loved it with a passion. I loved the secrecy of its hidden life shut away in its green baize case, the soft snuggle of the pad under my chin, the smoothness of the horsehair when I drew my bow across the inside of my wrist to test its tautness. I loved playing my violin too, but I had always hated practising, and in particular I hated being told to practise. Once I could forget that I was practising, once I could lose myself in the music, then I could play quite happily for hours on end and not even notice the passing of time.

I was just beginning to enjoy it, just beginning to feel at one with my violin. I was playing Handel's *Largo* so well I could feel my skin pricking with pleasure all down my arms. But then the doorbell rang. The magic was broken. I was immediately back to hateful practising. The bell rang again. Any excuse to avoid practising was good enough. I put the violin down on my bed, and my bow too, and went to the top of the stairs to see who it was. I heard the front door opening. There was a shadow down in the hallway, and my mother was standing beside it, motionless.

'Who is it?' I said, as I came down the stairs.

The shadow moved suddenly into the light of the hallway and became the old man from across the road. He was standing there, dripping. 'I'm sorry,' he said. 'I don't want to intrude.'

His face tremored into a smile as he saw me. 'Cessie?' He knew my name! 'You must be Cessie. I know this is going to sound a bit odd, but I'm your grandad. I'm your dad's dad, so that makes me your grandad, doesn't it?' He looked full at my mother now. 'It's true, true as I'm standing here. I'm young Arthur's dad. When I knew him last he was only little, five years old, and that's near enough fifty years ago. Long time.' For a moment or two, he didn't seem to know what else to say. 'Big ears. Born with big ears, he was, like a baby elephant. That's why we called him Arthur. You know those Babar books, do you?' I nodded because I couldn't speak. 'I was Babar, if you see what I mean. His mum was Celeste, and so the little fellow, our son, was called Arthur. He didn't have a trunk of course.' I smiled at that, and he caught it and tossed it back at me, his eyes suddenly bright.

'You'd be a bit old for all that now, I suppose. All grown up, I expect.' He was scrutinising me now. 'Come to think of it, you look a bit like little Arthur too, except for the ears of course. You've got nice ears, nice and neat, like they should be. Not flapping around in the wind like his were. What are you? Thirteen? Fourteen?'

'Eleven,' I said. I felt my mother take my hand and hold on to it tightly, so tightly it was hurting me.

'Seventy-five.' The old man was pointing to himself. 'I'm seventy-five. Old as the hills, eh? Do you know what your dad used to call me when he was little? "Popsicle". "Pops" to start off with. Then it was Popsicle. Don't know why. It's what everyone's always called me ever since – Popsicle, Popsicle Stevens.'

'You can't be,' my mother whispered, pulling me close to her. 'You can't be him. Arthur hasn't got a father.' The old man seemed suddenly unsteady on his feet. He swayed and staggered forward. Instinctively we both backed away from him. He was dripping from his ears, from his chin, from his fingers too. It was as if his whole body was weeping tears. His hair, I noticed, wasn't really white at all, but creamy, almost yellow in places. It didn't look very clean. None of him did.

'Everyone's got a father,' he said, and he was holding out his arms towards us – just like ghosts do, I thought. 'I'm not a ghost, Cessie.' We backed further away. Ghosts can read minds. 'I'm telling you, I'm Popsicle Stevens and I'm Arthur's father, and I'm alive, alive, oh. I mean ghosts don't get hungry, do they? And they don't get fruzzed either.' He reached out suddenly and caught me by my wrist. 'Feel that?' He was as cold as stone, but he was real. He was no ghost. 'You wouldn't have a nice cup of tea, would you, just to warm a fellow through?'

My mother stood her ground now, pulling me behind her, clasping my hand even tighter still. 'How do

I know? You could be anyone, couldn't you? Coming in off the street like that, you could be anyone. How do I know you're who you say you are?'

The old man took a deep breath before he spoke. 'Listen, these old grey cells up here' – he was tapping his temple – 'they may not be what they once were, but there's some things you don't get wrong. If you've got an Arthur Stevens living here, and he grew up in a little place called Bradwell-on-Sea – on the Essex coast it is – if he's your husband, and if he's your dad, then, unless I'm mistaken – which I don't think I am – we're kith and kin, all of us. I just thought I'd look him up, that's all. I didn't think it could do any harm – not now, not any more.'

In the silence of the hallway I could almost hear my mother thinking, perhaps because we were thinking the same thing. My father *had* grown up on the Essex coast. We'd been there. We'd seen the house where he was born. His childhood was a bit of a mystery. He'd been a Barnado's boy – I knew that much. His mother, my grandmother, had died young – I knew that too – a long time before I was born. As for his father, I'd known little or nothing of him. My father had never spoken of him, not in my hearing anyway. If I had thought about him at all, and I am not sure that I had, then I suppose I had simply presumed he was dead, like my grandmother was.

The old man was unbuttoning his jacket now, and fumbling deep inside. My mother still held me by the hand in a grip of steel. The wallet he took out was stuffed full, like some battered leather sandwich. He opened it up with great care, almost reverently. With shaky fingers he pulled out an old photograph, faded to sepia, torn at the edges and criss-crossed with creases. He gave it to us. A young man looked at me out of the photograph. He was standing in front of a clapperboard house with roses growing up around the windows. Astride his shoulders sat a small boy clutching his hair with both fists. Beside them stood a young woman who was looking up at them adoringly.

'That's your grandmother,' he said, 'and there's me with little Arthur, your dad, that is, pulling my hair by the roots. He was always doing that, little rascal. Summer 1950. That was the last summer we were all together.'

'What was she called?' My mother was still interrogating him. 'Arthur's mother. What was she called?'

The question clearly troubled him. He seemed reluctant to answer, but when he spoke at last he spoke very deliberately. 'Cecilia,' he said. 'She was called Cecilia.' Then he was looking at me and beaming. 'Of course. I didn't think of it till now, Cessie. That'd be after your grandmother, wouldn't it?'

He was right. He'd been right about everything. I felt a warm shiver creeping up the back of my neck. My grandmother *had* been called Cecilia, and I *had* been named after her, I'd always known that. There was a photograph of her on top of the piano in the sitting-room. She was young in the photograph, somehow too young for me to have ever thought of her as a grandmother.

I looked up into his face. The eyes were deep-set and gentle. They were blue. He had blue eyes. My father had blue eyes. I had blue eyes. That was the moment the last doubts vanished. This man had to be my father's father, my grandfather.

For some time we just stood there and stared at him.

I squeezed my mother's hand, urging her to do something, say something, anything. She looked down at me. I could see she was still unsure. But I knew he was not lying. I knew what lying was all about. I did it a lot. This man was not doing it. It takes a liar to know a liar.

'You'd better come in,' I said.

I broke free of my mother's grasp, took my grandfather gently by the arm and led him into the warmth of the kitchen.

2 WATER MUSIC

'I'M AFRAID I'VE GOT A VERY SWEET TOOTH,' HE
said, stirring five heaped teaspoons of sugar into his tea.
We sat watching him as he sipped and slurped, both
hands holding the mug. He was savouring it. In between
sips he set about the plate of chocolate digestive biscuits,
dunking every one till it was soggy all through, and
devouring one after another with scarcely a pause for
breath. He must have been really famished. His face was
weathered brown and crinkled and craggy, like the bark
of an old oak tree. I'd never seen a face like it. I couldn't
take my eyes off him.

I did all the talking. Someone had to. I can't stand
silences – they make me uncomfortable. He was
obviously too intent on his tea and biscuits to say
anything at all, and my mother just sat there staring

across the kitchen table at him. How many times had she told me not to stare at people? And here she was gawping at him shamelessly. It was as if Quasimodo had dropped in for tea.

I had to think of something sensible to talk about, and I reasoned that he might want to know something about me, about his new-found granddaughter. After all, he had my whole life to catch up on. So I gave him a potted autobiography, heavily selective, just the bits I thought might be interesting: how we'd just moved here six months ago, where I went to school, who my worst enemies were. I told him in particular about Shirley Watson and Mandy Bethel, and about how they'd always baited me at school, because I was new perhaps, or maybe because I kept myself to myself and was never one of the girls. All the while he kept on chomping and slurping, but he was listening too. I could tell he was because he was smiling at all the right places. I'd told him just about everything I could think of, when I remembered my violin.

'I'm Grade Five now. I started when I was three, didn't I, Mum? Suzuki method. I do two lessons a week with Madame Poitou – she's French and she's a lot better than my old teacher. She says I've got a good ear, but I'm a bit lazy. I have to practise every day for forty minutes. Not much good at anything else, except swimming. Butterfly, I'm really good at butterfly. Oh, yes, and I like sailing too. Dad's got a friend who works at the radio station with him, and he's got a twenty-six footer called *Seaventure*. He keeps it down at the marina. We went all the way down the coast, didn't we, Mum? Dartmouth or somewhere. Bit rough, but it was great.'

'Nothing like it,' he said, nodding away. 'Nothing like the sea. "I must go down to the sea again, to the lonely sea and the sky . . ." you know that poem, do you? Not true, of course. You're never lonely at sea. It's people that make you feel lonely, don't you think? You like poetry, do you? Always liked poems, I have. I've got dozens of them up here in my head.'

My mother spoke up suddenly: 'How did you know where to find us? How did you know?'

'It was luck, just luck. It wasn't as if I was looking for him. It just happened. I was at home, a couple of weeks ago, and I had the radio on. Had it on for the weather, matter of fact. I always listen to the weather. I heard him, on that programme he does in the mornings. I didn't recognise his voice of course, but there was something about how he said what he said that I had to listen to. And then I heard his name. "Arthur Stevens'

Morning Chat", they called it. I'm not a fool. I knew well enough there was likely to be more than one Arthur Stevens in the world, I knew that. But I just had this feeling, like it was a meant-to-be thing. Do you understand what I'm saying? It was like we were supposed to meet up again after all this time.

'So, the same afternoon it was, I went and had a look. I walked right in the front door of the radio station. And there he was, larger than life up on the wall, a huge great smiling poster of him. I took one look and, I'm telling you, I didn't have to read the signature across the bottom. It was him. Same big ears, same cheeky smile, same little Arthur. Just fifty years older, that's all. Couldn't mistake him. And then, whilst I was standing there looking up at him, he comes right past me, close enough I could've reached out and touched him. And I wanted to, believe me I wanted to; but I couldn't, I didn't dare. Then he was gone out of the door and it was too late.'

He swept the biscuit crumbs up into a little pile with his finger, and went on. 'Anyway, after that I came over all giddy in the head. I get that from time to time. I had to sit down to steady myself, and there was this young lady at the desk who helped me. She was nice too. She brought me a glass of water. I reckon she

15

was a bit worried about me. After a bit, we got talking, her and me. I asked her about Arthur and she told me all about him – and about the two of you as well. She said how good he is to work with, how he cares about what he does. "Never stops," she said. "Works himself to a frazzle." She told me about all the shows he does, how they phone in with all their cares and woes, and how he talks to them and makes them feel better about themselves. "You should listen in some time," she said. So I did. I've heard every one of his pro-grammes ever since – never missed. Not once. Plays my kind of music too.'

He was looking at us hard. 'I know what you're thinking. You're thinking I'm maybe a bit crazed in the head, a bit barmy. Well, maybe I am at that. Maybe I shouldn't have come at all. I've got no business being here, I suppose, not really, not after all these years.' His eyes were welling with tears. 'It was an agreement, a sort of understanding, between Arthur's mother and me. Don't get me wrong. I don't blame her – I wasn't much good to her, I know that now. One day she just said she'd had enough. She was leaving and she was taking young Arthur with her. She wanted a fresh start, she said. There was this other man – these things happen. Anyway it wasn't nasty, nothing like that. It'd be best all round if I stayed out of it, she said, best for the boy. He'd soon get used to a new father. So I said I'd keep away, for the boy's sake. And that's what I've done. I kept my promise, and it wasn't easy sometimes, I can tell you. A father always wants to know how his son's grown up. So I never went looking; but when I heard his name on the radio, well, like I said, I thought it was a meant thing. And here I am. He sounded grand on the radio, just grand.' He brushed away the tears with the back of his hand. He had massively broad hands, brown and engrained with dirt. 'It took me two weeks thinking about it, and then a whole day standing out there in the rain before I could bring myself to knock on the door.'

He composed himself again before he went on. He was looking directly at my mother. 'I haven't come to bother you, nor him. I promise. I just wanted to see him, see you all, and then I'll be on my way.'

My mother glanced up at the kitchen clock. 'Well, I'm afraid he's not going to be home for quite a while yet. Half an hour at least, maybe longer.' Then, quite suddenly, she snapped into teacher mode again – positive, confident, organising. 'All right,' she said. 'Cessie, you can go and run a bath.'

'What?' Sometimes I just could not understand her

at all. Why on earth should I have a bath all of a sudden, and before supper too?

'Not for you, Cessie, for Mr Stevens.' She clapped her hands at me. 'Go on, hop to it. And he'll need a towel too, from the airing cupboard – the big green one. We can't have Mr Stevens sitting around in those wet clothes till your father comes home, can we now? He'll catch his death.'

'Not Mr Stevens, please. Popsicle. I'm Popsicle,' my grandfather said quietly. 'I'd like it very much if you'd call me Popsicle. It's what everyone calls me. It's what I'm used to.'

My mother had been interrupted in full flow, but she was only momentarily taken aback. 'Popsicle it is then,' she said, and she bustled me out of the kitchen. 'I'll look out some of Arthur's clothes for you,' I heard her telling him as I went up the stairs. 'They'll be a bit on the large side, I shouldn't wonder. We'll have those wet things of yours dry in a jiffy.' She was talking to him as if she'd known him for years, as if he was one of the family.

I was thinking about that as I ran the bath, but it wasn't until I was fetching the towel from the airing cupboard that it began to sink in, that I began to under-stand what all this really meant. Until then I had believed it, but I hadn't felt it. I had a new grandfather. Out of nowhere I had a new grandfather! A flush of sudden joy surged through me. As I watched him coming slowly up the stairs, hauling himself up by the banisters, all I wanted to do was to throw my arms round his neck and hug him. I waited until he reached the top, and then I did it. He looked a bit bewildered. I'd taken him by surprise but I think he was pleased all the same.

'Do you have a loofah, Cessie?' he asked me. 'I don't have baths very often. Bit difficult where I live. Bit cramped. Never enough water either. But when I do have a bath I always have my loofah.'

'What's that?' I asked.

'It's a sort of backscrubber. Reaches the parts you can't reach otherwise.'

'I don't think we've got one,' I laughed. 'But you can have a duck, if you want. I've got a yellow plastic one called Patsy. Had it ever since I was little.'

'What more could a fellow want?' He smiled at me as I handed him the towel. 'Tell you what, Cessie, why don't you give us a tune on that fiddle of yours, eh? Same tune you were playing when I was out in the street. I liked that. I liked that a lot. You could do me a sort of serenade in the bath.'

So, with my bedroom door open, I serenaded him with Handel's *Largo*. I could hear him humming away and splashing next door in the bathroom. I was playing so well, I was so wrapped up in it, that at first I didn't notice my mother standing at the door of my room. I could tell she'd been listening for some time. When I stopped playing she said, 'You play so well, Cessie. When you mean it, you play so well.' She came over and sat down on my bed. 'I don't know what it is. I don't feel right in myself,' she said. 'Shock, I suppose. I can't explain it. It's like someone's just walked over my grave.' I sat down beside her. She seemed to want me to. 'It *is* him, you know,' she went on. 'I can see your dad in his face, in his gestures. You can't fake that.' She was hugging herself. 'Maybe I'm frightened, Cessie.'

'Of him?'

'No, of course not. Of what might happen when your dad gets back. I don't understand. I just don't know what to make of it. I mean he'll talk occasionally about his mum, and, very occasionally, about his stepfather too. But in all the time I've known him I don't think he's ever said a single word to me about his real dad. It's as if he never existed, like he was almost a non-person. Perhaps I should have asked, but I always felt it was . . .

well . . . like forbidden territory, almost as if there was something to hide, something he didn't want to remember. I don't know, I don't know; but what I do know is that any minute now your dad's going to walk in this house, and I'm going to have to tell him his father's here. It's going to be a big surprise, but I'm not sure what kind of surprise, that's all.'

'I'll tell him, if you like,' I said. I didn't make the offer just to help her out. I offered because I wanted to be quite sure I was there when he was told, that this wouldn't be one of those private, important things they went out into the garden to discuss earnestly. Popsicle may be my father's father, but when all was said and done, he was my grandfather not theirs.

My mother put her hand on mine. 'We'll do it together, shall we?'

That was the moment we heard the front door open, and then slam. My father always slammed the door. It was part of his homecoming ritual. He'd toss the car keys next.

'Anyone home?' We heard the car keys land on the hall table. He was walking into the kitchen. 'Anyone home?'

I don't know who was squeezing whose hand the harder as we walked together along the landing past

21

the bathroom door. We went down the stairs side by side, holding hands, and into the kitchen, holding hands. My father had his back to us. He was by the sink pouring himself a can of beer. He turned round and took a couple of deep swigs. I had never noticed how big his ears were, but I noticed now. I had to smile in spite of myself. My mother was right. You could see Popsicle in him. He was younger of course, and without the long, yellow hair, but they were so alike.

He smothered a burp and patted his chest. 'Pardon me,' he said. 'Throat's as dry as a bone.'

'It's all that talking you do,' my mother said, clearing her throat nervously.

'What's up?' He was looking at us, from one to the other. We looked back. 'Nothing the matter, is there? You all right, Cessie?' I looked away.

My mother began clearing the table, busily. She wasn't a very convincing actress. 'So,' she said, 'so you won't be wanting a cup of tea then, not after a beer.'

My father was looking down at the kitchen table. He was counting the mugs, I was sure of it. 'Seems like tea's over and done with anyway. You been having a party, have you?' I smiled weakly. I could think of nothing to say.

'Cessie's done her violin practice.' My mother was prattling now. 'And I have to say that she's playing the *Largo* quite beautifully.' She was bent over the table, wiping it down, but with far too much enthusiasm. As I watched her I could see she was never going to be able to bring herself even to look at him, let alone to break the news. I was bursting to tell him, but I didn't know how to begin. I couldn't find the words. I couldn't just blurt it out, could I? I couldn't say: 'Your long lost father's come back to see you. He's upstairs having a bath, with Patsy.'

I was still trying to work out how to tell him, when we heard the bathroom door open, and slow, heavy footfalls coming down the stairs.

'Who's that?' My father had put down his beer. He knew now for sure that there was some sort of conspiracy going on.

'Are you in there? Are you in the kitchen?' Popsicle was talking all the time as he came down the stairs, as he came across the hallway towards the kitchen. 'The clothes are fine. Jacket's bit big in the sleeve. I may look like a right old scarecrow, but at least I'm a clean old scarecrow now, and warm too. Warmed right through, I am. Best bath I've had in years. And it's been a very long time, I can tell you, since I had a bath with a duck.

Friendly sort of a duck too, never leaves you alone. Always nibbling at something.'

The kitchen door opened. My father looked at his father. My grandfather looked at his son.

3 BARNARDO'S BOYS

POPSICLE SHUFFLED FORWARD, HESITANTLY, offering his hand as he came, but my father didn't take it, not at first. Even when he did, it was obvious to me that he had little idea whose hand he was shaking. But he knew he should know. He wanted help. He needed someone to tell him who this was. So I told him.

'He's your dad.' I said it straight out. It seemed the only way.

'You don't recognise me, do you, Arthur?' Popsicle held on to my father's hand for a moment longer. 'Why should you? Been fifty years, near enough. Last time I saw you was in Bradwell, in the village. You were catching a bus across the road from the church, a green bus, I remember that. You and your mum were off to live in Maldon, just down the coast. You were looking out the back window and you were waving. Never saw you again after that, nor your mum.'

Still my father said nothing. He seemed to be in some kind of a trance, incapable of movement, incapable of speech. I had never seen him like this and it frightened me.

My mother was trying to explain. 'He heard you on the radio, Arthur,' she said. 'And then he went to the radio station. He saw your picture on the wall. Recognised you right away, didn't you, Popsicle?'

'Bradwell-on-Sea?' My father spoke at last.

Popsicle nodded. 'Remember the house, do you, Arthur? Down by the quay, next to the Green Man. Good pub that. Too good.'

My father said nothing more. The silence was becoming long and awkward. I suppose I had been anticipating a joyous reunion, huge hugs, tears even. I certainly hadn't expected this. My father was usually so spontaneous. This wasn't like him at all.

'Maybe I shouldn't have come, Arthur,' said Popsicle at last. 'Not without warning you anyway. I should have written a letter perhaps. That would've been better. Well, maybe I'd better be off then.' And he turned away towards the door.

'You'll do no such thing,' said my mother firmly. She

had Popsicle by the arm now. 'No one's going anywhere. If this man is who he says he is, then there's more than just the two of you involved in this. There's Cessie and there's me.' She sat Popsicle down on a kitchen chair, none too gently. Then she stood behind him, hands on his shoulders, facing my father.

'Well, Arthur, we need to know. Is this your father, or isn't it?'

My father took his time before replying. 'Yes.' He spoke softly, so softly I could hardly hear him. 'I remember the bus. The window was steamed up and I had to rub a hole in it to see him. I wasn't waving, not exactly.'

'Maybe Cessie and I should just leave you both alone for a while. There'll be a fair bit you want to talk about, I shouldn't wonder. We'll make ourselves scarce. Come along, Cessie.'

I was reluctant to go, but it looked as if I had no choice. I was being ushered out of the door when my father called us back.

'Don't go,' he said, and he said it in such a way that I knew he needed us.

My mother was the life and soul of that first gathering around the kitchen table. She brought out the sloe gin. 'Only for very special occasions, very special people,' she said, opening the bottle. 'Five years old.

Should be perfect. Not every day a father turns up out of the blue.'

'Nor a grandfather,' I added. I was allowed a taste, but that was all. Popsicle emptied his glass in one gulp and declared that it was 'beautiful'. My father was watching him, scrutinising him all the while, but it was a long time before he said anything.

'I went back, you know.' My father spoke up suddenly. He was looking into his glass. He still hadn't touched a drop.

'Back where?' Popsicle asked.

'Bradwell. To our house.'

'What for?'

'I went looking for you. After Mum died, I ran off. But you weren't there. I asked in the pub, but you'd gone, years before, they said.'

'She's dead, Arthur? Your mum's dead?'

'A long time ago,' said my father.

'I never knew, Arthur. Honest to God, I never knew.' His face seemed suddenly very sunken and exhausted. 'When? How?'

'I was ten. Boating accident. They were both drowned, her and Bill. No one knows what happened, not really. They looked for you. Well, they told me they did anyway, but no one could find you. They packed me off to a home, a children's home. Nothing else they could do, I suppose. That's when I ran off back to Bradwell. They caught me of course. Brought me back. A Dr Barnardo's place it was, by the sea. Wasn't home exactly, but it wasn't too bad.' He took a sip of sloe gin, and then, looking directly across the table at Popsicle, he went on: 'Do you know what I'd do sometimes? Summer evenings, I'd sit on the brick wall by the gate and wait for you. I really thought that one day you'd come back and take me away. I was sure of it.'

Popsicle seemed suddenly breathless. He clutched at the table for support. 'You all right?' my mother asked, crouching down beside him.

'I'm fine, fine,' said Popsicle.

'Sure?'

Popsicle put a hand to his neck. 'There's a thing,' he said. 'Be funny if it weren't so sad. Runs in the family. Father and son, both of us Barnardo's boys. There's a thing, there's a thing.'

Without any warning at all he slumped forward off the chair. His head smashed against the corner of the table and hit the floor at my feet with a sickening, hollow crack. There was blood at once.

I had always longed to be in an ambulance on an emergency dash to hospital. When I'd twisted my ankle

I'd gone by car and there had been no drama at all, no excitement. But with Popsicle it was the real thing. The ambulance arrived at the house, lights flashing, sirens wailing. Green-overalled paramedics came dashing into the house. They were struggling to save a life under my very eyes.

As he lay there, crumpled on the kitchen floor, all the colour drained from his face, Popsicle looked very dead. I couldn't detect any sign of breathing. And there was so much blood. The paramedics felt him, listened to him, injected him and put a mask on his face. They told us again and again not to worry, that everything would be all right.

They stretchered him out to the waiting ambulance, where the radio was crackling with messages, and around which a dozen or more of our neighbours were gathered. Mandy Bethel was there, Shirley Watson's scandal-mongering sidekick from school, so I knew the news would be all over the estate in no time. Mr Goldsmith from next door was there too. And Mrs Martin from across the road, who'd hardly even spoken to me before, put her arm round my shoulder and asked me who it was that was ill. 'My grandfather,' I said, and I said it very proudly, and very loudly too, so that everyone should hear.

Then we all climbed into the ambulance with him and we were driven away at speed, sirens wailing. I only wished they hadn't closed the doors, because I should have liked to have seen their faces for a little longer, especially Mandy Bethel's. I felt suddenly very important, very much at the centre of things.

It was only when I was inside the ambulance and looking down at Popsicle, deathly white under the scarlet of the blanket, that I realised this was not a performance at all. Suddenly it was serious and I could think only that I didn't want Popsicle to die. I didn't say prayers all that often, only when I really needed to. I needed to now, badly. I had just found myself a grandfather, or he had found me, and I did not want to lose him. So I sat in the ambulance and prayed, with my eyes closed tight. My mother thought I was crying and hugged me to her. That was when she began blaming herself.

'Maybe it was the bath,' she said. 'Maybe I shouldn't have made him have a bath. Maybe we should have warmed him up more slowly.' And later: 'He was soaked to the skin, he was shivering. And I just left him sitting there, all that time, in those wet things.'

'It wasn't you,' said my father. 'It was me. I shouldn't have told him about Mum, not straight out like that. I didn't think.'

We sat in casualty at St Margaret's until the early hours of the morning. When I'd come before with my ankle it had been busy, full of interesting injuries. This time there was hardly anyone there to distract me. I tried not to think of Popsicle. I kept picturing him lying there under a white sheet not breathing, not moving. I flicked through all the *Hello!* magazines, all the *National Geographics* and the *Readers Digests* I could find, but I was quite unable to concentrate on any of them. My mother and father both sat grey-faced, like stony statues, and didn't speak to each other, nor to me.

We hadn't had supper and I was hungry. I begged some change off my mother and fed the vending machine. There wasn't much to choose from. I had a meal of Coca Cola, chocolate biscuits and two packets of cheese and onion crisps. I was feeling a bit queasy by the time the doctor finally came to see us.

She was a lot younger than I thought doctors could ever be. She wore jeans and a T-shirt under her white coat, and twiddled her dangling stethoscope around her fingers as if it was a necklace. She smiled an encouraging smile at me, and I knew then that the news was going to be good news. Popsicle was not going to die after all. I wasn't going to lose him. I felt like whooping with joy, but I couldn't, not in a hospital.

'How is he?' my mother asked.

'Stable. We think he's had a stroke, a mild stroke. We'd like to keep him in for a while under observation. We'll do some tests. All being well, he can go back home in a couple of weeks or so. He'll need a bit of looking after. He lives with you, does he?'

'Not really,' said my father. 'Not exactly.'

My mother looked at him meaningfully.

'Well,' my father went on, 'perhaps he does. For the moment anyway.'

The doctor was looking from one to the other in some bewilderment. 'I'm afraid he does seem to have lost some movement in his right side. But given time that should right itself. For a man of his age I'd say he has a very strong constitution. He's very fit. But there is one other thing. He's got a very nasty head wound – fractured his skull in two places. We won't know the extent of the damage – if any – for a while yet. Another reason for keeping a good eye on him.'

'Can we see him?' I asked.

Her bleeper went off. 'No peace for the wicked,' she said. 'The nurse will show you the way.' I watched her walk off down the corridor and decided that if I didn't end up as a concert violinist, or a round-the-world singlehanded yachtswoman, then I'd be a doctor like her – maybe.

Popsicle was lying in a bed surrounded by a fearsome array of monitors and drips. There was a tube in his nose and another in his arm. His hair was gold against the white of the pillows. There was a wide strip of plaster across his forehead, and a dark grey bruise round his eye. He wasn't a pretty sight, but at least the dreadful pallor had gone. He was asleep and breathing deeply, regularly, his mouth wide open. He must have sensed we were there. His eyes opened. For some moments he looked from one to the other of us. He didn't seem to know who we were.

'Not angryla,' he murmured, looking around him. He was more than bewildered, he was frightened, and agitated too. 'Not angryla.' He wasn't making much sense.

'It's me,' I said. 'Cessie. It's all right. You had an accident. You're in hospital. It's all right.' At that he seemed to calm down, and a sudden smile came over his face.

He knew us. He knew me. He beckoned me closer. I bent over him. I was so close I could feel his breath on my cheek. 'See what happens if you eat too many chocolate digestives.'

'It was the sloe gin,' I said, and he managed a smile.

My mother was beside me and taking his hand. 'You've had a bit of a turn,' she said. She was speaking slowly, deliberately and loudly too, as if he were deaf. 'The doctor says you'll be right as rain. We'll come and see you tomorrow, shall we?' Popsicle lifted his hand and touched his forehead. 'You clunked your head, when you fell. You'll have a bit of a shiner too, a black eye. You'll be all right, Popsicle, you'll be fine.'

Popsicle was looking up at my father, trying to lift his head, trying to say something to him. 'Popsicle. You remember, Arthur? It's what you used to call me when you were little. D'you remember?'

'Yes,' said my father.

'And you had big ears in those days too,'

'Did I?'

'And you still have,' Popsicle chuckled just once, and then drifted off to sleep. My father stood there looking down at him. He reached down, took Popsicle's hand and laid it tenderly on the sheet. His hands so wrinkled, so ancient.

'Let's go home,' he said, and he turned on his heel and walked out of the ward without another word.

By the time we got home there wasn't much of the night left, but I spent what there was quite unable to sleep. I kept going over and over in my mind everything that had happened that day. I knew as I lay there in bed that my ordinary life was over, that from now on everything was going to be extraordinary. Popsicle had come out of nowhere, out of the blue, to be my grandfather; and nothing and no one would or could ever be the same again.

4 THE PRODIGAL FATHER

EVERYTHING HAPPENED VERY FAST AFTER THAT. They didn't want to keep Popsicle in hospital for long, so we had a lot to do and very little time to do it. The spare room needed a good lick of paint, and some new curtains. We set up a radio by his bed, fixed up a television for him on top of the chest of drawers, and brought one of the armchairs up from the sitting-room so he could sit by the window and look out over the garden.

My father took very little part in all this flurry of activity, indeed he was scarcely ever home. He did, at my mother's suggestion, add legs to a wooden tray so that Popsicle could eat his meals in bed if need be. And my father took his time over that, disappearing for long hours into the garden shed where he did his carpentry

– joinery he called it. But whenever he emerged he seemed distant, uneasy somehow. And if ever I asked him about Popsicle – which I often did, and so did my mother – he'd simply shrug and say that it was all a long time ago. Then came the argument over the patchwork quilt.

It was the morning we were due to bring Popsicle home from the hospital. My mother and I were upstairs in what was to be Popsicle's room and I was helping her to spread out the old family patchwork quilt. It fitted the bed perfectly.

'1925,' she said, showing me the date sewn into one of the corners. 'The year Popsicle was born, if I've worked it out right. Looks fine, doesn't it, Cessie?'

She stood back and looked around the room. 'I want it all to be special for him, Cessie, really special.'

At that moment my father came in and at once noticed the quilt. 'Don't you think you're overdoing it a bit?' he said. 'You always said that quilt was too good to use. Unique, you said. Part of your family history. He'll get food on it. Bound to. It'll spoil.'

'What is the matter with you, Arthur?' my mother said. 'It's for your father, isn't it? To make him feel at home. Don't you want him to feel at home?' She didn't wait for him to reply. 'Well, I do. This is *my* family heirloom, made by *my* great aunt, and I want him to have it on his bed.' She touched his arm as she passed him to open the window. 'Come on, Arthur. I just want him to feel welcome, that's all – you know, like the fatted calf and the prodigal son.'

'With one big difference,' my father said. 'This isn't the prodigal son come back home, it's the prodigal father. And we hardly know him. You don't know him. I don't know him. I just think you're laying it on too much, that's all.' My mother was looking at him long and hard. I knew that look, and my father did too. He turned away.

'I may not be back till late,' he said, and he was gone.

'Won't you even be here when we bring him back?' she called after him. He didn't reply.

My father wasn't there when we came home with Popsicle that evening. Popsicle never asked where he was, so we didn't need to excuse or explain or lie. 'He'll be busy at work, I expect,' was all he said. But he caught my eye, and I could see how hurt he was, how disappointed.

Popsicle spent those first ten days or so of his convalescence up in the bedroom that had become his. He slept a lot, either propped up on his pillows in bed, or in his armchair by the window. With his head bandaged, he looked less like the Viking warlord I had first known, and more like an Apache warrior. He had his meals up there, and the bathroom was right next door, so he never needed to come downstairs at all.

Whenever my father wasn't about – and he wasn't about these days – the three of us settled into a routine of our own. My mother would cook. I would ferry trays up and down the stairs. I would cut up Popsicle's food and she would help bathe him – his right arm was almost useless, though he could walk unaided by now. I'd play him my violin whenever he wanted me to, and that was often. 'I love a good tune,' he told me. 'Scott Joplin, George Formby, Vera Lynn, Elvis, the Beatles, you name it and I'll sing it. I know them all, off the radio.' I soon discovered he was particularly passionate about the Beatles. He'd hum me through one of their songs. I'd practise it and then play it back for him. 'Yesterday', 'Yellow Submarine', 'Norwegian Wood' – he taught me them all, and then sang along with me, once I'd got the hang of the tunes. Strictly speaking this wasn't violin practice, but I counted it as such – and it was a lot more fun.

Sometimes, though, he was happy just to sit in his chair for hours and watch the goldcrests flitting about the garden or the swallows swooping down to drink from the goldfish pond. Watching alongside him, I learnt more about birds in a few days than I'd learnt in my entire life.

But whether it was birdwatching or the Beatles, when it was time for one of my father's radio shows, everything else was forgotten. We had to promise always to remind him, even to wake him if he was asleep.

The radio had to be turned on well before time, just to be sure he didn't miss the beginning of each show. It was the highlight of his day. He had only to hear my father's voice and his whole face would at once be suffused with loving pride.

I just wished my father would be home more often, for Popsicle's sake, and for mine too. He never came to hear me play my violin these days. He just didn't seem interested any more. My mother said he was overtired, working too hard, but I felt there was more to it than that.

Dr Wickens used to come in every few days to check on Popsicle, and a nurse would call daily to change the dressing on his head. There would be hushed and confidential discussions as my mother, or my father, or both, walked them out of the front door and up the path, always out of earshot. From their faces and from everyone's reluctance to answer my questions, I knew something was not quite right, but I had no idea what it was. I wasn't that worried either, because Popsicle was getting out and about now much more. There was already more use in his arm, that was obvious, and he was up and down the stairs like a yo-yo.

Dr Wickens had recommended gentle exercise; but said he mustn't get cold. So, every day now, with Popsicle well wrapped up in his coat, and in what he called my 'Rupert Bear' scarf, we would walk slowly down the road to the park. It wasn't far. My mother made him carry a stick, on the principle that three legs are safer, more reliable, than two. Popsicle didn't like it but he went along with it.

To begin with, I dreaded going on these walks. I was forever worried about bumping into Shirley and Mandy, my tormentors from school; but once we'd discovered the ducks, I forgot all about them. Popsicle adored ducks. To sweeten them in close he'd make wonderful ducky noises, quite indistinguishable from the real thing. We'd sit there on the bench, and wait till we were completely surrounded, and deafened by a chorus of raucous quacking. When he was quite sure they were all there, he'd dig deep into his bag of crusts and hurl them as far as he could out on to the pond. How he'd chuckle to watch them go, and how he hated to leave them when the time came. 'Back tomorrow,' he'd tell them. And we always were.

He loved the garden too. When it was warm we'd often find him out there, picking weeds off the rockery or raking the lawn. He liked to be up and doing, he said.

But I did notice that he was a little wrapped up in himself these days, as if he were lost in his thoughts and didn't know the way out. I'd often find him sitting in his armchair just staring ahead into space. Sometimes he wouldn't even know I was there till I spoke to him.

If he was brooding, I thought, then perhaps he had good reason. My father hardly ever seemed to speak to him, not unless he had to. Whenever they were in the same room together, it was always uncomfortable. All too often, my father would find it suddenly very important to be elsewhere. As he left the room, the hurt on Popsicle's face was plain to see.

It wasn't until some time later that I was to discover what all this was about. My father was home late again after work. They must have thought I was already asleep, but I wasn't. Popsicle had turned off his radio in his room so I could hear quite plainly every word they were saying downstairs in the kitchen.

'But have you asked him again?' My father's voice.

'I can't keep asking him, Arthur. It upsets him. And,

anyway, asking him isn't going to help. It isn't going to make it come back, is it? You just have to accept it. You know what Dr Wickens said. It wasn't the stroke that's caused it. He told us. He explained it all. The brain's nothing more than a jelly, a blancmange, and the skull's there to protect it. You jolt the skull violently enough, you bash the brain up against the inside of the skull, and it can cause serious damage, bruising, bleeding, whatever. The result can be some loss of memory, temporary or otherwise. So it's hardly surprising that Popsicle can't seem to remember much, is it? If he says he can't remember where he lives, where he's from or anything else, then I believe him. And I simply can't understand why you don't.'

'All right, then tell me this, how come he still remembers Bradwell? Answer me that. He goes on and on about the old days when I was a kid in Bradwell. As far as I can see he remembers anyone and everyone from those days. And that was forty, fifty years ago. Yet he can't seem to remember where he lived before he walked in here four weeks ago. Now doesn't that strike you as a little strange?'

'Not really. My memory's fairly patchy already, and I'm only thirty-six years old, and I haven't just fractured my skull in two places. But you don't mean "strange" do you, Arthur? You mean convenient. Why don't you come right out with it. You just don't want him here, do you?'

'What do you expect? He's a complete stranger to me. I don't know the man.' He was almost shouting now. I could hear my mother shushing him to lower his voice. 'Listen,' he went on, just as loudly. 'Let's say you're right, let's say he *has* lost his memory – which I doubt – who says it'll ever come back again? Who says he'll ever remember where he comes from? He can't go on living here for ever, can he?'

'I don't know why not. He's not much trouble. And, besides, you're never here these days, are you? What's it matter to you?' He seemed temporarily silenced by that. My mother hadn't finished with him yet. 'For God's sake, Arthur. He's an old man. He's got no one else, so far as we can tell, and nowhere else to go. After all those years he's found his son and you've found your father. Doesn't that mean anything to you?'

My father was speaking much more calmly now, so that I had to get out of bed and put my ear to the floor-boards to be able to hear him at all. 'Of course it means something,' he was saying, 'but I'm not sure what, that's all.' He didn't go on for some moments. 'Listen, there's things you don't know, things I haven't told you.'

'What things?'

'It's what my mother told me about him. She said he'd get mad in the head sometimes. "Mad with sadness", she called it. One moment high as a kite, the next down in the dumps. And he was a bit of a layabout, couldn't hold down a job, always in trouble, drank too much, that sort of thing. My mother didn't want to leave him. She had to. That's what she told me, and I believe her. I didn't ask him to come here, did I? He just landed on us, and now he comes up with this fantastical tale that he can't remember where he's from, nor where he lives. And you believe him, just like that! Well, I'm afraid I don't. And now maybe you understand why I don't. I've had enough. I'm going to bed.'

I heard the kitchen door open and my father's footsteps on the stairs. I was tempted to jump out of bed and confront him there and then, and tell him just what I thought of him. But I didn't dare. I heard my mother crying down below in the kitchen. Whenever she cried, I cried. I couldn't help myself. I cried into my pillow, not only in sympathy but in anger too. I hated my father that night for making her cry and I hated him too for saying what he had about Popsicle. I hardly slept at all. I lay there full of doubts and forebodings.

By morning I had determined to find out how much

of what I'd overheard was true. I would talk to Popsicle and find out for myself exactly how much he could remember, and how much he couldn't. I would try to do it in such a way that I wouldn't upset him. I would try to be casual.

The next morning we were both in Popsicle's room. I was tightening my violin bow. 'But before you came here, Popsicle,' I began as nonchalantly as I could, 'where did you live?'

'Ah,' he said. 'You too.' And I wished at once I hadn't asked. 'So they told you. I asked them not to. Didn't want you worrying.' He sighed. 'How I wish I knew, Cessie, but I don't. And that's the honest truth of it. I don't remember. I remember ringing the bell on your front door. I can remember you coming down the stairs, and I can remember Patsy too in the bath. But that's all. I remember bits and pieces from long ago: Bradwell, and Cecilia, and little Arthur – all that. We had some good times, Cessie, good times, believe me. And songs. Don't know why, but I seem to remember songs. "Yellow Submarine", "Nowhere Man", lots of them. Clear as a bell, I remember them. And my poems too, I haven't lost them, thank God. Keep me sane, they do. But as for the rest, Cessie, it's gone, all gone. It's like living in a fog. I'm not lying to you, Cessie. Honestly.'

I thought of asking more, of probing more deeply, but I couldn't. I knew enough anyway, enough to know that I believed him, believed him absolutely.

I waited until my father came home that evening, late again. Popsicle had gone up to bed. I'd been waiting all day for just the moment and now the moment was right. I went storming into the sitting-room.

'It's not fair.' I was in tears already. 'It's not fair. I heard you. Last night, I heard you. Popsicle can't help it. He fell and hit his head. He had a stroke. That's not his fault, is it?' I had the advantage of surprise. They were both gaping at me. 'He'd never have had a stroke in the first place if you hadn't . . .'

'Cessie!' My mother was trying to stop me, but I was steaming with fury. Nothing would stop me now.

'He's not making it up, Dad. I know he isn't. But even if he was, I wouldn't mind. I like having him here and I want him to stay. I want him to stay forever if he wants to. I hate all this . . . feeling in the air. Do you know what I wish? I wish . . . I wish you weren't my father.' I ran out and upstairs to my room where I slammed my door as hard as I could.

They left me for a few minutes, and then my father came up to my room and sat on my bed. I kept my back to him.

'It's not easy for you to understand what's going on here, Cessie,' he began. 'Not easy for me either. I never had a real father, you see, not till now. I had a stepfather for a while, of course, but it's not the same; and anyway, Bill and me, we never got on. I don't know what you do with a father, how you talk to a father. You've got to trust me. I'll do right by him, I promise you that. But you don't love a father just because he's your father. You can't love someone you don't know, and I don't know him. You've got to give me time, Cessie.'

I was still seething, still too angry to turn over. I wanted to, but I couldn't bring myself to do it. I'd said things I shouldn't have said, and I knew it. He leant over and kissed the back of my head. 'I'm not an ogre, Cessie,' he whispered. 'Honestly.' When he said 'honestly', he sounded just like Popsicle.

The next morning I was up late. There was no sound of the radio from Popsicle's room, so I thought he must be downstairs, having his breakfast already. But I found my mother alone in the kitchen. She was pouring herself a cup of coffee as I came in. 'Well,' she said, 'that was some performance last night.'

'Sorry,' I said.

'No, you're not.' She was not angry with me, but she was not pleased either. 'Popsicle up yet?' she went on.

49

'He can do almost everything for himself now, you know, except for cutting his food up. Marvellous how that arm of his has come on. Let's just hope his memory does the same. Go and see if he's all right, Cessie, will you?'

The bathroom door was ajar. He was not in there. There was no reply when I knocked on his bedroom door. I went in. His bed was made. The wardrobe door was open. His clothes were gone, his coat too, and there were no shoes by the bed. He'd gone. Popsicle had gone.

5 NOWHERE MAN

MY MOTHER SAT DOWN ON THE BED, THE POINTS of her fingers pressed against her temples, her eyes closed for a moment in concentration. 'Think,' she said. 'We've got to think.'

It came to me at once. 'Ducks,' I said. 'Maybe he's feeding the ducks.' We dashed downstairs. We found what we'd hoped to find, that the bag of accumulated bread-crusts we kept for the ducks was no longer hanging on the back of the kitchen door. A further search revealed that his stick was gone too.

'I'll take the car,' said my mother. 'You stay here, in case he comes home. He'll be in the park, bound to be. Shan't be long. And don't worry.'

She *was* long and I *was* worried. It seemed like an age before she came back, but when she did she was alone.

I met her at the front door. She had Popsicle's stick in her hand. 'He's been there, but he's not there any more. I've looked everywhere. He left it on the bench. And this too.' She held out the breadcrust bag. It was empty. 'I asked around. No one's seen him. It's like he's just disappeared.'

'He can't have,' I cried. 'You can't just disappear. No one can.'

She reached out and smoothed my hair tenderly. 'You're right, Cessie. We'll find him, I promise we will. I've tried ringing your dad at work, but he's off somewhere, doing an interview or something. I tried his mobile too. Nothing. Only one thing to do. I'm going down to the police station. You'd better stay here. He'll probably walk in just as soon as I've gone. Worrying won't help, Cessie. Go and practise your violin or something – it'll keep your mind off it.' And she was gone.

I tried practising. I tried reading. I tried the television. Nothing worked. It was impossible not to think of all the dreadful things that might have happened to Popsicle. He'd had another stroke. He'd been run over. He'd fallen into the canal. Or maybe he'd just gone off as suddenly as he'd arrived, and would never be coming back again.

As the minutes passed by like hours, I was more and more certain that this was in fact what had happened. Perhaps he'd suddenly remembered where he lived and had just gone home. Miserable though this made me, I consoled myself with the thought that at least he wasn't hurt, at least he wasn't dead.

My mother did come back eventually, and when she did she was beside herself with indignation. 'If it was a child, they'd be out there looking for him right now – dogs, helicopters, the lot. "How long has he been gone?" he says. "Maybe he's just wandered off, madam. They do, y'know. We can't go looking for every OAP who decides to take a longer walk than usual, can we now, madam?" God, did I give him an earful! So finally he says, "All right, madam, all right. We'll give it an hour or two and if he's still not back then we'll go looking, how's that? Meanwhile, I'll ask the lads to keep an eye out, madam." I'll give him madam! Well if they won't look, I will. I'm going to drive around town till I find him. He can't have gone far. I want you to stay here, Cessie, and I want you to try your dad, and keep trying. Understand?' And despite all my protestations, she went running off up the path, leaving me alone in the house again.

I rang my father every few minutes, both at work

and on his mobile. When at long last he answered, it took me a bit by surprise. 'Popsicle's gone,' I said. 'He's gone, and we can't find him.' He didn't say anything, so I told him the rest. Even after I'd finished the whole story, he still said nothing.

'Dad?' I said. 'You there?'

'I'm here.'

'Mum's gone off looking for him,' I repeated. 'And the police won't do anything.'

I have no idea what he said, nor to whom he said it, but within five minutes there was a police car outside the house and two policemen at the front door. 'So you've lost your grandaddy, have you?' said the taller of the two, taking off his cap. The other one had a mermaid tattooed on his arm. 'Your mum and dad in, are they?' said the tattooed one. And they walked right past me into the house as if they owned the place. They never asked. They just wandered about the house, peering into this room and that. They even went out into the garden and searched the garden shed. Did they really imagine they'd find Popsicle hiding away in the garden shed?

My father came home, and then my mother shortly after. There followed a prolonged question-and-answer session around the kitchen table over endless cups of tea, all about Popsicle, where he went, what he did.

'Have you got any photos of him?'

'No.'

'Not one?'

'No. Well, there is one of him as a young man. But it's in his wallet and he must have his wallet with him.'

'Do you know who his friends are?'

'I'm afraid not.'

'How long has he been living with you?'

'A month or so.'

'And before that?'

'We don't know,' said my father.

The more we didn't know, the more strange they seemed to find it all. A third policeman came in, filling the doorway. They had already checked all the hospitals for miles around, he said, and no one of Popsicle's description had been brought in. No one had seen him. It was just as my mother had said, Popsicle had disappeared.

She seemed suddenly very dejected. The tattooed policeman leant forward across the table. 'Listen,' he said. 'It's true what they say: no news *is* good news. You just sit right here, and we'll keep on looking till we find him.' He gave me a cheery wink as he stood up again.

But by six o'clock that evening, after the longest day

of my life, there was still no news of Popsicle, good or bad. 'I need a walk,' said my mother. 'I've got to get out. I can't stand any more of this waiting.'

'Nor me,' I said.

This time my father stayed by the phone. As we left, he said, 'He'll turn up, you'll see. That old man's a survivor. He'll turn up.' He never called him 'my father' or 'Popsicle', and I wished he would.

We ended up in the park – I'm not sure why. There was a large crowd gathered round the duck pond, so we couldn't even see the bench where we usually sat with Popsicle, nor the pond beyond. We had to force our way through the crowd to see what was going on. There were a couple of policemen holding everyone back, not the same ones who had come to the house. I heard a sudden agitated quacking commotion from the middle of the pond, and a flurry of ducks took off and circled over the park. My mother grasped me by the arm. I looked where she was looking. Out of the pond rose first one head, then two. Frogmen. Frogmen in goggles and wetsuits, with oxygen tanks on their backs. My mother had her hand to her mouth. She knew what I knew, that they were dragging the pond for Popsicle.

I led her home in tears, and the three of us sat in the kitchen in silence, just waiting, fearing the worst, believing the worst. There were more encouraging words of reassurance from my father, but we didn't believe them, and I don't think he did either. I tried to pray as I had in the ambulance. After all, it had worked that time, hadn't it? But I couldn't concentrate long enough even to finish a prayer. I had a picture floating in my head that would not go away, a picture of Popsicle, drowned, lying face down in the pond, his hair spread out over the water like golden seaweed.

Then came the knock on the door. Both my mother and father seemed paralysed, so I had to go and open it myself. It was the police again. This time one of them was a woman, and behind her was the one with the tattoo on his arm.

'May we come in?' she said. Dark and dreadful words that fell like stones on my heart. Tears choked my throat. They'd found Popsicle, I knew it. They'd found him dead and drowned and I'd never even said goodbye. I took them into the kitchen. 'We've found him,' said the policewoman. 'Down by the harbour. He was just sitting there looking at the boats. Just sitting there. He's fine, fine.'

My mother was sobbing. I found myself sobbing too and I couldn't stop myself. My father had his arms round both of us. 'Didn't I tell you?' he said. 'Didn't I tell you?'

'He's a very confused old man,' the policewoman went on. 'Didn't seem to know where he was nor how he'd got himself there. We took him off to the hospital. Routine check-up. Can't be too careful, can you? Not when they get to that age.'

'They'll be bringing him home soon,' said the tattooed policeman. 'All being well, he should be back in time for supper. Bit scatty in the head, I'd say. Bit forgetful like, is he?'

The ambulance brought Popsicle home from the hospital that same evening. I was overjoyed to see that the neighbours were out in numbers yet again. As we fetched him into the house, I waved regally at Mandy Bethel. I enjoyed that.

All through supper no one said a word about Popsicle's disappearance – that had been my mother's idea. 'He'll tell us when he wants to,' she'd said. Popsicle carried on as if nothing had happened. He sat there, quite at home, waiting for me to cut up his pork chop for him. Then he ate ravenously, chuckling to himself as he chased his peas around his plate with his fork until he'd speared the very last one.

'Gotcha,' he laughed, popping it in his mouth with a flourish. He pushed his plate away and sat back. There came the moment then when we were all looking at him, and waiting, and he knew well enough what we were waiting for.

'Was I hungry!' he said. 'I haven't eaten since breakfast, you know.'

'You could have come home sooner,' said my father, and I could sense him reining in his exasperation, with some difficulty. 'For goodness' sake, you were gone all day.'

Popsicle was looking straight at my father as he spoke. 'What Cessie said last night, I heard every word. I didn't want to cause any more upsets, that's all. Time to pack up and go, I thought. So I did. I got up early and I just went. I was sitting there down in the park, feeding the ducks, and I was wondering what to do with myself, where to go. That's when it came to me. This is just like where I live, I thought, by the water, with ducks and gulls and all sorts. So I went off looking, looking for my place. I thought the best bet would be down by the harbour, along the seafront. I thought I'd maybe see something, something I'd recognise. Where I live, I can see water out of every window. I can smell the sea too, I know I can. So I went looking. Walked miles, I did. I looked at every house along the sea front, in the windows of some of them. Got myself shouted at too. But it wasn't any good. I didn't recognise a thing.'

'I still don't understand,' my father said. 'All right, so you upped and went, went off looking for your house. But when you couldn't find it, why didn't you just come back here? We've been worried sick, all of us.'

'I couldn't,' said Popsicle. 'I didn't know where I was, where I'd come from, or anything. I couldn't even remember the name of this street, so I couldn't ask, could I? I mean, you don't want to look stupid, do you? So I just sat myself down and tried to piece it all together, you know, work it out, make some sense of it. I could see you all up here in my head. I could see this house, this kitchen, my room upstairs, the garden, everything; but I didn't know where you all were, nor how to get to you. That's my trouble. Sometimes things are as clear as day, and sometimes . . . well, ever since I was in the hospital . . . You take your mum for instance, Arthur. I can't picture her like I used to. I know what she looked like from her photo; but I can't see her up here.' He tapped his head with his knuckles. 'When I think of your mum now, it's not her face that comes into my head, I know it's not. It's someone else, always someone else altogether, but I don't know who.' For a few moments, he seemed quite unable to find his voice. He looked at us, his eyes brimming with sadness. He was trying to smile, but he couldn't. 'A nowhere man, that's me. A real nowhere man, like the song says.'

'Things'll come back, Popsicle,' said my mother. 'Time's a great healer. Things'll sort themselves out.' She reached out and took his hand in hers. 'You're family now,' she said. 'You're family, and you're staying. You belong here with us. We want you to stay as long as you like. Isn't that right, Arthur?'

We had to wait some moments for my father to reply, and when he did it was not at all fulsome. 'Of course,' he said. 'Of course we do.' That was all. I was angry at him again, angry at his thinly disguised reluctance. Maybe he had his reasons, but he could pretend a little, couldn't he? Just to make Popsicle feel at home and welcome. He could pretend.

'But you've got to promise you won't go off on your wanders again,' said my mother, wagging her finger playfully at Popsicle. 'Frightened us half to death, you did. Promise?'

'Promise,' Popsicle replied, holding up his hand. 'Cross my heart and hope to die.'

'We don't want you doing that either,' she said, and we all laughed at that, even my father.

'Well,' my mother went on, getting to her feet, 'now that's settled, we can get on with life, can't we? And you know what that means, don't you, Cessie Stevens?'

'No.' But I knew exactly what she was getting at.

'I have this feeling that, in all the excitement, you might have forgotten something.' I played dumb. 'Your violin practice?' There was no point in arguing. I made the best of it and got up to leave.

'You want me to come up and hear you?' my father asked.

'It's all right,' I replied. I was so angry with him, and I wanted him to know it. 'Popsicle'll come, won't you? We'll do some Beatles songs.'

'"Nowhere Man",' said Popsicle, as I helped him to his feet. 'We'll do "Nowhere Man".'

So we went upstairs and, sitting on the bed in my room, Popsicle taught me 'Nowhere Man' till I knew it through and through. I played. He sang. We were good together, very good. But my mind wasn't on it. I just couldn't enjoy it as much as I usually did. I kept thinking of my father downstairs, and I kept wishing I hadn't been so cruel.

When I'd finished, Popsicle looked at me for a while, and then he said, 'You and me, we're friends, aren't we? And friends have to be honest with each other, right?'

'Yes.'

'You've always been good to me, Cessie. You spoke up for me last night, and I shan't forget that, not ever.

But you mustn't judge your dad like you do. You mustn't hurt him. You're the apple of his eye, you are. So you be kind to him, eh? There's a girl.'

Popsicle had been reading my mind again, and I wondered how he did it.

6 AND ALL SHALL BE WELL

IT WAS SOON AFTER THIS THAT I BEGAN TO NOTICE Popsicle talking to himself. I'd hear him in his bedroom, a muffled monologue, so muffled that I could never make out much of what he was saying. I noticed too that he was becoming more and more absent-minded. Once, he went wandering out into the garden in the rain with just his socks on; and time and again he'd make the tea and forget to put any tea in the pot. He'd think that lunch-time was tea-time and tea-time was lunch-time. Every time he'd try to laugh it off and call himself a 'silly old codger', but I could see that it worried him as much as it worried us.

Then one day he lit a bonfire too close to the garden shed and Mr Goldsmith's fence. I wasn't at home when it happened. I was out at Madame Poitou's for my violin lesson. When I came back the fire-engine was already there and a pall of brown smoke was hanging over the house. I ran inside. Popsicle was sitting on the bottom stair in the hallway, his face in his hands, and my mother was crouched down beside him trying to comfort him.

'It's not your fault, Popsicle,' she was saying. 'These things happen. Why don't you go upstairs and have a nice wash? You'll feel a lot better.' His eyes were red, his face tear-stained and besmirched. He went up the stairs very slowly.

I followed my mother out into the garden. It was a mess out there, a real mess. The fire-fighters were packing up and going. As one of them passed us, he stopped. 'Could have been a lot worse, missus. Whatever does he think he was doing anyway? First he builds a bonfire too close to the shed and then he goes off and leaves it. Got to be a bit doolally, if you ask me.'

When they had all gone I gave her a hand tidying up what we could in the garden. We raked all that was left of the garden shed into a pile of charred timbers and soggy ashes. She worried on and on about what Mr Goldsmith from next door would say about his fence when he got home from work. And she worried on about Popsicle too.

We were an hour or so clearing up the worst of it. My wellingtons were covered in mud by this time, so I had to take them off at the back door before I went in. I was padding through the hallway into the kitchen when I felt it. The carpet was sodden under my bare feet. I charged upstairs to find the basin overflowing, and the bathroom awash. I turned off the tap and pulled out the plug.

Popsicle was in his room, sitting on his bed and staring into space. I sat down beside him.

'It doesn't matter, Popsicle,' I said. 'It's just a rotten old garden shed. It was falling down anyway. Dad's been moaning on about it ever since we moved here. He was going to get a new one. Honestly he was.' But nothing I could say seemed to bring him any comfort.

Then he muttered something, something I couldn't quite hear. 'Sorry?' I said, leaning closer.

'Shangri-La.' He clutched at my hand as he spoke. 'Shangri-La, I don't want to go to Shangri-La.' I could see in his eyes that he was terrified. He was pleading with me, begging me.

'What's Shangri-La?' There was an echo in my head, an echo of something he'd said before.

'I don't know. I don't know.' The tears were running down his cheeks, and he didn't even trouble to wipe them away.

'If you don't want to go there,' I said, 'then no one's going to make you, I promise.' He seemed happier at that.

'You promise?' he said. I laid my head on his shoulder, and after a while I felt his arm come round me. That was how my mother found us some time later. She helped Popsicle to wash, and put him to bed.

We spent the rest of the day mopping up. But there was still water dripping from the lightbulb into a bucket in the hallway when my father came in from work. I explained what had happened, how none of it had been Popsicle's fault, just bad luck, that's all. 'Anyway,' I said, 'now you can have your new garden shed like you wanted.'

They exchanged knowing glances. I knew then that they were both, in some way, blaming Popsicle for what had happened. My father walked out into the garden to inspect the damage and left the two of us alone. It was then I remembered what Popsicle had said to me earlier.

'Where's Shangri-La?' I asked my mother.

'Why?' she said.

'I just wondered. Read it in a book somewhere.' I didn't want to say any more.

'Well,' she said, 'it's a sort of imaginary paradise, high up in the mountains, the Himalayas, I think. A kind of heaven on earth, you could call it. Just a story of course. Doesn't exist, not really.'

But I couldn't forget the fear in Popsicle's eyes when he'd spoken of it. Imaginary or not, Shangri-La was real enough to him.

After the garden-shed fire, I would often find myself alone in the house with Popsicle. My mother was in and out of school getting ready for the new school year; and my father, of course, was as busy as ever down at the radio station, always leaving the house early and getting home late. I was to keep a watchful eye on Popsicle; and above all, they said, I mustn't let him wander off on his own. As it turned out, he didn't seem to want to. He seemed to be as content with my company as I was with his. Having Popsicle at home was a boon for me. I was dreading going back to school, because I knew I'd have to face Shirley Watson and the others. Just the thought of them looking at me, laughing at me, made me go cold inside, but Popsicle kept my mind off all that – most of the time anyway.

We did everything together. He'd listen to me playing my violin, and I'd listen to him reciting his favourite poems. It was strange. He couldn't even remember where he lived, but he knew his poems off by heart, dozens of them. I wasn't sure I always understood them, but I loved listening to him, because when Popsicle read poetry he made the words sing.

What he still looked forward to most though was our daily walk to the park to feed the ducks. Once out there in the park he just loved to talk, never about his past though, and never about my father. He loved to think out loud. As with the poems, I have to say I couldn't always follow all of it, but I listened all the same because I knew he was confiding in me, trusting in me, and I felt honoured by that.

The day it happened we were on our way back home from the park. We had to stop at the shop for some milk. He was tired by this time, but that never stopped him talking. 'Have you ever thought, Cessie?' he was saying. 'Have you ever thought that this is all a dream? All of it, the ducks, the pond, this shop, you, me, all of it, nothing but a funny old dream. Maybe all you do when you die is wake up, and then you don't remember anything anyway because you never remember dreams, do you? You know what they say, Cessie? They say in the last two minutes before you die you live your whole life over again. Looks like I'll have to wait till then to remember. Be a bit late by then, bit late to do anything about it, I mean.' He was frowning now. There's something I've still got to put right, Cessie, I know there is, something I've got to do. Trouble is, I can't for the life of me remember what it is.'

We were inside the shop by now and walking along past the breakfast cereals and the coffee and the tea, towards the fridge at the back. Popsicle had stopped talking. I was a while finding the two-litre carton of semi-skimmed I was looking for. When I turned round Popsicle had vanished. I panicked, but I needn't have. I found him almost at once near the check-out desk. He had taken a tin off the shelf.

'What've you got?' I asked him.

'There's something, Cessie, something I've remembered,' he said.

I read the label out loud. 'Condensed milk?'

'All I know is that I like it,' he went on, 'that I've always liked it.' He was looking at me strangely, as if I wasn't there. 'There were searchlights. There were searchlights and I couldn't get out. I couldn't get out.'

'What d'you mean?' I asked.

'I don't know, Cessie. That's the trouble, I don't know what I mean. But this, this tin is part of what I've got to remember, I know it is. I can't think, Cessie, I can't think.' His eyes were tight closed and he was banging the tin repeatedly against the side of his head. Everyone was looking at us now, so I bought the milk and the tin of condensed milk, took Popsicle by the arm and left the shop as quickly as I could. All the way home he was lost in himself, and that was how he stayed.

After that he wouldn't go out for his walk any more. He wouldn't read his poetry. He'd simply sit in his chair in the sitting-room, frowning incessantly and gazing into nowhere. If ever I offered to play my violin for him, he'd just shake his head. Whatever my mother put on his plate he refused to touch, not even pancakes and maple syrup, and he adored pancakes and maple syrup. 'The look of it doesn't taste nice,' he said. He said such odd things these days. She was worried about him, and I could see my father was too; but I wasn't. I knew what they didn't know, that he'd discovered a clue to his past and was struggling to work out what it meant. Once he'd worked it out, then the door to his memory would open and everything would be fine. I was sure of it.

Each night I lay awake wondering what the significance of a tin of condensed milk could possibly be. I asked myself again and again whether or not I should tell anyone about it, but I decided that what passed between Popsicle and me when we were alone was our private business and no one else's. I felt it would be like informing on him, like breaking a confidence. So I said nothing.

Popsicle had hardly eaten a thing now for a week. He was so frail he had to be helped up the stairs to bed. He didn't shave any more. He didn't wash any more. He never got out of his dressing-gown and slippers. Nothing seemed to interest him. He'd even stopped listening to my father on the radio. All day and every day, he'd just sit there rocking back and forth, humming tunes to himself and rubbing his knees. Like Aladdin, I thought, like Aladdin rubbing his lamp. He was making a wish and rubbing, but, unlike Aladdin, no amount of rubbing brought out the genie to make his wish come true. I was watching him sink deeper and deeper into despair and there was nothing I could do about it.

My mother tried all she knew. She tried threats. 'You don't eat this and I won't ever make you pancakes again.' She tried blackmail. 'You don't go out and feed those ducks of yours and they'll die.'

My father tried sweet-talking Popsicle out of it, but he very soon gave up in exasperation.

'If you ask me,' he said, 'he's just being downright difficult. My mother always said he was a moody devil. She wasn't far wrong either.'

'How can you say that?' I cried. 'He's not doing it deliberately. He's just sad, that's all. He's trying to remember, and he can't. How would you like it, if you'd lost your memory?' Tears of anger always came too easily to me, and I wished they wouldn't. He was judging Popsicle, blaming him, and that was so unjust, and so unfair.

Then one evening they called in Dr Wickens. He spent a good half hour alone with Popsicle. I sat on the stairs outside and tried to eavesdrop – unsuccessfully – until my mother found me and fetched me into the kitchen, where all three of us sat and waited.

It was some time before the doctor came into the kitchen. He sat down heavily, and packed his stethoscope into his black bag. He smiled at me over his glasses.

'Well,' he began, 'I've had a good look at him. The good news is that he's continuing to make a good recovery from the stroke. His right arm's not as strong as I'd like it to be just yet, but apart from that he's got the constitution of an ox. He's got a thumping strong heart, and his blood pressure's fine. Lungs as clear as a bell.' He paused.

'So what's the bad news?' my father asked.

'Well, I don't think it's that serious, not yet, but he is depressed. He won't talk to me much, so I can't say how depressed exactly. Depression is not uncommon after a stroke. And of course there's this loss of memory. That can't have helped. So he's going to need some treatment.'

73

'What sort of treatment?' my mother asked.

'Hopefully, it can be dealt with by a short course of antidepressant pills. And perhaps a spell in a nursing home may be necessary for a while. We'll see. Let's hope it won't come to that. The pills should set him right, get him eating again, get him on his feet, help him take more of an interest in life.'

So they did, and when the transformation came, it came so soon and so suddenly that it took us all completely by surprise. It was two or three days later, on Sunday afternoon. My father was out in the garden, rebuilding the fence with Mr Goldsmith, who had been very good about it, considering everything. My mother was ironing in the sitting-room – again. I was curled up with a book on the sofa – a six-pages-a-minute horror book. Popsicle was upstairs lying down on his bed, as he had been more and more often just recently. He'd eaten a little bit of his lunch – we'd all noticed that – but he'd been just as uncommunicative as ever. Suddenly we heard him calling out. 'Up here,' he cried. 'Cessie, come up here!' I was upstairs in an instant, my mother hard on my heels.

He was sitting up in his bed and chuckling. The tin of condensed milk was open on his lap and he was licking the spoon clean. He held up the tin to show us. It was quite empty. 'Cessie,' he said, 'I've got a riddle for you. Do you know why elephants have good memories?'

'No,' I said. 'Why do elephants have good memories?'

'Because they eat a lot,' he said, wagging the spoon at me. '*And* . . .' Now he was wagging it at my mother. '*And* because they wash themselves too.' He rubbed his stubbly chin, and was grinning hugely. '*And* maybe, just maybe, because they shave as well, every day.'

'Popsicle.' My mother put her arms round him and hugged him. 'Popsicle, you're better. You're feeling better, aren't you?'

'A whole heap, and I'm not talking elephants either – if you know what I mean.' And at that his chuckling broke into guffaws of laughter.

'What *is* this stuff?' my mother asked, taking the empty tin off him. She was wrinkling her nose at it disapprovingly.

'Ah,' said Popsicle enigmatically. 'That's magic that is, pure magic.' He swung his legs off the bed. 'Give us a hand up, Cessie, there's a girl.' He was standing between us, still holding on to my arm, when my father came into the room.

The two of them looked at each other, and for a while neither seemed to know what to say.

'Put you all through it a bit, didn't I?' said Popsicle.

'A bit,' my father agreed.

'Black dog days. I've always had them, all my life. I don't rightly know how I get into them. But I'm out now, and all on account of a tin of condensed milk. Got me thinking.' He steadied himself against my shoulder.

'Well, I suppose it's about time this old elephant had a wash and brush-up,' he said, and without another word he went off to the bathroom. It wasn't long before we heard him singing 'Yellow Submarine', full volume too.

To my mother's huge delight and relief, before he went to bed that night he ate three syrupy pancakes, and downed two mugs of hot chocolate, five spoonfuls of sugar in each. That tin of condensed milk had reminded him of something, and something important too, I was sure of it. I waited until he was in bed, and then I went in to see him. He was reading.

'T.S. Eliot,' he said. 'Good poet, he is. Listen to this:

"And all shall be well and
All manner of things shall be well"

He's right too.'

'You know something, don't you?' I said. 'You know where you live. You've remembered, haven't you?'

'No. I'm afraid not, Cessie. But I'm getting there. I've made a start.'

'What then? What've you remembered?'

'It's only a little thing, but a little thing is something. Every night when I'm home, I have three teaspoons of condensed milk, always have done. Helps me sleep. Helps me think straight. I can see them lined up on the shelf above the sink in my kitchen – dozens of tins of condensed milk. I can see them, up here in my head. Only a little kitchen – not enough room to swing a rat, let alone a cat. I'm telling you, Cessie, it's coming. All I need is my condensed milk each night to oil the old memory. It'll get it working again, I know it will.'

'Are you having me on?'

'Cross my heart, Cessie. It works. Honestly. I mean, look at me. I'm feeling better already. That's proof enough, isn't it? You should try some. Do you good.' I shook my head. It looked revolting. 'Please yourself,' he said.

'It could've been the pills, couldn't it?' I ventured.

'Don't think so,' said Popsicle, smiling sheepishly. 'I haven't taken them, have I? Not one. Just pretended. Spat them out again. Don't like pills. Don't trust 'em. Give me my old condensed milk any day. I'll be right as rain now, in no time, you'll see.'

A sudden frown came over his face like a shadow.

He beckoned me closer, and gripped me by the arm. There was a wildness in his eyes that frightened me. 'Remember what I said, Cessie. Whatever happens, I don't ever want to go up to Shangri-La. Never, d'you hear me? Never.'

7 SHANGRI-LA

WHETHER IT WAS THE CONDENSED MILK OR NOT, Popsicle was certainly a changed man. He was using his bad arm more and more every day, so that I now had difficulty in remembering which arm was supposed to be the weaker of the two. No one cut his food up for him any more. No one tied his shoe-laces. He did everything for himself. He was still absent-minded occasionally; but he was much happier in himself, so much so that by the time term began the following Monday morning, we were confident enough to leave him on his own in the house for the day.

To my huge relief, school turned out not to be the nightmare I had been dreading – Shirley Watson was off sick, and she wouldn't be back for a couple of weeks at least. When I got back after school the house had been cleaned from top to bottom and tea was ready for me on the kitchen table.

'Marmite and hot buttered toast,' Popsicle said. 'Is that all right for you, madam?' And he sat me down, pushing my chair in behind me. Normally I would have come home to an empty house and my own company.

To her huge delight, my mother had the same waiter service when she came back from school, exhausted as usual. She could not believe what Popsicle had done around the house.

Every day that followed was the same. The garden, muddied and blackened by the fire, was slowly being restored, and he had set about the building of a new garden shed. In fine weather, the patio became his carpenter's shop. When it rained he used the garage. Within weeks the garden shed was up, much bigger and much better than it had ever been before.

One windy autumn afternoon we held an opening ceremony. My father was speechless as he cut the ribbon, and still speechless when we were allowed inside for the first time.

Popsicle, it seemed to me, was like a small boy out to impress his father – in this case my father – and my father was impressed, I could see he was. But he simply would not say so. All he said was, 'Lot of work gone into this, I should think. Looks sound; but don't go lighting fires too close, will you?' It was supposed to be a joke, I think, but it just wasn't funny.

By now it was as if Popsicle had always lived with us. He'd wash the cars on Sundays, put the rubbish out for the dustmen on Tuesday. He'd even help me with my French homework – so much about him was completely unexpected.

When I asked him once how it was that he knew so much French, he went strangely quiet on me. I should have known better than to ask. It was always the same. Any question that related in some way to his past he would deflect or simply ignore. He would sometimes talk wistfully about his years as a boatbuilder in Bradwell when he was a young father and a young husband, but that still seemed to be all he could remember – in spite of the condensed milk, which he took religiously every night. But at least his inability to remember did not seem to be lowering his spirits as it had before. No one was more chirpy about the house than Popsicle. He was the whistling outside in the garden and the singing up in the bathroom. He was the life and soul of the place.

Home was happier now than it ever had been, despite my father's continuing coolness towards Popsicle. And at school too life was proving unexpectedly good. Shirley Watson was back, but was ignoring me – so far. Things were set fair, I thought.

These days, I noticed, Popsicle would often disappear into the new garden shed and lock himself in for hours on end. I asked him time and again what he was doing in there. 'Tell you when I'm ready,' he'd say, tapping his nose conspiratorially. 'And you're not to peek.' I tried to peek of course, but he'd hung an old sack over the window. All I could see through a knot-hole low down in the door was a tray of onions on the floor. I was none the wiser.

20th of October. My twelfth birthday. It was a Saturday. When I came down there were three wrapped presents waiting for me on the kitchen table. Everyone was sitting there and singing happy birthday. I opened the cards first and then attacked the presents. I had a CD of Yehudi Menuhin playing Beethoven's Violin Concerto from my father, and from my mother a video of *The Black Stallion*, my favourite film in all the world. I left Popsicle's till last.

'Go careful,' he said, as I tore the paper away. It was a shoe box, but it wasn't shoes inside. It was a boat, a model boat, blue with a single yellow funnel. I took it out. It looked like some sort of a lifeboat, with looping ropes along the sides. Below the funnel a man stood at the huge steering-wheel. He was dressed in a yellow sou'wester and oils, and he really looked as if he was clinging to the wheel in the teeth of a gale. The name *Lucie Alice* was painted in red on the side of the boat.

I put it down very gently beside the Grape Nuts in the middle of the table. I looked at Popsicle. 'That was my boat,' he said proudly. 'The *Lucie Alice*.'

'Beautiful,' my mother breathed. 'Just beautiful.'

'You made it?' I said. 'In the shed?' Popsicle nodded. 'Built in 1939 she was. Served at Lowestoft for thirty years. Reserve boat down in Exmouth after that. Know every plank of her, every nail. Don't know why, but I do. She went to Dunkirk in 1940 too, in the war. Took hundreds of our lads off the beaches, she did.'

'Where is she now?' my father asked.

Popsicle got up suddenly from the table. 'How should I know?' he said. 'I just made it, that's all.' I went after him and caught him by the arm before he reached the door.

'It's lovely, Popsicle,' I said. 'Will it float? Can I float it in the bath, with Patsy?'

'In the bath! With Patsy!' he laughed. 'This is my lifeboat you're talking about.'

'All right then. What about the pond? Could we

float him out on the pond, in the park?'

'Not him,' he said. 'She's a she. All boats are shes. She'll float all right, but she'll do a lot more than just float, you mark my words. She's got engines. I've tried her out. She's had her sea trials. Goes like the clappers, she does. And she's unsinkable too. Got to be if she's a lifeboat. You want to see?'

'Now?'

'Why not? We'll all go, shall we?'

The ducks were not at all pleased with us. They must have thought we'd come over with our usual offering of breadcrusts. Popsicle ignored all their raucous clamour, started the engines and set her chugging off across the pond on her maiden voyage. Transfixed, we all stood there and watched her, until Popsicle said that one of us had better run across the other side to catch her before she ran aground and got herself stuck in the mud. My father raced round. He was there just in time.

'She looks such a brave little boat,' said my mother.

'She was,' Popsicle replied. 'Saved a lot of lives in her time.'

'You crewed on her, did you?' my mother was delving, prying, and I wished she wouldn't. 'So you were a lifeboat-man, then?' I expected Popsicle to clam up, but he didn't, not this time.

'I wish I knew.' He was looking out over the pond as he spoke. 'I know that she was mine once, that's all.' He put an arm round my shoulder. 'And now she's yours, Cessie, all yours. You'll take good care of her, won't you? Course, you can let your dad play with her from time to time.' He chuckled. 'Look at him. Just like he was. Always loved boats, did your dad.' My father was crouched down by the pond pointing the bow of the lifeboat right at us.

'Ready?' he called out.

'Ready,' said Popsicle.

My father released the boat and then stood up to watch, hands on hips. He was beaming like a little boy.

By now a dozen people or more had gathered around the pond to watch, Shirley Watson amongst them with her dog. Mandy Bethel was there too. The dog, a snuffling puggy-looking thing with pop eyes, yapped incessantly from the edge of the pond. That dog and Shirley Watson, I was thinking, they really suit each other.

'It's mine. My grandad made it,' I crowed. I knew as soon as I'd said it that I should have kept my mouth shut. The trouble was that I felt safe. Popsicle was nearby. My mother and father too. I felt suddenly brave, so I bragged on. 'It's called the *Lucie Alice*. It's got real engines. It's an exact replica of a 1939 lifeboat, a real one.'

'Kids' stuff, if you ask me,' Shirley Watson sneered.

'Well,' I said, still full of bravado, 'if you don't like it, you don't have to watch, do you?'

Mandy Bethel gaped. She could not believe what she was hearing. Neither could I. No one spoke like that to Shirley Watson, no one in her right mind.

Shirley Watson glared at me and stomped off in a fury. I knew, as I watched her go, that I had done something I would live to regret. I knew she was best not roused, not confronted, and I had done both. I knew there would be trouble.

I soon discovered that Shirley Watson was putting it about at school that I had a crazy grandfather back at home, a drifter, a tramp, who wore his hair in a ponytail and looked like a pirate. That I could ignore, but there was worse to come – just looks at first, then whispers.

Shirley Watson was spreading poison about Popsicle. She was telling everyone. He looked like a druggie, a weirdo. He was probably a dealer too, hanging around the park like he did. And she'd seen him talking to small children. It was a deliberate campaign of innuendo and gossip, and I hated her for it from the bottom of my heart.

The mud was sticking. People were treating me differently. Some would not speak to me at all. I wanted to rise above it, to face them down, to be brave. I wanted to go out with Popsicle as often as I could, and be seen with him, just to show them exactly what I thought of them. And to begin with I really did try. But every time I went out with Popsicle, I was looking over my shoulder, dreading seeing anyone from school.

Gradually my courage ebbed away, and I was cowed into staying at home. I had homework, it was raining, I had violin practice to do – any excuse to avoid bumping into that gaggle of sniggering tormentors in the park. I wasn't proud of myself.

Popsicle kept making minor adjustments to improve the *Lucie Alice*'s performance or her stability in the water. He had to test his refinements on the duckpond in the park. There wasn't anywhere else. Luckily, there were long periods when he didn't want to go there at all – whilst he was working on her on his bench in the garden shed. 'Any boatbuilder worth his salt can't be satisfied with getting it almost right,' he told me one day, as I watched him at work. 'He has to get it perfect. And I'm going to get this boat perfect for you, Cessie, perfect.'

It looked quite perfect enough for me already, but I

wasn't going to argue. I was more than happy to sit and watch him at work, and happier still not to have to venture out into the park. But I knew the day must come when he would want to test the *Lucie Alice* out on the water again, and that unless I had a ready excuse, I'd have to go with him, my heart in my mouth all the time.

One Sunday afternoon I was reading on my bed when he came into my room with his coat on, the *Lucie Alice* in the shoe box under his arm. 'She's ready,' he said.

'It's raining,' I told him.

'Only drizzling, Cessie girl,' he said. 'Come on.' I had no choice.

I knew that Sunday afternoon was always the most likely time to meet some of Shirley Watson's crowd in the park. They could be on their way down to the bus shelter, a favourite hang-out at weekends, particularly when it was raining. I was thinking about that as I followed him down the stairs. 'But I haven't done my violin practice,' I said, stopping where I was.

'It won't take us long,' said Popsicle, and I could see how disappointed he was at my reluctance.

My father had heard us from the sitting-room. 'She needs to practise,' he said. 'She won't get her Grade Six by playing with boats, will she?' There was no need to say it like that. I very nearly changed my mind, just to show solidarity with Popsicle. But I didn't. Instead, to my everlasting shame, I gave Popsicle my scarf and sent him off to the park on his own in the rain.

I went up to my room and pretended to practise, but of course my heart wasn't in it. I spent all the time excusing my excuse, rationalising my chickening out. I just couldn't concentrate. I kept thinking of Popsicle out there in the park, of what Shirley's cronies might say to him if they caught up with him, how bewildered he'd be, how hurt. Then, quite suddenly, I could picture him in my mind. I knew they were there, all around him, laughing at him, jeering.

I was down the stairs and out of the house before anyone could stop me. I could hear my father calling after me as I slammed the door.

The traffic lights turned red at the right moment. I dashed across the main road, past the library and the bus shelter, and into the park. I hurdled the children's play-ground fence and got a shrill rebuke from an angry mother seesawing her little girl, before I hurdled out again. I was almost there.

To my intense relief there was no chanting, no jeering, just a commotion of quacking. There was no one about, only the ducks – that was how it seemed at first. But then I saw that the ducks were not alone in their pond. Popsicle was standing waist-high in the water, with his back to me. I called to him and ran down to the water's edge. He didn't turn; I ran round so that he'd have to hear me, have to see me. He had something in his hand. There was debris floating in the water all around him. I knew in an instant what had happened. I ran into the water and waded out towards him. He was holding the bow of the lifeboat in one hand, the stern in the other. The yellow funnel was floating towards me. I picked it up. I saw the wheel just under the surface and retrieved it. I looked for the lifeboatman in the sou'wester, but he was gone.

'They just came,' he said. 'They were shouting things, horrible things. Then they threw stones, hundreds of them. They went on and on. I don't know why. I don't know why.'

Nothing I said would persuade him to come out of the pond. He had to stay, he said, until he'd picked up every last bit of her. Then my father was there, and my mother too, wading out towards us. They took an elbow each and, ignoring all his protestations, led him out of the pond. When I looked back, the ducks were moving in amongst the last of the flotsam, pecking at it, then discarding it and finally swimming away in disgust.

After the sinking of the *Lucie Alice* Popsicle went

downhill again fast. Dr Wickens said he wasn't seriously ill. He had a chest cold, that was all. But even I could see it was a lot more than that. He was sinking further and further into despair. Every day now was a black-dog day. He'd sit there in his chair, his eyes glazed, and unseeing. He wasn't with us. He seemed lost in a deep sadness and could not bring himself out of it. I told him it didn't matter about the *Luice Alice*, that he could always build another. I stroked his hand and told him we'd do it together. I think he barely knew I was there. He didn't feel like eating. He even refused his condensed milk.

The doctor came back one evening to give Popsicle an injection, just to help him along, I was told. I was sent upstairs for a while. They wanted to talk to the doctor in private. I heard the hushed discussions down in the kitchen, but the tap was running or the kettle was boiling and I could make no sense of what they were saying.

At school it took a few days to screw up my courage before I could bring myself to do what I had to do, to say what I had to say. Shirley Watson knew it was coming. There was guilt written all over her face. She couldn't hide it. Day in, day out, I had eyed her from across the classroom, from across the playground, just to let her know that I knew it was her that had sunk the *Lucie Alice*, her and her friends. At first she tried to stare me out, but each time I won the battle of the eyes, and she'd have to look away.

I waited for my moment. It came in break one day when I saw she was alone. I walked right up to her. We were face to face now. Somehow my courage held firm. 'Why? What did you do it for?' My voice was steadier than I dared hope. 'My grandad made me that boat. It took him weeks and weeks. What you did, it's made him ill, really ill. Does that make you feel good?' I looked her full in the eye, unflinching. 'Well, does it? Does it?' Then, without a word, she turned and ran off.

As I went home that afternoon I was singing inside with triumph. I told Popsicle all about how I'd faced down Shirley Watson. I wasn't sure how much he understood, but he seemed to listen. After I'd finished he just touched my face, and smiled wanly. 'Lucie Alice,' he said. 'Lucie Alice.' And that was all.

If there were warnings of what was about to happen, then I didn't see them. Perhaps I didn't want to see them. For a week or so over half-term, a nurse came each day to see to Popsicle, and the doctor was in and out almost daily too. I would see my mother and father walking around the garden, deep in earnest discussion from which I was always excluded. There would be long knowing looks across the table at supper, and my father, I noticed, was being unusually attentive and kind towards Popsicle.

I had just come home from school. I was hanging up my coat in the front hall. I remember thinking how odd it was that both cars were parked outside, that my father and my mother must both be home early. They were waiting for me as I walked into the kitchen. She should have been at school. He should have been at work. Something was definitely wrong.

'Where's Popsicle?' I said, dumping my bag on the floor.

'Sit down, Cessie,' said my father. 'We've got something to tell you.' Then he was looking across to my mother for help.

'It's Popsicle, Cessie.' She was trying to tell me something she didn't want to tell me. 'Don't worry, it's nothing terrible,' she went on. 'It's just that . . . just that we've had to send him away for a while. We can't cope with him here, not like he is. He wasn't taking his pills like he should. He was just getting worse. We had to do something.'

'What do you mean "send him away"?'

'Well . . .' she began, and she wouldn't look at me as she spoke. 'It's a sort of home for the elderly, a nursing home where he can be looked after properly. He'll have everything he needs.'

'Shangri-La,' said my father. 'It's called Shangri-La. Lovely place. He'll be fine there, Cessie. It's what's best for him, honestly it is.'

'Come to think of it,' my mother went on, 'Cessie was asking about Shangri-La only the other day, weren't you, Cessie? Funny that.'

There was nothing funny about it, nothing at all.

8 THE *LUCIE ALICE*

FOR DAYS I WOULDN'T SPEAK TO EITHER OF THEM. As far as I was concerned they were both as guilty as each other. I spent much of my time alone in my room brooding over the dreadful thing they had done to Popsicle. They would come up, sit on the bed and try to talk me round. I had to understand that, at the moment, Shangri-La was the best place for him, and it was a perfectly nice place too. You couldn't hope for better. But I was deaf to all explanations, all excuses.

'It won't be for ever, you know,' my mother told me. 'Just for a while, till he gets better.'

'Don't think badly of us, Cessie,' my father pleaded. 'I know how upset you must be, but what else could we have done? The way he is, he needs proper full-time care. I've got to go out to work. Your mother's got to go out to work. You've got to go to school. We just couldn't leave him alone in the house, not as he is. Remember the fire? It's no use carrying on like this, you know. It won't achieve anything, Cessie. It won't bring Popsicle home.'

But it wasn't only the sending away of Popsicle that grieved me, nor even where he'd been sent – that wasn't their fault – it was how it had been done, covertly, on the sly. I wasn't stupid. I could understand that Popsicle shouldn't be left all on his own. I could even understand that in his state of mind he could possibly do himself some accidental damage. But they had packed him off to Shangri-La, to the very place Popsicle most dreaded, and without even telling me. I could have warned them. I could have told them.

On the principle that I would never again let them have the satisfaction of hearing me play my violin, I waited until I was sure I was alone in the house before I began my practice. I always ended with 'Nowhere Man', dedicating it each time to Popsicle, and promising him as I played that somehow I would get him out of Shangri-La. I could never play that tune without crying for him. It was while I was playing it one afternoon that I decided the time had come to stop moping, and to do what I should have done in the first place.

I packed away my violin and got my bike out of the back of the garage. If I was to rescue him, then I had to get to see him. The first step was to find out where the Shangri-La nursing home was. I asked a postman. 'Cliff Road,' he said, 'on the coast road, going west out of town, top of the hill.'

It turned out to be a long way out of town, beyond the harbour, beyond the marina, a couple of kilometres at least. The hill was horribly steep, but I was determined to keep pedalling right to the top. Once I reached it, I got off, gasping for breath, and rested. There it was across the road – 'Shangri-La. Residential Nursing Home for the Elderly'. Beyond the closed white gate was a driveway, and an avenue of trees, every one of them slanted and stunted by the wind. There were lawns and rhododendron bushes and, just visible from the road, a great gabled house, cream-painted with neat, white windows.

There didn't seem to be anyone about, so I opened the gate and wheeled my bike up the drive. The porch alone was as big as the front of our entire house. It had fluted pillars all around like a temple, and two stone lions glared at me from either side of the front door. I pressed the brass bell and stood back. I didn't think I was frightened but I could hear my heart pounding in my ears. No one came. I rang again. Still no one came. I wheeled my bike round the side of the house and peered in at the first window I came to.

They were sitting around the room, ancient men and ancient women, some with their heads lolling in sleep, their mouths wide open; others staring vacantly into space, their hands trembling in their laps. A few were reading magazines. One of them looked up at me, looked straight at me I thought, but she didn't see me.

It was a huge square room with a high ceiling and a chandelier. On the walls there were pictures in gold frames of cart horses and sailing boats and village feasts, and beneath them the room was lined with grey-green chairs with wooden armrests. A television was on in the corner, but no one seemed to be watching it.

I was searching amongst the faces for Popsicle, but I couldn't find him, not at first. Only when he stood up and came walking towards me across the room did I know him. His cheeks seemed sunken, his skin sallow. His hand was reaching out towards me.

'Cessie,' he mouthed.

A voice spoke from behind me. 'And what have we

here?' Her grey hair was as starched and stiff as her white uniform. She was a thin-lipped, peaky-faced woman with sharp little eyes. 'You do this often, do you, peering in people's windows?'

I ran for it across the lawn, leapt on my bike and was gone down the drive. I dismounted at the gate, fought with the latch that wouldn't budge, flung the gate back and at last made my escape. I never looked back, not once.

I wasn't going to give up. One way or another I had to see Popsicle. I had to talk to him, to tell him I hadn't been part of the conspiracy, that I'd known nothing at all about it. So that evening I broke my silence for the first time. 'I want to visit Popsicle,' I said. 'Even in prison you're allowed visits, aren't you?'

They seemed relieved that I was talking to them again.

'Soon,' said my mother. 'They said we should let him settle in for a while. But it's been two weeks now – we could go on Saturday, couldn't we, Arthur? What d'you think?'

'Why not?' my father replied, and then he smiled at me. 'Truce?'

'Truce,' I said, but I didn't mean it.

I had several long days at school to endure before Saturday. Word had got around that Popsicle was up at

Shangri-La. It seemed Mandy Bethel's aunt worked there as a part-time nurse. Ever since I had confronted Shirley Watson, she and Mandy Bethel and the others were giving me a wide berth – thank goodness. But there were some who felt they had to say something. They were meaning to be sympathetic, but sometimes it didn't come out like that. 'They're all really old up there.' 'Must be horrible for him – with all those wrinklies, I mean.' 'I've seen them out in their bus on outings. They look prehistoric, if you ask me.' And so on. I endured it as best I could, but it wasn't easy.

On the Friday morning, we had RE with Mrs Morecambe. It all got silly and out of hand, as it often did with Mrs Morecambe. Her crowd control was never much good, but at least she was always interesting. She was talking about Hinduism, about the transmigration of souls. Some people saw this as an opportunity to wind her up by suggesting what they'd most like to be when they came back in their next life. There were all sorts of ridicidulous ideas: elephants, kangaroos, dung-beetles, daddy-long-legs, even a flea. Finally she'd had enough. She banged the table. 'It is not a joking matter,' she stormed, her eyes flashing. 'It's about time some of you learnt that life is not one long joke, and nor is death either.' There was still some tittering. 'You won't think it's so funny when your time comes, and it will come. It comes to us all. I've got an aunt. She's up at the Shangri-La nursing home right now. And she won't ever come out. Just sixty. Been there five years now. Alzheimer's. She can't feed herself. Some days she doesn't even know who she is any more. She hasn't known me for two years.' Suddenly everyone was looking at me. Mrs Morecambe went on: 'Believe you me, getting old is no laughing matter.' No one was laughing any more.

Mrs Morecambe called me up after the lesson. 'It's not too bad up at Shangri-La, Cessie. They do what they can,' she said. So she knew too. 'Don't let it worry you.' It was kind of her, but it was no comfort to me. The memory of Popsicle's pained face through the window haunted me night and day. His worst nightmare had come true, and I was to blame, in part at least. I had promised him he would never have to go to Shangri-La, and I had broken that promise. Somehow I would get him out of there. Somehow.

I thought about little else. I had the notion that Popsicle and I could steal away together in the middle of the night and make our way down to the railway station. We'd catch the first train out in the morning – it didn't matter where it was going. I had nearly a hundred pounds in the building society, enough to take us a long way away. He could make ship models, and we could sell them. I'd look after him. He'd be fine. We'd both be fine. We'd find a house somewhere remote, somewhere no one would even think of looking for us.

I knew all along that it was a dream, but I clung to it all the same, and just hoped that there was some way I could make at least some of it come true.

I was still hoping, still dreaming as we drove up to Shangri-La that Saturday morning. We turned in off the road and up the drive. 'See?' my mother was saying. 'We told you, Cessie. Isn't it lovely? Wonderful views, rose gardens. They've got croquet too, look. And you should see inside. Library. Television room. Carpets everywhere. Paradise on a hill. Lovely views of the harbour. They don't call it Shangri-La for nothing.'

We weren't the only people visiting. Half a dozen cars were parked on the front drive, and on the front lawn they were playing croquet, with a couple of little children jumping the hoops as if they were hurdles.

'Our future Olympic champions perhaps, Mr Stevens,' said a voice from behind me, a voice I recognised at once. Striding across the drive was the starched lady in the white uniform whom I'd met on my previous visit, the lady with the sharp little eyes and the thin lips. I tried to hide behind my mother.

'I heard your programme yesterday evening, Mr Stevens. Excellent as usual, quite excellent. And who is this then?'

'This is Cessie, Popsicle's granddaughter,' said my mother, stepping aside so that I was now completely exposed. 'Cessie, this is Mrs Davidson. She's the matron here, and she's looking after Popsicle for us.' I need not have worried about being recognised. Mrs Davidson wasn't interested in me. She was soon deep in discussion with my mother and father. They'd forgotten all about me.

'It's early days,' Mrs Davidson was saying, 'but your father's making very good progress already, Mr Stevens. He can be a bit cantankerous, of course, but we're used to that at Shangri-La. He still won't take his pills, but there we are. You can lead a horse to water . . .'

'But is he eating better now?' my mother asked.

They had all turned away from me and were walking towards the house. I took my chance and made off. I had it in mind that I would find Popsicle before they did and tell him of my plans for his escape. He had to know that I hadn't abandoned him, and that I never would.

I must have been preoccupied. I was making my way across the lawn, past the rose garden towards the window where I'd seen Popsicle before, when I walked right into a man in a wheelchair.

'Where you off to in such a hurry, young lady?' I expected him to be furious, but he wasn't. 'Visiting someone, are you?'

'I'm looking for Popsicle, for my grandad,' I said.

When he smiled I saw he had very even, very yellow teeth. He held out his hand. 'I'm Harry,' he said, 'and you must be Cessie. Never stops talking about you. Pretty as a picture, just like he said you were. Grand fellow, your grandad. Won't stand any nonsense from the Dragon-woman.' I knew well enough who he was talking about. He looked around him and then beckoned me closer. 'All smiles she is on visiting days. Different story when they've gone. Shouts at us like we're all deaf. Treats us like we're a bunch of loonies. I'm telling you. It's not right what she does. Not right at all. Popsicle – he's the only one that talks back at her. And she doesn't like it, not one bit. Got it in for him already, she has, but Popsicle doesn't take no notice.'

'Where is he?' I asked.

'He goes down to the gun emplacement on the cliffs. Just sits there, looking at the boats going in and out, birdwatching sometimes, or reading his poetry. Potty about poetry, isn't he? Best place to think his thoughts, he says.' He pointed through the trees. 'Over there he doesn't like to be disturbed. But he won't mind, not if it's you.' I began to move away, but he hadn't finished yet. 'I'll tell you something else, young lady. He may not have been here long, but your grandad, he's like a breath of fresh air. Keeps us smiling, he does. And that's a lot to be thankful for. Off you go now.'

I found Popsicle standing on top of a concrete bunker. There were holes in the sides where I supposed the guns had once been. He was looking out to sea through a pair of binoculars. He hadn't heard me, so I climbed up behind him and tapped him on the shoulder. The moment he saw me his face lit up.

He hugged me to him tight for a moment or two, and then held me at arm's length. He seemed so much happier than the last time I'd seen him, more his old self again. 'Oh, Cessie, I've been hoping you'd come back. Every day I've been hoping. That woman, that Dragon-woman, she didn't catch you when you came before? She didn't catch you?' I shook my head. I had every-thing ready to tell him, my whole escape plan, but I didn't get the chance even to begin. 'Good, good. Now listen, Cessie. I've got news for you, good news. I've remembered something, something important. That boat I made you, it's more than just a boat.'

'What d'you mean?'

His eyes shone with excitement. 'It's where I live, Cessie. It's my home. That boat's my home. I live on the *Lucie Alice*.' I must have looked a bit doubtful. 'It's true, Cessie. I live on that boat. Honestly. I woke up a couple of days ago and I just knew it. Don't ask me how. I reckon it's the old memory waking himself up at last. About time too, if you ask me. It's just like the one I made you, the one they went and sunk. I'm not barmy, Cessie, honestly I'm not. For a while I really thought I was, and it frightened the living daylights out of me. You do believe me, don't you?'

'Of course I do,' I said, but I wasn't at all sure that I did. I had to ask: 'But where is it then? Where you live, the boat, where is it?'

He looked suddenly downcast. 'That's the thing, Cessie. That's the bit I don't know. I mean, it's got to be moored somewhere, hasn't it? I'm still trying to work it out, and I will too. I will. You'll see.'

A pair of gulls wheeled above our heads and flew out to sea. 'Lesser Blackbacks,' he said. 'Have a look.' He took off his binoculars and gave them to me. It was a few moments before I had them in focus. I found them floating out on the thermals over the cliffs. 'That's what I'd like to be, free as they are,' said Popsicle. 'All my life there's one thing I've hated, Cessie. You know what it is? Being cooped up, shut in, told what to do. That's why I always dreaded coming up here to Shangri-La. I heard all about it from a friend of mine – Sam he's called. Sam had an older brother, and he went a bit barmy in the head. So Sam had to send him up here to be looked after. He hated it up here, and he never came out. That's not going to happen to me, Cessie. I'm getting out of here, soon as ever I can.' He was angry now, angrier than I'd ever seen him. 'There's fine people in this place, good people, but that Mrs Davidson, that Dragon-woman, she who must be obeyed, I've seen her scream-ing at them, Cessie. Maybe we're a bit slow. Maybe some of us wet ourselves. But that's not our fault, is it? And all she does is scream at us. Not right, Cessie, not fair. Little Hitler she is. I'm telling you, Cessie, I'm getting out – and for two pins I'd take Harry and the others with me. Honest I would. Soon as I remember where that boat of mine is, I'll be gone, out of here for good.'

That was when I heard my mother's voice from in amongst the trees.

'Popsicle!' She was hurrying down towards us, and with her were Mrs Davidson and my father.

'We've been looking for you, Mr Stevens. I thought

I told you to stay inside to meet your visitors, in the dayroom,' said Mrs Davidson. There was an edge to her voice that hadn't been there before.

'How are you, Popsicle?' My mother was helping Popsicle down off the gun emplacement. 'Mrs Davidson says you're eating really well these days. That's good, very good.' She breathed deep of the air as she looked out to sea. 'Isn't this the perfect place?'

'You doing all right, then?' my father asked.

'Better all the time, Arthur. And d'ya know why? I was telling Cessie. I've remembered. I've remembered where I live. It's on the *Lucie Alice*.' They were all looking at him, nonplussed. 'That's right. It's a boat, just like the one I made for Cessie. It's a lifeboat, and I live on it.'

We didn't stay talking for very long. Popsicle did his best to explain how it was that he could be so sure about the *Lucie Alice*; but how, even so, he still couldn't remember where it was moored. 'That'll come,' he said. 'That'll come.' But I could see what Popsicle couldn't see, that they all thought he was losing his mind, that Shangri-La was just where he should be, and where he'd have to stay.

All the while Mrs Davidson was eyeing me. I was sure she was beginning to recognise me.

As we were leaving she took Popsicle by the elbow.

'I think you'd better come inside now, Mr Stevens, don't you? Bit breezy out here.'

'I'll be fine where I am,' Popsicle pulled away. 'I like a good breeze. Gets rid of bad smells, if you know what I mean.' Mrs Davidson glared at him.

When we said goodbye I held him as long and as tight as I could, so that he'd remember it when I was gone. It was all I could do to choke back my tears. 'Don't you go crying on me, girl,' he whispered. 'I've got enough on my plate without that.'

My mother kissed him goodbye too. 'It's not for ever Popsicle,' she said. 'You do understand that. Just till you're better. We'll come again soon.'

My father shook Popsicle by the hand. There was just a nod between them and a brief meeting of eyes.

'You do see what I mean,' said Mrs Davidson as we walked away. 'He says such bizarre things. He does live in a bit of a fantasy world, I'm afraid, but he'll settle down. They all take time to settle. I'll look after him, don't you worry.' To me, that sounded more like a threat than anything else.

We drove home in silence. I waited till the engine was turned off before I let them both know exactly what I was thinking. 'I don't know how you can do it, how you can leave him up there in that place with that horrible woman.' They stayed silent, which simply provoked me to go further. 'You don't believe him, do you? You never do. If he says he lives on a lifeboat, then he does. Why should he make it up? You think he's mad, do you? Well, you're the mad ones. Why don't you just trust him? Why don't you ever trust him?'

I lay there that night asking myself that very same question. Try as I did to dispel them, my doubts still nagged at me. Was Popsicle really in his right mind? How could he be living on a lifeboat? If I could find the *Lucie Alice*, if only I could prove there was such a boat . . . I knew what I had to do. I don't think I slept at all.

I was up early. I told them I was going for a cycle ride. I searched the marina from end to end, and the harbour beyond. There was no lifeboat. I went out after lunch and tried again. There was no *Lucie Alice*. No one had ever heard of her. So maybe they were right after all. Maybe Popsicle *was* sick in his head. Maybe he was barmy. I remembered what Mrs Morecambe had said about her aunt in the RE lesson, how she was dying of Alzheimer's. I went and looked up Alzheimer's in a medical dictionary from my mother's bookshelf. It took me some time to find it, because I didn't know how to spell it. Everything I read confirmed my worst fears. Alzheimer's began with muddled thinking, with intermittent loss of memory. When I'd finished reading I was quite sure that Popsicle was in the early stages of Alzheimer's.

With two sleepless nights behind me, I was so tired the next day and so worried that I could hardly think straight at all. The last person in the world I wanted to have to face at school was Shirley Watson. I was sitting under a tree eating my lunch on my own, when I looked up and saw her coming towards me. There was nothing I could do to avoid her. She stood for a moment looking down at me out of the sun. I thought she was going to kick my head in.

'You know that boat?' Her tone was conciliatory, ingratiating almost. 'Well, I've seen it,' she said.

'What do you mean, you've seen it? You bust it up, remember?'

'No, I mean a big one, a real one. Down by the canal. By the lock. You been there?' I shook my head. 'I was fishing down there yesterday with my brother. There's a whole lot of barges moored down by the old ware-houses, and right at the end there's this boat, and it's just like the one your grandad made. Just the same it is. I'm not having you on, Cessie, promise. It's there, really there. "*Lucie* . . ." something or other, it's called. Great big yellow funnel. Blue, just like the one . . .' She was shifting nervously from one foot to the other. 'I'll show you, if you like. After school?'

9 GONE MISSING

IT WAS A LONG WALK FROM SCHOOL TO THE canal, right across the other side of town. All the way I felt uneasy. Shirley Watson didn't say very much. There was never a mention of the sinking of the *Lucie Alice*. She asked after Popsicle, and she seemed genuinely concerned, as if she really cared about him. It wasn't like her at all. All the while I felt I might be being led into some kind of a trap. I stayed with her only because I knew there had to be some truth in her story. No one else could possibly have known what Popsicle had told me up at Shangri-La, about the *Lucie Alice*. She couldn't have plucked the idea out of thin air. But Shirley Watson was Shirley Watson, so I stayed on my guard.

As we neared the lock gates I was becoming ever more intrigued, but ever more anxious too. She stopped on the bridge and pointed. 'There. See?' I could see only the funnel at first, a yellow funnel beyond the line of brightly painted pleasure barges. But then I saw the side of the boat, dark blue, broader than the barges, her hull bellying out into the canal, a rope looping the length of her, just as there had been on the model Popsicle had made me. I looked around nervously, half expecting some kind of an ambush.

'What's the matter?' Shirley Watson asked.

'You,' I said. And then I asked her straight. 'What are you doing this for? Why did you bring me?'

I didn't know Shirley Watson could cry, but suddenly there were real tears in her eyes. 'What happened to your grandad, I didn't mean it to happen like it did. It just got out of hand. I don't know why we did it, and I wish . . .' She couldn't say any more. She turned away and went off, leaving me alone by the canal.

As I walked over the bridge it was coming on to rain. I hurried along the towpath past the barges – they had names like *Kontiki* and *Hispaniola* – and there in front of one was the vertical prow of the lifeboat rising majestically from the water, her name painted in large red letters on her side: *Lucie Alice*. I stepped over the mooring ropes and ran my hand along her side. She felt so solid, so sturdy.

The towpath in front of me and behind me looked deserted, and so it seemed was the boat. I called out. 'Anyone there? Anyone on board?' Then I saw the huge wheel – polished wood and brass – as high as a man, and beyond it the dark of the cabin down below. The only difference between this boat and Popsicle's model, apart from size of course, was that no man stood at the wheel in his sou'wester. In every other detail this was the same boat. I called out once more just to be sure. There was no reply, and there was no one watching except a pair of swans gliding past on the canal. It looked safe enough for me to go on board.

For a few moments I stood at the wheel and just held it. It wasn't hard to imagine the towering seas and the throb of the engines and the cries of the shipwrecked sailors. I could almost feel the spray on my face and the cruel wind whipping the seas into a frenzy all around me. I clung to the wheel now for dear life, just like the man in the sou'wester. I looked up at the funnel, but the rain stung my eyes at once so I had to look away. There was a gangway of some kind leading down, to the cabin perhaps, or to the engine-room.

In the oily darkness below decks it was difficult at first to make things out. I could see the shapes of two bulky engines amidships, and beyond them a small door with a brass handle. I tried to open it, but it was locked firmly. I turned the handle again and shook it. I put my shoulder to the door and pushed. It wouldn't give. Only then did it occur to me that I was trespassing, and more serious still, that I could be caught trespassing.

The boat breathed and groaned around me like a living thing, as if she knew I was an intruder and was telling me exactly what she thought of me. My eyes were becoming more accustomed to the dark now, and I saw to my left, down a small flight of steps, what looked like a ship's galley – a small sink, a worktop, a gas ring. There was a bottle of washing-up liquid on the shelf, and a couple of saucepans and a frying-pan hanging up on hooks above the sink. Everything was very tidy and in its place.

I was reaching out to try the tap, to see if it worked, when I heard a footfall on the deck right above my head.

'Come on up, whoever you are.' A man's voice and it was not friendly. 'I know you're down there.' I thought of hiding down there in the dark, but I knew there was no point. I had nowhere to run to. Sooner or later he'd find me. I had no choice. I climbed up into the glare of the daylight.

He had a sailor's peaked cap on the back of his head and wore a navy blue sweater that was full of holes. He was pointing his pipe at me as if it was a weapon.

'And what the blazes do you think you're doing down there?' My mind was racing. I knew how guilty I must have looked. 'Vandal, are you? One of those vandals?'

'No,' was all I could manage.

'What then? It's private property this. You can't just go snooping about on private property whenever you feel like it. All the same these days, you young ones. Think you can do what you please. Well you can't, not on my patch. I'm the lock-keeper. I look after all the canal moorings. My job. This boat belongs to a friend of mine, and a good friend too. Done it up himself. Pride and joy of his life it is.'

'My grandad,' I said. Gulls screamed overhead and suddenly I could see how it all fitted. 'He's my grandad.' Everything Popsicle had said all along had been true. He *could* see the water from his windows. There *were* ducks on the canal, and gulls *were* always screaming around his house. His house *was* the boat, and the boat *was* called the *Lucie Alice*, all just as he'd said.

'This grandad of yours,' the lock-keeper went on, and I could tell from his tone he didn't believe me, 'what's his name then?'

'Stevens. Same name as me. But we call him Popsicle. Everyone does.' He seemed taken aback, disappointed almost. I went on: 'And he's got long, yellow hair and it's tied back in a ponytail.' The lock-keeper took a moment or two to recover.

'He really is your grandad then?' I nodded. 'Didn't know he had any family. Is he all right? I haven't seen him down here for ages. Must be a couple of months now at least. I know he's always going off on his wanders; but he's been gone a long time. I was getting worried.'

'He's been ill. He's been staying with us,' I said.

'Not serious, is it?'

'No, he's better now, thanks. Trouble is . . .' I said, inventing hard as I went along. 'He wants me to fetch some things from the boat for him. But he never told me where he keeps the key to the cabin. It's locked.'

The lock-keeper smiled at me, and I knew then that I'd won him over. 'That's easy; and what with you being his relation, like you say, I don't suppose he'd mind me telling you, would he? In the galley. He keeps it in the tea-tin under the sink. You tell him Sam sends his best, will you?'

'You're Sam?' I asked.

'That's me,' he said. 'He's told you about me, has he?'

So this was the friend Popsicle had spoken of, the friend whose brother had been taken off up to Shangri-La, never to come out again.

'Popsicle, he'll be coming back soon, will he?' said the lock-keeper.

'Very soon,' I replied.

'Good,' he said. 'You take care now.' And he was gone.

I found the key in the tea-tin just where he'd said. The cabin door unlocked easily and I stepped inside. It was a whole house in one long room. The floor was strewn with overlapping rugs, all of them threadbare. His bed was at the far end, a radio on his bedside table. There were three armchairs grouped under a single oil-lamp which hung from the ceiling in the middle of the cabin, and the walls were stacked high with books all around. Huge though the cabin was – the full width of the lifeboat and half its entire length I guessed – it was somehow still snug and homely.

To one side of me was a writing-desk covered with charts, a pair of binoculars and a photograph in a frame. I walked round the desk and sat down. I noticed then that not all of the books were in English. Some were in French. On every ledge and shelf where there weren't books, there were models of ships: fishing smacks, clippers, super-tankers and dozens of different yachts. Across the cabin, opposite me was a workbench under the roof light. An unfinished model of what looked like a warship lay on its side, a chisel nearby, and a squeezed-out tube of glue; and there were pieces of used sandpaper scattered all over the place.

I turned the photograph into the light so I could see it better. It was of my father. It was a photo with his printed signature on it, the one he gives away to his fans when they write in. I didn't like him smiling at me, so I looked away. That was when I first noticed the wall behind Popsicle's bed, in the darkest corner of the cabin. It was covered with a collage of newspaper cuttings. I knelt up on the bed to get a closer look. The biggest cutting was a photograph of a beach, a wide beach stretching away into the distance, with high dunes behind and plumes of black smoke rising from a town in the background. In the foreground there were long lines of men in the sea, soldiers in helmets, some with rifles held above their heads. Another photograph was of a lifeboat crammed from end to end with soldiers, a lifeboat with a funnel amidships and a bow that rose vertically from the water.

The headline above it read: *Dunkirk. Lowestoft lifeboat rescues hundreds.* I could just about read the story below:

> *The* Michael Hardy *of Lowestoft was one of sixteen lifeboats that took part in the recent heroic evacuation of the British Expeditionary Force from Dunkirk.*

Along with hundreds of other small ships, she went in and took the troops off the beaches, ferrying them to bigger ships standing offshore outside the harbour. Bombed and strafed continuously, the Michael Hardy *went back and forth for two nights and two days. She was twice rammed in the darkness by German motor torpedo boats but returned under her own steam to Lowestoft, her brave work accomplished.*

There were several more articles like it, all with photographs. Some were of ships sinking, some of soldiers trooping wearily off ships. Others were of soldiers with their hands on their heads being marched away into captivity. Then I saw, right in the middle of this collage of war, a tiny sepia photograph – the only one that wasn't a newspaper photograph – of a young woman standing in front of a town house. She was laughing into the camera. She was pushing her hair back out of her eyes. I unpinned it and took it to the light. Something was written on the back of it. *Lucie Alice. Dunkerque 1940. Pour toujours.* The writing was faded but just legible.

I sat for a long time in the half dark of the cabin with the photograph of Lucie Alice on Popsicle's desk in front of me, trying to make sense of it all. By the time I left, taking with me the photo of Lucie Alice and one of the newspaper cuttings, both pressed flat inside my English book, I had solved very little. This lifeboat, the one I was on, had been at Dunkirk – that was very evident. It looked exactly the same as the one in the newspaper cuttings. Then she had been called the *Michael Hardy*, and now she was the *Lucie Alice*, no doubt after the girl in the photo. But why the change? I stood on the towpath and looked up at the lifeboat. She was massive – I wondered how many soldiers she had carried out at a time, 200? 300? Popsicle must have been there. Had he been one of the soldiers rescued from the beaches perhaps? Or had he been a sailor on the *Michael Hardy*? And who was this Lucie Alice anyway? What did *pour toujours* mean? Was it Lucie Alice who had taught him French? Was that how Popsicle knew so much French?

As I walked home in the drizzle, my head reeling with unanswered questions, it occurred to me that, for the moment at least, I probably knew more about Popsicle's past than he did.

I was home late, very late. They'd both been out of their minds with worry, they told me. They had been ringing everywhere to find out where I was. 'I've just been for a walk,' I said. 'That's all.'

'That's all!' My father lost all patience. He glared at

me for a while, and then stormed out, leaving me with my mother in the kitchen.

'Why do you do these things, Cessie?' she said, shaking her head sadly. 'No one minds you going out for a walk, but you should've told us.'

'Like you told me about sending Popsicle to Shangri-La, I suppose,' I retorted.

I could see that she too was at the end of her tether. 'That was different. You know it was. I can't talk to you when you're like this. I've got some marking to do.'

I helped myself to a yoghurt from the fridge and sat down to think things through. I couldn't just leave it until visiting day the next Saturday to tell Popsicle of my discovery. The sooner he knew I'd found the *Lucie Alice*, the sooner he saw the photograph of Lucie Alice and the newspaper cutting, the sooner he might remember the rest. And, besides, I was burning to tell him. Perhaps, with these new pieces of the jigsaw puzzle in place, he might be able to put the whole picture together at last. I would cut school tomorrow and go up to Shangri-La. I'd forge a sick note and take it in the following day. Other people had done it and got away with it. No one would find out, not if I was careful. And I would be very careful.

Playing truant was not nearly as easy as I had

imagined. I left home at the normal time. That was a mistake for a start. I had planned to double back, wait for my mother and father to leave, take my bicycle from the garage and cycle up to Shangri-La. But I had forgotten something: on the way to school in the mornings, you were never alone, you were always one of a crowd.

Mandy Bethel was there, as usual. So were all the Martins from across the road, and then Shirley Watson and a dozen others joined us too. We were all of us walking to school, not necessarily together, but we were all going the same way. I couldn't just double back, not without questions being asked anyway.

I was almost at the park gates before I finally worked out something that had a chance of being believed. I stopped dead and pretended to search frantically in my bag. As she came past, Shirley Watson asked just the right question.

'Forgotten something?' She stopped beside me.

'Maths homework,' I replied.

'It *was* the same one, wasn't it?' she asked.

'What?' I couldn't think what she was talking about.

'That boat, that old boat on the canal.'

'Oh, that . . . Yes . . . Thanks . . . I'd better go back home and fetch it . . . I'll catch you up.' I ran off back across the road and into the estate without ever once looking behind me. I wasn't sure I'd been entirely convincing, but at least I'd got away.

I skulked in a bus shelter for a while, just until I was quite sure the house would be empty, and it was just as well I did. I'd been there only a few minutes when I saw my mother coming along the road in her car. I looked the other way hard, and hoped. Fortunately, she went by without seeing me. At least now I knew the coast was clear.

After that it was plain-sailing, except that the hill up to Shangri-La seemed a lot steeper and a lot longer than before. In the end I had to get off and walk, which was just as well because it gave me time to think. I couldn't just walk in there and announce that I wanted to see Popsicle. That Mrs Davidson, the Dragonwoman, would be bound to ask searching questions. I was in school uniform. Why wasn't I at school? I was alone. Where were my parents? At all costs I was going to have to avoid the Dragonwoman.

I left my bicycle hidden deep in the rhododendron bushes beside the drive, and then crawled the rest of the way through the undergrowth, until I was as close to the house as I dared. A white minibus was parked outside the pillared porch. I could just make out the writing on its side, in large pink lettering: 'Shangri-La. Residential Nursing Home'. I thought of making a dash for it, across the drive to the dayroom window overlooking the front lawn. It wasn't far, but I just couldn't summon up the courage to do it. I could see people moving about inside the house, but they were too far away, too shadowy for me to be able to identify any of them as Popsicle.

Then I had a stroke of luck. I'd been sitting there in the bushes for some time, wracked by indecision, hugging myself against the cold of the wind and with terrible pins and needles in my legs, when the front door opened. It was Harry, in his wheelchair. He was wheeling himself out from the shadow of the porch towards the rose garden on the other side of the drive from me. He had some kind of basket on his lap, a gardening trug perhaps. It crossed my mind that this might be the moment to make my move. The front door was open and inviting, and Harry would know where Popsicle was. It was a very good thing that caution got the better of me.

Suddenly Mrs Davidson was at the door and shouting after him. 'Half an hour only, Mr Mason. Do you hear me?'

Harry ignored her and went on wheeling.

The front door closed. Harry was bumping himself up on to the lawn. He reached the rose garden, took a pair of secateurs out of his trug and began clipping. I watched him, cowering in the undergrowth, and wondered what to do next.

'Cessie!' He wasn't looking at me, but it was Harry's voice – I was sure of it. 'Cessie! Don't say anything, and whatever you do, don't move. If I spotted you, then she could too. If you want to play hide-and-seek in dark green bushes then you shouldn't go wearing a red blazer – if you understand my meaning. I don't know what you're up to, young lady, but my guess is you've bunked off school to come and see your Popsicle. That right? Well you can't, not this morning. He didn't like the scrambled egg at breakfast, and he said so. She didn't like that, so she's gated him. He's got to stay in his room till lunch.'

'But I must see him. I've got something for him,' I said. 'It's important. It's really important.'

'All right, Cessie. Here's what I'm going to do. I'll clip off a few more of these deadheads, then I'll come over your side of the drive and park myself as close as I can. Give me a few moments. But don't move. Don't move a muscle.'

He clipped a last deadhead, glanced up casually at

127

the house, and then came wheeling across the drive towards me. There was a single rosebush in the centre of a small flower-bed. He stopped beside it with his back to me, so that he was between me and the house, and put his brake on. Then he reached out, caught a bloom between his fingers and pulled it gently to his nose.

'Old Velvet Tuscany,' he said, sniffing deeply and savouring it. 'Lovely old-fashioned rose. Scent of paradise. Beautiful. All right, so what do you want me to do then?'

'Tell him,' I was speaking as loudly as I dared. 'Tell Popsicle I've found his boat, I've found his home. It's down on the canal, by the barges. I've been there. And it *is* called the *Lucie Alice*, just like he said it was. And I found things, all sorts of things, photos, newspaper cuttings, all about the war, about the boat. I've got one or two of them with me. If he sees them, then maybe it'll help him remember. He fell over. He hit his head, lost his memory. But it's coming back, and this'll help, I know it will.'

'He's told us, Cessie,' Harry said. 'He told us everything, everything he can remember, that is. He'll be happy as pie about this, over the moon. Be a real fillip. It gets him down a bit sometimes, you know, when he can't remember. Thinks he's going barmy, round the twist; but he isn't, not our Popsicle. Don't you worry, Cessie, he's amongst friends up here. We've most of us got dicky memories, including me. Popsicle's no nutter. The Dragonwoman thinks he is, of course, but then she thinks we're all nutters. Where are the photos then?'

'In my bag. In my English book.'

'Now listen, Cessie, and listen good. You put it down, right where you are, and then get out of here, quick, before anyone spots you. I'll see he gets it, don't you worry.' I took out my English book and checked the cutting and the photo were still there. They were. I left it on the ground under the rhododendrons, backed away slowly on my hands and knees, retrieved my bicycle, jumped on, and made off like a bat out of hell.

For the rest of the day I loafed about the house behind closed curtains, worrying that some busybody might have seen me coming home from school in the morning, that someone might say something to my mother. I thought of playing my violin, but I couldn't, in case I was heard. In the end I went up to my room and finished my maths homework, and then read my book – *Animal Farm* it was.

When my mother came in, I played the exhausted schoolgirl and complained, bitterly and very convincingly I thought, about all the homework I'd been given that

129

day. She wasn't at all sympathetic, but then I didn't expect her to be. I wasn't exactly in her good books. 'Then you'd better get on with it, hadn't you?' she said.

So it was that I found myself up in my room again doing more homework, or pretending to. I was still there when I heard my father come home. I didn't go down. I heard their confidential murmuring downstairs in the kitchen. They'd be talking about me, I was sure of it. I knelt down and put my ear to the floor. I was right.

'She'll get over it in time,' my mother was saying. 'You've got to remember, she's twelve; and believe you me, that's an awkward age for any girl. All right, so she's being a pain, a real pain; but when all's said and done, you can't blame her.'

'So you're blaming me then, I suppose?'

'No, I'm not blaming you either, nor Popsicle, nor anyone. We took a decision that was maybe the most difficult decision we've ever had to take. You didn't enjoy sending your father up there to that place, and neither did I. But it was the only thing we could do. You know something, Arthur? I hate myself for what we've done, and what's more I think you do too. And if we hate ourselves for sending him off to that place like we did, then we can hardly blame her for hating us too, can we? She loves that old man, and we sent him away. For God's sake, how do you expect her to feel?'

The doorbell rang. I heard my father leave the kitchen and go out into the hallway. I crept out on to the landing so that I could hear better. The door opened.

'Yes?' my father was saying.

'Is Cessie in?' It was Shirley Watson. She'd never ever called at my place before.

'She's upstairs.' My mother's voice.

'So she's all right then?'

'Yes, of course. Why do you ask?'

'Well . . .' Shirley began, and a cold shiver went up my spine. I knew already what she was about to say. 'Well, it's just that we were on our way to school this morning, and she forgot her homework and she went back to fetch it, and then she never came to school. I looked for her everywhere. Thought something might have happened to her that's all, but if she's here . . .' She knew then that she'd dropped me in it. To be fair to her, she did try to put it right, but it was too late. 'Well, maybe . . . maybe she wasn't feeling well or something.'

'Probably,' said my father, and I could sense the fury in him rising already.

'That's all right then,' said Shirley Watson. 'I'd better be going. I'll see her tomorrow. Bye.' The door closed.

'Cessie!' my father bellowed up the stairs. 'Get down here this minute. This minute!'

I appeared at the top of the stairs and came down slowly. I had no wish to hurry. They stood there in the hallway watching me. They waited until I was halfway down, until I was in range, before they began.

'How could you, Cessie?' said my mother. She was going to try the patient teacher approach. 'Where were you? Why? Why would you do such a thing?' I stayed inside myself, behind my wall of defiance. I would offer no explanations, no apologies, nothing.

'You go on like this, Cessie.' It was my father this time, stabbing his finger at me and fast losing all control. 'You go on like this and we're going to have to take steps, d'you hear me?' How could I not? He was shouting at the top of his voice, not two metres away.

'Leave it, Arthur,' my mother was trying again. 'I'll talk to her. Just leave it to me.' She came towards me. 'Is it something at school, Cessie? Are you in trouble? Has someone been bullying you, is that it?' She put her hand on mine on the banister. I pulled my hand away. 'This isn't like you, Cessie. How can we help you if we don't know what the problem is?' She looked deep into me and I did not flinch from her gaze. 'It isn't school at all, is it? This is a protest for Popsicle, isn't it? You stayed away from school to get back at us, didn't you? That's it, isn't it?'

My father was about to wade in again, but the phone rang and cut him off short. My mother picked it up. 'Mrs Davidson . . .?' The Dragonwoman. She'd seen me up at Shangri-La and was reporting it. I sat down on the stairs and prepared myself for the worst. 'When was this?' my mother was asking.

'What is it?' my father tried to interrupt. She shushed him, but he went on in spite of her. 'Is he all right? Is he ill?'

She put her hand over the mouthpiece and shook her head. 'No, it's not that. He's gone missing. Popsicle's gone missing. They haven't seen him since just after lunch. No one has. They've looked everywhere.'

Not quite everywhere, I thought, trying to hide my joy as best I could. Not quite everywhere.

10 DUNKIRK

THEY WERE GOING UP TO SHANGRI-LA RIGHT AWAY, they said, to see Mrs Davidson. I was to stay behind just in case Popsicle decided to come home in the meantime, and I had to be sure to call them at Shangri-La if he did. They were full of last-minute panicky instructions as they went out of the door. I looked suitably concerned and nodded away, willing them to be gone.

I waited only till I saw the tail-lights of the car disappear round the corner. Then I was out of the house and away on my bicycle, head down and pedalling like a mad thing towards the canal. I ran into traffic jams, but I managed to keep moving, weaving in and out of the cars, cutting across carparks. Then at long last I was clear of the traffic and bowling along under the prison walls, the canal running darkly across the other side of the road. I always hated going past the prison, especially in the evening. The whole place glowered at me, but it gave me an even greater incentive to pedal harder. I never stopped the whole way, not once.

From the lock gates I could see there was a light in Popsicle's boat. He was there, and as I cycled along the towpath past the barges, I was sure that he knew I was coming, that he would be waiting for me. I'd barely set foot on the gangplank when I heard him calling out to me.

'Cessie? Is that you? Come aboard. Come aboard.'

I found him down below in the glow of his cabin, lying on his bed, and grinning like the Cheshire cat. He was propped up on a pile of cushions, with his knees drawn up in front of him. His shoes were off and he wore no socks. He was wriggling his toes at me.

'Long walk. My feet are killing me.' He had a tin in his hand. I knew at once it had to be condensed milk. He held it up. 'Remember this, Cessie?' He swung his legs off the bed, stood up and came towards me. 'Well, what do you think of the old *Lucie Alice*? Isn't she the most beautiful thing you ever saw? And she's not just pretty either. Two forty-horsepower diesel engines. You can hardly hear yourself thinking when she's at full throttle. Eight and a half knots, two hundred miles without refuelling, and – unlike yours – she's quite unsinkable.' He was close to me now, his hands on my shoulders, and his eyes were burning bright into mine.

'Thanks to you, Cessie, I know it all now. It's all here, in this boat, all around me, and you found her for me, Cessie. I got your school book. Harry said it was important, and it was too.' I looked down and saw my English book lying open beside the half-finished model of the battleship. 'Lucie Alice . . . Dunkirk,' he went on. 'You gave it all back to me, Cessie; but this old tin helped a bit, I'm sure of it. You can smile, but it was like Popeye with his spinach. Like a flood it was, Cessie. The moment I lay there on that bed and tasted it, all the memories came flooding through me. I'm telling you, Cessie, I was dizzy with it.'

He picked up another tin from the desk behind him. 'Here,' he said. 'I've got dozens more in the cupboard. You can have a whole tin to yourself, if you like. You've had it before, have you? You turned your nose up at it, if I remember rightly. One taste and you won't put it down. Guaranteed.' And he stabbed two holes in it with his knife, settled me down in one of the big armchairs in the middle of the cabin, and sat himself down opposite me.

I had never tasted anything so sickly sweet, nor so

completely and overwhelmingly delicious.

'They'll be out looking for you, you know,' I said.

'Well, they won't find us here, will they? You haven't said anything, have you?' I shook my head, and sucked in another mouthful of condensed milk.

Then I asked the one question I'd been longing to ask him: 'Who's Lucie Alice, the girl in the photo?'

It was some time before he replied. 'Well, after all you've done for me, Cessie, if anyone's got a right to know, then you have. I'm warning you before I start, there's things I'm going to tell you you'll find hard to believe. But it'll all be true, true as I'm sitting here. You keep knocking back your condensed milk and I'll tell you the lot, beginning to end.'

He took a deep breath, and then he began.

'I don't rightly know where I was born, Cessie. Never knew who my mother was, nor my father. So that bit's easy. First thing I remember was the house in Lowestoft. Barnardo's home it was – fifteen, maybe twenty of us. And it was all right too. I wasn't miserable, nothing like that. If you don't have a proper family in the first place, then you can't miss them, can you? I'm afraid I was a bit of a tearaway as a young lad, always in trouble: bunking off school, scrumping for apples, and poaching too – rabbits, pheasants, trout – whatever I could find. Time and again I'd get myself caught, and of course I'd get a good wigging for my trouble. Didn't stop me. Never seemed to learn my lesson somehow.

'You could see the sea from my bedroom window, and I never wanted to be away from it. All I wanted to do when I grew up was go to sea. And do you know why? It wasn't just the beauty of it, nor the wildness of it. It wasn't the salt on your lips, or the shrieking of the gulls, not for me. It was the boats, and one boat in particular – the Lowestoft lifeboat. To watch that lifeboat shooting down the slipway and go plunging into the sea, to see her ploughing her way out into the waves – it's all I lived for. Nothing like it, nothing in all the world. Whenever she went out, all weathers, I'd be there, down on the beach waiting for them to come back. And afterwards, I'd follow the crew through the streets, as they walked up to the pub. I'd be outside the window listening to their talk. All I wanted as a lad was to be near them, to be like them, to be one of them.

'I was fifteen years old, big for my age and strong too. I was out there, along with half the town, when the new lifeboat was launched. Forty-six foot, Watson cabin-type, she was; bright yellow funnel, shining blue with a red stripe round the gunwales. I never saw anything so beautiful in all my life.

'Later that day, I was walking round her in the shed at the top of the slipway, stroking her from end to end, when I first saw her name: *Michael Hardy*. Now I don't know who gave me my name when I was little, but all my life I'd been called Michael, Michael Stevens. And here was this lifeboat with half my own name on her. Silly, maybe, but I knew then that it was a meant thing with me and the *Michael Hardy*, that we belonged together. One day I would be a lifeboatman in that boat. I would pull on the blue jersey and the yellow oilskins. I would climb up into that boat and go roaring down the slipway. I would go to sea in her and save lives. So I went right up to the coxswain – I can't remember his name now, a great big bearded fellow – I walked right up to him next day in the town and I asked him, point blank. He laughed, and shook his head. "You're far too young," he says. "Come back in a couple of years," he says. I'll tell you, Cessie, I went away and I cried like a baby.

'By now everyone was talking about the war they knew was coming, but all I could think about was how they wouldn't let me join the crew of the *Michael Hardy*. I mooched about the beach all that summer. Every time I saw the lifeboat go down the slipway it was just more salt in the wound.'

The boat creaked above our heads and Popsicle looked up and smiled. 'I swear she talks to me sometimes. She listens too. The things she's seen in her time. The things she's heard. You know about Dunkirk, d'you?'

'Not much,' I said.

'And why should you? Long time ago, all of it. Summer of 1940, and there was a right old mess going on over there in France. The German army was knocking all hell out of everyone. They pushed the whole jolly lot of us back to the sea at Dunkirk: British, French, Belgians, all sorts. There were 250,000 men on the beaches of Northern France that had to be fetched back home; the whole army, or what was left of it. It was all on the radio, in the papers too. Next thing I heard, the navy were in Lowestoft, looking for all the boats they could find to bring the boys back home off the beaches. They were going to take the *Michael Hardy* over to Dunkirk. Well, I wasn't going to miss out on that, was I?

'No one was looking for stowaways, so it was easy enough. I crept on board the night before and found myself a hiding-place in the locker right under the bow, just about where my bed is now. I was too cold to sleep, too excited. Next morning there was a lot of stamping about and shouting up on deck. Then we were thundering down the slipway. We hit the sea with a great crash – it fairly shook me up, I can tell you. I thought I had broken every bone in my body. I remember the engines were pounding, and I was sick, sick as a dog with all the pitching and rolling. And it was cold, Cessie, bitter cold down there, and dark too. Never been so cold in all my life. I couldn't feel my feet at all. But honest to God, I'd never been so happy. I was at sea at last, in a lifeboat, in the *Michael Hardy*.

'I can't be sure, but I think I was more than a day down there in that locker before they found me. And do you know how they found me? I sneezed. They found me because I sneezed. I was hauled up on deck to explain myself. The officer wasn't best pleased, I can tell you. But what could he do? We were in the middle of the English Channel and the weather was blowing up a gale. He could hardly have me chucked overboard, could he? So he just gave me a right rollicking and sent me down to the galley to brew up the tea.

'Pretty soon after that they were all far too busy to bother with me anyway. There were fighter planes, Stukas, Messerschmitts, all diving at us out of nowhere; and ahead of us were great plumes of black smoke along the coast as if the whole place was on fire. And the little ships. All shapes and sizes. Hundreds of them, all ferrying the soldiers from the beaches to the Navy ships standing offshore. We waited until nightfall and then we went in close, into the harbour – or what was left of it. The whole sky was red with fire.

'We heard the soldiers first, and then we saw them. Lines and lines of them waist high, shoulder high in the water, helmets askew, rifles held over their heads. They were shouting at us, and some of them were crying. First time I'd ever seen grown men cry. They were grabbing at the ropes and we were hauling them on board. And off we went packed to the gunwales. You couldn't move for soldiers.

'Awful terrible wounds they had, some of them; and they were sea-sick too. Poor blighters. It doesn't bear thinking about. Terrified they were, some of them. And I was too. We were all frightened. I mean you couldn't not be. You could see the sea on fire where a ship had gone down, and there were men in the water screaming, and the shells kept coming and coming; and you knew that sooner or later one of them had to hit you.

'We'd done a couple of trips to and from the beaches when it happened. I was sitting high up on the bow of the boat, a crowd of soldiers all round me, when I saw this shape come towards us out of the darkness. It took me a few seconds before I realised it was a boat, and a few more before I saw that it was coming straight for us. She rammed us amidships and I was knocked right over the side and into the cold of the sea. Down I went. I never thought I'd come up, but I did. I was kicking and screaming for all I was worth, but it didn't do me any good. I just sank again like a stone.'

'Couldn't you swim?' I asked.

'Still can't,' said Popsicle, shaking his head. 'Isn't that mad? I've spent all my silly life on boats, and I still can't swim. So, anyway, I thought I was going to drown for certain; but suddenly there were arms round me and lifting me, and at last I was breathing blessed air again. It was one of the soldiers. He still had his tin hat on too. I remember that. "Hang on," he says. And I did, for dear life. He swum me ashore and we staggered up the sand and into the dunes.

'Of course we didn't sleep a wink. We were wet through to the skin, and freezing. The shelling never stopped all night long. Not a night I'd care to live through again, I can tell you.

'He was a nice young fellow, the one who pulled me out. We got chatting, the two of us. He'd only been in the army a few months, he said, and he'd done nothing but retreat the whole time. I told him about how I'd stowed away on the *Michael Hardy*. "Well," he says, "you'd better find yourself a uniform, and be quick about it; because if we don't get off the beaches and the Germans catch us, then they'll think you're a spy and they'll shoot you for certain." Do you know what he did? He took off his battledress top and gave it to me, there and then. "Here," he says. "You'd best have this, just in case. About the same size, we are." And it was true, too. Him and me, like two peas in a pod. So I put it on.

'Five minutes later, that's all, and we were sitting there side by side shivering in the dunes, when the fighters came back, strafing and bombing all along the beach. Everyone was running for it; but there was nowhere to run to, I could see that. The soldier and me, we just stayed where we were and flattened ourselves in the sand. The ground shook, like an earthquake it was, and the sand showered down on us. I thought it would never stop. There was a horrible silence after that. Then I heard the crying and the moaning. I felt blood on my face, warm blood. I knew I'd been hit in the head. There wasn't much pain, but my head was spinning. I seemed to be floating, almost like I was in the sea, and it was getting darker all around me, darker than it should have been. I remember the soldier's eyes were open in the darkness. They were looking straight at me, but he wasn't seeing me. I knew he was dead. I knew then that I would soon be dead, just like he was. I was sure of it. I wasn't frightened any more. Funny that.

'I woke up and there were gulls flying overhead, screeching just like they did at home. I thought for a moment I was back home in Lowestoft. I really did. But not for long. I sat up and looked around me. The tide was up. There was no more shelling. It was quiet, like the quiet after a storm. The place was littered with trucks, jeeps, guns – some still burning – and there were bodies, everywhere bodies lying on the sand. One of the soldiers rolled over in the shallows, and he seemed for a moment to be alive. He wasn't. No one was, except me. The armada of little ships was gone, except for the wrecks left behind out at sea – or beached – and there were dozens of them, dozens. The soldier who had saved me was still looking at me. I had to get away.

'I got to my feet and climbed up over the dunes. No one was moving in the town. Everyone was dead, or everyone was gone – that's what it felt like anyway. I wandered up into the smoking ruins of the town, not knowing where I was going nor why. I suppose I was just looking for someone who was alive, anyone. My legs wouldn't work like they should and I kept reeling and stumbling up against the walls of the houses. Then they just gave way completely, and I found myself sitting down in the doorway of a house and I couldn't move any more. I heard a sort of rumbling and a rattling, and it was coming closer and getting louder all the time.

'Suddenly the door opened behind me and I was dragged in off the street. I found myself in a darkened room and there was this lady standing over me, her finger to her lips. She didn't want me to talk. So I didn't. She was peeping out through the closed shutters. I crawled over to have a look. Tanks, and there were soldiers behind them, German soldiers, hundreds of them.

'That poor woman, she had to drag me all the way up the stairs. I couldn't help myself much. By the time we got to the top I knew there were two of them, one had me by the legs, the other had her arms under my shoulders. They took me into a bedroom and I thought they'd put me on the bed, but they didn't. They put me in a clothes cupboard instead, a great big thing it was and it smelled of mothballs. They turned out to be mother and daughter, and they looked like it too. Same dark hair, pale skin. They were terrified, just like I was. But the young one, she gave me a smile, the sort of smile that said it was going to be all right. "Lucie Alice," she whispered, "*Je suis Lucie Alice*." Then she closed the cupboard door and I was left in the darkness lying at the bottom of that musty old cupboard, the clothes dangling all around my face.'

Popsicle's voice was faltering now as he went on. 'The things they did for me, those two. Patched me up, fed me, cared for me, just like I was their family. No one ever treated me like that before, not in my whole life. For days and days, they let me out only for five minutes at a time, to stretch my legs, go to the toilet – that sort of thing. I knew why, of course. I could hear the soldiers, plain enough, just outside, down in the street. I had to stay in the cupboard, and I wasn't ever to come out unless they said so. I did as I was told and stayed put, and it was just as well I did too. They came looking. One evening it was. I was half asleep in the bottom of my cupboard. I heard them coming up the stairs and into the room, stamping around in their boots. I curled myself up tight under the clothes, closed my eyes, and stopped breathing. They opened the cupboard door too, had a look, but they never moved the clothes, so they never found me. But if they had . . .

'You've got to remember, Cessie, that if they'd found me they'd have shot the two of them for sure. That's something, eh? They did that for me, and they didn't even know me. After the house had been searched that time, they reckoned it was safer. So they let me out of my cupboard a bit more often, and for longer too; but I still had to stay in my room and stay away from the window. I was never to open the shutters, Lucie Alice told me, never to look out of the window.

'Of course, I couldn't understand much of what they were saying, not to start with; but I got the gist of it all right. They were going to find a way to get me out and back home to England. But it would take time. I had to be patient. I didn't mind waiting, I can tell you. The more I saw of Lucie Alice, the less I wanted to go home anyway. She'd come to my room often, and not only to bring me my meals either. She did most of the talking, and every day I understood better and better what she was saying.

'We only had a month together, Cessie, but I loved that girl. I really loved her.' He picked up the photograph. 'She gave me this. "So you won't forget me," she said. See what she wrote on the back? *"Pour toujours."* Means "For ever". And she meant it too, I know she did.' He turned the photograph over in his hand. 'Great brown eyes she had, Cessie, and her hair . . . I never touched anyone else's hair before hers. Soft as air.' It was a moment or two before he was able to go on.

148

'She kept warning me and warning me to stay in the cupboard, just in case. But I hated it in that cupboard, Cessie. I couldn't stand being shut up; and, besides, I couldn't read my book in there. I had this book of poems called *The Golden Treasury*. I'd found it in the pocket of that soldier's battledress. Bit wrinkled with the damp it was, but you could read it, just about. First time I'd ever read any poems. Wonderful they were. Wonderful. So anyway, from time to time, I'd come out of my cupboard and read my poems. I'd read them out loud too, and learn them off by heart. One morning I was on my own in the house and I'd been reading a few of my poems. Maybe I was feeling a bit restless. I don't know. But I did what Lucie Alice always told me not to do – I went to the window. I thought it was safe enough. I couldn't see anyone down in the street, so I opened the shutter just a little and peeked out.

'I hadn't noticed the soldier. He was standing just across the street from me, under the lamppost, and he was smoking. He was blowing smoke rings in the air and watching them float away up towards me. Our eyes met just for a moment, but that was all it took. Before I even reached my cupboard I heard the street door crash open and boots pounding up the stairs. I had the cupboard door almost closed, but I was too late. He wrenched it out of my hand and there I was crouching in amongst the clothes, and he was smiling down at me like a cat that's got a mouse. Then there were other soldiers in the room. They hauled me out and I was marched off down the street with my hands in the air, a rifle jabbing into my back. We'd just turned the corner into the wide road along the seafront, when I saw Lucie Alice coming towards us on the same pavement, a loaf of bread under her arm. We both knew there mustn't be a flicker of recognition between us. That was the last I ever saw of her.

'I always kept her photo in my book of poems. When they searched me they found the book, of course, and the photo of Lucie Alice inside, but they never took much notice of it. They must've thought it was my girl back home. They let me keep my book of poems and the photo too.

'I spent a few uncomfortable nights in a prison cell, with a few other soldiers they'd rounded up. They questioned me over and over again about the people who had hidden me, but I just played dumb and shrugged my way through it. I kept saying I didn't know who they were, nor anything about them. In the end, I think they believed me. "We'll find them anyway. We know their names. They can't run for ever," said the officer. "And when we do, we'll put them up against a wall and shoot them." Then he wished me a happy war in my prison camp and packed me off with the others in a lorry to Germany.'

I was so wrapped up in his story that I had quite forgotten my condensed milk. I remembered now. I sucked in another mouthful and waited for him to begin again.

'Prison camp was all boredom, cabbagey old soup, black bread and boredom. And the winters were cold, Cessie, so cold you couldn't sleep. Still, I had my *Golden Treasury* and my photo of Lucie Alice. That was something. Worst of all was not knowing all that time about what had happened to Lucie Alice and her mother. I wanted to write to them, but I couldn't, could I? I didn't want to give them away. They'd read your letters, everything you wrote. There were so many things I hated about that place: the locked doors at night, the searchlights, and the dogs and the wire all around us; and always these little Hitlers bawling at us, telling us what to do, what not to do. I'd look at the birds, Cessie. I'd watch them take off and fly out over the wire, go wherever they wanted. And I'd look out of the window of my hut sometimes, and I'd think those are the same stars they're looking at back in Lowestoft, the same stars Lucie Alice is looking at, if she's still alive. I never stopped thinking about her.

'I taught myself French. It was hard at first, but I had a pal in the camp who knew a bit of French, and he gave me a hand. We got hold of all the French books we could – you can learn an awful lot in five years if you haven't got much else to do. And I wanted to learn because I wanted to be able to talk her language when I got out, when the war was over.

'The best thing of all though wasn't the French lessons, it was the Red Cross parcels. It was like Christmas every time they came.' He held up his tin of condensed milk. 'That's when I first tasted this – out of a Red Cross parcel in the camp.

'Those five years behind the wire were like a lifetime. Then one morning we woke up and the guards were gone. The gates were open and there were American soldiers marching down the road towards the camp! It was all over and done with. I was twenty-one years old and there was only one thing I was sure about – I was never ever going to allow myself to be shut up again. The war ended soon after and I was sent back home to England.

'I wrote to Lucie Alice, telling what had happened, asking how she was, thanking her and her mother for all they'd done for me. I told her I still loved her and I always would. I even asked her to marry me. But she never wrote back. I wrote again and again. No reply. Then one of the letters was sent back. "Not known", it said on the envelope. After that, I'll be honest with you, I tried to put her out of my mind. If she was dead, it had been my fault. Then I met your grandmother, and things took another turn.

'I'd found a job boatbuilding in Hull, and I was delivering a fishing boat from Hull down to Bradwell. I liked the place, liked the people. There was a job in a small boatyard, and so I stayed. Then one evening I bumped into Cecilia down on the quay. She was looking at the sunset and I was looking at her. Pretty as a picture, she was. Six months later we were married. We found a place to live, and then little Arthur comes along. The boatbuilding business wasn't going that well. I did a bit of fishing too on the side to make ends meet. Things weren't easy, but we were doing all right, I thought, making a living of sorts.'

For a few moments Popsicle said nothing more. I thought he'd finished, but then he went on. 'The truth is, Cessie, I should never have done what I did. I should never have got married. Sometimes I think I only did it to make myself forget Lucie Alice, and that wasn't fair on your grandmother. We were never suited. She knew it. I knew it. We were just making each other more and more miserable every day. I was off drinking in the Green Man, drowning my sorrows, and she began to hate me for not loving her like I should have. I don't blame her. Then she met this other fellow, this Bill; and off she went, her and Bill and little Arthur, and that's the last I saw of them. Not exactly a happy-ever-after story, is it?'

'Not exactly,' I said. 'What about the lifeboat? You must've found it again somehow.'

'I was coming to that. After Cecilia left, and little Arthur, I never lived in a proper house again, not till I come to live with you anyway. I picked up work here and there in boatyards all over the country, and I made decent money too. But I always lived on a boat, always on the water. I moved around, became a bit of a water gypsy, I suppose. I went where the work was, wherever I felt like going. Then, maybe ten years ago, I came across this old lifeboat rotting away in a boatyard in Poole. You guessed it, it was the *Michael Hardy*. Pure luck. I'd saved a bit, over the years – nothing much to spend it on, I suppose. She was going for a song, and so I bought her. It took me five years to put her to rights, back to what she was. I only changed one thing, her name. I called her *Lucie Alice*. I don't have to tell you why, do I?'

I needed to ask something else and now seemed the right moment.

'But I still don't understand, Popsicle. Why didn't you go back to France and look for her, for Lucie Alice?'

He sighed, and then smiled sadly. 'I've been asking myself that same question, just about every day of my life, I should think. Up to now it's always been the same answer, and it's not easy to explain, Cessie. But I'll try. It's like this. Whilst I don't know what happened to her, I've got hope, some little hope that she's still alive somewhere. The chances are of course that she's been dead all these years, I know that; but if I don't know that for certain, then at least I can think of her as if she's still alive, can't I? Once I'd found out that she was dead, then it'd be the end of all my hope, wouldn't it? And let's say I did find her and she was alive after all, what would she think of me, I mean after what I'd done? I'd betrayed her, hadn't I? Her and her mother. I looked out of that window when I shouldn't have. So I'd lose both ways, wouldn't I? That's what I thought, until . . . until now that is.'

'What d'you mean?'

'Well, I was sitting here thinking, just before you

came. That little stroke I had – it was a warning, that's how I see it. It was telling me something, telling me that for better or worse, and before it's too late, I'd better go and look for Lucie Alice and find out what really did happen all those years ago. And then maybe, just maybe, I can put things right between us. I've been running away from this all my life, Cessie. Not any more. Not any more. I even know the street where she lived. It's in the photo. You've got to look carefully, but it's there.'

He showed me the photo again and, sure enough, I could just make out the street name above Lucie Alice's head: *Rue de la Paix*.

'It's not far,' Popsicle went on. 'And you never know, Cessie, I could get lucky. Maybe I'll find her. Maybe she'll still be there.'

The idea came into my head at once and I didn't hesitate. 'Can I come? Please, Popsicle, I can help. Honest I can. You'll need someone to help, won't you? I can do the mooring ropes. I can be on look-out. I can cook. Anything. Please?'

He was looking at me long and thoughtfully. 'You and me, Cessie, we think like one person sometimes, I swear we do. I was just wondering how I was going to manage the old girl all the way over to Dunkirk on my own.' He reached forward suddenly and took my hand. 'Would you do it?' he asked. 'Would you really come with me?'

'When?' I said. 'When do we go?'

'Soon as I've fixed a few things up,' he said. 'Soon as the tide's right.'

11 THE GREAT ESCAPE

AN HOUR LATER POPSICLE WAS STILL BENDING over his charts. There were tins of condensed milk all around to hold the edges down. He'd done his calcula-tions in complete silence, his brow furrowed in deep concentration.

'Almost there, Cessie,' he said at last, reaching across the table for a slim grey booklet. 'Tides,' he went on, as he searched for the right page. 'Mariner's bible, this is. You've got to know the time of the tides, high tide, low tide. You can't move unless you know that. It should be just about right Saturday next, that's what I'm hoping. One thing you've always got to remember about the sea, Cessie, is that you can only do what she'll let you do.' He found what he was looking for. 'I thought so. I thought so. Full moon Saturday night. High tide just after midnight. Perfect. Could be cloud cover, of course, but that doesn't matter. We'll have enough light to see our way out of here. We don't want it blowing a gale of course. Keep our fingers crossed, eh? With a bit of luck we'll make it in five or six hours. It's sixty-three miles to Dunkirk, less than I thought. We should be there before first light. We'll come in in the dark. Better that way. If they don't see us, then there won't be any questions, will there? And if they do see us, well then, we'll just have to talk our way out of trouble, won't we? Done it before.' He closed the book. 'So, you'll need to be here by midnight next Saturday. Are you sure you can make it?'

'Sure,' I said. But I wasn't at all sure of any of it. I only knew that I wanted to go with him. Of that I was quite sure.

'Good girl. But there's one thing you've got to do for me, and I don't want you forgetting it. I want you to leave a note for your mum and your dad. We don't want them worrying themselves to death, do we? Just tell them that you've gone off with me for a couple of days, that I'll bring you back home again soon. And whilst you're at it, tell them goodbye from me. Tell them no hard feelings. Time for me to move on, that's all.'

'What d'you mean?' I asked.

'I told you, Cessie. I can't abide being shut in – cupboards, prison camps, Shangri-La – all the same to me. I don't ever want to go back. Don't get me wrong. It's not a bad place, except for that Dragonwoman. I've got good friends up there, and I'll miss them. But it's not for me, not in a million years. No, Cessie, this is my home, this boat. Whatever happens over there in Dunkirk, whether I go barmy or not, here's where I'll end my days, on my own boat, with the sky above me and the sea all around me. It's where I belong.'

I pleaded with him even though I knew it was useless. 'But I'll tell them. I'll tell Mum and Dad what's happened, that you've remembered everything, and you're better, completely better. You'll be able to come home. They won't send you back to Shangri-La. I know they won't. I won't let them.'

He was shaking his head as I was talking. 'No, Cessie, don't you go telling them anything of the kind, anything at all come to that. And don't you go blaming them for sending me up to Shangri-La. The way I was carrying on, they had no choice. I was a liability. That's what I was, a liability. I've caused them enough trouble, enough pain.'

'But you're better,' I insisted, quite unable now to hold back my tears.

'Yes, I'm better, better than I've ever been, thanks to you – and now I'm going to do just what I should've done all those years ago. I'm going to go over there and find out what happened to Lucie Alice, and I don't want anyone trying to stop me. So we'll keep everything just between the two of us. No one else must know a thing. Promise me, Cessie.'

'Promise,' I said.

He reached forward and wiped my face with his sleeve. 'And no more tears either, Cessie. I can't cope at all if you do that.' I did what I could to sniff them back. 'That's better,' he said. 'Now, I'll get myself back to Shangri-La, and you'd best get off home quick. They'll be getting anxious, and we don't want that. I've got a thing or two to finish off here, before I go – check the batteries, see if I've got enough diesel in the tanks, that sort of thing. We don't want the engines packing up on us in mid-channel, do we? Not with all those giant tankers steaming up and down.'

He took me up on deck and walked with me as far as the gangplank. 'Saturday midnight,' he said. 'Don't be late.' I looked up into his face. It was ghostly white against the dark of the night sky. The thought came over me that Popsicle might not be real at all, that he was a mere figment of my imagination, that maybe I was

161

living all this only inside a dream. I needed to reassure myself. I stood on tiptoe and threw my arms round his neck. He was real enough. I was down on the towpath before he spoke again.

'Oh and, Cessie, bring lots of warm clothes, there's a girl. You'll need them. And that fiddle of yours too. Nothing like the sound of music out at sea. It'll keep our spirits up.'

There was plenty of music to face when I got back home. I was hardly in through the front door before it began. I didn't argue, but I did defend myself.

'I just went looking for him, that's all. What's so wrong with that?' Then I remembered to ask: 'Haven't they found him yet?'

'Not yet,' said my mother. I could see that she had been crying. 'But they will,' she went on. 'They will find him, won't they, Arthur?' She turned away from me and buried her head in my father's shoulder. It was only then that I realised how much they were suffering, my father as much as my mother. I had a sudden longing to comfort them, to tell them everything I knew, everything that had happened to me that night. But I could not bring myself to do it. Popsicle had confided in me. I'd given him my promise.

'I bet,' I said, inventing as I went along, 'I bet he's

just gone off for a wander or something. He'll find his way back sooner or later, you'll see.' It was the best I could do without giving anything away.

Later I made them a cup of tea – not something I often did – and brought it into the sitting-room. They were sitting side by side on the sofa and holding hands. Their faces lit up when they saw me come in with the tray, and I liked that. 'Popsicle can take care of himself,' I said, pouring the tea. 'He's a survivor, Dad; you said it yourself. Wherever he is, he'll be all right. I know he will.'

As we sat there waiting, I was trying to think of more reassuring things to say, but I knew I had to be careful. I had to be seen to be anxious too. So I kept silent. It was the safest way.

Suddenly my father was on his feet and standing with his back to the fireplace, his hands thrust deep in his pockets. 'I'm going to say something, something that's got to be said.' He looked uncertain as to whether he should go on. 'You're going to hate me for this,' he said, catching my eye.

'What? What is it?' my mother was on the edge of the sofa.

'All right, all right.' He still didn't want to let it out. 'All along, ever since he came here, I haven't been fair to him. I know that, and I'm not proud of it either. The truth is, I think I may have sent him up to Shangri-La, not just for his own good, but partly to hurt him, like he hurt me when I was a kid. I think I really wanted him to sit up there and long for us to come and visit, just so he'd know what it was like.' His whole face was overwhelmed with tears now. 'Day after day, year after year, I'd be sitting up on that wall outside the home, and I'd be looking down the road, believing he'd come round the corner and take me away, and he never did. I've always hated him for that, always. I know I shouldn't have, but I did.'

'But you're not like that,' my mother whispered. 'That's spiteful, vengeful.'

'Yes, all of that,' my father went on, 'and worse, too. He could be lying out there under a bus right now, or mugged in some dark alleyway; and if he is, it'll be like I killed him myself, my own father.' He was reaching out for understanding, for comfort, and I didn't know how to give it. 'I should've been like you, like both of you. I should've welcomed him and with open arms, but I couldn't. I should have forgiven him by now. I'm a grown man, for Christ's sake. I should have had it in me to . . .'

The telephone rang. My mother was there first. We

followed her into the front hall. She wasn't doing much of the talking. All she said was: 'Yes . . . Yes . . . thank you.' Then she put the phone down and turned to us. She was beaming through her tears. 'He's all right. Popsicle's all right. It seems he just walked up to a policeman in town and said he'd like a lift up to Shangri-La. He's fine. He's safe.'

The hug that followed was a threesome one, and lasted and lasted. 'We'll bring him home,' said my father when it was over. 'We'll bring him home.'

The week that followed seemed more like a month. Every night, every day I spent thinking of Popsicle, of Saturday, of Dunkirk, of Lucie Alice. At school Shirley Watson plied me with endless questions about the *Lucie Alice*, questions I fended off as best I could without offending her. I told her as much of the truth as I dared – it always helps when you're telling a lie. I explained that Popsicle loved lifeboats because he'd worked on one long ago, when he was a young man. He must've seen the *Lucie Alice* down on the canal, and used her as a model for my boat. She believed me, I thought, but I wasn't quite sure. I couldn't be sure of anything with Shirley Watson. Certainly, she seemed to have become an ally, a friend even; a turn-around I welcomed but still could not quite trust.

At home hurried preparations were under way to have Popsicle home again. My father was arranging for a nurse to come in to be with him each weekday until he was well enough to be on his own. But the nurse couldn't come until after the weekend. We'd surprise Popsicle, he said. We'd go up there on Sunday and we'd just tell him out of the blue that he was coming home. We'd pick up his things there and then and bring him home with us.

They were so much looking forward to it all; but of course, all the time they were planning I knew it was never going to happen, that by Sunday, Popsicle and I would be gone to France, they'd have found my letter – the letter I was still trying to compose – and they'd know the worst. So many times I nearly told them. I longed to unburden myself of my secret, but I could not and I would not betray Popsicle. I held my secret inside me and willed the days to pass.

I didn't finish my letter until the Saturday morning. I'd tried to write it all out, to explain everything, to tell Popsicle's whole life story; but when I read it through it seemed so unlikely, as if I'd concocted the whole thing. Maybe it was the way I'd written it. I wrote pages and pages, but it all ended up in the wastepaper basket. In the end I settled for the briefest of notes:

Dear Mum and Dad,

Please don't worry about me. I've gone off with Popsicle for a couple of days. There's something he's got to do and he needs me to help him. That's why I'm not here. Don't worry. I'll be quite safe and I'll be home soon.

Love from

Cessie.

We spent the Saturday afternoon making 'Welcome Home Popsicle' signs, one for the front door, one for his bedroom door. We brought out the box of Christmas decorations from under the stairs, and festooned the sitting-room with streamers and balloons. We hung the Christmas tree lights over the mantelpiece. I blew up so many balloons that my head ached with it.

In spite of the deception I was playing out, it was a lovely time, because the three of us were together, really together as we hadn't been for a long time. My father never once talked of going to work, nor even answered the phone. And my mother hardly mentioned 'her' school or 'her' children. I wished it could always be like this.

I hoped they'd get off to bed early, and I tried to encourage them to do so by going up to have my bath straight after supper.

167

'See you in the morning,' said my father. I think it took him by surprise when I kissed him goodnight. I hadn't done that for weeks. 'Tomorrow's the great day then,' he said, holding on to my hand for a moment longer.

'Yes, Dad,' I said, hating myself for what I was about to do to them.

'Don't run all the hot water off,' my mother called after me. 'I'll come up and see you. Won't be long.'

When she did come up an hour or so later, she found me in bed seemingly asleep with my light turned out. Over the chair my clothes were all ready to step into, and behind the chair two extra jumpers, and my anorak. My violin was under the bed – I hadn't forgotten it.

'Asleep?' she whispered. I didn't reply because, in my state of high excitement, I couldn't trust my voice not to give me away. She closed the door quietly. I lay there in the darkness, riven with guilt. I knew well enough how much anguish I was about to cause, but I could see no other way I could fulfil my promise to Popsicle.

I tried not to shut my eyes. I had to stay awake. The last thing I wanted to do was to fall asleep and not wake up in time. I just wished they'd turn off the television and come up to bed. But they didn't. The television hummed and burbled downstairs, lulling me out of my resolve.

Only when I woke did I realise I'd been asleep. I sat up with a jolt. My bedside clock said eleven fifteen. The house was dark and quiet all around me. I knew where everything was without turning on the light. I was dressed, down the stairs, and out of the front door within a couple of minutes. With my violin clipped to the rack behind me, I cycled out of the estate and into town as fast as I could go. The roads were practically empty. I heard midnight strike from the church as I cycled over the canal bridge. I'd made it, just.

I could see the barges quite clearly in the moonlight, and beyond them the wider hull of the *Lucie Alice*. But there were no lights on board. She was as dark as the barge next to her. There was no one there. As I wheeled my bike along the towpath, I began to think, and worry and doubt. Perhaps Popsicle wasn't that much better after all. Perhaps he still had bouts of forgetfulness. Perhaps he was barmy. Or maybe the whole story about Lucie Alice, about Dunkirk, was some kind of old man's fantasy. Perhaps Popsicle was lying fast asleep in his bed up at Shangri-La, our rendezvous quite forgotten.

I left my bike lying in the undergrowth beside the towpath, and went on board. I called out for him as loudly as I dared. The moon slipped behind a cloud and the world darkened suddenly. A warm shiver of fear crept up the back of my neck. I went below. The cabin door was still locked. I felt for and found the key in the tea tin. Popsicle was definitely not there. I thought then that maybe he'd said Sunday night, not Saturday night. I went up on deck. The moon was out again and gave me new hope. It was as round, as perfectly full, as it could possibly be. Full moon was Saturday, Popsicle had said so. It had to be tonight, midnight tonight.

There was the sound of an approaching car, headlights sweeping out over the canal, briefly illuminating the entire length of the *Lucie Alice*, and blinding me as they did so. I ducked down below the gunwales. I could hear the car bumping along the towpath towards me. It stopped. The engine died and there was silence again. I had to look. It wasn't a car. It was a minibus, a white minibus with writing on the side. One of the words was definitely 'Shangri-La'. Popsicle was getting out of the driver's side and coming round the front of the minibus. He smiled up at me.

'Bit late, Cessie. Beggar wouldn't start,' he said.

The nearside door opened and the side doors slid back. I counted them as they got out. I could not believe what I was seeing. Twelve. I recognised Harry as one of them. He wasn't in his wheelchair. He was walking, bent between two sticks. There was an old lady beside him, helping him along. 'You know Harry, don't you?' said Popsicle, 'and this is Mary. Used to be a nurse, did Mary. She's seeing to all the medicines for us, aren't you, Mary?' He clapped his hands. 'Everyone, everyone. This is my granddaughter, this is the Cessie I've been telling you all about.'

They were all coming on board and they all seemed to know exactly where to go as well.

Popsicle was beside me, his arm round my shoulder. He was showing me off. Some of them ruffled my hair as they passed; one of the old ladies – later I found out that everyone called her 'Big Bethany' – touched my cheek with her cold hand and said, 'Just like you said, Popsicle, a princess. That's what we'll call her then, Princessie.' And they all laughed at that.

'Ancient mariners we may be,' Popsicle told me proudly. 'But we'll do fine. We've got blankets, food, water, all we need.'

I watched Harry's wheelchair being carried on board and the gangplank hauled in. 'Don't worry, Cessie. We did a dummy run, two nights ago. "Borrowed" the minibus for a couple of hours,' Popsicle went on. 'I showed them what was what. Everyone's got a job to do. They all know what they're doing.'

I could only stand and watch and admire as they bustled purposefully about the boat.

'Do they know everything? About Lucie Alice?' I asked.

'Everything,' Popsicle replied. 'The whole thing, beginning to end. I reckoned we were going to need all the help we could get. They volunteered, Cessie, to a man, to a woman. Of course there's some that couldn't make it; not well enough. But those we've got are raring to go. Isn't that right, Harry?'

'Only one thing I'm going to miss,' said Harry, 'and that's the Dragonwoman's face in the morning when she finds out that half her inmates have done a bunk!' Harry had settled himself down in his wheelchair and Mary was wrapping his legs in a blanket. 'Some ship, eh Cessie?' he said.

Some ship, some crew, I was thinking. All about me the ancient mariners went about making the lifeboat ready for sea. The lights came on down below, tarpaulins were rolled and stowed away. Popsicle was everywhere it seemed, helping, reminding, cajoling. There was no doubt who the skipper was. Everyone had a part to play – except me, it seemed. I was beginning to feel a bit redundant, until Popsicle took me to one side.

'Soon as I start up the engines, Cessie,' he said, 'I

want you to go and tell Sam up at the lock-keeper's house that we're ready. You know him already, don't you? He told me all about your little meeting. He'll be expecting you. Give him a hand with the lock gates, will you? Then, once we're through, I want you back on board and for'ard, keeping your eyes peeled for buoys and ropes and what have you. We won't get to Dunkirk with a rope wrapped round our propellers, will we?'

As the engines roared to life, I dashed along the towpath, over the canal bridge and hammered on Sam's door. He must have been ready and waiting, because the door opened almost at once, and he was standing there in his wellies and his dressing-gown, a torch in his hand. He looked at the *Lucie Alice*, all lit up like a Christmas cake from bow to stern, her ancient crew hauling in the lines, Popsicle at the wheel, with Harry beside him in his wheelchair.

'I need pinching,' said Sam. He never stopped chortling the whole time as we opened the lock gate and let in the *Lucie Alice*. The wheel was heavy and stiff, and there was a lot of huffing and puffing before the gate was fully open. She inched into the lock, engines chuntering sonorously. It was a very tight fit. We closed the gates behind her. As the lock flooded, she rose majestically up towards us. Only now that she was away from the barges and on her own, did I see just how magnificent she really was. Sam spoke my thoughts. 'Never seen anything like it,' he said. 'I just hope Popsicle knows what he's doing, that's all. It's an awful long way over to Dunkirk. Still, you've got the weather. Should be like a millpond out there tonight.'

As the deck of the *Lucie Alice* reached ground level, Popsicle was there to help me jump back on board. 'You see anything for'ard, Cessie, you let me know – loud,' he said. I made my way to the bow, stood on tiptoe, hooked my elbows over and looked down into the black of the water.

Minutes later we were out of the lock. The engines throttled up and we moved slowly into the harbour itself. The sea was bright with the moon and clear ahead as far as I could see. Below me the bow of the *Lucie Alice* was cutting her way through the water, and I felt the first salt spray on my face. I licked the salt off my lips, and breathed in deep.

As we steamed out across the harbour. I could see the silhouettes of fishing boats by the quay, and the cranes standing guard over them like skeletal sentinels. The lighthouse at the end of the harbour wall was closer now and flashing brighter all the time. Then we were underneath it and the swell of the open sea took us and rocked us. Sam had been wrong. It was no millpond out there. I heard laughter behind me as we crashed into our first significant wave – nervous laughter it was. The old lifeboat groaned and shuddered and ploughed on.

The cold of the spray took my breath away. Above me the moon rode the clouds, at just the same speed as the *Lucie Alice* rode the sea. She would be keeping up with us all the way, I thought. Out ahead of me, the sea glistened and glowed, and I knew that beyond the dark horizon lay Dunkirk and France. I thought of the last time she had made this trip all those years ago to pick up the soldiers off the beaches. I just hoped and prayed (and I really did pray) that Lucie Alice would be there in Dunkirk, just as she had been then.

Once we were well out to sea, I made my way back to Popsicle at the wheel. Harry's chair was being lashed down and Mary was wrapping him in another blanket, all the time urging him to come below with the others. But Harry would have none of it. 'I'm not going to miss this, Mary, not in a million years. So you can stop your fussing, I'm staying put.'

Popsicle enveloped me in his coat and let me take the wheel with him. 'We're on our way then,' he said. 'You did leave a note for your mum and dad, like I told you?'

'Yes.'

'That's good. Keep her steady now. Can you feel her, Cessie? Can you feel the heart of her?' I could too. 'Excited, isn't she? I reckon she knows exactly where she's going. Back to Dunkirk. And, please God, let it be back to Lucie Alice too.'

12 EARLIE IN THE MORNING

IT WAS AS IF I WAS SETTING OFF ON SOME GREAT and grand adventure, some wonderful quest, with a bunch of silverhaired Argonauts, and with Popsicle at the helm as our Jason. But these Argonauts around me were not strapping, muscle-bound Greek heroes. They were a dozen very old-age pensioners whose combined age, I worked out, must have totalled nearly a thousand years.

From their incessant jovial banter and the warmth of their camaraderie it would have been easy to believe that they were all on some Sunday outing; but Popsicle only had to say the word and they at once became a crew, slow about the boat maybe, but serious and purposeful. There were always four up on deck on watch, two for'ard, two aft, and Popsicle himself never left the wheel. We did hour-long shifts, and when we went below there was always a mug of hot sweet tea waiting, jam sandwiches for some, baked beans on toast for others.

I never did get to know all of them – there were too many for that – and besides no one really introduced me. They all treated me as if they knew me already, and I liked that. I got to know Benny though because he told me all about himself. The galley was Benny's domain – he made that quite clear. Benny liked talking, he liked talking loudly and repeated himself often. Everyone shouted at him, and at first I wondered why. It wasn't long before I discovered that he was almost completely deaf. He'd been a chef in a hotel in Bournemouth for most of his working life, he said, and he'd never allowed hangers-on in his kitchen. So I could come into his galley only if I lent a hand. I found myself doing everything from washing up, to stirring beans, to spreading butter, to cutting crusts off bread.

'You got to give the customers what they want,' he explained, waving a wooden spoon at me for emphasis. 'I said, you got to give the customers what they want. Most of us can't be doing with crusts, not any more. Not any more. You know something, Princessie? You might not believe this, but I had 'em all out for my twenty-first birthday, the whole lot of them.' He wasn't always easy to understand. 'I said, the whole lot of them. Present from my mum, bless her heart. Have your teeth out, she says, and you won't have no trouble with them later on. And she was right too. I said, she was right too. Not many of us up at Shangri-La still got our teeth left. You take Chalky, he's like me. Not a tooth of his own left in his head, not one.'

Chalky, as everyone called him, scarcely ever left the engines. He'd grin toothlessly at me and wave an oily rag whenever he saw me. 'Loves engines, does Chalky – knows 'em inside out. Train driver in his time. Easy-going sort, wouldn't hurt a fly,' Benny told me, and then in a more confidential tone: 'But you watch out for Mac. Different kettle of fish altogether. Used to be a Sergeant Major in the Guards. Stickler for everything. I said, he's a stickler for everything. Everything got to be just so or he's not happy, not happy at all. And when he's not happy . . . You've got to watch out for Mac. I'm saying, you've got to watch out for Mac.'

I knew Mac already – Harry had pointed him out. He was the dapper one with the natty moustache, the only one of them who never seemed to smile at me. He patrolled the deck constantly, making sure we were all properly secured on our lifelines whenever we were up on deck. He kept checking Harry's chair was properly lashed down. He was there too whenever the watch changed, making sure no one slipped or stumbled as they came out on deck. Benny told me he had a glass eye, but I never did find out which it was.

Then there were the twin brothers, still identical at eighty-four, and known to everyone as Tweedledum and Tweedledee – both of them unsteady on their legs, and both of them always insisting on taking their turn on watch together. Benny told me all about them: 'Tweedledum and Tweedledee, they've been up at Shangri-La near enough fifteen years now – oldest inmates. Hardly been out of the place in all that time. Never been in a boat before, neither of them. Never been nowhere much. Kept an ironmongers shop all their lives up in Bradford. Never done nothing like this. Well, nor have any of us, come to that, except Popsicle of course. Those beans'll be sticking if you don't stir them, Princessie. I said, those beans'll be sticking if you don't stir them.'

It was hot and stifling down below. I don't know if it was the oily smell of the engines, or the bubbling beans in the galley, or just the roll of the boat, but whatever it was I began to feel queasy. I went up on deck to breathe in the fresh air and felt better at once. Popsicle called me over to him. He patted the wheel. 'Isn't she the best? Isn't she something? More than fifty years old and she still purrs like a kitten.' It sounded more like a roaring lion to me, but I didn't argue.

Harry handed me his empty tea mug to take back down to the galley. 'I'll tell you something, girl,' he said, 'I've never been so cold in all my life, and I've never had so much fun either. A real live adventure, isn't it? Even if your grandad has got us all here under false pretences, even if that whole story of his about Dunkirk and Lucie Alice is just a load of old cobblers, if it's one great big porky pie, I won't mind. None of us would. We're having the time of our lives, all of us. Being out here, like this, it makes a fellow feel alive again.'

'But it's not a story,' I protested. 'It's true . . .'

'Of course it is,' Harry said. 'I know that. And d'you know how I know? Because it's too fantastical, that's why. He couldn't make up a story like that even if he wanted to. Mind you, I had my doubts to start with – we all of us did. But once he'd brought us down to see the *Lucie Alice* a couple of nights back, we were well and truly hooked. And now here we are, out in the middle of the ocean with nothing but water all around us. Like a dream it is, like the best dream I ever had.'

'Never mind about the dreaming, Harry,' said

Popsicle. 'Just you keep your watch. We'll be getting out to mid-Channel soon and there's bigger ships than us out here, a lot bigger; and I want to see 'em coming in plenty of time. So you keep your eyes skinned, Harry, you hear me?'

'Aye, aye, skip,' said Harry, and he dragged his hand out from under his blanket and gave a mock salute.

It wasn't long after that that Mary and Harry had a real set-to. It all began when she said he'd catch his death if he stayed up on deck much longer. He told her it was his death and he'd catch it if he wanted to. Popsicle had to intervene and send him down below to the warmth of the cabin. 'You can always come up again later, Harry,' he said. Harry muttered something un-repeatable, and gave in gracelessly. Between them, Mac and Mary got him down the gangway, Harry grumbling all the way.

'You fetch that fiddle of yours, Cessie,' said Popsicle. 'It'll cheer him up, cheer us all up.'

So I sat in Harry's wheelchair and began to play. 'Yesterday', 'Michelle', 'When I'm Sixty-Four' – I played all the tunes I could remember. Popsicle sang along, and after each one they clapped, from all around me on the deck, from down below in the cabin. Even Chalky left his engines for a while and came up to listen. After

'Nowhere Man' – we'd done it really well, the best we'd ever done it – they even called for an encore. Big Bethany then suggested I should play something on my own. I did the *Largo* because I knew I wouldn't make any mistakes. The sound of the violin seemed thin and reedy to me. Much of it was smothered by the pulsating throb of the engine, any resonance whipped away and lost at once over the vastness of the sea; but they seemed to like it.

'Lovely,' said Big Bethany quietly. 'Lovely that was.' She *was* big too, big smile, big everything. I liked her the best of all of them, I think. My fingers were aching with the cold now. I put the violin down on my knees and blew into my hands. I thought I'd finished.

'Princessie?' It was Harry's voice from down below. 'How about "Sailing"? Do you know "Sailing"?' So we did 'Sailing' again and again and again. Everyone seemed to know it – better than I did. Then, over the pounding of the engine, Benny shouted up that he wanted 'What shall we do with the drunken sailor?' I couldn't feel my fingers by now, I was playing so far out of tune that it was almost unrecognisable, but they didn't seem to mind. We ended the very last chorus with a thunderous 'Earlie in the morning', and then, to my great relief, Popsicle brought the sing-song to an end. He called up the new watch and sent the rest of us below to get some sleep. No one argued, least of all me. I was exhausted by now, frozen through and longing for the warmth of the cabin, however smelly, however stifling. I went down and lay on Popsicle's bed. Big Bethany came and covered me with an eiderdown. She said she'd never in her life heard a violin played so sweetly. Until then I never knew that words could really warm you physically, but hers did. I curled myself into myself and fell asleep almost at once.

A bell was ringing in my ears as I woke. Then I discovered it wasn't in my ears at all. It was ringing somewhere above my head. I looked around me. There was no one with me in the cabin, no one at all. The engines were turning over gently and I could feel that the boat was barely moving through the water. I swung my legs off the bed and ran out of the cabin. I saw Chalky bending over his engines.

'Anything wrong?' I asked.

'Fog,' he said, without looking up. 'Lousy fog.'

Moments later I was up on deck and it was swirling all around me. The bell was sounding again somewhere forward. I couldn't see the bow of the boat at all. Popsicle was at the wheel. Everyone else, including Harry, was on watch all around the boat, like dark statues, each of them wrapped in a cocoon of their own fog. None of them moved. None of them spoke. Popsicle saw me.

'We're listening,' he whispered.

'For what?'

'For anything. An engine perhaps, foghorn, ship's bell. All we've got's our ears and a compass. Thank God for the compass.'

'How long's it been like this?'

'A couple of hours maybe. We've had one near miss already, and one's enough. Get listening, Cessie, there's a girl.'

So I found myself a place at the gunwales. I scanned the impenetrable greyness around me, and listened, listened as hard as I could. But my ears, I discovered, were almost as useless as my eyes. All I could hear was the throb of our own engine and the sea running against the side of the boat.

The shape beside me moved and became Big Bethany. 'Can't be far now, Princessie,' she said, putting her arm round me. 'Can't be far.' Big Bethany mothered me, and everyone else, through the terrors of that night, a little word here, a little hug there.

It seemed as if we were entombed out there in the fog for hours. All the while the world was becoming lighter around us as the dawn filtered through the fog, but I could neither see any better nor hear any better. The harder I looked into it, the more fearsome were the shapes I began to imagine: a charging bull, a rearing dragon, a lion crouched and ready to pounce. Our shroud was a whiter shade of grey now, but it still felt like a shroud.

There was a shout from behind me. I turned. Harry was pointing out into the fog over the starboard side. 'There! There!' he cried. And even as he spoke there was a deafening blast of a foghorn, so thunderous, so close that we all looked now for the looming prow of a ship that must come out of the fog and run us down at any moment.

'Hang on! Hang on tight!' Popsicle called out, and the engines roared to full throttle. The boat surged forward underneath me. I clutched at Big Bethany and hung on to her. I saw Mary fall and go rolling over and over across the deck. Mac went after her, caught her and held her. Mary clung to him, sobbing. We didn't see it, until the last moment, a vast wall of a giant tanker, or a ferry perhaps, that passed astern of us by barely fifty metres and then vanished into the fog. I thought the danger was over, but it wasn't.

'Look out for the wash!' Popsicle stood now like the

lifeboatman on the model he'd made me, his feet apart, braced, fighting the wheel as the wash hit us broadside on and tossed us like a cork. It was as if we'd been suddenly thrown into the path of a raging typhoon.

I know I screamed – and I wasn't the only one. I could not stop myself. The sea crashed over the gunwales, smacking me in the chest and chilling me to the bone. Big Bethany clung on to me tight, and then we were suddenly out of it and into calmer water. I looked around me again. Popsicle was still at his wheel, and he was laughing out loud, wiping the water from his face.

'Look, you beggars, look what I see!' he cried. The fog ahead was wispy. It was thinning, it was quite definitely thinning. Moments later we saw a flashing light and the emerging shape of a lighthouse, and then a harbour wall. Popsicle throttled back. 'Dunkirk dead ahead,' he said. 'Dunkirk or I'm a Dutchman.'

I went over to be near him. 'Do you recognise it?' I asked. In the grey gloom of the dawn I could just make out a strand of beach stretching away into the murky distance.

'Not a thing,' Popsicle replied. 'I wouldn't, would I? It was a long time ago and, besides, the place was in ruins last time I saw it. But it's Dunkirk all right. If I plotted it right, Cessie, and I think I did – hope I did – then what you're looking at is Dunkirk town.'

As we entered the shelter of the harbour we left the last vestiges of the fog behind us. There was a solitary angler fishing from the harbour wall. He waved at us and we waved back. There didn't seem to be much happening in the harbour except for a couple of fishing boats unloading at the quayside. The fishermen stopped what they were doing and watched us come in. They were still watching us as we tied up behind them.

'*Magnifique*,' one of them called out. '*Le bateau, il est superbe, magnifique.*'

'*Bonjour*,' Harry shouted in reply, as Mac and Mary between them settled him in his wheelchair on the quayside. '*Allez la France!*' And the fishermen laughed and echoed it back at us.

'*Allez la France! Allez la France!*'

'What's that?' I asked.

'It's what they always shout at rugby matches,' said Harry. 'It's all the French I know – and *bonjour* of course.'

Once everyone was off the boat – and that took some while – Popsicle gathered us all together. 'If anyone asks,' he was saying, 'just remember we got lost, lost in the fog. We had to put in somewhere for safety. Blame it on the skipper if you like.' I looked out across the harbour towards the town. The streetlights were going off everywhere. It was almost daylight. But hardly a car was moving. There was still scarcely anyone about.

'Popsicle,' said Harry. 'That street where Lucie Alice lived, do you know where to find it?'

'There was a church just up the road from their house, I know that much. I used to hear the bells. That's all I remember. I'll ask. Someone'll be bound to know. I'll ask.'

So we all set off into town, Popsicle leading us, his photo of Lucie Alice in his hand. He asked and he asked. He asked everyone he met – a couple of dustbin-men, a postman, a motorist who had stopped at a red light. The response was always the same – first, a look of utter disbelief when they saw us coming, and then, when they'd had a look at Popsicle's photograph, a shrug and a shake of the head. No one seemed to recognise Lucie Alice – that didn't surprise me, it was obvious they were all too young to have known her – but none of them had heard of the Rue de la Paix either, and that did seem strange.

Mac shepherded us along the pavements, taking particular charge of Tweedledum and Tweedledee who seemed intent on stopping to look in every shop window. Whenever we had to cross a road, Mac was there to marshall us – at one point even holding up his hand to stop an approaching lorry, so that we could all cross over safely. But the further we walked the more exhausted we were all becoming, except Popsicle. Big Bethany had to sit down to catch her breath whenever she could. She had a wheezing cough that she kept apologising for. Now that a few of the shops were opening, Popsicle would dart in and show his photograph at every possible opportunity. We would stand and wait for him outside. It was hopeless. Every shake of the head, every shrug of the shoulders, told us so. But Popsicle never once lost heart.

He was walking on ahead up a narrow cobbled sidestreet, when he called for me to catch him up. He took my hand in his and squeezed it. 'The street where she lived, Cessie, it was like this, just like this. Little houses. Grey shutters. If I could find the church . . . I could hear church bells, Cessie, in my cupboard. And they were close, very close.' He wasn't looking at me at all as he spoke. 'The trouble is, Cessie, I'm beginning to wish I'd never started out on this whole caper. I'm thinking that maybe there's some things it's better not to know.'

I squeezed his hand back because it was all I could think to do. 'Popsicle!' It was Mac, calling from behind us. 'How about some breakfast? There's some of us could do with it. Warm us up. Army marches on its stomach, y'know.'

There was a café across the street. The lights were on inside. The door was open. A lady in a headscarf and a coat was sweeping the pavement outside vigorously. She saw us coming and stopped her sweeping. Like everyone else we'd met, I think she thought we were a bit strange at first, but as soon as she realised what we were after, she ushered us inside only too gladly.

With her coat and scarf off, she turned out to be a lot older than I had imagined. Not that she behaved old. She bustled about the place like a beaver, putting three tables together, arranging the chairs and talking nineteen to the dozen as she did so – all in French, so I didn't understand a word. When we had all finally sat down, she turned to Mac and said: 'English? *Anglais*?'

'Scots,' said Mac firmly, and she seemed puzzled by that.

'*Café*? Coffee? *Thé*? Breakfast?' she asked.

'Breakfast,' said Harry, patting his belly. 'Famished, we are.'

And so we found ourselves for the next hour or so thawing out in the warmth of the café, with baskets of freshly baked croissants and endless glasses of tea. No one wanted coffee. And Popsicle, I noticed, didn't want anything at all. He just sat there beside me staring down at the table, at the photograph of Lucie Alice, smoothing out the corners and saying nothing.

The old lady brought over yet more glasses of tea. 'You don't like it? The breakfast, it is not good?' she asked Popsicle. That was when Popsicle suddenly broke into French. It took us all by surprise, the old lady too. For a while it was difficult for me to understand what it was that they were talking about. Then Popsicle gave her the photograph and she looked at it closely. I began to recognise some of the words they were saying: 'Rue de la Paix' and 'Lucie Alice'. But that was all. After a while she spoke in English again – perhaps she hadn't entirely understood Popsicle's French. Perhaps it wasn't so good after all. 'You were here, in Dunkirk?' she said. 'In 1940?'

Popsicle nodded and turned the photo over in her hands. A long look passed between them.

'I have come to find her,' said Popsicle, speaking very slowly. *'Vous la connaissez*? You know Lucie Alice? Maillol, her last name was Maillol. You know where she is?' The old lady was studying the photograph closely, frowning at it. She took it to the door where the light was better. 'I can show my husband?' she said.

'Of course,' said Popsicle, and she hurried away out through the door at the back of the bar. We watched her go. It was Harry that broke the silence. 'I've just thought of something,' he said. 'Who's going to pay for this little lot? We haven't got any francs, have we? Didn't think of that, did you, Popsicle?'

But Popsicle wasn't listening to him. His eyes were fixed on the door behind the bar.

'She'll take pounds, won't she?' said Chalky. 'And if she won't, then we'll just have to get Benny to do the washing-up, won't we, Benny?' We were still laughing at that when she came back into the café. With her was an old man in a collarless shirt and braces. He was scrawny round the neck and unshaven. He had the photograph in his hand. He looked at us over the top of his glasses, suspicious, hostile almost. Popsicle got to his feet.

'You are the one who is looking for Lucie Alice Maillol?' the old man asked.

'Yes,' said Popsicle.

'Why? *Pourquoi*?'

'She's a friend. She saved my life. *Elle m'a aidé pendant la guerre. Elle m'a sauvé la vie.*'

I wasn't sure the old man understood. He came closer and looked up into Popsicle's face. 'She hid me,'

Popsicle went on. 'She hid me in her cupboard, in her house, in the Rue de la Paix.'

'But it is no longer there, *monsieur*. La Rue de la Paix, the old street, it is gone. How you say it? *Bombardée*. Destroyed. And Lucie Alice . . .'

'You know her?' Popsicle breathed.

'*Elle était dans la même école*, in the same school, *monsieur*, the same class. My wife, myself, Lucie Alice. We were friends, all of us. *Mais . . . nous sommes désolés, monsieur*. We are very sorry, but Lucie Alice, we have not seen her since 1940, since the war. No one has. One day, we go to see her, and she is gone. *Disparue. Sa mère aussi. Elles sont disparues toutes les deux.* Disappeared. They take them away. We never see them again.'

13 MESSAGE TO MY FATHER

POPSICLE FELT FOR THE CHAIR BEHIND HIM TO steady himself.

'You are sure?' he asked. 'You are quite sure?' The old man nodded as he handed back the photograph.

'Rue de la Paix, it is still there,' he said. 'They built it again after the war, like many other streets in Dunkirk. But Lucie Alice and her mother, we hear nothing of them ever again, nothing.'

Popsicle took a deep breath before he spoke again. 'I'll go for a walk, I think,' he said, more to himself than anyone else. 'Yes, I think I'll go for a little walk.' He tried to smile at us, but he couldn't do it. 'I won't be long. Why don't I meet you all back at the boat in a couple of hours? You'll see they're all there, won't you, Mac? Then we'll all go home.' And he was gone out of the door.

Harry put a hand on my arm. 'Best not leave him on his own, eh Princessie?' So I went after Popsicle and caught him up in the street.

'Where are we going?' I asked.

'Don't rightly know,' said Popsicle. 'Maybe we'll sit on the beach for a while, just for old time's sake. We can hardly come all this way for nothing, can we?' He took my hand and held on to it tight as if he needed me to be with him. I wanted to say something about Lucie Alice, something to comfort him, but I couldn't find the words. We walked on together in silence.

There were more people about in the streets now. We passed by the open door of a large baker's shop where they were busy stacking loaves and baguettes. The smell of them seemed to follow us down the street. 'Lovely,' I said, breathing it in. Popsicle hadn't heard me.

'Well,' he said. 'I suppose I got what I came looking for, didn't I? I wanted the truth and I got it. I wanted to know, and now I do. All I want now is to unknow it, if you see what I mean. But that's one thing you can never do, can you, Cessie?'

A bell rang out, loud and close by, a church bell. I stood there on the pavement and waited for it to finish. 'Eight o'clock,' I said. Popsicle was hurrying on without me. I ran after him.

'The bells, Cessie.' He grabbed my arm as I came alongside him. 'I know them. I know those bells.'

We turned into a small square with a fountain in the middle, and beyond it a huge, grey, stone church with gulls ranged along its rooftop.

We gazed up at the tower. 'They were the same bells,' said Popsicle, 'I'm sure of it. This is the church, it must be. Every Sunday she'd go to church, her and her mother. They'd leave me back in the house, shut up in my cupboard. I'd sit there in the dark and listen to those bells. I'd say a prayer or two for them, and for me too. Never been much of a churchgoing sort, not before, not since; but I prayed hard in that cupboard, Cessie, so hard. It doesn't seem like anyone was listening very much, does it?'

Popsicle was still trying to work out where the old Rue de la Paix might have been, when we saw a lady come into the square walking her dog. The dog looked just like Shirley Watson's dog back home – pop-eyed and snuffly and yappy. When he asked her for directions, the lady led us across the square and pointed to a narrow street that led down towards the sea. She was a lot more friendly than her dog. So at last we found the Rue de la Paix, and stood across the street from where Popsicle thought the house might have been.

'Nothing's the same. Different street, different house – except the shutters,' said Popsicle. 'The shutters were grey then too, grey and peeling. God, what a silly little beggar I was. I had to do it, didn't I? I had to open those shutters. I had to have a look out. The soldier who saw me, he must've been standing just about where we are now. Then they hauled me off that way, down towards the beaches. And that's the corner, that's where I saw Lucie Alice coming home with her bread. Oh, Cessie, what I'd give to see her come walking round that corner right now.'

We crossed the wide road that ran along the seafront, and walked along the beach. There was a chill breeze off the sea, so we went to sit down in the shelter of the dunes, where I discovered that French sand-hoppers were just the same as English ones, only there seemed to be more of them. The sea was murky grey and limpid. Each wave seemed so tired it barely had the strength to curl itself over and run up the sand. There were miles of beach, and miles of dunes, as far as the eye could see, all completely deserted, except for a couple of walkers out with their gambolling dogs.

Popsicle was looking out to sea. 'That young soldier,' he said, 'the one who pulled me out of the sea. I never even knew his name. I've still got that poetry book of his, *The Golden Treasury*, always kept it. Sitting here like this, Cessie, it's all so peaceful. You can hardly believe it happened, all those ships out there, and the planes screaming down on us, and the bombs, and the bodies. I remember walking away from him. He was a body, like the others, and I never even knew his name.'

'Names don't matter,' I said.

Popsicle seemed suddenly cheered by that. He put his arm round me and hugged me to him. 'That's a true fact, Cessie,' he said. 'That's a powerful fact. I may not know his name, but I have the memory of him, of what he did. Same with Lucie Alice. I'll never see her again, I know that now, but I have the memory of her, haven't I? And that's a whole lot better than nothing. If anyone should know that, then I should.'

He talked on and on, but I really didn't hear much of what he was saying. I was too cold, too tired to follow his thinking. After a while he seemed to sense it. 'Come on, Cessie,' he said, at last, helping me to my feet and brushing the sand off me. 'I'd better be getting you home. I'd better be getting us all home.'

We must have walked further than we thought – it seemed a very long way back to the harbour and the *Lucie Alice*. They were all on board and waiting for us, and so were the harbourmaster and the customs men.

Popsicle explained, in French and in English, how we'd got lost in the fog, that we had no passports, and that we were on our way home anyway. They complained a bit, and shrugged a lot, and then complained some more, but that was the end of it.

As we cast off there was a sense of deep sadness about the boat. They were clearly not at all the same cheery crew they had been. Even Harry had lost his sparkle and sat hunched and dejected in his wheelchair. I told him we'd been to the beaches. I told him about the sandhoppers, but he didn't seem to want to know. Big Bethany stood on her own, gazing back at Dunkirk. She had her handkerchief out and, because I knew why, I left her alone. Benny grumbled down in his galley, about all the washing-up he had to do. He didn't seem to want any help. Some of them had that vacant look on their faces, the same look I'd seen through the window up at Shangri-La.

I thought at first that it might be a kind of solidarity for Popsicle in his disappointment, but in that case you'd have thought they'd have been all over him with consideration and kindness, and they weren't. Then I thought they might be blaming him for bringing them on what had turned out to be a fool's errand, but that wasn't how they were, any of them. It wasn't only fatigue either, although that was evident on every face around me as we steamed out of Dunkirk harbour and into the swell of the open sea. As I was sitting on my own under the red ensign at the stern of the boat, I finally worked out what it was that must be making them all feel so wretched. It could be one of two things, or maybe both: an unspoken dread in each of them, the dread of going back to Shangri-La, or an aching sadness that their grand adventure, our grand adventure, would soon be over.

There had been an hour or so of this all-pervading gloom, when Popsicle called everyone together up on deck. He handed each of us a tin of condensed milk. 'To sweeten you up, you miserable beggars. Come on, it's not that bad. Do you think it's the last time we'll be doing this? Of course it's not. Don't you worry, I'll see to it.' He patted his wheel. 'We'll go out in the old girl whenever you want to. She's my boat, isn't she? I'll take her out whenever I want to. They can't stop us. Promise.'

They seemed to brighten a little at that. Popsicle hadn't finished. 'All right, so we didn't find what we came for. It didn't work out like I wanted. But we've had the time of our lives, haven't we? We may be a lot of old crocks, but I'm telling you, this old girl never had a finer crew, not even in her heyday. So let's not mope, eh? We'll scoff down our condensed milk, warm ourselves up with Benny's tea, and we'll all come home smiling. I want them to see us smiling. And they'll be waiting, you can be sure of that. There'll be quite a kerfuffle when we get back, I shouldn't wonder. And the Dragonwoman'll be there too, bound to be. So let's just show the old crow what a time we've had. Let's show her what we're made of. How about it?'

The first of the sun broke through and flooded the deck with sudden warmth. 'Here comes the sun,' cried Popsicle. 'Come on, Cessie. Get your fiddle out. Play us a tune, there's a girl.'

How Popsicle did it, I'll never know, but somehow he transformed all of us. Within minutes we were the same happy bunch we had been on the way over – well, almost. Popsicle said later it was the magical properties of condensed milk that did the trick. Whatever it was, it certainly wasn't my violin playing. I just couldn't get into my stride. My fingers wouldn't work as they should, and then my 'e' string broke and I didn't have a spare in my violin case. You can't play very much without an 'e' string.

'No matter,' said Popsicle. 'We'll have the radio instead. There'll be some music on. There always is.' He asked Mac to turn it on full volume so we could all hear it.

After a lot of wheezing and whistling and foreign-sounding stations, the radio at last settled on a clear signal, some jingly music, and then an English voice – a voice I knew at once, the voice of my father. Popsicle had recognised it too. He cut the engines at once.

'That's him!' he said. 'That's Arthur, that's my son! Listen, listen.'

'This then is a message to my father. I just hope and pray that you're listening out there, Popsicle.'

'He called you Popsicle,' I whispered.

'So he did, Cessie, so he did. Hush now and listen, there's a girl.' There was a pause so long that I thought the radio must have gone wrong. My father cleared his throat, and went on.

'All those years sitting on that wall I longed for you to come back. All my life ever since I've been wanting you to come home – that's the truth of it. And then when you did come, all I did was give you the cold shoulder and send you away again. What I did was shameful, I know that now; but just how shameful it was I never really understood until we found Cessie gone this morning, until we read your letter, Cessie, the one you threw away. Lowestoft, the *Michael Hardy*, Dunkirk, Lucie Alice, my mother – I know it all now, I know you've gone off to look for Lucie Alice in Dunkirk.

I pray you find her alive and well, but if you do not, then please come home and be with us. We want you with us. I want you with me. There'll be no more Shangri-La, I promise you that. And, Cessie, if you're listening out there, come home safe and sound and bring Popsicle with you. Take care, both of you.' I thought he'd finished, but he hadn't, not quite. 'I've played a lot of requests on my shows over the years, but this is the first one I've ever requested myself. This is for you, Popsicle, to serenade you home. I know you're a lot older than sixty-four, but it'll have to do. Here it is then: "When I'm Sixty-four" by the Beatles. God bless. We'll be waiting for you.'

Those who knew it – and that was most of us – hummed or sang or clapped along. But Popsicle stood at his wheel and just listened, gazing out to sea all the while. When it had finished, he rubbed his hands together and blew on them. 'Cold. It's cold out here,' he said. 'Let's go home, shall we, Cessie?' And he started up the engines.

As Popsicle had predicted, there was indeed quite a reception committee waiting for us. In mid-Channel a helicopter found us and circled overhead for a while. We were still several kilometres off when the first boat came out to meet us, a police launch. They came alongside and, through a loudhailer, offered to put a couple of officers on board – to help us, they said. Popsicle refused, and made it very plain that we were quite capable of bringing the *Lucie Alice* in under her own steam and needed no help whatsoever. They seemed a bit disgruntled at that and told us rather curtly to follow them in. Popsicle replied that we were a lot bigger than they were and faster too, so they could follow us – if they could keep up, that is.

Word had clearly got about, because before long there was a flotilla of small ships all around us escorting us in. The closer we came to the shore, the more there were. Another helicopter was hovering overhead now. There was a cameraman on board, hanging out of the side as he filmed us. It was as if we'd been single-handed round the world, not just over to Dunkirk and back.

Once inside the harbour there was a cacophony of hooting all around us, and one ship had even turned on its fire hoses to greet us. The quay was lined with people cheering and waving. My arms were aching with waving back; but I never stopped, not once. Popsicle stayed at the helm, as he had done all the way. I looked up at him and I could see that, tired though he was, he was enjoying every moment of it, as I was, as were all the ancient Argonauts. You may not have brought back your Golden Fleece, Jason Popsicle, I thought, but even if you had, the welcome could not possibly have been any better.

We were edging our way back into the lock when I first saw my father and my mother. They were standing side by side in front of the lock-keeper's house, slightly apart from the rest of the crowd, as if they wanted to enjoy it all by themselves, in private.

It seemed an age before we were through the lock and tied up once again, the great engines silent at last. I saw Chalky give them a last wipe, and kissing each of them a fond goodbye. Big Bethany enveloped me against her warm softness and said I was to come and play my violin for them one day up at Shangri-La. I promised, and I meant it too.

My mother was first on board. It was while we were still clinging to each other that I saw Shirley Watson and Mandy Bethel, and a few others besides, watching from the towpath. I wriggled my fingers at them. They wriggled theirs back. After a time I managed to disengage from my mother. My father was looking at his father.

'We heard you, Arthur, on the radio,' Popsicle said.

'Welcome home, Popsicle,' said my father. And there on the deck of the *Lucie Alice* they hugged each other, for all the world to see; and judging from the applause, all the world seemed to be enjoying it hugely. They hugged and hugged, long enough, I thought – and I hoped – to make up for all the years they hadn't.

Which type of book do you like best?

Take the quiz . . . then read the book!

Who would you like to have an adventure with?
a) On my own
b) A ghost
c) Someone in my family
d) My best friend
e) My pet

Where would you like to go on holiday?
a) A remote island or a far-away mountain
b) A fantasy world
c) Anywhere as long as my family and friends are there
d) A different time period
e) The countryside

I would like to be . . .
a) Explorer
b) Author
c) Someone who helps others
d) Warrior
e) Circus ringmaster

My favourite stories are . . .
a) Full of adventure
b) Magical
c) About friendships and family
d) War stories
e) About animals

If you answered mostly with A you'll enjoy . . .

KENSUKE'S KINGDOM

Washed up on an island
with no food and water,
Michael cannot survive.
But he is not alone . . .

If you answered mostly with B you'll enjoy . . .

THE GHOST OF GRANIA O'MALLEY

There is gold in the Big
Hill, but Jessie and Jake
can't bear for the hill to be
destroyed. Can they save
it before it's too late?

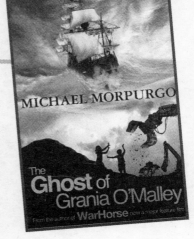

If you answered mostly with C you'll enjoy . . .

LONG WAY HOME

George doesn't want to spend his summer with another foster family . . . but this time he may have found somewhere to call home.

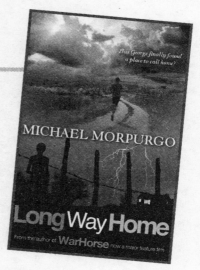

If you answered mostly with D you'll enjoy . . .

FRIEND OR FOE

It is the Blitz. One night David and his friend see a German plane crash on the moors. Do they leave the airmen to die?

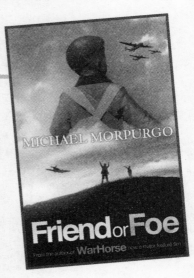